The Study of Policy Formation

Edited by
RAYMOND A. BAUER
and KENNETH J. GERGEN

THE FREE PRESS, New York
COLLIER-MACMILLAN LIMITED, London

Collier-Macmillan Canada, Ltd., Toronto,
Ontario

Library of Congress Catalog Card Number:
68-10789

First Printing

Foreword

"Our problem is not to do what is right," Lyndon Johnson declared in characterizing the national choices of the White House. "Our problem is to know what is right." *The Study of Policy Formation* is a first-rate response to that confession of the dilemmas of policy making.

When the research that underlies this book began, I served as a some-time adviser in its design. By the time the work was completed, I was deeply immersed in the process the volume analyzes.

From both perspectives, I applaud the final result. Raymond Bauer and his associates began and remained scholars in this enterprise. Their probes of the policy process—of how the great societal choices occur—pay due homage to work that has gone before. In fact, one immediate contribution of this book is the skillful synthesis of past approaches and the ready and accurate references provided to contemporary techniques of study. These summaries of the state of the art, in themselves, justify the volume.

But Bauer and his associates have research contributions of their own. They identify the existing kit of tools available to the empirically oriented scholar; they acknowledge, in their methodological essays, their limitations. Then they are bold enough to try honestly to apply the techniques and methods available to actual cases and to test a research strategy of their own.

Not all of these efforts in application are successful—nor are all the theoretical and methodological problems resolved. Undoubtedly none of the participants in any of the specific cases analyzed would be satisfied with the accuracy of the account. *More important, however, they would be less satisfied with the accuracy of their own accounts of how the policy process in which they participated in fact worked.*

This is, at any rate, the overwhelming judgment I carry from my second and present perspective as practitioner. More than a year of steady involvement in national policy making in urban affairs persuades one that whatever the limitations of outside analysis, the risks of evaluation by the insider are greater. What one gains by access to detail in one part of the process, one loses by being barricaded from other sectors.

It is in both recognizing and responding to this fact that *The Study of Policy Formation* makes its great contribution. Bauer does not scorn nor dally with the practitioner—he is concerned with helping him. The key concepts of bargaining, problem definitions, interest definitions, institution filter, and leverage point are operative terms. The emphasis on the "open system," the acknowledgment of uncertainty, is especially welcome to the policy maker. They are *his* concepts, if not usually so precisely and astutely expressed.

Thus, scholarship appears as a positive support to action by its superior powers of conceptualization and more orderly analysis, increasing our appreciation of the policy process in a way the memoirs of past actors never can. This in my judgment is where scholarship belongs—not disenchanted from or afraid of the world about it, but committed to its service and competent in its assistance.

It is Bauer and his colleagues' contribution that they demonstrate social science's growing capacity to respond to the President's request—"to know," in the accurate sense of the word, "what is right." And, accordingly, this may help in the hard choices of policy making.

ROBERT C. WOOD
UNDERSECRETARY
DEPARTMENT OF HOUSING AND
URBAN DEVELOPMENT

The Study of Policy Formation

Preface

Like many another book this one represents the convergence of more than one stream of interest.

The National Planning Association has for several decades been one of the most effective and influential private organizations dealing with problems of national policy. The NPA with its chief economist Gerhard Colm is credited with being one of the most important instruments in the acceptance of the "new economics" that has flourished in this country in recent decades. But the conduct of analyses of policy problems and the effective communication of such analyses to the men who can act on such problems is another matter. The staff of the NPA, and especially John Miller, its executive officer, have been long concerned with the more effective communication of their studies.

I have at various times been involved in the conduct of policy studies. After the completion of one book (*American Business and Public Policy*) with Ithiel de Sola Pool and Lewis A. Dexter, I felt the need for some positive statement of an up-to-date view of how policy is formed and some notion as to how to go about studying such a complex process in an orderly fashion.

Early in 1964, the NPA staff and I joined forces in an effort to forward our complementary interests, which converged on the question of "What do we need to know about the policy process in order to do a better job of feeding useful information into that process?" Under a grant from the Ford Foundation we launched a project to clarify the existing state of the art on the *study* of policy formation and to suggest further steps that could increase our ability to improve the policy process.

The early intention of the discussions in which we engaged was to design empirical research for the improvement of the role of information in the policy process. However, it soon became apparent that during recent years a number of areas of related research had been advancing at a rapid rate, and that if we were to take advantage of these advances in designing research on the role of information in the policy process, it would be necessary to undertake appropriate reviews of these other areas of study.

The essence of the work plan was a series of position papers that would furnish the background for the design of empirical research on the process of policy formation, such that this research would reflect developments in several disparate areas that had not as yet been brought together. It was also planned that this same group of position papers, appropriately edited, should be made available to a wider group of scholars who might find them similarly useful.

This book serves these purposes. Its core consists of the position papers that were prepared: on the use and limitation of formal models for determining optimum policies; on the state of public policy studies, of organizational studies, of the methodological problems associated with policy problems; and three examples of policy problems to serve as raw material for our analysis. Based on these papers, the reading to which they directed me, and the contributions of my collaborators and others, I wrote the introductory essay, which is in part an introduction to the remaining chapters. More importantly it is a statement of the conceptual premises that seem to me to lie behind the modern view of the policy process and a proposal for a research strategy that will make it possible to gather orderly data on complex processes more efficiently and effectively.

The conceptual model of how policy is formed cannot be considered novel in any one detail. Perhaps some formulations are phrased more sharply than others have stated them. Perhaps the over-all picture is more coherently drawn. Perhaps—we hope—there are novelties in our proposals as to how policy research is to be done. If there be any sort of novelty, we are delighted that this is so. However, the intent of our effort is not to produce novelty, but to pull together in as useful a fashion as possible a point of view that will have utility.

Our experience since beginning this work has been encouraging. Men who have to deal with important, complex problems have said that our depiction of them mirrors their experience. Our conceptualizations and methodological suggestions have found their way into research done by ourselves and others. In these ways our earlier hopes have been confirmed.

Any conceptual scheme stands midway between past and future evidence. It grows out of data and it anticipates future data. It tries to make sense out of what we have observed in the past, and it tells us what to look for in the future. Its validity rests primarily on its usefulness either in helping us to understand what we observe, or in guiding us to make observations that will expand our understanding. In these senses the judgment of our proposals must be a personal one. The reader will have to make his own judgment.

The project out of which this publication grew was guided by a Steering

Committee consisting of Messers. John Miller, Gerhard Colm, and myself. I wish to record my personal pleasure at having had the opportunity to work with them and to become better acquainted. The contributors to this volume have each provided me a personal and professional reward in our work together: Richard Zeckhauser, Elmer Schaefer, Enid Bok Schoettle, Joseph Bower, Lewis Schneider, Edward Furash, Theodore Geiger, Roger Hansen, and most especially, of course, my co-editor Kenneth Gergen. During the active life of the project, we were all carefully, capably, and cheerfully shepherded by Alice Courtney, who served as administrator, editor, and chaplain, and whose substantive contributions were so numerous that no one of us can be sure just which are his ideas and which are hers.

One of the working arrangements of our groups—and a vital one—was that we should from time to time expose our thinking and writing to a group of friendly but firm critics. This group met formally on two occasions and supplied us with many helpful reactions over a period of two years of correspondence. The familiarity and distinction of their names speaks of itself for the quality of the help they gave us. I wish to extend my own gratitude to Neil Chamberlin, Richard Cyert, W. Phillips Davison, William Dill, Robert Dorfman, Roger Fisher, Harold Guetzkow, and Robert Wood. Professor Wood, now Undersecretary of HUD, has done us the additional honor of writing the Foreword.

Finally, my secretary during these years, Mrs. Laura Snow, is to be thanked not merely for her help, but for her patience and good humor.

RAYMOND A. BAUER

Contributors

RAYMOND A. BAUER
is a social psychologist and Professor of Business Administration, Harvard Graduate School of Business.

JOSEPH L. BOWER
is Assistant Professor of Business Administration at the Harvard Graduate School of Business and is a student of business policy.

EDWARD E. FURASH
is Vice President of Shawmut National Bank, Boston, Massachusetts. At the time of writing his paper he was a management consultant at Arthur D. Little, Inc.

THEODORE GEIGER
is Chief of International Studies, National Planning Association, Washington, D.C.

KENNETH GERGEN
is a social psychologist and Chairman of the Psychology Department, Swarthmore College.

ROGER D. HANSEN
is Project Director for the Studies of Development Progress, National Planning Association, Washington, D.C.

ELMER SCHAEFER
when writing his paper with Zeckhauser, was a graduate student in the Department of Economics at Harvard University.

LEWIS M. SCHNEIDER
is Assistant Professor of Business Administration, Harvard Graduate School of Business.

ENID CURTIS BOK SCHOETTLE
is Assistant Professor of Political Science at The University of Minnesota.

RICHARD ZECKHAUSER
is an economist and junior fellow at Harvard University.

Contents

Analytical Table of Contents

The Study of
Policy
Formation

Chapter 1

RAYMOND A. BAUER

The Study of Policy Formation: An Introduction*

The Nature of Policy Formation

One way or another, in a complex and changing world, men and institutions are constantly accepting or rejecting new courses of action or maintaining or forsaking old courses. The federal government continues to extend cultural and trade relations with European Communist countries while continuing to pursue an anti-Communist policy in Vietnam. A business firm diversifies to give itself a hedge against fluctuations in its original business while simultaneously taking on the dangerous burden of developing new competencies on the part of the top officers of the company. A general hospital builds a psychiatric wing and adds to the demands on the competence of its staff, at least in proportion to the additional facilities. Or a university concludes that it should give tenure to scholars whose salaries are not underwritten by endowments.

Various labels are applied to decisions and actions we take, depending in general on the breadth of their implications. If they are trivial and repetitive

---

* In part, this chapter is a revision and expansion of an article, "Social Psychology and the Study of Policy Formation," *American Psychologist*, Vol. 21, No. 10, 1966, pp. 933–42, copyright 1966 by the American Psychological Association, and reproduced by permission. Certain passages appear verbatim.

and demand little cogitation, they may be called routine actions. If they are somewhat more complex, have wider ramifications, and demand more thought, we may refer to them as tactical decisions. For those which have the widest ramifications and the longest time perspective, and which generally require the most information and contemplation, we tend to reserve the term *policy*. We assume that the sorts of course-setting described in the opening paragraph would be regarded as "policy" setting by most persons. Those familiar with Philip Selznick's[1] discussions of leadership in institutions will recognize what we have called "policy matters" as his "critical decisions."

It is true that one man's policy may be another man's tactics inasmuch as the level of organization is critical. The superintendent of a factory may pass along a directive to his foremen which then becomes policy for them, that is, it forms the general framework of principles within which the foremen make their own "tactical" decisions, which in turn become policy for their subordinates. Thus, agreement on which courses of action constitute "policy decisions" is somewhat dependent on the perspective of the individual who views the event. However, regardless of how chary one may be in applying the term, it is in all instances reserved for those parameter-shaping acts which are taken most seriously, which are presumably most difficult to arrive at, and at the same time most difficult and most important to study.

It is important to recognize that this definition of policy extends the implications of the activity "policy formation" well beyond the traditional concern for the intrinsic importance of issues. When we focus on those strategic moves that direct an organization's critical resources toward perceived opportunities in a changing environment, we are at once concerned with the (1) intellectual activities of perception, analysis, and choice which often are subsumed under the rubric "decision making"; (2) social process of implementing policies formulated by means of organizational structure, systems of measurement and allocation, and systems for reward and punishment; and finally (3) the dynamic process of revising policy as changes in organizational resources and the environment change the context of the original policy problem.[2]

At once it is evident that simplistic models of the policy process will have to be abandoned. There is every evidence that in complex policy situations, so-called decision makers do not strive to optimize some value nor is the notion of optimization a useful way of ordering and analyzing their behavior regardless of their intentions. Possibly a less stringent term such as *problem solving* could be applied, but many of the central features of the intellectual

1. Philip Selznick, *Leadership and Administration* (New York: Harper & Row, 1957).

2. Joseph Bower, "Capital Budgeting Is a General Management Problem," mimeographed, Cambridge, Mass., 1966.

aspects of policy formation are not ones which have ordinarily been dealt with in the empirical study of problem solving. I refer to such matters as the individual's allocation of time, attention, and other resources among problems that are competing for these resources; and to the formulation and communication of policies in such a way as to articulate the interests of a sufficient number of involved parties so as to identify a policy that has a good potential for implementation. This latter activity, the formulation of policies in such a way as to meet at least the minimal objectives of the policy maker while simultaneously generating adequate support for the policy, can demand a high degree of inventiveness.

Since the social and intellectual processes of policy formation will be the main topic of this essay, we may defer further discussion of them until later. At this point we take note of another feature of the policy process as we have defined it which distinguishes it from common usage, namely, that moralizing and generalizing are not the same thing as policy making.

Unfortunately, all the difficult aspects of policy formation lie outside of what is *morally correct* from the point of view of a given set of values and scientifically correct for a given class of problems. It is the distinctive mission of the policy maker that he must allocate scarce resources and must mediate among conflicting sets of values and interests. He must form judgments specific to the situation with which he is confronted rather than those which are correct in general for a class of situations. Finally, he must balance each individual issue off against a wide range of other issues, including not only those that presently exist but those that might exist in the future.

There is an essential role for moralizing in the policy process. Moralizing is the mechanism for making one's values evident. But policy making is the setting of courses of action designed to implement the values, usually of a fairly large group of persons, on a given issue without unduly compromising other values on other issues. As Learned, Christensen, Andrews, and Guth put it in their exposition of the problems of business policy:[3]

> The professional manager of a large, publicly held corporation is clearly in some sense responsible to the owners of this business, to its suppliers and customers, and even to his competitors—since he owes it to them to compete "fairly." He is also responsible in some ways to certain institutions, including the local government and community, the national government and community, and the fraternity of businessmen with which he identifies himself. It is clear at once that if the interests of any one of these groups are pursued exclusively, the interests of the others will suffer.

Americans have traditionally been moralizers and activists. They have also been apolitical in the sense of denigrating the practice of politics. The

3. Edmund P. Learned, C. R. Christensen, Kenneth R. Andrews, and W. D. Guth, *Business Policy: Text and Cases* (Homewood, Ill.: Richard D. Irwin, Inc., 1965), p. 523.

three tendencies are neatly intertwined. Politics (or policy making) demands the sort of concrete thinking that tells us that no value is absolute, that in the real world we have to trade off units of one value against units of another. Politics (or policy making) also demands a frank acceptance of the limitations on our ability to act and a willingness to face up to the full range of possible consequences of our actions, including those consequences that are against our values and intentions. In short, if we expose ourselves to the intellectual and moral discipline of policy formation, we are stripped both of the complacency of easy virtue and the illusion of omnipotence. Americans have been reluctant to pay this price. However, unless we are willing and able to think "politically"—if only as a matter of role playing—we will not be able to enter the phenomenological world of the policy maker and understand the policy process. And this is probably the most important intellectual problem with which we are faced.

To say that the study of the policy process is the most important task with which we are confronted may well sound presumptuous. The setting and implementation of policy are such regular activities and wise men have commented on them for so many centuries that, some will say, the process must be quite thoroughly understood. But men have regularly exercised wisdom and skill when their knowledge was incomplete. Rocks were thrown, arrows fired from bows, and guns and cannon constructed before the science of ballistics was mastered. Bridges were built before the basic data on strength of materials and the mechanics of stress were well mastered. Man has proceeded and succeeded in many enterprises by rule-of-thumb. The fact that he has done better than chance and often been quite successful has not diminished our general faith that a fuller understanding of the phenomena with which he deals will be of use. On the whole, it has been mankind's experience that we are able to guide our affairs more to our liking as we better understand what we are doing.

This is about where our understanding of the process of policy formation stands: We have the accumulated experience of human history, many men who have mastered much skill and judgment, but we are merely beginning to systematize our comprehension of what the process of policy formation is about. One initial attempt focusing on the sphere of business organization has already been cited.[4]

This book exists because of the relatively recent acceleration in the study of and understanding of the policy process. Although the design and rationale of the book will be explained in greater detail below, it may suffice to say here that the intent has been to serve the reader in three ways:

1. To acquaint him with the main bodies of intellectual work that bear immediately on the formation of policy both on the public and private

4. *Ibid.,* p. 5.

level while stressing both the contributions and limitations of these approaches;

2. To review the distinctive methodological problems that are associated with studying the policy process while making some suggestions for the advance of the art;

3. To present several concrete policy areas from the point of view developed in the discussions relevant to points 1 and 2.

Although we have not aimed our efforts directly at the practitioner, we hope that what we have written will be of benefit to him, at least to those men of affairs who find profit in expanding their understanding of the murky matters with which they daily deal. If, however, there are any prescriptions of "good practice" here, they have slipped in inadvertently. It is true that in many areas of administration and in the operation of complex institutions, highly sophisticated methods for solutions of particular problems have been developed. This is not true, however, of more complex policy problems. Hence, our immediate gift to the practitioner, if a gift it be, is not to supply specific solutions to specific problems. It is rather to deepen his comprehension of the range of problems with which he is accustomed to deal and thereby to help him to invent better solutions of his own.

Our long-range aspirations for improvement of practice, however, are considerably more ambitious. To say that policy formation is a social process in which an intellectual process is imbedded does not mean that the relative effectiveness of the intellectual process can not be increased, or that the social process can not be "improved"—that is, made to serve better the purposes of the parties involved, and to do so more efficiently.

As we note at various points in our discussions, considerable work has been done recently in the discipline of making better decisions. The prescriptions for making better decisions generally indicate the need for a considerable change in customary behavior. If this were not so, they would not offer much prospect of improvement. The prospects of widespread adoption of such improved procedures must, however, depend upon a better understanding of present practice. The understanding will serve three purposes: (1) to indicate realistic limitations on the type of "improved" behavior to which we can aspire; (2) to supply that understanding of ongoing practices and existing forms of organization which will facilitate the introduction of better procedures; and, (3) to improve those aspects of the process of policy formation which fall outside the framework of formal decision theory— for example, to facilitate the process of negotiation by supplying improved procedures whereby the parties involved may assess more rapidly which among the possible propositions that may be advanced stand some chance of being accepted.

To a large extent, the enterprise on which we have embarked approximates what has been called descriptive decision theory. Although its contribution to our understanding of our own behavior in complex situations is a worthwhile thing in itself, it may also be regarded as the establishment of a natural science basis for the engineering of better organizational processes.

Past History of Policy Studies

Certainly the study of policy formation, whether it be on the level of the nation, state, or the international community, or on the level of the individual organization, is far from a new venture. It has been the principal business of political philosophers for centuries, although they suffered the occupational disability of continually (and without due warning) mixing up their ideas of how they wished the world to be with their best guesses as to how it actually was. An occasional writer such as Machiavelli, who attempted to keep separate his notions of what should be and what actually was, earned a reputation for being immoral. At this point, I would not care to venture a guess as to Machiavelli's true state of virtue. But I would cheerfully assert that his passion for attempting to separate his understanding of how Florentine politics actually worked from his wish as to the type of state he would like to see in existence was rare.

Students of organizations smaller than the state (business organizations, educational institutions, hospitals, and other nonprofit organizations) have been almost as flagrant in their assumption of wisdom. Only a relatively few students of such organizations have been sufficiently informed and self-critical to be aware of the flimsy base on which prescriptions for running such organizations have been posed. When we remember that most such organizations have existed essentially in their modern form for decades and perhaps centuries, it is sobering to note that only a few decades ago Chester Barnard, with long years of organizational experience and great familiarity with the established wisdom, wrote:[5]

> Nothing of which I knew treated organization in a way which seemed to me to correspond either to my experience or to the understanding implicit in the conduct of those recognized to be adept in executive practice or in the leadership of organizations.

The present book would not exist if this state of affairs had not been under radical change in recent decades. For approximately 40 years, American political scientists have increasingly insisted on a more naturalistic reporting of what has actually happened as policies have been formed or as people have

5. Chester Barnard, *The Functions of the Executive* (Cambridge, Mass.: Harvard University Press, 1938), p. viii.

tried to implement existing policies. In still more recent years, the meaning of the phrase "behavioral approach" in political science has taken on additional import. It has implied, among other things, a more extensive use of both the concepts and data-gathering techniques of psychology, sociology, and anthropology. In place of analyses of printed or written records and of relatively unsystematic observation of behavior and loosely conducted interviews, we are now getting detailed systematic observations amounting at times almost to 24-hour surveillance of key persons, verbatim transcripts of interviews and meetings, minute descriptions of behavior, and studies based on precise samples of individuals and incidents.

In addition there is an increased emphasis on understanding before judging. Particularly in the study of politics, there is a decreasing tendency to label the actions of politicians "irrational," and an increased sense of responsibility for discovering the rationale that lies behind seemingly inexplicable behavior.

Probably this trend of developments has been most rapid in the field of political science. One conceivable reason for this is the prevailing sense of the disparity between the way politicians behave and the stereotyped version of American politics that appears in the traditional civics book. (This circumstance was, of course, the source of much critical comment, whether warranted or not, about the conduct of the Presidency under Dwight D. Eisenhower.) It is conceivable that there has been just as much disparity between the actual and idealized behavior of businessmen, educational administrators, and other men of action. But they have not come under the same sort of critical scrutiny and, therefore, there has been less pressure for reconciliation of actual and ideal behavior. The conduct of the businessman has been something of an exception to this generalization. Scholars have tended to assume that businessmen were "rational" in their behavior but pursuing goals that most intellectuals did not approve of.

All the above is compounded by the greater volume of traffic between educational and governmental institutions as compared to that between educational and business institutions. As a result of the fact that since the early years of Franklin D. Roosevelt, many economists, political scientists, and lawyers have served the Federal government and returned to academic posts, there developed a large group of scholars who came to accept the goals and values of governmental institutions and also realized that the working of these institutions did not conform to what they had been reading (and, worse yet, teaching!). Hence, there has been a strong motivation on their part to bring about a better understanding of the governmental process of policy formation and a concomitant attempt to make some systematic sense out of behavior that has tended to be viewed as chaotic and/or immoral.

Many teachers of business administration, many consultants, and many articulate businessmen have presented their notions as to how businesses might be better run. But few had the driving intellectual curiosity, coupled with the capacity for conceptualization, to create any profound understanding as to why business institutions actually function as they do. At the same time, the "theorizers" among the intellectuals have seldom had the day-to-day contact with the operation of business concerns even to be aware of the problems and activities that most occupied a businessman's time. Furthermore, they were, and are, generally at such ideological odds with the business community that the job of understanding before evaluating is often not even attempted. But we shall see in the chapters that follow, that more recently, substantial progress has been made both in the conceptualization of how policy is formed in business institutions and in how one may research the process.

Governmental institutions and private profit-making institutions comprise such a large portion of our institutional life that one tends to forget about the administration of such private nonprofit organizations as hospitals and educational institutions. Yet we shall see that they too have been scrutinized in our attempts to understand the policy process.

Although attempts to understand policy formation in the many areas of our institutional life have moved forward, this area of knowledge is at a peculiar point in its development at which a reassessment of the situation is necessary if further progress is to be made.

Organization of the Book

The content of the various chapters and their implications both for our understanding of policy formation and the design of research on the problem will be discussed in more detail later in this introductory essay. At this point I would like only to indicate briefly the rationale for each of the chapters and their relationship to each other and to the overall problem. The eight chapters following this one group themselves conveniently under three quite familiar labels: Theoretical, Methodological, and Applied (or Substantive).

The three theoretical papers are each based on one of the established traditions of intellectual inquiry which, in recent times, have been relevant to the study of broad policy problems.

In recent years there has been an increasing development and use of sophisticated quantitative techniques for the solving of complex problems. The use of formal methods for assessing the relative value of various programs and assigning a money value to their utility has received a good deal of publicity as a result of Robert McNamara's methods of running the Department of Defense. These methods for finding a best solution to complex problems have been developed under the labels of Operations Research, Statistical Decision Theory, and Welfare Economics, among others. As publicized in some quarters, these methods might appear to give a promise of similar clean solutions to major policy problems. For this reason, it is imperative that the student of policy formation understand quite precisely what are the capabilities and limitations of such formal models.

Richard Zeckhauser and Elmer Schaefer undertook the task of introducing the reader to this vital although demanding topic. Despite the inherent difficulty of the subject matter to one who encounters it for the first time, we felt that it was logically necessary that this essay be presented first. Although I will expand on some of their arguments in the following pages of this introduction, it can be said that the central conclusion of their exposition is that for complex problems involving large numbers of interested parties the concept of a single best solution is misleading. Quantitative techniques of decision making are of great value in solving many problems; however, they offer little prospect of serving as an impartial, irrefutable arbiter of the conflicts of interest involved in large policy problems. We shall see that there is not even a single unarguable way of thinking about what is "best for everybody." The acceptance of this limitation as inevitable has the valuable consequence of turning our attention to a closer study of how people do in fact work out their conflicts of interest while freeing us from the arrogant assumption that they would certainly come to a wiser solution if they left the problem in the hands of some competent scholar.

The study of decision making and policy formation falls into two traditions. One, so-called normative decision theory (such as that discussed immediately above), is concerned with how people *should* act in order to achieve better (or best) results. The other tradition, so-called descriptive or behavioral decision theory, is concerned with how people *actually* go about handling such problems, whether the outcomes be admirable or not. The distinction may be thought of as a parallel to the contrast between the natural sciences and engineering in the physical world. The engineer tries to build the best structures or systems he can (within practical constraints). But in order to do this, he can proceed effectively to the extent that he understands the natural laws that his materials and processes would follow without his constructive intervention. Similarly, any proposals we may have for improving the way in which policy should be formed must take into cognizance the ways in which people and institutions function under present circumstances. Minimally, normative proposals must at least be compatible with what it is possible for people and institutions to do.

In recent decades, descriptive and analytic studies of policy formation have been done in two related but somewhat distinct traditions. One treated by Joseph Bower has focused primarily on the making of decisions within formal, particularly business, organizations. The other, treated by Enid

Schoettle, is more squarely in the tradition of political science and concentrates more on policy formation in the public arena. Each of the authors traces the evolution of increasingly more sophisticated models of organizational and political processes, although neither reviewer is able to conclude that fully satisfactory models have been developed. The fact that one tradition treats policy formation as something that occurs in a formal institutional setting and the other takes the opposite point of view offers us an interesting opportunity to think afresh about the actual role of formal organizational arrangements.

The implications of what Bower and Schoettle have written will be the subject of much of what I will have to say and therefore the substance of their papers can be treated later. Each, however, will bring the reader up to date on the state of the art on the study of policy formation in formal organizations and in public policy. Because the state of the art is readily seen to be imperfect, the focus of the two essays is more on where research and thinking should be directed in order to improve our understanding rather than on spelling out the present practical value of our state of knowledge.

Whereas our model of the policy process is, as I have indicated, incomplete and not entirely crystallized, recent students of the process are in sufficient agreement as to the broad approach that must be taken; there is reasonable consensus as to the distinctive research problems with which we are confronted. Gergen devotes his two chapters to identifying these problems, reviewing the merits and limitations of existing methods and, where possible, suggesting new procedures. One of the central problems on which there has not been agreement is the actual identification of the key actors who influence the outcome of a particular policy problem. The available evidence on the complications of this problem are so much at variance with the ordinary conceptions of a well-identified "power elite" that Gergen devotes one entire essay to just this question. The other essay treats, in lesser detail, methodological problems that seem particularly relevant to our general view of the policy process. Again, further discussion of these problems will follow in this essay, but the reader will have to rely on Gergen's treatment for a systematic coverage.

Finally, we asked Schneider, Furash, Geiger, and Hansen to look at three substantive issues that involved actual or potential policy problems: urban mass transportation; transfer of aerospace and military technology to the civilian economy; and United States foreign aid. *The intention of these three papers is to identify the research problems that would be uncovered by viewing such issues in broad systematic terms and then, to see whether or not, having taken such a broad view, it would be possible to identify those points in the policy process at which it would be most efficient to begin empirical research.* This latter objective, the development of a research strategy that does not immediately sacrifice the complexity of the process yet makes systematic data gathering possible, is one of the more difficult tasks with which students of policy formation are confronted.

In a sense, the three substantive papers can be regarded as the raw material on which to test the ideas presented in theoretical and methodological papers. The authors, inasmuch as the available evidence permitted, attempted to present these concrete problems in terms consistent with the earlier systematic papers.

This then is the plan of the book and of the work that went into the production of the separate chapters. Since in a cooperative project of this sort, each worker is constantly learning from the others, it is impossible to achieve complete consistency of each chapter with the others. Every one of the chapters has been revised one or more times in the light of the other papers. Because each such revision represents a move forward in the thinking of the individual author, this means that on some points the other authors will not have caught up with him.

The Policy
Process

The best point of departure for an understanding of the policy process is to consider more fully the assertion made earlier that "decision making" is an inappropriate concept for characterizing policy formation and the conclusion reached by Zeckhauser and Schaefer that there is no determinate *best* solution to a policy problem. The two propositions are closely linked.

The term decision making, when used by psychologists, decision theorists and other students of the phenomenon ordinarily implies a specific model of cognitive activity. This model assumes a single decision-making unit with a single set of utility preferences; knowledge of a reasonably full range of action alternatives and of their consequences; this intention of selecting that course of action of maximum utility; and, the opportunity, disposition, and capacity to make the appropriate calculations.[6] In the process of policy formation every one of these assumptions is violated. However, both the connotations of the term *decision making* and the ordinary discussion of decision making on policy issues preserve the illusion of these assumptions. The difficulty created by this circumstance is dual. It diverts the attention of the student of the process from what actually occurs and thereby hampers our efforts to understand the process. Furthermore, it furnishes the policy

6. For a fuller discussion of how these assumptions are not appropriate to what happens in policy formation, see Martin Patchen, "Decision Theory in the Study of National Action: Problems and a Proposal," *Journal of Conflict Resolution* (June 1965).

maker with an inappropriate model of how he ought to behave. It does not help him, and it will confuse him if he takes the phrase seriously.

Some of the ways in which the assumptions of decision making are violated in the policy process are amenable to practical solutions. Specifically, to the extent that an individual's information and capacity to process information are finite he can operate as rationally as possible by formalizing the state of his imperfect information. Thus, there is a sophisticated modern approach to decision making that is based on formalizing one's judgments, however subjective they may be and however tenuous the information may be, with the view of reaching the best decision that can be made on the basis of this imperfect knowledge.[7] Nevertheless, even this approach tells *an individual* what he *ought* to do. Furthermore, it does not and is not designed to help us understand what people *actually* do. Most important is the fact that it does not touch on the impossibility of hitting on a single "best" solution for a group of people. Any optimizing model for decision making (a model for a best solution) is built around the notion that some preference scheme can be established according to which the solution is optimal. Such a preference schedule, in turn, assumes some single set of values against which possible future outcomes can be matched in order to establish the order of their desirability. (If more than one set of values is involved, it must be translatable into a common set. There is the rub.) The key difficulty in conceiving of an "optimal" public policy is that of conceiving what would constitute the single system of values against which to judge the solution. Any group of individuals of reasonable size will not have identical values. Furthermore, individuals, although having substantially identical values, will be located at different points in the organization and therefore would receive different benefits from the same policy.

If we conceive of the organization as an abstraction, it is possible to say that a given policy is or is not "in the interest of the firm" or "in the national interest." The implication of such an assertion is that at some future time the firm or the nation will in some sense be better off as a result of a given policy (than it would be as a result of some other set of circumstances). However, it is worth noting that concepts such as "the interest of the firm" or "the national interest" are never invoked except when the policy in question is one for which *someone* will, or thinks he will, suffer an immediate and perhaps permanent disadvantage. Often, when the benefits are widely distributed the costs are highly concentrated. This, for example, has been the essence of the controversy over foreign trade policy in recent decades. While there can be general agreement that a liberal trade policy is good for "the economy," the fact is that there will be some small number of firms and people who will pay a cost, and in some instances that cost will be disastrous.

7. The pioneering work in this field is Robert Schlaifer, *Probability and Statistics for Business Decisions* (New York: McGraw-Hill, 1959).

Any notion of judging a policy by its contribution to an overall system, as Zeckhauser and Schaefer demonstrate by their review to the relevant literature, poses the possibility and usually the inevitability of an inequity to some person or unit within the system. Overall contribution of benefit to the system usually produces some perceived inequity in the distribution of benefits. For example, it is well known that the rich in any society have never as a group looked favorably on any redistribution of property. At the opposite extreme, however, one way of looking at the welfare of "this group" would favor a policy that benefited a rich man by $1 million if it cost a group of poorer people any measurably smaller sum.

In principle, it has been argued that such inequities can be handled by side payments to the disadvantaged parties. If the gain to the system as a whole is sufficient, the magnitude of such payments can be such that everybody is better off. A policy that produced such a situation could unequivocally be called a "good" policy. But, in no meaningful sense is it an optimal policy, because different people will have different preferences among the many "good" policies that might be pursued.

In the absence of any method of determining a "best" public policy (even in principle), there are but two alternatives for selection of policies. The first is the delegation to or usurpation of this task by some small group of persons. The other possibility is negotiation among interested parties to arrive at some policy sufficiently satisfactory to enough of them so that they can or will impose it on the others. Examples of the delegation of preference setting are the granting of formal authority in business organizations or the making of the federal budget. However, any such situation, whether authority is delegated or usurped, can be regarded as a form of deferred negotiation.

The federal budget is based on the assumption that it is acceptable to the American people and to the Congress which, in varying ways, represents the American people. It must also be acceptable to the agencies that will imple-ment it. These agencies are not merely rote executors of the Presidential will, nor could they ever be, since they are faced with the day-to-day opportunity and necessity of interpreting that policy. Similarly, the head of a business organization can initiate policies, but these policies must produce results over the reasonably short run that will maintain the morale of his organization. Even a dictator can only, at best, defer negotiation. It is true that he may be able to impose his will for a long time, perhaps even for the duration of his life. But to the extent that his policies do not build him a base of support, he will have to spend organizational resources to maintain his position.

It would appear that the bargaining process is at the heart of the policy process. One of the functions of a formal organization is to build a delay into the bargaining. Formal delegation of authority makes it possible for certain persons to exercise initiative in establishing and implementing policies. Exercise of that authority involves the formulation of policies and their articulation such that a minimum winning coalition of parties will be aligned behind those policies. This idea of the "minimum winning coalition" was first posed by Riker as the basis on which public policies are formed, but as Bower points out in Chapter 3, the work of Cyert and March suggests that this is also a useful way of looking at how policies are formed in business organizations.

From a research point of view, one disconcerting characteristic of policy problems is that they do not exist as units. The student of policy tends to think of "the problem" such as urban mass transportation as a unitary problem. In fact, there is no unity with respect to the problems people actually have, the way in which they perceive the problem or, as has been pointed out, of their interests and their values. Furthermore, since the policy process has a time dimension, each of these elements changes over time.

Let us consider the question of the lack of unity of "the problem" through an example from urban mass transportation: in a given case, should the city build a subway or an elevated road? A businessman in an adjacent suburb may be concerned with parking space for his executives who would not take mass transportation under any circumstances but might benefit from less congestion on the highways. He may also be concerned with how to get competent secretaries to commute to his plant as well as with the changing local tax rate. Perhaps, but not necessarily, he will see all these separate issues as part of *the problem* of urban mass transportation. It may even be that he will see that his interest is simply that *some* form of transportation be built but with a reasonable impact on the local tax rate.

This businessman has no "problems" in common with his local politician in the core city. The local politician may concentrate most of his attention on the question of whether the transportation goes underground or above the ground. His concerns will be the possible displacement of people, a changing ethnic composition of his constituency, a changing tax *base* if taxable land is usurped, and so on.

We can quickly imagine various other groups which have different versions of "the problem." One might be concerned with preservation of historical sites and "the traditional appearance of our city," and so forth.

Even when their actual and their perceived problems are identical, and they have the same values, the interests of actors may differ. The mayors of two towns may be in wholehearted agreement over the need for a particular type of transit service but differ widely in the preferred methods of financing the service. Their perceptions and values may be identical but their interests conflict because one method of financing will benefit one community more than the other.

This lack of unity of the problem is important to us in two ways. In the first instance the diversity of interests and values precludes, as pointed out, the sort of determinate identification of a single "best" policy that is implied in the conception of decision making. The second implication of the lack of unity of "the problem" is a problem for the researcher. Because the problem cannot be taken as given, it becomes necessary to establish the pattern of distribution of perceptions of the problem held by the various relevant actors in the system of action. But in saying this, we pose a whole series of questions for research.

Who are the relevant actors? The policy system is an "open system" in that the relevant actors in any policy issue cannot be specified in advance. Attempts both to use the formal system of authority and the reputation of a supposed "power elite" have been tested and found inadequate for identifying the relevant actors in any specific policy problem. Both the system of formal authority and the reputation of some persons as being influential are *relevant* in the sense that persons identified by such routes are more likely to be involved in a policy problem than people selected randomly from the population. However, such persons are never completely involved in every policy problem. Furthermore, for any one problem some of the crucial actors will be persons who have neither formal authority nor a general position of informal influence. Their role is highly specific to the particular issue. Both Schoettle and Gergen review the failures of the traditional approaches, and Gergen addresses himself specifically to the devising of a procedure for identifying those persons who are in a position of leverage at various stages of the policy process.

Once such persons (or the institutions they represent) are identified, we find that other traditionally cherished concepts must be reexamined. The notion that people (or organizations) act in their "self-interest" turns out to be an uninformative tautology. As this assertion is usually used in the discussion of policy formation, it clearly implies that an organization or an individual has an obvious, unitary, unequivocal interest in any given issue. It further implies that the organization or individual is aware of what this is and that certainly any intelligent observer ought to be able to infer this interest from the clear logic of the situation.

In point of fact, the "interests" of people and organizations are multiple and complex and policy problems are sufficiently complex that for the vast majority of individuals or organizations it is conceivable—given the objective features of the situation—to imagine them ending up on *any* side of the issue.

We are also faced with the definition of the "self" which has a self-interest. Does a British-owned American distributor of Scotch whiskey consider his obligation to be to the parent company or to the American subsidiary? Is the "self" interest of a firm that of the chief executive officer, the top executive group, the firm as an abstraction, or does it include the stockholders and the customers? On the governmental level, various bureaus of the executive branch have developed constituencies for whose interests they are expected to work. However, under certain circumstances the executive branch stands more unified. The question of the self whose interest is pursued cannot be settled on an a priori basis.

Once the self has been identified, there is still the latitude of definition of interest to which we have referred. "Interests" are articulated by the various participants in the policy process and an integral part of the process of negotiation is the presentation of policy proposals in such a form as to engage the perceived interests of members of a winning coalition.

Of course, there are constraints of reality beyond which a sane man cannot be persuaded his interests lie. But within these limits there is sufficient latitude that self-interests cannot be taken for granted. We need to determine empirically not only how the persons in the policy process define their self-interest, but how the social process of communication brings about the definition and redefinition of self-interest over the course of time.

The definition and redefinition of the issue are central to the process of debate and negotiation that takes place over time. In this view of the policy process, a key skill of leadership is that of formulating policy so that a winning coalition can be mobilized behind it. The skill does not end with the formulation of the policy but extends to spelling out to the potential members of the potential winning coalition the ways in which the policy will serve their interest.

It will probably be agreed that negotiation of the sort we have been describing is a social as well as an intellectual process. Additionally, there is a certain amount of social context implied in what we have said so far. We have already referred to the question of who are the relevant actors. But these actors exist and act in a series of structured relationships. Certainly people, institutions, and groups vary not only in values, interests, and perceptions of the issue, but also in their access to means of communication, ability to formulate and communicate issues, and in access to resources that can be used for persuasion or coercion.

Up to this point we have treated the policy process as a *relatively* closed system that can, for practical purposes, be isolated for analysis. Regrettably this is an exaggeration. The parties involved in any policy issue have other responsibilities and obligations. They also have a past and a future. They live in an institutional context that has relevance beyond any one policy issue. One of the fallacies of treating the policy process simply as "decision making" is that it assumes that someone is aware of the problem, that he can devote full time and attention to it, and that the issue has a clear-cut beginning and end. This picture does describe to some extent the situation of the staff analyst who, by virtue of the extent to which he is able to free his time and attention to analyze a given issue, can thereby be misled to assume that this is true of the man with action responsibility whom he is advising.

Regardless of the amount and quality of analysis done, the men who must take final responsibility for policy setting are faced with other events that compete for their time, attention, and energy. These other events involve interests and values that must be traded off against the interests and values involved in the policy issue in which the researcher is interested. Some events, which might actually have low priority in a given actor's scheme of values, may have the capacity to grab and hold his attention and command his resources. For these reasons we have coined the phrase "the envelope of events and issues" to refer to those events and issues that must be considered as the context within which to analyze a given policy problem. This "envelope" will be distinctive of individuals, or at least of classes of individuals.

Because of the formidable (although hopefully feasible) data-gathering demands that this context of events and issues poses, a fairly strong case should be made that this exploration of the broader context in which actors deal with specific issues is more than interesting, more than important, but (at least in some cases) crucial. The argument and evidence to support the preceding assertions about the importance of context follow.

The simplest aspect of the importance of context of the problem is that busy men do not have the resources to treat many issues as salient and that their strategies for handling salient and nonsalient issues are probably quite different. Furthermore, the researcher, because *he* is interested in the problem, tacitly assumes that other people find it equally important. Because people are polite they will answer the researcher's questions generally, but not always, in his terms. In the study of the making of foreign trade policy by Bauer, Pool, and Dexter,[8] it became gradually apparent to them that the issue was for most of the businessmen and most of the Congressmen interviewed one of very low priority.

In any ongoing institution, the ability to get important things done is dependent upon maintaining a reservoir of goodwill. The person who fights every issue as though it were vital exhausts his resources including, most especially, the patience and goodwill of those on whom he has to depend to get things done. Therefore, it should be considered neither surprising nor immoral that, when an issue is of low salience the sensible individual may use it to build goodwill for the future, or pay off past obligations, by going along with some individual for whom the issue is of high salience. Bauer, Pool, and Dexter found many men in Congress treating foreign trade legislation in this way. On the other hand, businessmen for whom this was an issue of low salience were careful not to expend an excessive amount of their finite goodwill on it.

Hence, in order to understand or predict the way in which a given issue will be handled, we must determine the salience which the issue has relative to other things with which the individual has to cope. And this is seldom self-evident.

The salience of an issue *can* be considered in an atemporal sense in that, at a given moment in time, a person has a limitation on the resources, including time, that he can muster. But as we have already hinted, an issue

8. Raymond A. Bauer, Ithiel de Sola Pool, and Lewis A. Dexter, *American Business and Public Policy* (New York: Atherton Press, 1963).

of low salience may be used to settle past debts and build up future goodwill. The time-binding nature of the policy process manifested itself in many ways in the Bauer, Pool, and Dexter study. During one session of Congress the Eisenhower Administration had put considerable demands on the chairman of a relevant committee to secure the passage of another bill. As a result of the amount of goodwill and committee time they had expended on the previous bill, the Administration was reluctant to, and did not, ask the chairman to hold full hearings on the Reciprocal Trade Act. In effect, what had happened before foreign trade legislation came to the committee was decisive in determining how the bill was handled.

On the other hand, since policy making is by definition setting a course to be followed in the future, it is redundant to say that consideration of future consequences is part of the "envelope" that affects the policy process. However, the policy maker's view of the future world, if he has wisdom, is different from that implied in concepts like decision making, problem solving, or goal seeking. All these usual concepts imply a discreet sequence of events with a single definite point of termination.[9] Serious policy making does not involve such decisive resolutions of a problem. A Supreme Court ruling of 1954 did not abolish segregation in public education, nor did the Civil Rights Act of 1965 eliminate discrimination in politics. Each of these events redefined the terms in which an ongoing struggle was conducted. The experienced policy maker knows that as he resolves one issue he is posing others. He realizes that he is frequently not settling an issue but redefining the rules of the game and if, in any meaningful sense, he has been "victorious" he hedges his victory to give himself room for maneuver in the future.

One of the ways in which he does this is not to force on the losing coalition terms that will make it unduly difficult to work with the losing parties in the future. In 1965, a private study that involved a considerable number of interviews with key figures in Congress, indicated that the relative speed with which Civil Rights legislation has been passed—or if you prefer, not been passed—has not been a result of lack of sufficient support for such legislation in the Congress. It has been more a result of the reluctance of many Congressmen and Senators to force such measures on their southern colleagues more rapidly than the Southerners could adjust *vis-à-vis* their constituents. A similar explanation would apply to President Johnson's behavior during the crucial week of turmoil in Selma, Alabama. Johnson appeared to be waiting for public pressure to build up to the point that when he made his address to the Congress he could not be viewed by the Southerners as arbitrarily "pushing them around."

9. For an articulate and detailed discussion of this distinction, see the contrast between the views of human behavior held by psychologists and that held by policy makers in Sir Geoffrey Vickers, *The Art of Judgment* (New York: Basic Books, 1965), pp. 31-34.

It is true that this model of an intellectual process embedded in a social process which, in turn, has to be understood in the context of past, present, and future events and issues, can be masked. For one thing I have not denied that there are situations in which men have enough power for a finite period of time to override the sort of negotiating process to which we referred. Such actions generally build up future trouble. Nor do I deny that negotiation is sometimes deferred. This occurs most often in situations in which authority is delegated to handle some range of issues. Thus an office holder is not in constant explicit negotiation with his constituents but returns to them from time to time to seek out their reaction, in the form of votes, to what he has been doing.

Finally, I do not deny that there are situations in which the formation of policy is a highly intellectual, highly deliberate process. It is conceivable that the Kennedy Administration's reaction to the Cuban missile crisis was of that nature. However, the published accounts of the Bay of Pigs episode suggest that the earlier crisis is better understood as a complex social process in which circumstances kept the new President from understanding the nature of the commitment he was making; his recent campaign had made him sensitive to being seen as "soft on Castro," he envisaged a group of disgruntled, disappointed refugees spreading anti-American sentiment throughout Latin America if he called it off; some advisers were afraid to speak up; others had become so committed to the invasion plan that they glossed over the difficulties; and so on.

What I am suggesting is that we should approach each policy issue as though the process were as complex as has been suggested, and converge on the intellectual or "decision" aspects of the problem rather than hope that the problem can be understood in terms of its solely intellectual component. There are two reasons for *not* working *outward* to the social context. The first is that much of the record and people's verbalization of what has happened and is happening will be highly rationalized, and the researcher may be deceived into believing he has an adequate picture of what is transpiring or has transpired. The other is that much of what occurs will not make sense in the more limited context. This is the reason that much behavior of congressmen and businessmen is labeled "irrational." And this, in turn, is also deceptive, at least in many instances in which the man involved is concerned with more issues than the observer has taken account of.

Our position that the student of any policy problem should proceed with the assumption that the process may be as complex and as social as we have described should not be taken as a statement of our preference of the way in which people *ought* to solve such problems. We do believe that to some extent it is impossible and undesirable that individual policy decisions be approached in isolation or as though they did not impinge on a wider range of issues. And we also believe that, even though it might be desirable, it is not possible to eliminate entirely the essentially irrelevant factors that influence policy formation.

It is difficult to conceive of a way in which the intellectual aspects of policy formation can ever be completely isolated from their social context. Policies will always be made by and for human beings who inhabit human institutions. But, to the extent that we can handle deliberately those variables that have influenced us without our knowledge or with which we have been able to cope only vaguely, we can with a certain amount of justification say that we have been able to bring the policy process closer to the intellectual models of "problem solving" or "decision making." We would hope, therefore, that as the individuals faced with specific policy problems understand better the complexity of the events with which they are confronted, they will become less the victims and more the masters of those events.

Strategy of Research

In the social sciences in recent years we have had frequent espousal of such open systems and transactional models as we have been proposing here. The approach is in very many ways akin to the clinical approach and is ordinarily set in opposition to the experimental approach and to more rigorous procedures in general. The authors of this book do not share the notion that rigorous research procedures and the acceptance of complex process models are inherently incompatible. In fact, one of our main objectives is to reconcile the two. However, we believe that there are implicit in the experimental method certain limitations that must be recognized and dealt with intelligently. I refer, for example, to the necessity in most experimenting for developing an explicitly closed system so that we may know on what set of variables we presumably are acting and the accompanying tendency to view the sequence of acts studied as having a prescribed beginning and end. On the other hand, we cannot study every conceivable variable and every conceivable pattern of interacting influence. There seems to be a consensus among students of the policy process who adhere to our point of view that the way of looking at things must be made more "operational." One of our major objectives is to think through the question of how the notion of anything being possibly related to everything else can be made tractable for the empirical researcher. To accomplish this it is necessary to increase the effectiveness and efficiency of research strategies and procedures for the study of such issues. The related goals involve identifying what information is needed and improving the methods of gathering and presenting it.

The basic strategy we devised is reflected in the three substantive position chapters on foreign aid policy, the transfer of technological information, and urban mass transportation. The writers of these chapters, each a specialist in his area, were exposed to an earlier view of the policy process of the sort outlined above. Each writer was then asked to outline a model of this process which he could accept as adequate to include all the variables that he thought might be relevant to the problem with which he was concerned. The next move was to reduce the magnitude of the research task by a sequence of steps I will now outline. We asked each writer to identify the points of "leverage" in his system. By a "point of leverage" we mean a person, institution, issue, or subsystem of the overall system that has the capacity to effect a substantial influence on the output of the system. The chairman of an appropriate sub-committee of the House would be an example of a person with high leverage in the instance of foreign aid.

The reason for the use of the term "leverage point" was to invoke a concept that was both more general and freer of excess semantic baggage than the term "power." It should be noted that ability to influence events may occur without any of the trappings ordinarily associated with power. Hence, we chose a concept that is defined only in terms of that in which we are interested.

In any system, all elements do not have equal leverage for influencing the output of the system. In computer simulation such elements are located via sensitivity analysis by experimentally varying the "behavior" of elements and observing the relationship between these variations and the output of the model. Sometimes the model will be very insensitive to variations in the behavior of given elements but very sensitive to slight variations in others. Our analysts were asked to make such an analysis on a judgmental basis. Specifically, they were asked to identify the leverage points on the basis of their ability to influence the output of the system.

Actually this type of an analysis is carried on in three stages: the system of action, the system of information, and the system of research. I will explain what these mean.

I have been referring to the system of action. Here we asked about the ability of a person, institution, issue, or subsystem to influence the outcome of a policy issue. We lose interest in elements of the system of action if they have little leverage on the system. In addition, it is sometimes the case that the behavior of a high leverage element is as predictable as it would be if we had more information. For example, in Chapter 9, which provides an analysis of the politics of foreign aid, the author concluded that public opinion is an important subsystem in the formation of policy on foreign aid. However, attitudes toward foreign aid are so deeply rooted in broader aspects of the American ethos—and the relationship between these attitudes and the more general features of the American ethos is so understandable—that there is little prospect that further research would improve our understanding of our ability to influence public opinion. Hence, the subsystem of the foreign aid policy system was screened out in the "system of information."

Finally, if an element of the system has survived the screening on the levels of action and information, we screen it once more in terms of the extent to which at this time it is researchable. Let me give an example.

The three major subsystems Geiger and Hansen identified in Chapter 9 were the public (already screened out for the reasons mentioned), the executive branch, notably AID, and the Congress. Unquestionably Congress, particularly in the form of the subcommittee of the Appropriations Committee, has important leverage in the system of action, and there are many elements in the Congressional subsystem about which one might want further information. However, many of these elements seem at the moment to be virtually unresearchable.

Congressional reaction is primarily influenced by the committee structure, relations between the Congress and the Administration, and Congressional responsiveness to public opinion. In a word, the reaction of Congress to foreign aid proposals is at least as much a function of the institutional context and of other issues occupying the attention of the Congress as it is a response to the particular program and information brought to it by the Agency for International Development in a given year. Congress has a great deal of leverage on the outcome of the foreign aid issue, but the main variables seem so "noisy" that it does not appear worthwhile, *at this point in time*, to expend much research effort on this subsystem except to monitor it with the hope of possibly gaining some additional insight as to the type of information that would take the noise out of the system. It presents a completely opposite picture from that of public opinion. In the latter case our understanding is sufficiently complete that it does not seem worthwhile to gather new information. In the case of the Congress the situation in recent years has been sufficiently complex and indeterminate that it is now difficult to decide what data to gather.

This brings us down to the last of the three subsystems, the Executive Branch, particularly AID. There is a series of interesting questions here, such as the use or nonuse of information from disciplines other than economics, the flow of information to and from the academic community that might improve the planning models, and so on. It appears that empirical research should thus start with the study of the Executive Branch.

This is an example of the first stage of reducing the complexity of our model of the issue for the purpose of deciding where to begin empirical work. Naturally this screening process would be reassessed from time to time, and one area of empirical work might be abandoned for another in the course of this reassessment. I am assuming that the reader will not be particularly bothered by whether or not he and I are in agreement on any substantive statement about the foreign aid process. I have intended merely to illustrate how one set of judgments were used to accomplish this reduction of complexity. If another's judgment differs, he may still follow the procedure, but, as is appropriate, he will conclude that he should start research on different parts of the system.

In practice the initial screening may identify some specific individuals or institutions or it may merely locate subsystems and issues of high importance. Thus, in the case of urban mass transportation it seems important to study the process in the local community for the approval of specific projects. This procedure rules out immediate investigation of policy discussions on the national level and a series of issues on the local level, such as the adoption of a broad transportation policy and allocation of funds for mass transportation. That is to say, we would begin—in the instance of mass transportation—at a stage where broad policy had been established and general funds allocated, and look at how the funds are spent on specific projects within the broad policy. I have not indicated how the analyst narrowed our choice down this much. It is sufficient to note here that such narrowing has taken place and then consider the research problems with which one is then faced.

Study of Individual Actors in the Policy Process

This initial phase, carried out by the subject-matter specialist, can serve only to identify subsystems and issues that are judged to be the most important point at which to research the policy process. From this point, we must turn to the methods proposed by Gergen for identifying the specific policy system appropriate to the problem which has been isolated for study. This consists of identifying institutions, groups, and eventually individuals who are to be the points of analysis and observation. Schoettle reviews the evidence for the necessity of concentrating initially on the individual as the point of observation and analysis. Her longer treatment of the issue is commended to the reader who is not already persuaded by what has been said thus far.

Taking individuals as the unit of observation and analysis by no means implies ignoring their interaction, or assumes that all individuals in the system of action represent the same research problems. Because the policy process is a dynamic one extending over a span of time, and because different people play different roles, provision must be made for studying the changes that take place over time and for more intensive observation of those persons who play more central roles. As people are increasingly central to the process it will be necessary to study each individual[10] and on a relatively continuing basis;

10. I am aware of the fact that in some instances the key individuals may be exceedingly important people who may, in fact, not be amenable to direct observation

or, conversely, as they are further from the center of influence, sampling of individuals will suffice and reobservation at fairly long intervals will be possible.

To a large extent the approach to the individuals being studied is dictated by the preceding discussion of leverage in the policy process. Perhaps it would be better to make it explicit: Once an individual is identified as being in a position of leverage, a role analysis might be done. Because of the importance we have assigned the problem of context, we would want to know, before turning our attention directly to his involvement in the issue, his range of responsibility, involvements, resources, information, and any other aspects of his role that may bear on how he might handle the issue in question. Once these facts had been established we could then consider his involvement in the specific issue. Nevertheless, the host of subproblems is formidable. To what extent can retrospective evidence be used? Can a person tell you what he did and thought in the past without absorbing his report to some scheme of how he thinks he ought to have behaved? How do we find out what problems he *perceives* himself as having among the multitude of variants of the issue which are possible? These of course are bread-and-butter problems of research that require diligence but are not of a new order. Gergen treats them in Chapter 6.

The main thrust of our assessment of the problems of studying the role of the individual actors in the policy process is that, for the immediate future, the job of data gathering is going to have to be more extensive and more systematic than it has been in the past. Generally speaking the policy research that has carried us to this point has been of two sorts. There has been research on large-scale problems with modest data-gathering activities, and the use of intuition to bridge the gaps in the data. There have also been very intensive data-gathering jobs involving minute-to-minute observation of important actors. However, the cost of such data gathering and the vast task of processing data of this sort have made it impossible to extend this sort of operation to coverage of very elaborate systems.

We are assuming that both of the types of research described above will continue to play a vital role in our understanding of the policy process. However, we are aiming in the present context at developing an approach which uses very intensive data gathering selectively in key spots and which, at the same time, can attempt to deal with broad problems and processes.

---

at all. Obviously the words "study" and "observe" have to be stretched in some cases. In the Bauer, Pool, and Dexter study, for example, President Eisenhower was never seen personally but perhaps a half-dozen persons working with him were interviewed, in some cases several times.

Conclusion

The purpose of this introductory chapter has been to make the reader acquainted with the plan of the book, the content of the chapters that form the body of the book, the relationship of the chapters to each other, and the major ideas that are developed in greater elaboration in those chapters.

The formation of policies is one of the most serious types of activities in which man ordinarily engages. Precisely because the process is so complicated, it has been resistant to both adequate conceptualization and adequate research. Our goal is to move forward toward both these goals without in any way being presumptuous about what we can at present achieve.

The major difficulties in forming a conceptualization of the policy process are to overcome the misleading notions that have prevailed because of confusion of what happens with what many people *wish* would happen, to distinguish what was intended from what occurred, and to reflect the complexity of the process in contrast to the simpler models that have been applied to it. We hope that in the main we have overcome these obstacles and have presented a view of the policy process that will at least encourage the reader to criticize, supplement, modify, and build on the present orientation. In the course of this being done, it may well be possible that much that has been said will have to be abandoned.

Our intention in presenting a view of the policy process is not particularly to gain immediate acceptance of a viewpoint, although we would be delighted if it met with some approval and seemed of direct utility. Our major purpose, however, is to present an approach that we believe is appropriate to further empirical research. There is a paradox in this effort, however, in that we are simultaneously advocating more systematic data gathering and complicating the model of the phenomena to be investigated. The two tendencies are ordinarily in opposition to each other. Certainly it is an unusual way to encourage systematic research to remind the researcher that he is dealing with an open system in which anything may be relevant.

It is because of the difficulty of gathering systematic data on policy formation without sacrificing the essential complexity of the process that we have proposed the particular research strategy outlined above for identifying the points in the policy system at which to begin making observations.

We recognize many limitations on the approach we propose. To study any policy problem of major dimensions as systematically as the various essays in this volume would indicate would require an expenditure of effort at least as large as that to which we are accustomed in the largest of our undertakings. However, the use of the approach (or approaches) suggested here need not be viewed in an all-or-none fashion. Several of us involved in this work have found that elements of it fit easily into various other pieces of research in which we have been engaged.

Another difficulty with our way of looking at things is that it does not fit with many usual notions of what research is about. We are not proposing "hypothesis testing," for example, but rather the testing of the utility of some assumptions about the policy process. These assumptions are not likely to prove either "right" or "wrong." It is difficult to imagine, for instance, how one could negate the proposition that negotiation underlies all policy processes *even though the mechanism of negotiation may be masked.* Obviously every negative instance can be explained away by the qualifying clause that the process may be masked. One can judge only after one or more attempts at acting on this assumption whether or not it leads research in fruitful directions.

Similarly, our urging of the inclusion of a wider range of variables in the model of the process must be judged against the question of whether the extra effort produces sufficient additional knowledge to justify it.

Judgments such as we have suggested are matters for the future and are dependent on whether or not the readers of this book choose to attempt to exploit the ideas presented here. We hope only that we have presented them well enough so that they may engender an informed judgment.

Chapter 2

RICHARD ZECKHAUSER and ELMER SCHAEFER

Public Policy and Normative Economic Theory

Introduction

An economist approaches a decision by asking, "What do we want and what can we get?" Generally, we want more than we can get.

> ... the will is infinite and the execution confined ...
> the desire is boundless and the act a slave to limit.
>> *Troilus and Cressida*
>> Act III, Scene ii

Because our capabilities are limited, choices must be made among our competing desires. Methods for making these choices—"the allocation of scarce resources among competing ends"—are the stuff of economics and the subject of this chapter.

At the outset it might be helpful to clarify the relationship set forth in our title. Of what use is the economic model of choice to the decision maker? Is not the ability to make difficult choices among competing ends the very asset that has placed him in his policy-making position? The economist would answer that systematic analyses and formal statements of procedure can be valuable. He might invoke an analogy to the well-worn example of

Molière's M. Jourdain who discovered he had been speaking prose all his life. What grammar is to prose, the model of choice is to decisions.

But public policy decisions do not always fit neatly into the model of choice. The choice between undertaking an urban renewal program and increasing our foreign aid commitment is conceptually more difficult than the choice familiar in economics between alternative bundles of goods. Even in the evaluation of individual projects we may encounter exceptional difficulties. How can we weigh the loss of those families displaced by our hypothetical urban renewal project against the gain of those who will be treated to improved living conditions in the completed housing? In recent years economics has become more concerned with developing techniques for dealing with public policy decisions. This chapter attempts to relate these new techniques and methods, but in end product it may also serve to point out the inadequacies as well as the strengths of normative economic methods for dealing with public policy problems. With this warning in mind we proceed to our more formal analysis.

Our starting point is a simple model of choice, from which we deduce the characteristics of best decisions. The rest of the paper extends this model in an effort to make it more applicable to the complex problems that confront the public policy maker. This extension is needed to deal with three basic difficulties:

1. Decisions may affect more than one individual;
2. The outcome resulting from a decision may not be known with certainty;
3. All the consequences of a decision may not occur immediately; they may be spread out into the future.

The Model
of Choice

There are two elements in an act of choice: the set of alternatives from which the choice is to be made, and the set of preferences according to which the chooser ranks these alternatives. The set of feasible alternatives can be specified by listing all the members of the set (for example, purchasing a new suit, taking a trip to Chicago, buying a new hat and taking a trip to New York, buying two shares of Stock X . . .), or by stating the constraints that the alternatives must satisfy, (for example, spending no more than $100). The decision maker attempts to select the one alternative that is preferred to all others in the feasible set. There will be such a uniformly preferred alternative, if his preference rankings have the property of transitivity: if alternative A is preferred in the paired comparison (A, B), and alternative B is preferred in the paired comparison (*B*, *C*), then alternative *A* will be preferred in the paired comparison (*A*, *C*). Such a transitive preference ordering is called an ordinal-utility ranking. Most theories of rational individual decision making under conditions of certainty require that the decision maker behave in accord with some ordinal ranking of the available alternatives. An ordinal ranking can be conveniently described by assigning a number to each alternative in such a way that if *A* is preferred to *B*, *A* is assigned a higher number. The decision maker chooses that alternative with the highest number; he maximizes his utility.

We will be concerned with the two primary elements in the model of choice: the set of alternatives, and the set of preferences by which they are evaluated. The model can be interpreted in various ways. The alternatives can be combinations of goods, such uncertain prospects as lottery tickets, elaborate plans for an individual's entire life, or even sweeping programs of social reform. The chooser in turn can be an individual, a group, or a government. The principle of rational choice is unchanged. The decision maker should attempt to select the alternative that he values the highest in terms of his own preferences.

The model of choice can be interpreted as a theory of behavior, a theory that can be tested by seeing whether actual choices correspond to those choices predicted by the model. However, we place considerable importance on the normative value of the model; we wish to assess its ability to tell the decision maker what he should do, and to assist him in making choices. We need neither a model nor a theory to help us choose among differently flavored ice-cream cones. This chapter is written on the assumption that decision problems in the public policy area are not this simple, that they are sufficiently complex as to benefit from

1. An explicit statement of the decision maker's preferences;
2. A careful exposition of the alternative actions that are open to him; and
3. A model that relates these alternative actions to the stated preferences in a manner that permits an efficient choice to be made among the alternatives.

We proceed to develop a model that conveniently represents the preferences and alternatives which characterize that decision situation. From these representations will emerge the efficiency properties that characterize optimal decisions.

Frequently the available alternatives combine many attributes, all of which are valued by the decision maker. The problem of choice would not be difficult if one alternative were favored for all attributes—in technical language, if one alternative were dominant. In the left-hand part of Table 2-1, alternative *A* dominates alternatives *B* and *C* because it is preferred to them for all (in this case, two) relevant attributes. Unfortunately, dominant alternatives rarely present themselves. The right-hand part of the same table show.s a choice situation with no dominant alternative; the prettiest girl is not the most intelligent. It might even be the case that one's preference function would rank Brenda, who is neither prettiest nor most intelligent, over the two alternative dates.

Difficult choice problems in which attribute rankings conflict lie at the core of the decisions that must be made by public policy makers. These difficulties may arise because their decisions affect many individuals. Though policy A might be better for one group in our society, policy B might be better for another. If time is a crucial element we may find for example that policy A is more immediately beneficial, but that policy B will be better twenty years from today. In a third context, policy A might be superior if some uncertain events turn out favorably, but policy B may be a better hedge against

Table 2-1   Rankings on Attributes

	ATTRIBUTE I	ATTRIBUTE II	ALTERNATIVE DATE POSSIBILITIES	ATTRIBUTE Intelligence	ATTRIBUTE Beauty
A	1st	1st	Alice	1st	3rd
B	3rd	2nd	Brenda	2nd	2nd
C	2nd	3rd	Carol	3rd	1st

disaster. Conceptually, these conflicts between attributes are no different from the conflict between the attribute rankings of Alice, Brenda, and Carol. What is needed is a method of displaying the decision maker's preferences between different combinations of attributes. If we develop a perfectly general formulation we will be able to apply it to some of the more complex problems we will encounter further on in our discussion.

INDIFFERENCE MAPS

Economists have developed indifference maps as a method of displaying a decision maker's preferences. We can think of an indifference map as a graphical representation of the decision maker's ordinal utility function. For any two points on the map, each of which represents a pair of attributes,[1] we can say whether the decision maker prefers the first to the second, the second to the first, or if he is indifferent between them. Figure 2-1 shows a planner's indifference map relating his preferences between different combinations of the possible outputs of a dam project.

1. In general, more than two attributes will enter into the decision-maker's utility function. It would seem that this would lead to a breakdown of indifference-map analysis—for example, a four-attribute function would require that a complete indifference map be constructed in four dimensions. The word *complete* is the clue to the solution. It is usual practice to deal with incomplete, two-dimensional maps. Other attributes are held constant, or one of the two attributes on the map is chosen to play a summary role (for example, in consumption theory we represent "all other goods" as the money left in our budget).

Electricity is measured on the vertical axis, the horizontal axis measures the output of water for irrigation. Thus, point *A* represents an electricity output of 11,000 kw per day and a daily water output of 20,000 gallons. Each curve on the map represents a different level of ordinal utility; accordingly, the decision maker is indifferent between any two points on the same "indifference curve." The decision maker is indifferent between point *A* and point *B* which offers more electricity but less water. Thus the curve represents the way in which he is willing to trade water for electricity. The negative slope of the indifference curves (by negative slope we mean that from up and to the left they run down and to the right) shows that he is willing to give up some electrical production if he can increase his irrigation output and vice

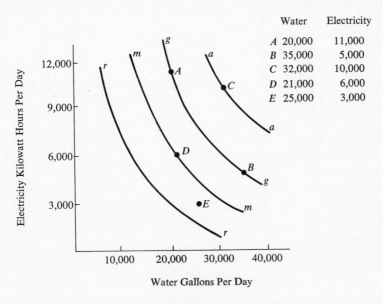

	Water	Electricity
A	20,000	11,000
B	35,000	5,000
C	32,000	10,000
D	21,000	6,000
E	25,000	3,000

FIGURE 2-1

versa. The steepness of the curves indicates at what rate he is willing to trade off between the two outputs: the steeper the curve the greater the amount of electrical output he is willing to trade for a unit of water production. Thus at point *A* he would give up more electricity for an extra unit of water than he would at point *B*.

Increases in both outputs would clearly be desired by the decision maker.[2] Thus, northeasterly movements across the indifference map bring the decision maker to continually higher levels of utility. For example, the decision maker

2. It is economic convention to choose one's variables so that movements away from the origin are desirable. Thus on an indifference map we represent positive values such as the employment level rather than negative values such as the level of unemployment.

would prefer any combination of outputs represents by a point on curve *aa* to any combination represented on curve *gg*.[3]

The planner is asked to choose among five alternative dam projects: *A, B, C, D,* and *E.* He should choose alternative *C* as the project preferred according to his own ranking; it is the project that places him on the highest indifference curve.

It need not be the case, as above, that the planner has only a small set of discrete alternatives. It could well be that he could vary the output combinations in small steps so that he could always get a little more hydroelectric power by giving up a little more water for irrigation. If it is possible to make

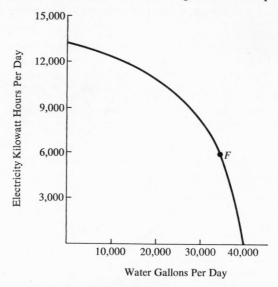

FIGURE 2-2

these continual trade-offs between the two outputs we will have what is known as a *production-possibility frontier* or *transformation curve.* This frontier represents all efficient combinations of water and electricity output; by an *efficient* combination of outputs we mean a combination in which more of any one output cannot be obtained except by giving up some of another output. The frontier is not merely five or eight or even twenty-five points, rather it is a continuous curve that gives the maximum possible water output for every given output of electricity. In this sense it is a locus of constrained maxima; each point on the frontier shows the best that can be done on one attribute for a given value of the other attribute. For example, point *F* indicates that with an electrical output of 6,000 kw hours the maximum possible water output is 33,000 gallons (Figure 2-2).

3. Given this information, the geometrically adept reader should be able to prove that indifference curves can never cross each other.

Increases in both outputs are clearly to be desired. Before proceeding further, the reader should convince himself that it is always in the interest of the decision maker to select an alternative that lies on the production-possibility frontier. The reason is simply that every point which lies within the frontier is dominated by a point on the frontier (there is a point on the frontier that yields more of both outputs).

The planner should choose from the dam whose output combination corresponds to point *G* in Figure 2-3. No other point among his production possibilities reaches as high an indifference curve as does point *G*. (Indifference curve *dd* is preferred to indifference curves *tt* and *nn* for example, and indifference curve *aa* is not attainable.) At point *G* the production-possibility frontier is tangent to the planner's indifference curve, and the slopes of these two curves are equal. This is a geometric representation of an important characteristic of an economic optimum. Before we proceed further with our discussion of the significance of this equality, we must interpret the slopes of these two curves.

As we move along the transformation curve (production-possibility frontier) *TT* we are giving up the production of one output in return for the increased production of the other. The rate at which this trade-off is taking place is called, quite reasonably, the *rate of transformation*. In our example, *K* and *L* were points with the values shown in Table 2-2.

Table 2-2

	Electricity in KW	Water in Gallons
K	11,000	20,000
L	8,000	30,000
change	3,000	10,000

We now have a geometric representation of the two elements in the act of choice: the set of alternatives from which the choice is to be made, and the set of preferences according to which the chooser ranks the alternatives. We combine these representations into a single diagram (Figure 2-3) to show which alternative should be selected by the decision maker.

Over this range, we would say that the rate of transformation of electricity for water is 3,000 for 10,000, or three for ten. However, we are dealing with a case of continuously changing transformation possibilities. Although we can only average ten units of increased water production for every three units of electricity sacrificed over the entire range, we can get more than ten units of water for the first three units of electricity sacrificed at point *K*.[4] At any point, the rate at which one output can be transformed into another is given by

4. This is like a person's going from Chicago to Boston at an average rate of fifty miles an hour. Part of the time he is going faster than fifty, say seventy; part of the time he is going slower.

the slope of the transformation curve. The steeper slope at point L indicates that the rate of transformation between electricity and water is greater there than it is at point K. We refer to the rate at which two outputs can be transformed at a particular point as the *marginal rate of transformation* at that point.

We have already interpreted the slope of an individual's indifference curve as giving the rate at which he is willing to trade off between two outputs (or in the more general case, two attributes)—the rate at which he can trade and still remain on the same indifference curve. Economists refer to this rate

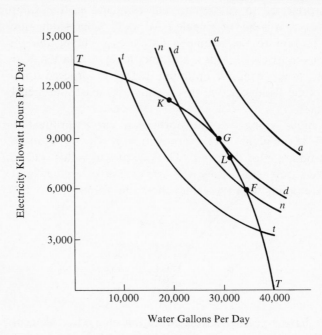

FIGURE 2-3

as the individual's *rate of substitution* between the two goods. We can see that this rate varies as we move along an indifference curve; it is clear that to be precise we will have to refer to the rate of substitution at a given point, and to the marginal rate of substitution at that point (sometimes abbreviated MRS). The reader should now return to Figure 2-1 and confirm that the planner's MRS between electricity and water is greater at point A than it is at point B.

The distinction between the marginal rate of transformation and the marginal rate of substitution is an important one to grasp. The former is the rate at which it is *possible* to exchange one good for another; the latter is the rate at which one is *willing* to exchange one good for another. The former is defined by the typical constraints on the production process; the latter by the subjective preferences of the decision maker.

We have found that at an optimum the slopes of the transformation curve and the indifference curve should be equal. Thus, it is seen that the marginal rate of transformation between two goods should equal the decision maker's marginal rate of substitution between them. The objective rate at which the planner is capable of carrying out the trade-off between electricity and water power is exactly equal to the subjective rate at which he is willing to substitute between these two outputs. Why must this be the case? Consider point K where the marginal rate of transformation between electricity and water (the rate at which electricity output can be traded for water output) is less than the planner's marginal rate of substitution. The planner will find it to his advantage to convert electricity into water at this point. He can give up x units

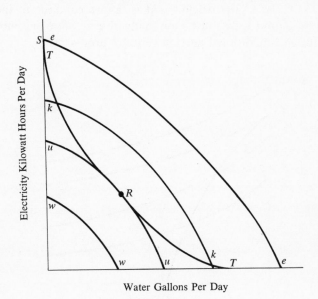

FIGURE 2-4

of electricity to get an additional unit of water output, whereas he would be willing to sacrifice y units of electricity for an additional unit of water. As x is less than y, it is in his interest to carry out this transformation. In this manner the decision maker will continue to move along the transformation curve until he reaches point G where the willingness rate and the possibility rate are equal.

When the decision maker is fortunate enough to be confronted with continuous transformation possibilities between different possible outputs, he will find it in his interest to think in terms of marginal trade-offs. He need never construct his entire indifference map; rather he need only be concerned with his transformation possibilities at a specific point and the rate at which he is willing to substitute between outputs at that point. By making continual beneficial trade-offs, so long as there is a divergence between these two rates, he can move until he reaches his economic optimum.

PATHOLOGICAL CASES

There are quite a few pathological cases for which the equality between these marginal rates will not hold at the optimum. We have followed conventional practice in constructing the shape of our indifference and transformation curves. It has been discovered that most decision makers behave as though they have convex indifference curves—the rate at which they are willing to trade output I for output II will decrease as they acquire more of output II. Furthermore, experience has shown that transformation curves are usually concave to the origin—that is, as we continue to increase our production of output I, we must continually give up more and more units of output II for each additional unit of output I produced.

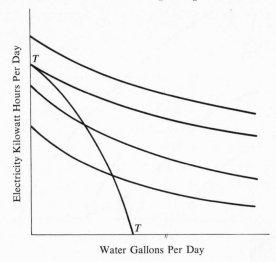

FIGURE 2-5

If for any particular decision problem some of these curves are not shaped in conventional fashion, the optimum may not be a point of tangency. In Figure 2-4 is shown a pathological transformation curve (convex to the origin) and pathological indifference curves (concave to the origin). There is equality between the marginal rates at the point of tangency, *R*. *R* is a terrible point. One can see by inspecting the transformation curve that the highest indifference curve is reached at *S*. The optimal solution involves the production of only one output. Economists would refer to this as a *corner solution* because the optimal choice lies in the corner of the production-possibility curve. It is possible to have corner solutions even if the curves are conventionally shaped. For example, see Figure 2-5.

INDIVISIBILITIES

A much more common problem is the one encountered when it is not possible to make continuous trade-offs between the outputs. If, for example, the outputs were aircraft carriers and bombers or sheep and goats, it would not be possible to carry out continuous trade-offs. One cannot fly two thirds of a bomber, or raise half a sheep. When the outputs are indivisible, feasible alternatives are indicated as a series of points (see Figure 2-1) rather than a continual transformation locus. Incremental (marginal) maximization procedures are of course ruled out, but the decision maker may find it helpful to move stepwise from point to point.[5]

IMPLICATIONS OF THE MODEL OF CHOICE

Although some complexities and difficulties may creep into the analysis, the basic nature of an economic choice is clear. Economists look at problems of choice in terms of trade-offs between the various desirable attributes. One desired output is gained only at the expense of another. In general, the problem is not to choose between different outputs, but rather to choose between different combinations of outputs. For example, the economist sees the problem of traffic safety

> ... not as an "all or nothing" problem, but as a "best mixture" problem whose solution involves some accidents plus some traffic. No accidents or no traffic are out of the question. ...[6]

The economist refuses to maximize the most valuable output (let us say human life) as though all other outputs and resources (for instance time, gasoline, traffic signals) were free. To the economist everything has an exchange rate, and his behavior and choice procedure reflect his willingness to trade.[7]

LEXICOGRAPHIC PREFERENCES AND PRIORITIES

Recently the idea has been advanced that individuals' preferences are sometimes lexicographic in nature.[8] A lexicographic ordering is one that ranks alternatives with regard to only one attribute; only if two alternatives are tied is the ranking on the second attribute considered. A priority approach to

5. The stepwise procedure will be helpful if his indifference curves are convex and if the scatter of discrete points can be connected by a curve that is concave to the origin.

6. Stefan Valavanis, p. 477. A complete list of all works cited is given in the Bibliography at the end of the chapter.

7. *Ibid.*, p. 478.

8. See John S. Chipman.

questions of choice is lexicographic in nature. We have often heard statements which express the dominance of a primary value. "There can be no justification for any action which increases the probability of nuclear war."

The pacifist might feel that he would be better Red than dead, but would he also choose to be Red rather than increase his chances of dying by .001 percent? A positive answer would require that no increase in the second attribute (freedom from communism) however large, could compensate a decrease, however small, in the second attribute (probability of survival).[9] A man would not agree to have his arms and legs cut off in exchange for any number of desserts, but if he were faced with the prospect of no desserts for the rest of his life he might accept a scratch on the finger.

The method of economic choice runs directly counter to any priority analysis—a method that makes one value or element preeminent. Therefore the economist may object to any kind of priority list. Hitch and McKean in their tour de force *The Economics of Defense in the Nuclear Age* make the following observation:

> Just how anyone can use such a list is not clear. Suppose a consumer lists possible items for his monthly budget in the order of their priorities . . . they rank as follows: (1) groceries, (2) gas and oil, . . . (5) liquor, (6) steam baths. This does not mean that he will spend all of his funds on groceries, nor does it mean that he will spend nothing on liquor or steam baths. His problem is really to allocate his budget among these different objects. He would like to choose the allocation such that an extra dollar on cigarettes is just as important to him as an extra dollar on groceries. At the margin, therefore, the objects of expenditure would be equally important.[10]

The economist is accustomed to think in terms of the problem of allocation. "A list of priorities does not face the problem or help solve it."

SPECIAL PROBLEMS CONFRONTING PUBLIC POLICY DECISIONS

As we mentioned above, ice-cream-flavor-type choice situations that form the standard examples of economic decision making do not adequately reflect the complexities involved in most decisions made in the public sphere. As the rest of this chapter will illustrate, the public decision maker is confronted with special difficulties, not all of which can be conveniently handled via present economic methods.

The decision maker in the public policy area may have to go beyond a

9. For an interesting discussion of thinking on this issue see Levine. Levine distinguishes between two groups—the maximizers, who concentrate on only one variable, say, probability of peace, and the optimizers, who would like to achieve some optimal mix between desirable variables.

10. Hitch and McKean, p. 123.

simple introspective evaluation to discover his preferences. Such an individual normally will have numerous competing goals and objectives by which to judge the alternatives open to him. He may well need a detailed and careful analysis before he can decide how these competing aims will be incorporated into his preference function. In the language of our model, he may have difficulty developing his indifference map or, more practically, a mental approximation to the indifference-map conception.

Thinking in terms of trade-offs between additional water or electricity production may be difficult. The task is all the more difficult if the competing objectives cannot be easily quantified. For example, we have no convenient standard equivalent to gallons or kwh by which to measure the output to be derived from an additional expenditure on foreign aid or urban renewal. These are the types of variables with which the public policy maker must deal. Even though they cannot always be adequately specified, the process of thinking in terms of trade-offs between such competing objectives may be of value. If nothing else, familiarity with economic methods encourages the decision maker to think in terms of all the variables that bear on his decision.

The literature of economics and operations research is replete with examples in which decision makers picked incorrect or too narrowly defined criteria on which to base their preferences.[11] The failure to carry out an explicit analysis of the preference function can readily lead to a choice that optimizes with respect to the wrong variables and in a sense answers the wrong question. The sole purpose of an economic analysis is to enable the decision maker to propose (and hopefully answer) the right question.

Policy-oriented decision makers may encounter special problems in connection with the other primary aspect of the model of choice, the setting forth of feasible alternatives. The constraints that restrict these alternatives may not be entirely concrete in nature. Government decision makers are often limited in their actions by constraints of a political nature. In this case, extensive political canvassing might be necessary before the decision maker could specify the alternatives which are open to him. Other constraint sets may demand economic, strategic, or engineering analyses before they can be converted into the format of feasible alternatives.

What combinations of kilowatt production, irrigation output, and flood control can be derived from a $5 million dam on the Red River?

11. Perhaps the best-known example of the choice of an inappropriate criterion has to do with mess-kit cleaning in the army. As the story goes, one analyst approached this task as that of minimizing the number of man hours needed to do the job. He converted the existing scheme of two wash tubs and two rinse tubs to a faster three wash, one rinse setup. Unfortunately, the analyst overlooked two crucial considerations: (1) the bacteria count in the rinse water soared beyond the critical level when there was but one rinse rub, (2) the "inefficient" old system led to the establishment of the long waiting lines the army employs to keep the men's legs in condition.

What alternative goals can be achieved through a $100 million aid program to Brazil?

What could we "buy" with an additional 1,000 soldiers in South Viet Nam?

Difficult questions such as these are basic to many of the choice problems that confront planners of policy. A complete answer to one of these questions might require a detailed analysis or may not be attainable at all. As we shall see later, an optimal-choice procedure must take into account the fact that a complete answer may not be worth the cost of obtaining it.

Individual
Welfare

In the discussion thus far we have not concerned ourselves with an elusive problem that must confront any policy decision—how should we go about defining our objectives, our goals? This question in turn rests on an even more fundamental inquiry—what are the values that underlie the goals and objectives to be established? When a policy maker chooses between different courses of action he is often concerned with the effect of his decision on the well-being of society. Similarly, when a policy maker sets up objectives and goals by which to guide his choices, he is merely establishing standards by which to judge alternative social states. Many people believe that it is ethically wrong to evaluate social states on a basis other than that of the welfare of individuals, and this primary value should be the base for any policy maker's set of objectives. We will base our further analysis on the acceptance of this ethic. Our criterion problem is thus translated to one of defining a policy maker's goals so that they adequately reflect the welfare positions of the individuals comprising his society. To date, normative theory has found this to be a most difficult and elusive problem. We feel that this is a profitable area for inquiry, both as a theoretical investigation and as an empirical study of actual policy decisions. We cannot deal adequately with the policy-making process without an understanding of the method by which tractable policy objectives can and should be derived from welfare judgments. We turn now to an underlying consideration, that of making individual welfare evaluations.

It would be helpful to have an unambiguous measure of an individual's welfare, just as we have a measure of his weight and height. In the past, economic theorists, in the tradition of Bentham, attempted to develop cardinal measures of individual welfare. A cardinal measure would tell us not only that the individual is better off in State A than in State B, but also how much better off he is; just as a scale can tell us not only that you weigh more this year than last, but how many pounds you gained.

Unfortunately, neither Bentham nor his successors were ever capable of making such a measurement process operational. As a consequence, discussions of "cardinal utility" went out of fashion and were left to those who talked of angels and pins. In later years, Von Neumann and Morgenstern rehabilitated the concept of cardinal utility to be employed in the limited context of choices made in uncertain situations (however, Von Neumann-Morgenstern utility can *not* be used to compare one person's welfare with another's). We shall return to their contribution in our discussion of uncertainty; for the present we confine ourselves to ordinal comparisons. "Is the individual better off in State *A* or State *B*?"

It is the usual procedure to judge this question by the individual's own actions. If when given the choice, the individual selects State *B* over State *A*, we say that he is better off in State *B*. That is, we rank the individual's welfare by means of his ordinal-utility function. This is the criterion of choice.

Sometimes it will not be possible to offer the individual a choice between different social states. Still it may be possible to establish his preferences between them. Suppose that the individual chooses a bundle of goods, *x*, from the alternative bundles offered in State *A*. Suppose that State *B* offers bundle *x* in addition to other new alternatives. The individual's welfare cannot be greater in State *A* than in State *B* though it could in fact be less.[12]

This principle can assist us in making judgments about economic welfare. Ralph chooses to buy six oranges when the price is set at six cents each (5 cents per orange plus a penny tax). If we accept the criterion of choice, we would agree that Ralph's welfare could not be decreased if he were assessed a lump-sum six-cent tax and the oranges were sold untaxed for a nickel apiece. The latter situation would still allow Ralph to reach his initial position of six oranges and an expenditure of 36 cents.

On what grounds can we justify a reliance on the individual's own ranking of his welfare in different situations? First, we might believe that he knows what is good for him, or second we might have an ethical belief that the individual choices as such should be respected as much as possible.

Some people reject both of these beliefs. They have raised some objections against the criterion of choice, and in particular against the common practice of confining comparisons solely to an individual's economic alternatives.

1. There may be reason to consider the alternatives that are open to other individuals. Following Veblen, we can say that given the same opportunities, the individual might feel that his welfare position has deteriorated if the lot of his neighbors has improved.

12. This concept lies at the heart of the theory of revealed preference, which in turn is the basis of much of index number and consumer-demand theory. The theory of revealed preference can be used to construct an individual's indifference map given his market purchases under different conditions of income and price. The crucial assumption of the theory is that the individual does not prefer any other available combination of goods to the one he actually purchases.

2. In ranking alternative social states an individual may include values which cannot be traded on an economic market. Even if centralized planning could improve the economic welfare of all individuals, it might not be a desirable innovation if it entailed a large sacrifice of individual liberty.

3. The choice procedure itself may affect an individual's rankings. An individual might prefer the establishment of a policy selected by a democratic process to the implementation by illegal means of an alternative policy for which he voted. A man's preference when all aspects of different situations are taken into account constitutes the most general form of an individual welfare function derived from the criterion of choice.

Sometimes we hear welfare judgments that seem to conflict directly with the criterion of choice. "He selects *A*, but *B* is better for him." Such statements might be defended on the grounds that the man would choose *B* if he knew better.

4. Under conditions of uncertainty it could be argued that the choice of the individual that should be respected is the one he would make if he had perfect knowledge.

5. Experience or education might be a prerequisite for the appreciation of the merits of *B*, which might be black olives or the music of Stravinsky.

6. Alternatively, the subject may not be able to comprehend or to evaluate the alternatives available to him, as in the case of a child or a madman.

7. One might justify a welfare judgment on the ground that the individual's freedom of choice is limited by a habit; as smoking cigarettes.

8. Finally, we might simply say that we disapprove of certain activities such as the use of narcotics whether the individual likes them or not.

Analysts are not agreed about the welfare criteria that should be employed for situations in which tastes are changing. Certainly we would agree that *A* should be ranked over *B* if it is preferred by the man both before and after the change in his tastes. Some observers feel that if there is a conflict the more recent preference should be given more weight because it may be the result of a learning process. Against this claim we might set the Epicurean argument that newly developed tastes that are created by advertising or by a desire for social emulation are artificial and should be discounted. Recently, attention has been called to the need for criteria to evaluate choices by which a man commits himself to actions in the future when his tastes may be different. Ulysses made such a commitment when he asked to be bound to the mast while he sailed past the sirens.[13] We should not underestimate the ability of policy makers to affect individual tastes, and in so doing to alter their welfare evaluations. This is an important consideration for normative theory, but it is often neglected.

13. See Rothenberg, Galbraith, and Strotz for further discussion of the material in this paragraph.

The Ranking of Public Policy Alternatives— The Pareto Criterion

There are some cases in which the ability to rank individual welfare enables us to provide a basis for comparing alternative social states. Such a basis is the Pareto criterion:

> State *A* is declared better than State *B* if some one is better off in State *A* and no one is worse off.

If for a State *C* there is no State *A* that is declared better by the Pareto criterion, we call State *C* a Pareto optimum. In choosing among all possible social states, we should like to select a Pareto optimum; a state in which it is not possible to make some one better off without making somebody else worse off.

The fundamental theorem of welfare economics, which economists have been busy proving under different assumptions since the days of Adam Smith, holds that under certain ideal conditions free competition working through the price system will produce a Pareto optimum. It will be worth our while to spend a moment examining this assertion.

THE PRICE SYSTEM AND PARETO OPTIMALITY

In the model of choice we defined the decision maker's best point as the highest ranked of all those points available to him. We also derived certain conditions that must hold at any such optimum: it is necessarily true that an optimal point be better than all the available points immediately surrounding it; that is, there is no small change, in any direction, that will lead to an improvement. Thus, we pointed out that decisions might be simplified by focusing on the marginal rate of substitution—the rate at which an individual is *willing* to substitute one attribute for another—and the marginal rate of transformation, the rate at which an individual is *able* to substitute one attribute for another. If these two rates are unequal, then the individual can make a substitution that will move him to a position that he prefers.[14]

If two people have marginal rates of substitution between two commodities which are unequal, then a trade can be arranged that will move each to a more preferred position. Suppose that George's marginal rate of substitution between apples and oranges is 3 and Peter's marginal rate of substitution is 4; George can exchange at the rate of three apples for one orange and remain on the same indifference curve. Since Peter is willing to exchange four apples for one orange, an exchange could be arranged to which both would agree. For example, Peter would be more than willing to give up three and

14. Unless, of course, no further substitutions are possible—if there is a corner solution.

one-half apples for one orange, and George would be receiving one-half apple more than is necessary to compensate for the loss of an orange. Because each participant in such a transaction moves to a position he prefers, he is made better off, according to the choice criterion for individual welfare. Because somebody is made better off, without making anybody else worse off, the Pareto criterion says that society is made better off by the voluntary trade. At a Pareto optimum, in which no such improvements remain to be made, it is necessarily true that all individuals have equal marginal rates of substitution for each pair of goods. (We extract from corner solutions, for which the appropriate marginal conditions are expressed in terms of inequalities.) Otherwise an exchange could be arranged that would make two people better off and no one worse off.

It is also possible to make an exchange with nature, by means of production. It follows that not only must everybody have the same marginal rate of substitution (MRS) for any pair of commodities, but that this MRS must equal the marginal rate at which one commodity can be transformed into the other. Suppose that in a two-man society Peter and George are each willing to give up four apples for one orange, but that if one less orange is grown, then five more apples can be produced. Then Peter and George can both be made better off by switching some resources—land, labor, and capital— from growing oranges to producing apples; by the Pareto criterion, society would be better off. In a Pareto optimum such beneficial alterations in production must not be possible. Each person's MRS between two commodities must be equal to the marginal rate of transformation between the commodities.

These are the necessary marginal conditions for a Pareto optimum. How can we be sure that they will be satisfied? How can an individual know whether his MRS between two commodities is equal to that of other people he does not know, or whether it is possible for him to make a mutually beneficial exchange with one of them? How can the productive sector of our economy be sure that it has allocated its resources in such a fashion that the rate at which it could transform one good into another is the rate at which consumers would be willing to trade their consumption of these goods? What we have set out to demonstrate is that prices can perform this function by signaling the relative values that the different elements in society place on different goods and resources.

We need speak only in terms of relative prices. Trade-off possibilities between apples and oranges would be the same whether their prices were 5 cents and 15 cents or perhaps 1 and 3 Martian Kroner. The trade-off possibilities available to a consumer are represented diagrammatically in Figure 2-6. Suppose that a man's income is sufficient to buy ten oranges if he purchases no apples. If the relative prices were as we specified above he could trade one orange for three apples, and move successively from his starting point *E* along the "budget line" *DE* until he reaches point *D* where he has thirty apples but no more oranges. He can stop at any point along the the way, for example, at point *P*, the optimum, where he has four and one-half oranges and sixteen and one-half apples.

In response to relative prices everyone adjusts his purchases so that his MRS is equal to the rate of exchange possible at those prices. Similarly, productive resources are continually transferred until the rate at which the economy could transform one good into another is equal to the rate of exchange in the market. Once all individuals' marginal rates of substitution and the economy's marginal rate of transformation between all pairs of goods are brought into equality we will be at a Pareto optimum. No profitable trades between producers, between consumers, or between combinations thereof will now be possible. The functioning of the price system as a signaling mechanism will allow this optimal equilibrium to come about.

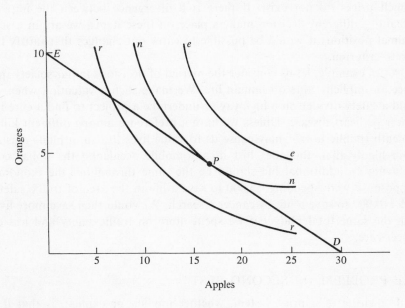

FIGURE 2-6

Our discussion has assumed that relative prices were set by some autonomous force. Actually, in a large market economy each consumer and most producers play such a minor role that their purchases and sales will have no effect on existing prices. However, the mass action of many consumers or producers can affect prices just as the mass movement of many motorists can create a traffic jam that no individual motorist could either prevent or create. The reader will recall Adam Smith's famous metaphor of the invisible hand at work in the market place. It is beyond the scope of this chapter to discuss how this invisible hand might work. It is sufficient for our purposes to state that if it is allowed to work via an unencumbered price system we will reach a Pareto-optimal position. Of course, certain ideal conditions (such as the absence of monopolies) would have to be satisfied and we would have to disregard such considerations as the psychological effects of pure competition.

IMPLICIT PRICES

The primary value of the price system is that it summarizes information in a form which can be readily conveyed to decision makers throughout the economy. Decisions made throughout the society, to be consistent, must place the same value on any specific trade-off.

In the absence of a price system we find it difficult to establish consistency between different decisions. Yet policy decisions must continually be made that involve items that are not traded on any economic market, or for which explicit prices do not exist. If there is a divergence between the implicit valuations different decision makers place on these items, we are in a sub-optimal position; it would be possible to carry out changes that satisfy the Pareto criterion.

As an example, let us consider the myriad of decisions in our society that place an implicit value on human life. We make such a valuation when we build a safety divider on a highway or undertake a project to find a cure for cancer or heart disease. Unless we have a preference among different kinds of death (public horror may cause us to value lives lost in airplane crashes more highly than the ones lost in automobile accidents) the dollar cost of saving an additional life should be the same throughout the economy. Suppose we were spending $5,000 to save a life in the area of traffic safety, and $10,000 to save a life by cancer research. We could then save more lives with the same total budget if we spent more on traffic safety and less on cancer care.[15]

THE PROBLEM OF SECOND BEST

The virtue of a price system, whether implicit or explicit, is that if it functions smoothly it is a guide to efficiency. We have demonstrated that in order to reach a Pareto optimum the market rate of exchange between any two commodities must be equal both to every individual's marginal rate of substitution between the two commodities and the marginal rate of transformation between them. Imperfections such as the existence of monopolies or excise taxes often lead to situations in which these conditions are not met.

15. We are abstracting from the difficult question as to how we should value the lives of different individuals. On the whole, leukemia victims are younger than the people who die of heart attacks; perhaps we should place different values on the lives of victims in these two classes.

If a monopolist is making a substantial profit, it is likely that his product is being overpriced in the market place, thus disturbing the desired equality between relative prices and marginal rates of substitution and transformation. It might be thought that if we can remove some imperfections, so that at least one more pair of relative prices satisfies the required equality, then we shall have moved to a Pareto-superior point. This need not be the case. All we know is that in order to reach a Pareto optimum *all* the specified equalities must be satisfied. This does not tell us whether a point with only five equalities unsatisfied will be Pareto superior to one where fifty-five are unsatisfied. We can only be sure of moving to a Pareto optimum if we correct every single imperfection.[16] In the real world we will never be in a situation in which we can eliminate all imperfections. In such situations it may be difficult for us to select the best of our feasible actions. This problem—what should we do if we cannot reach a Pareto-optimal point—is known as the problem of second best. We encounter second-best problems whenever we must make decisions in a world with market imperfections.

An example will show that when prices are imperfect they have, in a strict sense, no normative value. Suppose that we must ship supplies in order to carry out a project. We can ship the supplies by either rail or truck. The relevant prices for these two transport methods are shown in Table 2-3.

Table 2-3

	Market Price per Ton Mile	True Cost per Ton Mile
Rail	$50	$35
Truck	$40	$40

Actual market prices are given in the first column; the prices in the second column are those that would prevail if all markets were perfect and the ideal conditions necessary for a Pareto optimum were satisfied. The marginal rate of transformation between rail and trucking transport is given by the ratio of these prices (40/35 = 1.14 equals the number of units of rail services that must be sacrificed to produce one more unit of trucking services—equals the rate at which they could be exchanged in a market where prices reflected true costs).

The railroad, perhaps because it has a monopoly, is able to charge a price in excess of its marginal cost—the additional cost the railroad incurs when it produces an additional unit of services. True marginal cost reflects the resource

16. In correcting for these imperfections we may also alter the distribution of income. It is thus quite possible that some individuals will be hurt when we make these corrections—that the Pareto optimum will not be Pareto superior to the original point. For example, we will cut into the profits of monopolists if we make them charge a price equal to their marginal cost in accord with the requirements for ideal conditions.

cost to society for producing an additional unit of a good. A sophisticated public decision maker might choose to ship supplies by rail; although the market price of shipping by rail is greater, the cost to society in terms of resources sacrificed is less. If we "corrected" the price of rail services via regulatory action we could insure that private decision makers would ship by rail as well.

Should we correct imperfections in the pricing system wherever possible? What if, unbeknownst to us, the true marginal cost of trucking services is $30. In this case our decision to ship by rail would be inefficient from the point of view of society. Society must sacrifice $5 more in resources to ship a ton a mile by rail rather than by truck. We can see the dilemma which confronts us when the price system is unreliable, and at the same time we may appreciate even more the ability of a perfect price system to summarize vital information. If the price system fails to summarize the costs of production and value in exchange of every item in the economy, we can only be sure that we will reach an efficient position if we can obtain all of the missing information in some other way. The moral we wish to establish is that in some cases reliance on the price system, or even on a piecemeal improvement of the price system, may not make society better off. This does not mean that we are left in a hopeless position with respect to decision making. We must use the information that we have available, including information about any imperfections in the price system, and do as best we can to choose the alternative that is optimal for society. If the price system is not perfect, we may find it difficult to assemble all of the relevant information. We cannot place our faith in an imperfect price system, nor can we state that fewer imperfections make an imperfect price system a better guide to decision making.

PUBLIC GOODS AND EXTERNALITIES

Even if the price system were perfect in the sense that relative prices in the market reflected marginal rates of substitution and transformation, we could not rely on individual actions guided by the price system to lead to an efficient, Pareto-optimal situation. One condition necessary to insure that free competition working through a perfect price system leads to a Pareto optimum is that no individual's actions affect the welfare of another individual, that there are no externalities.

In many situations, an individual's actions may provide benefits and costs to others. If you construct a retaining wall you may help prevent gullies in your neighbor's land. If you allow your lawn to turn to crabgrass, your neighbors may soon find that their lawns have become infested as well. If you act in your individual self interest, you will not take into account these external benefits and costs that result from your actions, unless you are compensated for doing so. If society has not worked out such a compensation plan, we will find that self-interested behavior by each individual will not lead to actions that are optimal in terms of society as a whole. We will end up with too few retaining walls and too much crabgrass.[17] In the language of economics we say that because of the divergence between private and social (total community) returns, uncoordinated individual actions lead to less than optimal results.[18]

Normally an individual is *excluded* from the enjoyment of a good unless he is willing to pay for its use. If the good delivers external economies (diseconomies) an individual may receive some benefits (suffer some costs) so long as some other individual purchases the good. There are some goods for which the divergence between private and social returns may be more extreme, so that the benefit which the individual derives from the good is independent of his contribution to its provision—in technical terminology, the exclusion principle is inoperative. Economists call these goods public goods. Among the well-known examples of public goods we might list flood-control projects, public parks, justice, and the national defense. Neither retaining walls nor efforts to control crabgrass are perfect public goods, as their external effects are of a limited nature.

A common objective of a group of individuals can be thought of as a public good. If the common objective is achieved, everyone who shares the objective benefits regardless of his efforts to aid its achievement. The characteristic outputs of governments, those goods and services that affect the common interests of the citizenry, are public goods. The need for the provision of such goods provides one of the primary justifications for the existence of a public policy maker who assumes an economic function in our society.

In our discussion above we have shown that an individual can optimize his individual welfare by allocating his expenditures so that his marginal rate of substitution between any two goods is equal to their price ratio (the marginal rate at which one good can be exchanged for another). Using money as a common measure, we can state this condition as follows: his marginal rate of substitution of money for any good must equal its marginal cost (the cost of providing an additional unit of the good). Symbolically we would express this relationship:

$$_mMRS = MC$$

In a similar fashion, we can say that society should continue to provide a public good so long as the benefit derived from providing one more unit is greater than the marginal cost. The benefit that society derives from an

17. We are not arguing that the optimal situation is one with no gullies and no crabgrass. Such a situation would be clearly uneconomic if the cost of getting rid of them exceeded the total benefits (accruing to everyone) deriving from their elimination.

18. The ideal conditions we mentioned in our sections on pricing and Pareto optimality preclude the existence of external benefits or costs.

additional unit of a good can be measured by the total amount that the members of society would pay to insure that the additional unit is provided. Each member of society would be willing to pay up to his MRS of money for the good to insure the production of an additional unit. Total society benefit can be represented as

$$\sum_{i=1}^{n} {}_mMRS_i = {}_mMRS_1 + {}_mMRS_2 + \cdots + {}_mMRS_n$$

(the subscript distinguishes the n individual members of society). If this sum is in excess of marginal cost, it would be advantageous for society to continue to provide the good. Uncoordinated individual provision leads to a position in which ${}_mMRS = MC$ for each individual who provides some of the good. Clearly without coordination the sum of the individual's MRS's is greater than MC, and society should produce more of the good. In the absence of some coordinated or centrally administered production, any group of individuals will systematically fail to provide itself with an optimal amount of a public good or a good that possesses significant external economies.[19]

Let us return to our gullies and retaining walls to illustrate this phenomenon. To build an additional foot of retaining wall would cost you $100 and give you only $99 worth of benefit (your marginal benefit is your ${}_mMRS$ at this point). Shrewd calculation reveals that you would be ill-advised to add to your retaining wall. However, if your neighbor would receive $50 benefit from the additional wall, it would pay to build some more because total benefits $99 + $50 exceed total costs. You would be willing to continue building the wall if your neighbor offered you any bribe in excess of $1, and if necessary, he should be willing to pay you any extortionary charges up to $50.

It may seem strange that behavior that is best for each individual in isolation is not best for the group as a whole. There is actually no inconsistency, and we will observe phenomena of this type whenever there is a divergence between private and social costs or benefits. What is lacking is an element of compulsion.[20] Although you might not act voluntarily to install a smog-control device on your car, you might be willing to install one if all other motorists could be forced to do the same. You might not be willing to give land for a public park, but you might vote for a tax bill that would force the whole community to contribute on a nonvoluntary basis.[21]

19. The converse is of course true. If the production of a good yields external diseconomies, too much of it will be produced.

20. Some organizations that provide public goods manage to do so on a noncompulsory basis, but only because they provide some private benefit in a form of tied sale with the public good. Some religious organizations rely on voluntary individual contributions, but they offer in return prestige in the community and individual salvation.

21. Schelling discusses a most unusual example of a public good in a somewhat different context.

Edward Banfield showed me this irresistible quotation about the Bhats and

Some public goods are more abstract in nature. Were it not for the strictures of our patent system, technological developments and inventions would fall into this category. The even more important areas of education and scientific knowledge are in some ways public goods. If you receive a better education, all of your prospective employers and indeed all of society will benefit. In a similar way, what is scientific knowledge for one becomes scientific knowledge for all. It can be argued that only governmental action could enable us to devote sufficient resources to these ends.

INADEQUACY OF THE PARETO CRITERION FOR GOVERNMENT DECISION

The foregoing discussion has shown that we must rely on the government to undertake some public projects if we wish to improve the welfare position of society. The government decision maker might encounter two special difficulties if he attempted to rely solely on the price system and the Pareto criterion as a guide to his actions.

1. The public policy maker must often take actions that do not work through the market mechanism, for example, when he taxes the populace to pay for the national defence. There is no way to ensure that the individuals who pay for these government services will find that their welfare position has improved over a situation giving fewer services and lower taxes. Thus, these government actions may not always satisfy the Pareto criterion; they may make some individuals worse off.[22] For example, an increase in traffic safety will not satisfy the Pareto criterion unless compensation is paid to body shops.

Charans of the west of India, revered as bards. "In Guzerat they carry large sums in bullion, through tracts where a strong escort would be insufficient to protect it. They are also guarantees of all agreements of chiefs among themselves, and even with the government.

"Their power is derived from the sanctity of their character and their desperate resolution. If a man carrying treasure is approached, he announces that he will commit *traga*, as it is called: or if an engagement is not complied with, he issues the same threat unless it is fulfilled. If he is not attended to, he proceeds to gash his limbs with a dagger, which, if all other means fail, he will plunge into his heart; or he will first strike off the head of his child; or different guarantees to the agreement will cast lots who is to be first beheaded by his companions. The disgrace of these proceedings, and the fear of having a bard's blood on their head, generally reduce the most obstinate to reason. Their fidelity is exemplary, and they never hesitate to sacrifice their lives to keep up an ascendency on which the importance of their caste depends." [The Hon. Mountstuart Elphinstone, *History of India* (ed. 7; London, 1889), p. 211.]

22. Witness Joan Baez's attempted refusal to remit that portion of her income tax which goes to support the United States defense establishment.

2. Even if we could be sure whether or not a government action satisfied the Pareto criterion, we might encounter difficulties because the Pareto criterion falls far short of defining a complete ranking of all social states.

Table 2-4   Individual's Ranking of Social States

	Present	Under Policy A	Under Policy B
Bill	3rd	1st	2nd
John	3rd	2nd	1st

It is not operative when some individuals are better off in one state and some in another. In the example, the Pareto criterion would lead us to undertake either Policy *A* or Policy *B*, but it would not enable us to choose between them. It is to the intractable problem of defining such a ranking that we now turn.

THE UTILITY-POSSIBILITY FRONTIER

In Figure 2-7 we can represent all possible utility positions for Bill and John, the inhabitants of our two-member community. Before we can plot a social state as a point in this diagram we must first assign an index to the indifference curves of Bill. An arbitrary index will do so long as it assigns a higher indifference curve a higher number. Then we ascertain the indifference curve on which Bill will function in this social state. The number our index assigns to this curve is the vertical coordinate of the point that represents the social state on our diagram. We repeat this process with John's indifference curves in order to determine the horizontal coordinate. Four achievable social states are indicated on the diagram: *P, Q, R, S*. The curved boundary is called a utility-possibility frontier. The reader should recognize the direct analogy between the utility-possibility frontier and the production-possibility frontier discussed before. Just as the production-possibility frontier showed the maximum electricity output consistent with a given level of water production, the utility-possibility curve shows the highest indifference curve Bill can reach for each of John's possible indifference levels, given the resources and technology of society.

However, there is a significant distinction between these two possibility curves. We can measure electricity and water in cardinal units such as kilowatt hours and gallons. No such convenient measure is available for an individual's utility.[23] All that the utility diagram can tell us is whether one social state is

23. As a result, the shape of the utility-possibility frontier is somewhat arbitrary. We could, for example, double each number assigned to an indifference curve of John. This would move each point on the utility-possibility curve to the right; the curve as a whole would be flattened out somewhat. The curve must, however, have a negative slope. (If it had a positive slope at any point, this would mean that we were making both people better off. But then the previous points on the curve must not have been Pareto optima.)

There is an analogy here to the example of choosing a date among Alice, Brenda,

to the north or to the east of another; whether Bill prefers the first state and whether John prefers it. State Q lies to the north and to the west of state R; consequently, if given a choice between these two states Bill would select Q and John would choose R. The Pareto criterion would give us no way to choose, for example, between these two points, though it would enable us to

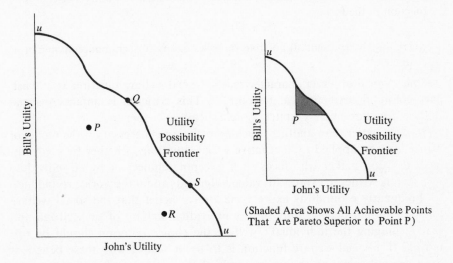

(Shaded Area Shows All Achievable Points That Are Pareto Superior to Point P)

FIGURE 2-7

choose point S over point R. It should be clear by now that the utility-possibility frontier is merely the locus of all Pareto-optimal points. At each point on this frontier, it is not possible to improve Bill's position without hurting John and vice versa.

SOCIAL WELFARE FUNCTIONS

We have seen that the Pareto criterion only allows us to make comparisons

and Carol. Suppose a friend of ours offered to get us a date with one of these girls, none of whom we have ever met. If he is only willing to tell us that one girl is more beautiful than another, but not how much more beautiful, and if he also only gives us an ordinal ranking of their intelligence, we would find it hard to choose among the girls. We face the same difficulty in our attempt to choose between different welfare positions. So long as Bill and John only have ordinal-utility rankings (indifference maps are ordinal tools), they can only tell us whether they prefer one solution to another, but not how much it is preferred. Of course, we might agree on a cardinal measurement of an individual's welfare (see the discussion of interpersonal comparisons of utility). This would be analogous to an intelligence quotient or to the famous scale for beauty drawn up by a group of Michigan State students. The unit on the latter scale was the millihelen, enough beauty to launch one ship. One could also speak of fractional millihelens, say enough beauty to launch two cabin boys.

among a very limited number of situations. A complete ranking of all social states is called a social welfare function:

> ... a function of all the economic magnitudes of a system which is supposed to characterize belief. ... We only require that the belief be such as to admit of an unequivocal answer as to whether one configuration of the economic system is "better" or "worse" than any other or "indifferent." We may write this function in the form

$$W = W(z_1, z_2, \ldots)$$

> where the z's represent all possible variables, many of them noneconomic in character.[24]

One cynical observer characterized the social welfare function as a "vast, parti-coloured mathematical balloon."[25] This criticism is unfair. A social welfare function merely states systematically whether one social state is considered better than another. Such an ordering is necessary if the model of choice is to be applied to alternative social situations, whether by a government decision maker who faces such sweeping choices or by an individual who merely wishes to express his value judgments about the world around him.

Frequently economists express the ethical belief that the social welfare function should depend only on the individual welfare of each citizen and that in judging the individual's welfare the choice criterion should be employed. If a social welfare function is to be in accord with these beliefs, it must depend solely on the utility levels of the members of the community:

$$W = W(u_1, u_2, \ldots, u_n),$$

where u_i represents the indifference curve on which individual i finds himself.

A social welfare function for our two-member society is shown in Figure 2-8. The indifference curves connect the points that represent all combinations of Bill's utility level and John's utility level among which the social welfare function expresses indifference. These curves are obviously analogous to the indifference curves of individual preferences: they are called *Bergson contours* in honor of the man who first expressed in the convenient language of a social welfare function the ethical beliefs that are prerequisite to the process of comparing one social state with another. As in a conventional indifference-curve diagram we can say that the point C is declared inferior to superior to E, and indifferent to point A. The social welfare function of Figure 2-8 is consistent with the Pareto criterion: whenever we move due north (Bill moves to a higher indifference curve and John stays on the same one), due east (John moves higher Bill stays the same), or to the northeast, we move to a higher Bergson contour. The social welfare function must make comparisons between points neither of which is Pareto superior to the other. For example point A is declared superior to point B.

24. Samuelson, p. 221.
25. Robertson, p. 41.

To choose an optimal point for society we combine the utility-possibility frontier of Figure 2-7 with the social welfare function of Figure 2-8. This is done in Figure 2-9. It is easily seen that the social welfare function declares point Q to be the best point attainable. The best attainable point will always be on the utility-possibility frontier, and hence will always be a Pareto optimum.[26]

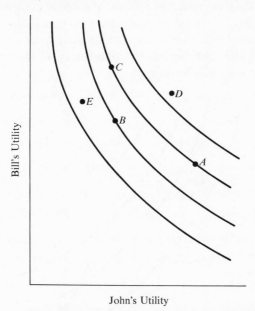

FIGURE 2-8

A social welfare function of the form $W = W(u_1, u_2, \ldots)$ calls for explicit judgments as to whether a change that moves one person to a higher indifference curve and another person to a lower indifference curve is an improvement; such judgments are know as interpersonal comparisons of welfare. The choice criterion of individual welfare unfortunately provides us no basis for making these interpersonal comparisons. We must attach some significance to the indifference curves of an individual to permit us to make comparisons with the indifference curves of others.

We must base our interpersonal comparisons on other considerations such as the following:

1. Although we cannot experience another's sensation, we can get an idea of his satisfactions or frustrations by observing him, or, if we do not know the individual, by interviewing him.

2. We may evaluate an individual's position by how we would ourselves

26. To test his understanding, the reader might wish to verify that it is possible for a point which is not a Pareto optimum to outrank a Pareto optimum, so long as the latter is not Pareto superior to the former. This does not affect our demonstration that the optimum for society will always be a Pareto optimum.

react to it. The difficulty with this is that his tastes may differ from our own. A partial solution would be to modify comparisons of this sort by also considering the individual's satisfactions, as mentioned in paragraph 1. But for rough comparisons of individual welfare, we may just be content with our own evaluation.

3. Instead of studying what the individual actually buys we might evaluate his economic welfare by what he could have bought. Thus, to compare the welfare of two people we would just look at the incomes each had and the prices each faced and rank higher the opportunity which would place us on the higher of our own indifference curves.

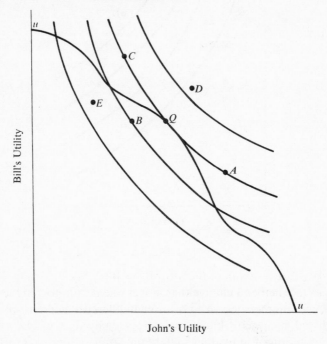

John's Utility

FIGURE 2-9

In order to compare the welfare of two people we move away from the choice criterion of individual welfare and interpret an individual's position either in terms of his satisfactions or in terms of our own reactions to such a situation. It is possible that when we use such bases to make interpersonal comparisons of welfare we may obtain a ranking of social states that is inconsistent with the choice criterion of individual welfare. We can only be sure of avoiding such inconsistencies if we know the indifference maps of all concerned and are thus sure when we say, perhaps on the basis of his "satisfactions," that Bill's welfare has been improved, or that he would not in fact choose his previous position. However, since interpersonal comparisons of welfare are likely to be made with wide margins for error, we may consider unimportant any inconsistency with the choice criterion and social welfare functions of the form $W = W(u_1, u_2, \ldots)$.

Once we have found a way to make interpersonal comparisons of welfare, we must consider whether we think it is better that certain individuals have higher welfare than others. That everybody should have equal welfare is only one of the ethical beliefs we might hold. We might believe that greater welfare should be the lot of those of more ability, more virtue, or more luck.

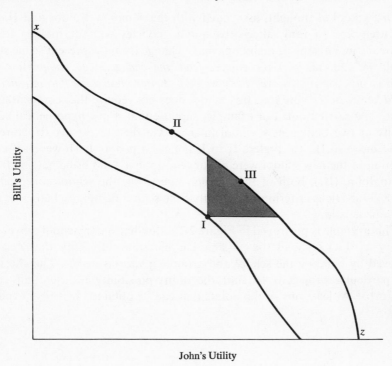

John's Utility

FIGURE 2-10

Samuelson has pointed out that the sort of distributional judgment called for by a social welfare function must be made when parents allocate a family's income. Roller skates for Bobby must be compared with a tennis racket for Susan and new shoes for Father. These comparisons may be based on the kind of pleasure that each individual will get from his good or on the importance that the parents themselves attach to the goods. Following these comparisons, ethical judgments must be made as to how "deserving" Bobby, Susan and Father are.

In practice, proposed social changes will affect great numbers of people, so that it will be impossible to consider how the welfare of each individual is affected. Interpersonal comparisons must then be based on considerations such as (2) and (3) which we previously discussed. It must be assumed that people who are alike with respect to one or two characteristics can be treated as if they were equal in economic welfare. Perhaps we can take comfort in Little's argument that "Most people who consider the welfare of society do not, I am sure, think of it as a logical construction from the welfares of individuals. They think rather in terms of social or economic groups, or in terms of average, or representative men."[27]

SOCIAL WELFARE CRITERIA

One school of thought, associated with the names of Kaldor and Hicks, has attempted to rank alternative public policies without making inter-personal comparisons. It maintains that a change from the present social state should be undertaken *if the gainers from the change could compensate the losers in such a way that everybody would be better off and the Pareto criterion would be satisfied.* Note that this school does not require that compensation actually be carried out. For example, suppose that if our hypothetical community of two built a new school financed via the present tax structure, it would move to II. Bill prefers II to I, but John prefers I. However, if construction of the new school were contingent upon a $100 bribe passing from Bill to John, (III), both of them would like to see the school constructed. The Kaldor-Hicks criterion requires that the school be built, whether or not the bribe is paid.

This example is portrayed in Figure 2-10. Building a new school moves the society to II. *XZ* shows the possible combinations of utility that can be achieved by building the school and arranging various bribes. The effect of this particular project is to shift the utility-possibility frontier uniformly outward.[28] At least one of the points that can be obtained by bribery (point

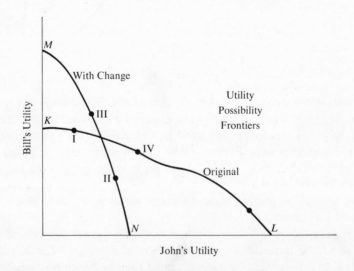

FIGURE 2-11

27. Little, p. 49.
28. In some cases, the new and old utility-possibility frontiers will cross. A change might shift our utility-possibility frontier from *KL* to *MN*. (See Figure 2-11). The

III) is Pareto-superior to I (the points that are Pareto-superior to I are shaded on the diagram). Both Bill and John prefer III to I.[29] Therefore, the Kaldor-Hicks criterion ranks II—or any other point on *XZ*—above I.

Many economists have been repelled by the insensitivity of the Kaldor-Hicks criterion to distributional aspects of changes. If a change would give John D. Rockefeller an additional $1 million and cost one thousand individuals of moderate means $999 each, the Kaldor-Hicks criterion says that the change should be undertaken.[30] Hicks has justified his criterion on the grounds that in the long run things would average out, and that the welfare position of each individual would be improved. I. M. D. Little has challenged Hick's argument:

> Some of the changes which might pass the Kaldor-Hicks criterion . . . will have quite significant real income distribution effects, so that it would be, at best, wishful thinking to suppose that they would cancel out the effects of other changes.[31]

We might still challenge the Hicks criterion even if we accept his contention that distributional changes will cancel out eventually. How long did it take before English landowners recovered from the repeal of the Corn Laws? In the words of John Maynard Keynes, "In the long run we are all dead."

Little proposes the rival criterion that a change should be adopted if it passes a two-part test: (1) the Kaldor-Hicks criterion is satisfied and (2) the redistributional effects of the change are beneficial. The most frequent criticism of the Little criterion is that it requires two separate tests if we are to make a comparison between situations, as I and II in the example above. As long as we are willing to make distributional judgments based on interpersonal comparisons of utility, it might be simpler and possibly more accu-

---

Kaldor-Hicks criterion tells us we should move from I to II and make this change, since with a bribe we could end up at point III. However, the Kaldor-Hicks criterion would also tell us to move from II to I and reverse our original change since a bribe would move us to point IV. Scitovsky recognized this inconsistency, and set up the additional requirement that after the change was undertaken it should not be possible for the losers to compensate the gainers to return to the original position.

29. The individual's rankings of I, II, and III are indicated for the reader's convenience in the following table. John's ranking can be found by ranking points higher as we move from left to right. For Bill the more northerly points rank higher.

	Status Quo-I	*Build School-II*	*Build School and Pay Bribe-III*
John	2nd	3rd	1st
Bill	3rd	1st	2nd

30. Rockefeller could pay each of the losers $999 and still have $1,000 left over for himself ($999 × 1,000 + $1,000 = $1,000,000). According to the Kaldor-Hicks criterion, the change should be undertaken even if Rockefeller does not carry out this payment scheme.

31. Little, p. 94.

rate to compare I and II directly. This is a moot point. We use different standards to evaluate efficiency and distribution, and it may be helpful to apply each standard separately.

Little's criterion is also subject to the criticism levied against any social welfare function which embodies distributional judgments; judgments may not meet with general acceptance. Little admits to this problem, but he manages to backpedal gracefully:

> People who differ on the subject of distribution will seldom agree on the desirability of economic changes. This is simply a fact which we have to accept. Even so, welfare economics may still help people who disagree on the subject of distribution to agree on the best way of bringing about any given redistribution.[32]

Criteria like those of Kaldor-Hicks and Little seek to provide sufficient conditions for the improvement of society's situation. It is not a grand optimum that is sought, but piecemeal reform. These criteria avoid having to rank all social states, but some of the advantages of a complete ranking are foregone.

1. A criterion is only a sufficient condition. It guarantees us that a change which satisfies it is an improvement; but it may fail to detect a change that we would actually rank as an improvement if we knew our social welfare function.

2. It may be that the adoption of one change precludes other alternative changes (for example, if we build one dam at a site we cannot build others). If we cannot adopt all possible improvements simultaneously, we want to know more than whether a proposed change is an improvement. We want to know whether it is the greatest improvement available.

3. In order to be sure that the satisfaction of a criterion is a sufficient condition for an improvement in welfare, we must prove in the context of a complete ranking of social states that any factors neglected by the criterion do not matter. For example, to prove the sufficiency of the Kaldor-Hicks criterion we must show that the distributional changes caused by its repeated application will cancel out or will not matter.

ARROW'S IMPOSSIBILITY THEOREM

We turn now to another approach to the problem of ranking social welfare. In Figure 2-7, Bill prefers P and John prefers R. We could rank social states P and R without making interpersonal comparisons of utility if we were willing to attach weights to each man's preference. Thus, if we were to give Bill's vote a heavier weight—say, if we gave it a weight of 1:5 and John's a weight of 1—we would rank P above R. This does not seem fair to John

32. *Ibid.*, p. 115.

because Bill's preferences would always be decisive, but in a society of more than two people such a method of deriving a social welfare function might work. We could rank each pair of states by seeing which one each member of the society prefers and giving a specified weight to his vote. After we make these pairwise comparisons, we would have to ask whether they are transitive. That is, if A is ranked above B when A and B are compared and B is ranked above C in the comparison (B, C), is A ranked above C in the comparison (A, C)? Unfortunately, the answer may be "No." Even with three people, preferences may be such that the pairwise comparisons lead to intransitivity.

We can illustrate this possibility in the simple case of majority rule in which each individual's preference received an equal weight. Suppose that we are serving breakfast to the three bears and that their preferences among our three alternative kinds of cereal are given in Table 2-5.

Table 2-5

| | RANKING | | |
Kind of Cereal	Papa Bear	Mama Bear	Baby Bear
Oatmeal	1	3	2
Grits	2	1	3
Corn flakes	3	2	1

Two bears prefer oatmeal to grits and two bears prefer grits to corn flakes. Therefore, if majority rule is transitive in this situation, we would find that it ranks oatmeal above corn flakes; but instead a majority of bears prefers corn flakes to oatmeal. The "ordering" is intransitive.

Kenneth Arrow's famous impossibility theorem is an elegant generalization of this example. It specifies five conditions such that it is impossible to combine individual preferences into a social welfare function that satisfies all of them. The theorem has caused some consternation because all five of the conditions are ethically appealing. One requires that the social welfare function be transitive. Another says that the social welfare function should be able to combine any conceivable configuration of individual preferences; in particular, the social welfare function must be defined when preferences are like those of Table 2-5. A third condition in effect rules out interpersonal comparisons of utility. In drawing up any social welfare function that depends on individual preferences we must violate at least one of Arrow's five conditions. If, for example, we are willing to make interpersonal comparisons of utility, as we did before, then Arrow's theorem has no terrors for us; we can still hope to satisfy his other four conditions.

ACCEPTING THE DECISION MAKER'S
SOCIAL WELFARE FUNCTION

When we are interested in Arrow's problem—how to resolve conflicting wishes of individuals—it is usually because the individuals belong to an organization or a society and decisions must be made that relate to all the members of that organization. An organization is formed when individuals feel that they have interests in common and therefore can benefit by coordinating their actions; in forming the organization they must agree upon a decision process. Arrow and Rothenberg have each suggested that the problem of obtaining a suitable social welfare function might be solved by using the ordering of social states produced by the society's decision process. This would require the decisions of this process to be accepted by all members of the society.[33]

Such acceptance means that the members of the society are more fundamentally interested in how a decision is made than in what the decision is. Consider the following four alternatives:

1. A set of traffic laws A, passed by the City Council;
2. A different set of traffic laws, B, passed by the City Council;
3. The set of traffic laws A, established by the police department;
4. A different set of traffic laws B, established by the police department.

Mr. Jones prefers the set of traffic laws B, he also prefers that traffic laws be passed by the City Council; therefore he prefers alternative (2) to both alternatives (1) and (4). However, if the City Council votes, it will pass the set of laws A; alternative (2) is not available. Mr. Jones may well prefer to have the decision made by the City Council than to have a decision he likes better made at the expense of an alteration in the method of choice: he may prefer alternative (1) to alternative (4). When all the members of a society attach such importance to a particular method of making a social choice, there is very good reason for adopting as a social welfare function the ordering produced by that method of decision.

Of course, as Arrow has pointed out, one's regard for a decision process depends in part on the decisions it reaches; if the outcome of the City Council's vote were the set of traffic laws C, Mr. Jones might have objected to that method of choice. This may remind the reader of our discussion of public goods. We said then that an individual may wish to have some restrictions placed on his own behavior if this is necessary for restrictions to be placed on others; he may accept a decision process because it is a means of reaching agreement on how much of a public good is to be provided and of compelling payment for it. This would be our explanation of Mr. Jones' behavior if he were to support installation of traffic lights and then run a red light. It might be that he is inconsistent, but it is also possible that traffic control is a public good: Mr. Jones' first choice is for everybody except him to stop at red lights, but he is willing to have the traffic laws enforced against himself in order that

33. Certain procedural rules that are followed in most democratic bodies (e.g., the order in which amendments are voted) prevent intransitivities from arising in the choices of these bodies.

they may also be enforced against everyone else; he prefers universal enforcement of traffic laws to a situation in which there are no red lights at all. This illustrates Arrow's point: one reason to value a decision process is the outcomes it makes possible.

However, in accordance with his ideas about justice and good government, one may value a decision process for political reasons as well. Mr. Jones, like the Congolese who were promised by their leaders that after independence they could drive on either side of the road, may prefer that there be no traffic laws at all. He may get no net benefit from the decision actually taken by the City Council, yet still he may think it important that the decision be made in this way.[34]

Although they may differ over what decision should be made, individuals usually agree on who should make it: this is a persuasive justification for taking as a social welfare function the ranking of the decision makers chosen by the members of society. Such an approach bypasses the problem of drawing up a social welfare function that evaluates the conflicting claims of individuals. Instead it focuses on the procedural systems by which society settles individual issues. Such systems can gain universal approval if each member of society recognizes that he benefits from a stable mechanism which resolves his conflicts with other members of society. According to this approach the analyst's job is to help the relevant decision process to reach efficient decisions. Such assistance can be facilitated by a better understanding of these processes. Abstract theoretical reasoning, as yet but little applied, can contribute to this understanding. However, there are quick returns to be gained from a descriptive analysis of decision processes.

An alternative approach views the political or administrative process as a constraint on the attainment of our preferences. Samuelson, for example, has proposed that we draw a *feasibility frontier* inside the utility-possibility frontier to indicate that in tracing out the latter we must adopt institutional arrangements, like lump-sum taxation, that are politically impossible. Clearly the two approaches are likely to lead to similar conclusions; assuming a constraint that is not technological is much like placing a restriction on one's preferences. But if we speak of feasibility constraints on our objectives, we should remember that political impossibility of a particular action may

34. For simplicity, we have been speaking as though the decision process is selected to make just one decision. Decision processes are of course established to make many decisions over a period of time. Mr. Jones may wish to retain a decision process even though he may be hurt by one of its particular decisions, because he expects to benefit from the series of decisions forthcoming from this process. This reason for a man to value a decision process is similar to the first one given in the text; he likes the outcome at which it arrives. But it differs from our second reason; he may like a decision process because of political virtues, such as "fairness." Of course, agreement on a decision process is partly like an agreement to settle a dispute by flipping a coin. People are not sure just what the outcome will be. See Schelling, p. 176.

reflect strong objections to that action on the part of many members of the society.

Applying the
Theory

We turn now to some problems that arise in applying the theory we have been developing. First, we shall use the Theil-Tinbergen model of stabilization policy to illustrate how a decision problem can be formulated in terms of the act of choice, what sort of work is involved in doing so, and how the calculations called for in the formulation can be carried out. Second, we shall illustrate how the model of choice is applied in benefit-cost analysis to guide decisions as to which expenditures should be undertaken by the government. Finally, we shall discuss the theory of sub-optimization: what should be done when many different decision makers are each responsible for a piece of a larger problem.

THE THEIL-TINBERGEN MODEL

Economic theory and statistical investigations have shown that there are relationships among variables like the price level, the rate of employment, tax rates, and monetary conditions. Using both theory and statistics, we can develop a model that describes these relationships. Some variables, such as the latter two, can be altered by the government, and when they are altered the other variables are affected. This is the basis of monetary and fiscal policy: variables in the control of the government, called *instruments*, are adjusted so that certain other variables, which we shall call *goal variables*, reach optimal values. Typical goal variables include the rate of employment, the balance of payments, the rate of change of the price level, the rate of growth, and the fair distribution of income. Typical instruments include the level of government expenditure, various rates of taxation, the rediscount rate, and the volume of central bank purchases of securities.

The Theil-Tinbergen model is intended to assist such decision makers as central bankers and Treasury officials by placing stabilization policy in the framework of the act of choice. From the model describing the economy, constraints are deduced that delimit the combinations of goal variables available to the policy maker. An objective function is then derived which describes the preferences of the policy maker. The problem is then the mathematical one of finding a constrained maximum: to maximize the objective function subject to the constraints. Such models are used, for example by The Netherlands Central Planning Bureau, an agency whose economic analysis has helped guide Dutch economic policy for many years.

Let us consider a very simple model of the economy.[35]

$$P = a(I+G) \qquad (2\text{-}1)$$
$$E = cP \qquad (2\text{-}2)$$
$$B = X - dP \qquad (2\text{-}3)$$

where

P = production		IRRELEVANT
I = investment	EXTERNAL	
G = government expenditure	INSTRUMENT	
E = employment		GOAL VARIABLE
B = balance of payments		GOAL VARIABLE
X = exports	EXTERNAL	

a, c, and d are constants.

Three of the variables are determined outside the model. Investments and exports are decided by the investors of the economy and foreign customers respectively; their values are given and assumed known by the government. Government expenditure is determined by the government; it is an instrument. Once these three variables are given, the values of the other three variables can be found by solving the three simultaneous equations; these values will differ depending on the value of G. The policy maker is interested in obtaining optimal levels of employment and the balance of payments; we assume that he is not interested in the level of production, which we have labeled "irrelevant."

There are three kinds of equations that we might find in such a model: behavioral, technological, and institutional. Equation (2-2) is a technological equation; it says that once we know how much is produced we know uniquely what percent of the labor force is needed for that production. The other two equations are both deduced from behavioral equations which for simplicity we have omitted. Equation (2-3) says that as production and income in the country rise more is imported; with the volume of exports given, the balance of payments decreases as production rises. Equation (2-1) is based on a behavioral equation telling what consumer expenditure is for each value of production (and hence income); the equation says that the amount of production depends on the amount of investment and the amount of government expenditure. (The reader need not be absorbed with such details. We merely wish to show what such relationships are like and how they can be used to deduce the constraints on the decision maker's choice.) Institutional equations involve a commitment by the policy maker not to alter the institutions in question.

The policy maker wishes to know which combinations of B and E are

35. Theil, pp. 381–83.

possible. To find out, we can eliminate P by substituting equation (2-1) into equations (2-3) and (2-2). We then have

$$E = ca\,(I+G), \tag{2-2}$$
$$B = X - da\,(I+G). \tag{2-4}$$

These two simultaneous equations can be solved for B and E, once G is given, because I and X are already known.[36] For each possible value of G there is a different combination of B and E. The goal variables conflict: the more the policy maker has of B, the less he has of E. These points are graphed in Figure 2-12. To each point on the frontier there corresponds a value of G, and the point can be reached by setting government expenditure equal to that

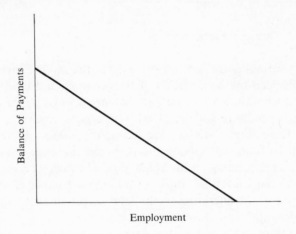

FIGURE 2-12

value. We have shown how the constraint which binds the policy maker can be deduced from the model of the economy. It remains to obtain the policy maker's preferences between B and E, so that we may determine his optimal choice of G.[37]

36. By substitution, we find that E and B are related by the following linear (see footnote 39) equation:

$$B = X - d\,E$$

The highest balance of payments that can be obtained for a given rate of employment is given by this equation.

37. Suppose we had another instrument M (such as monetary policy) which affected both the balance of payments and the rate of employment. Then we might be able to reduce the model to two equations like the following:

$$E = rM + s(I+G)$$
$$B = sM + t(I+G)$$

If these two equations satisfy the mathematical condition of independence (as do the equations shown) then we do not have to worry about maximizing subject to a constraint. By choosing appropriate values of G and M we can simultaneously

The most direct way to obtain a policy maker's ranking of the alternatives open to him is to ask him for it or, equivalently, to ask him to draw his indifference curves between the goal variables. It is of course inconvenient to ask a busy man to describe his objective function. It is also doubtful that a policy maker can answer such questions with enough precision to provide a basis for analysis. One alternative approach which has been tried[38] is for the analyst, on the basis of private interviews and public statements of the policy maker, to estimate the policy maker's objective function. Another possibility, which we have already mentioned, is for the analyst to describe the transformation frontier and have the policy maker pick the point on the frontier which he prefers; more simply, the analyst could tell the policy maker the rate at which he is able to exchange one goal variable for another (the marginal rate of transformation) and find in this way the point on the transformation frontier at which the policy maker is content to do no further exchanging.

FINDING CONSTRAINED MAXIMA

Once we have formulated the constraints that bind us and the objective function we wish to maximize, we must carry out the maximization. Drawing curves and finding tangencies is impractical for any but the simplest problem. However, computers, using algebraic rather than geometrical formulations, do just this; they can examine many points rapidly, using marginal techniques to test whether a point is optimal. Computer programs for finding maxima rely on iteration: find a point; see if it is a maximum; follow a certain routine to find a promising point to try next; see if that point is a maximum; and so on. Mathematicians have provided us with a number of such tools, and they are making rapid progress in finding new ones. Among the techniques for locating the constrained maxima are the following:

1. Suppose the equations of our model are linear.[39] We can simplify the mathematics if we do not try to maximize our goal variables but instead set a target for each one. Then the mathematical problem is to solve a number of simultaneous equations. Provided that the number of independent instruments is at least equal to the numbers of goal variables, the set of simultaneous equations can be solved. If the targets cannot be attained, it is of course necessary to adopt new targets. Even if one is trying to maximize, the ability

---

obtain any levels of B and E that we want. With existing instruments this is not possible; we must decide how much of one goal variable we are willing to give up for more of another goal variable.

38. See Van Eyk and Sandee.

39. By a linear equation we mean an equation in which the variables are only multiplied by constants and added; no variable is ever multiplied by itself or another variable. The following is an example of a linear equation: $X = by + cz + d$, where b, c, and d are constants.

to solve a large number of simultaneous equations can be of help in deducing constraints from the model.

2. Differential calculus is a familiar method of finding constrained maxima. This method is practical if the constraints are few and simple and if all mathematical expressions in the objective functions and the constraints satisfy the condition of differentiability. The marginal conditions we have developed in this paper are special applications of differential calculus.

3. Many practical maximizing problems can be solved by the linear-programming techniques that have been developed for computers. We can apply linear programming if both the constraints and the objective function are linear. Under these conditions it is known that the set of available points has corners; what is more important is that it is known that the optimum point will be one of these corners. In examining corners systematically to see if they are optimal and in selecting the most promising corner to investigate next, linear programming makes use of "shadow prices" which are analogous to the prices we have studied above.

4. Nonlinear programming must be adopted if either the constraints or the objective function is nonlinear. Effective solution procedures have been developed only for certain types of nonlinear-programming problems. It is interesting to note that one of these methods, the gradient method, uses a means of searching for an optimum that has been compared to a market mechanism.[40]

5. If the maximizing problem cannot be solved with the existing tools, it may be possible to simplify the model by omitting relations or by approximating the objective functions or the constraints with simpler expressions. For example, approximate solutions can be obtained by choosing suitable linear functions.

6. If it is impossible to find the constrained maximum, it may be possible to find a position better than the existing one. One can undertake, for example, those marginal changes which make the situation better.

7. If the solution cannot be found, we can console ourselves with the thought that formulating the problem in the form of the model of choice may have helped the policy maker to focus on the alternative open to him and the possible alterations he can make.

BENEFIT-COST

The benefit-cost model is the schema most frequently employed to evaluate public projects. The model proceeds on the reasonable assumption that in any public-decision problem we should attempt to maximize the net benefits accruing to society. It is easy to slip into the error of measuring the net benefits of various projects solely by the amount by which they increase the

40. See Baumol, p. 111.

economic pie that is to be divided among the members of the community. This approach concerns itself only with what are called efficiency benefits; it neglects the distributional benefits that may return from the projects: those benefits derived from an improved way of dividing the pie. To judge the economic welfare of a nation we would look not only at the size of its national product, but also at the distribution thereof. As we saw previously, it is not a simple task to define the social welfare function. The problem of combining efficiency and distribution benefits into a common objective function is much the same problem, and not surprisingly it may be a difficult one.

EFFICIENCY BENEFITS

Measuring the net efficiency benefits of a project (gross benefits minus gross costs) would seem to be a straightforward procedure. Benefits can be measured as the total willingness of all individuals to pay for the project rather than have no project at all. Costs are measured by the monetary value of the goods that are devoted to the project. Neglecting distributional considerations, we would say that a project should be undertaken if benefits exceed costs. The reader should realize that in essence this is the Kaldor-Hicks approach to problems of social choice. If the efficiency benefits from a project exceed its efficiency costs, the gainers from the project *could* compensate the losers so that all individuals would be placed in an improved welfare position.

Even if we confine ourselves to efficiency benefits we may encounter serious difficulties when we actually attempt to measure them. One method would be to value the benefits and costs of a project as the market value of the goods that it produces and consumes. This procedure will not be reliable unless the following conditions are satisfied:

1. There are no external effects in the consumption of any of the goods that the project provides.

2. Prices are equal to marginal cost throughout the economy.

3. The scale of the project is not sufficiently great as to alter prices in the economy.

4. All benefits produced and all resources used have market prices.

The first two conditions should be readily understandable in view of our discussion of externalities, public goods, and second-best considerations. The third condition may appear less plausible at first glance. An example should reveal the importance of the condition.

Let us assume that a water desalinization plant is installed in a parched, drought-ridden area. If the plant is sufficiently large and efficient the water can be sold for a low price, a price far lower than the price for which it was sold before the plant was built. The total market value of the water at this new low price will be far below the benefit that the area derives from the water.

The benefit derived from the water is the total amount of money that could be obtained from the residents of the area if the water were sold to them on an all-or-nothing basis by the most skillful of extortionary bargainers. Unfortunately, when a project effects significant changes in prices, this amount may be extremely difficult to measure.[41]

This brings to light an important distinction between private and public enterprises. A profit-maximizing corporation will not take into account the benefits its customers derive as the price of its product falls with increases in output. However, a public enterprise cannot neglect the benefits returned to the community it is trying to serve. The fall in price leads to benefits that cannot be transmitted via the market mechanism. Consider the following example:

Table 2-6

Price	$100	$98
Quantity	20	21
(which can be sold at price)		

The firm is producing twenty units selling for $100 a piece. Suppose that an additional unit costs $60 to produce.[42] It would only give the firm an additional $58 of revenue.

Table 2-7

Revenue with 20	Revenue with 21
20 × $100 = $2,000	21 × $98 = $2,058

As the additional cost of producing the twenty-first unit exceeds the additional revenue that will be realized, the firm decides not to produce the twenty-first unit. It produces only twenty.

What if the firm were instead a public agency? It could realize the $58 increment that was realized by the firm, and incur the $60, but it should also take into account the benefits that consumers of the first twenty units derive from the $2 fall in price. Total social benefits equal $38 + $2 (20) = $98, which is precisely equal to the price of the output. Therefore, the public agency produces more than twenty units; it expands production because total social benefits ($98) exceed marginal cost ($60). This is the general case. Following the net efficiency benefits approach, a public agency should continue to expand its output until the price at which another unit can be sold exactly equals the additional cost of producing that unit. An enterprise will

41. The reader familiar with economic theory will recognize the geometric equivalent to this "extraordinary price." (See Figure 2-13 where DD is the demand curve for the product, and the shaded area is the total which could be extracted from the community for the additional water.)

42. It is easy to establish that profits are maximized when marginal revenue (the additional revenue derived from selling another unit of output) equals marginal cost, and the latter is increasing faster than the former.

be larger under public as opposed to private control if the price of its product falls with increases in output. In deciding whether to increase its output the public enterprise will consider the benefits that consumers derive from a fall in price, benefits that must be neglected by a profit-maximizing private firm.

REDISTRIBUTION BENEFITS

As pointed out above, we might still encounter difficulties even if we could define the net efficiency benefits returning to each possible public project. We must have a method of measuring, in addition, benefits that result from a better distribution of income among members of the community. Often we

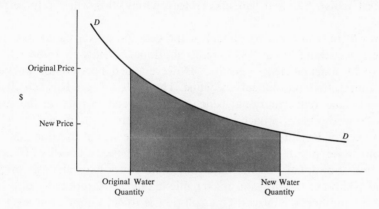

FIGURE 2-13

see fit to undertake projects, both private and public, that yield zero or negative efficiency benefits, but which are worthwhile because of the redistributional benefits. Direct monetary transfers to underprivileged individuals or areas are undertakings of this nature. Net efficiency benefits are negative to the extent of the cost of making these transfers, but redistributional benefits are considered sufficient to make the transfers worthwhile.

Measuring redistributional benefits is a tricky and intricate procedure. One method of attacking the problem is to measure net benefits returning to the group to which we wish to redistribute income. Let us say we wished to redistribute income from the landlords to the peasants.[43] Project *A* yields net efficiency benefits

Table 2-8

Project		Benefits to	Costs to
A	Landlords	$100	$90
	Peasants	$30	$20
B	Landlords	$40	$80
	Peasants	$40	$10

43. This is not to rule out the possibility that in some nations decision makers might be interested in redistributing income from the peasants to the landlords.

of $(\$100 - \$90) + (\$30 - \$20) = \$20$ and "redistributional benefits" of $\$30 - \$20 = \$10$. Project B yields net efficiency benefits of $(\$40 - \$80) + (\$40 - \$10) = -\$10$ and $(\$40 - \$10) = \$30$ of redistributional benefits. If no other projects were possible, and if all other income transfers were ruled out, we might prefer to undertake Project B rather than Project A.[44] For example, it might be desirable to parcel out a landlord's holdings among the peasants even though they would not produce as much as the landlord would if he were allowed to maintain control over his land. Once again we encounter the familiar problem of competing objectives.[45] We would have no difficulty in choosing a project if one of them offered the greatest efficiency as well as the greatest redistributional benefits. Unfortunately, this will rarely be the case.

Our problem would not be difficult if the decision maker could state his preferences in such a form as " $3 in redistributional benefits are to be valued as equal to $1 in net efficiency benefits." However, such a preference function may be complicated and difficult to define. The trade-off rate between efficiency benefits and redistributional benefits may depend in part on the level of each obtained. One approach would be an indifference-map analysis with the two forms of benefits measured on the axes. We would use this map to select from those points which offer the greatest efficiency benefits for each level of redistributional benefits. Even an indifference-map analysis might prove too complex; the decision maker might find it exceptionally difficult to define his indifference curves. One solution is to set a minimum level of redistributional benefits that we wish to achieve, and to maximize efficiency benefits subject to this constraint. For example, "maximize the total production (not efficiency benefits) that is possible while insuring that average annual peasant incomes are increased at least $50."[46]

RATIOS VERSUS ABSOLUTES

Our discussion of benefit-cost analysis has been in terms of absolute differences between benefits and costs. Some readers may have read discussions

44. We cannot add together these two different types of benefits any more than we can add together electricity production and water production. Efficiency benefits are not commensurate with redistribution benefits.

45. When we consider separately efficiency benefits and redistribution benefits, we are making a distinction similar to the one that Little makes (see footnote 31). Little of course says that a change should be made if it yields both efficiency and redistribution benefits. He does not consider the case in which these objectives conflict.

46. Similarly, we could maximize redistribution benefits for a given level of efficiency benefits. The reader should be able to see that if $\$X$ of efficiency benefits can be achieved with redistribution benefits of at least $\$Y$, then $\$Y$ of redistribution benefits can be achieved with efficiency benefits of at least $\$X$.

that talk in terms of ratios of benefits to costs as guides to action. The choice between these two methods of procedure has generated a great deal of confusion.

The proper approach depends upon the constraints which are relevant to the decision problem. Consider the following three projects:

Table 2-9

Project	Benefits	Costs	Ratio	Net Benefit
A	30	3	10	27
B	64	8	8	56
C	100	40	2.5	60

1. Let us assume that the projects are alternative highway systems which can be built to cross a given area. In the absence of a budgetary constraint it would clearly be desirable to build Project *C*, which would yield a net benefit of 60.

2. Assume that the projects are no longer mutually exclusive and that numerous versions of the same project can be undertaken up to the limit of the budget. An example might be teacher-training fellowships; *A, B* and *C* would be alternate forms of the fellowship. In such a case we should follow the ratio criterion, and if our budget were 120 we would undertake forty versions of Project *A*.

3. However, if the budget were relatively small in comparison to the costs of the projects we might run into the problem of indivisibilities. If the constraint were in fact 8, we would find that Project *B* should be our favored alternative.

Ratios are applicable when we are dealing with a budget constraint, but no constraint with respect to the number of projects that can be undertaken. The net-benefit approach is to be employed when the projects must be treated as mutually exclusive ventures.[47]

SUBOPTIMIZATION

The conceptually simple formulation of the problem of choice as a set of alternatives and a preference function to be applied to the set may pose a problem that is too complicated for any one decision maker to solve. We may be able to reduce the costs—perhaps prohibitive—of an overall solution by dividing the problem into pieces that allow a separate department to make the decisions relating to each piece of the problem. Each agency is given its

47. If all projects cost the same, there can never be a conflict between these two criteria.

own subcriterion, or objective function; all that it is told about those aspects of the problem that are in the hands of other agencies is the decisions that are made. Thus the range of choice available to each decision unit is restricted. There is a benefit to be derived from simplification. If the subdivisions were given broader responsibilities, information needs and calculation complexities might increase to the extent that the purpose of the suboptimized decision procedure would be vitiated.

Factoring a problem in this way may require the following steps:

1. For each individual decision unit, criteria must be chosen that are consistent with the optimization of the higher-level objective function. The problem is naturally simplified when all values are measurable in dollar terms. Diversified industrial empires may function quite effectively if each component enterprise attempts to maximize profits. However, we might encounter some difficulty if we attempted to define low-level criteria that individual units of our military establishment could employ as a guide for performance.

2. Responsibilities must be assigned to the various subdepartments in such a way as to minimize the spillovers among their decisions (spillovers occur when the activities of one agency affect the outputs or inputs of another agency directly; that is, in a way not reflected by the first agency's subcriterion). The problem is conceptually the same as that associated with public good procurement; if there be spillovers, the benefits and interest of different decision units are not independent. One subdepartment in maximizing its own objective function may hinder other subdepartments in attaining their own objectives. Spillovers are more likely the narrower the responsibilities of the subdepartments—that is, the further decentralization has been carried.

Interactions between the outputs of subdepartments are less troublesome than interactions between their inputs. When outputs interact—for example, the output of an air defense agency contributes to the effectiveness of strategic offensive forces by protecting them from enemy attack—the central decision maker can allow for this when he allocates the budget to each subdepartment. However, when the interaction is between inputs—for example, the deployment of SAC affects the costs of any warning system—correction for this interaction involves modification of the design of the offensive system and thus an alteration of the decision of the agency. One way to reduce the importance of spillover is to factor the problem so that interactions mainly involve outputs.[48]

3. Finally, the central decision maker allocates the budget available so that the contribution of the marginal dollar in each subdepartment to the fulfillment of the overall criterion is the same. In addition, subcriteria should be chosen so that trade-off rates between different objectives are roughly the same

48. See Enthoven and Rowen.

in all subdepartments. If there were divergencies among the trade-off rates in different subdepartments, it would be possible to increase the output of all objectives by bringing the trade-off rates into agreement.[49]

We can see that there are disadvantages to decentralization. It will not in general be possible to choose subcriteria in such a way that the many decisions of the subdepartments maximize the overall objective function; furthermore, the agencies may get in each other's way, and resources may be used in one agency that would make more of a contribution in another agency. It must also be borne in mind that as decentralization becomes more extensive, it may eventually be more costly to make many simple decisions than to make a few complicated ones. Decentralization of a decision process should be carried out until the disadvantages of coordinating agencies and the costs of making many decisions begin to outweigh the advantages of simplifying decisions and reducing the amount of information that must be transmitted.[50]

Considerations such as these have been applied to the organization of the Department of Defense. An effort was made to plan and budget on the basis of certain military outputs such as the ability to damage enemy targets. Criteria are selected for these outputs, and weapon systems are compared as to their effectiveness in satisfying these criteria. Criteria on which strategic offensive forces can be judged include the ability to deter enemy attack, the ability to limit damage to ourselves if war does occur, and the ability to bring an all-out war to an end on acceptable terms. On the basis of such criteria, comparisons are made among whole weapon systems, such as the Polaris submarine system, the land-based IRBM, and manned bombers. In the Navy's budget, a separate sub budget is set aside for the Polaris system, with its missiles, manpower, and special port facilities. Finally, comparison is

49. This concept, fundamental to the theory of international trade, may not be immediately evident. Consider the following example:

Table 2-10

Production of Objective	Subdepartment I	Subdepartment II
A	50	50
B	50	50
Trade-off Rate		
A for B	3	2

Let subdepartment I produce 3/4 of a unit less B and 2 1/4 more A, and let subdepartment II produce 1 more B and 2 less A. Total production will increase to 100 1/4 of each objective. The reader should recognize the similarity between this example and the problem of establishing the consistency of choice procedures in the absence of a price system, as illustrated above in connection with the implicit valuation of human life. In fact, it is the role of a price system to ensure that trade-offs are everywhere equal.

50. We are abstracting from such factors as the incentives of competition and the wastes of rivalry.

made among the criteria to determine how many resources should be devoted to deterring an enemy attack and how many to defending against such an attack if it occurs. It is at this stage that interaction between the objectives can be given explicit consideration.

This procedure is like telling a pitcher, "Don't walk him, but don't give him anything good to hit." The advice is good; the difficulty comes in following it. Each step given above is hard to carry out.

1. We listed several criteria for strategic offensive forces, which correspond to some of the many purposes for which these forces are maintained. To decide what emphasis should be placed on each purpose provides us with another example of our familiar problem of drawing up an objective function.

2. Suppose we agree that one criterion for judging strategic offensive forces will be the ability to deter enemy attack. We must find units in which to measure this ability and then calculate the contribution of each weapons system.

3. In organizing these weapons systems a balance must be struck between the advantages of simplifying each decision maker's problem and the disadvantages resulting from a lack of coordination.

4. In allocating the budget among different weapons systems so that the marginal contribution of each is equal, spillover costs must be estimated and compensated for.

This discussion of budgeting for defense may have reminded the reader of additional problems that we have been ignoring: the consequences of our actions do not all occur at once and we are not certain what these consequences will be. Having completed our discussion of decision making under certainty, we now turn to the latter problem.

Uncertainty

Often a decision maker must choose a course of action even though he is uncertain what the outcome resulting from his choice will be. It may then be impossible to make a decision that will turn out best in all cases; what is desired is a decision that is in some sense the decision maker's best bet. Consider the simple situation in which an individual must decide whether to carry an umbrella.

Table 2-11

		STATE OF NATURE	
		Sun	*Rain*
ACTION	Carry umbrella	Carry useless umbrella	Dry in the rain
	Leave umbrella	Unburdened	Wet in the rain

The outcomes in Table 2-11 depend not only on the man's choice, but also on the state of nature, which he does not know. If it is going to rain, his best choice is to carry the umbrella, but the umbrella will be a bother if the sun shines. We cannot always make accurate prediction about the weather, but we can make intelligent guesses. A sensible decision maker estimates the probability of rain, and carries his umbrella if he judges this probability to be above some crucial level. This is of course a relatively easy decision. The stakes are comparatively low, and it is doubtful whether any decision maker maker would feel the need to formulate a precise model of this form. However, such a model might well be a valuable aid to logical thinking if the decision were more complex or weighty.

Expected Value

Each action open to a decision maker can be thought of as involving a list of possible consequences, depending on what the state of nature turns out to be. The first row of Table 2-11 gives all the possible consequences of carrying an umbrella. Another set of alternatives is described in Table 2-12. We are given the opportunity to choose one of the alternative prospects *A* to *D*; the state of nature is selected by rolling a die. Since there are six faces to a die, each face will come up about one sixth of the time if the die is rolled many times. With

Table 2-12 Payoff Table

	Number Rolled						
	1	2	3	4	5	6	EV
A	$0	$0	$2	$0	$3	$0	$5/6
B	$1	$1	$1	$1	$1	$1	$1
C	$0	$0	$0	$0	$0	$6.06	$1.01
D	$0	$1.50	$1.50	$1.50	$1.50	$0	$1
probability	1/6	1/6	1/6	1/6	1/6	1/6	

such an interpretation in mind, the *probability* of rolling a five, say, is one sixth. In Table 2-12 the probability of each state of nature is shown in the last row. The probability of each outcome, if an action is taken, is equal to the probability of the corresponding state of nature. Thus the probability of winning $2 if lottery *A* is chosen is one sixth. Because an uncertain prospect can be described by giving the possible outcomes of the action together with their probabilities, we shall sometimes call it a "lottery ticket."

A decision maker's ranking of the possible outcomes of an action is not sufficient to guide his choice if he does not know which outcome will occur. For the model of choice to be applied to decisions under uncertainty it is necessary that lottery tickets as a whole be ranked and the most preferred one chosen. But comparing complicated uncertain prospects with many possible outcomes is not easy. In recent years theories of decision under uncertainty have been developed that recommend to the decision maker principles on which he *should* rank uncertain prospects, given the values he attaches to the possible outcomes and the probabilities of their occurrence. If the decision maker accepts some of these principles as sensible, he will wish to adjust his intuitive ranking of uncertain prospects in order to make it consistent with the theory he accepts.

One simple way in which to rank uncertain prospects whose outcomes are expressed as amounts of money is on the basis of expected value. The expected value of a lottery ticket is a weighted average of the monetary values of possible outcomes, the weight for each value being its probability of occurrence. That is, we multiply each payoff by its probability and add these terms up. The expected value of each prospect in Table 2-12 is given in the column headed EV; thus the expected value of alternative A is equal to

$$1/6 \times \$0 + 1/6 \times \$0 + 1/6 \times \$2 + 1/6 \times \$0 + 1/6 \times \$3 + 1/6 \times \$0 = \$5/6.$$

The expected value of an alternative is the average monetary amount that would be received if the alternative were selected on each of a large number of trials. If we were given the opportunity to receive the proceeds from lottery C on each of many trials, our average gain for each trial (our expected value) would be $1.01. However, expected value may not be a good criterion to use if a trial cannot be repeated. Many people would choose prospect B which offers $1 for certain rather than take prospect C which is more risky. On a more extreme level, most people would prefer to receive $50,000 for certain rather than take a 50-50 chance at $100,000.

VON NEUMANN-MORGENSTERN UTILITY

One explanation of this is to say that the individual prefers the sure $50,000 because he prefers, when gambling, the difference between $50,000 and $0 to the difference between $100,000 and $50,000. This idea, which was suggested by Daniel Bernoulli in the 1730's, is at the heart of the theory of decision under uncertainty developed by Von Neumann and Morgenstern two hundred years later. Von Neumann-Morgenstern theory seeks to assign numbers to all possible outcomes in such a way that (1) these numbers provide under certainty an ordinal ranking of the outcomes; and (2) the numbers reflect the decision maker's attitudes toward gambling with the outcomes, so that his ranking of any series of lottery tickets can be found by calculating their expected *utilities*.

The advantage of the VN-M theory is that it allows the most complex decision problems under uncertainty to be broken down into a number of elementary problems. The first step is for the decision maker to assign utilities to the possible outcomes. This can be done in the following manner:

1. Assign arbitrary utility values, say 100 and 0, to the most favoured and least favoured outcomes which we will call A and B respectively.

2. For any other outcome, C, find the crucial probability, P_c, such that the

individual is indifferent between two lottery tickets, one of which offers C for certain, the other of which offers A with probability P_c, and B with probability $1 - P_c$. We then assign C a utility value equal to the expected utility of the lottery with which the decision maker judges it to be indifferent:

$$U(C) = P_c \cdot U(A) + (1 - P_c) \cdot U(B).$$

Step 1 can be illustrated by a previous example. Using \$100,000 and \$0 as our benchmarks, we will calculate the utility for \$50,000. We assign the utility value 100 to the \$100,000 prize and 0 to the prize of \$0. Upon consultation, the decision maker tells us that his crucial probability, P_c, is 0.6. That is, he is indifferent between a lottery that offers a 60 per cent chance of \$100,000 and a 40% chance of \$0, and another lottery that offers \$50,000 for certain. Using the formula given above, we assign \$50,000 a utility of 60.

$$U(\$50,000) = 0.6 \, U(\$100,000) + (1 - 0.6)U(\$0) = 0.6 \times 100 + 0.4 \times 0 = 60.$$

Following this procedure, the decision maker can assign a utility to any prize, given the arbitrary utility values for his most favored and least favored outcomes. The decision maker is then at the point at which he can use these utilities to choose between different alternatives. As a second step the decision maker calculates the expected utilities of each of his alternative lotteries. The third step is simple: he selects that alternative which offers the highest expected utility. The reader can verify that in the following decision problem he should select Alternative II.

Table 2-13   Prize If Die Shows

	1	2	3	4	5	6
Alternative I	\$0	\$100,000	\$100,000	\$0	\$0	\$0
Alternative II	\$50,000	\$50,000	\$50,000	\$50,000	\$0	\$0

Expected Utility Alternative I

$$= \tfrac{1}{6} \times 0 + \tfrac{1}{6} \times 100 + \tfrac{1}{6} \times 100 + \tfrac{1}{6} \times 0 + \tfrac{1}{6} \times 0 + \tfrac{1}{6} \times 0 = 33\tfrac{1}{3}.$$

Expected Utility Alternative II

$$= \tfrac{1}{6} \times 60 + \tfrac{1}{6} \times 60 + \tfrac{1}{6} \times 60 + \tfrac{1}{6} \times 60 + \tfrac{1}{6} \times 0 + \tfrac{1}{6} \times 0 = 40.$$

Can this program be carried out? Can numbers be assigned to outcomes consistently so that the decision maker's ranking of uncertain prospects can be found by calculating expected utilities? A major contribution of Von Neumann and Morgenstern is to provide a set of axioms so that a consistent set of VN-M utilities exists for any decision maker who obeys all five axioms. The reader is referred to Luce and Raiffa for a discussion of these axioms;[51] we can indicate how persuasive these axioms are by discussing the most questioned one.

51. Luce and Raiffa, pp. 23–31.

This axiom says in essence that if there are two lotteries offering identical prizes (which may in fact be the right to play in another lottery) for all states of nature but one, then the first lottery will be preferred to the second if its unique prize is preferred to the unique prize of the second lottery. For example, let us say that you prefer prospect B ($1 for certain) to prospect C ($6.06 should we roll a 6), then, according to this axiom you should prefer prospect E to prospect F.[52]

Table 2-14

PROSPECT	State of Nature (Result of Flip of Coin)	
	HEADS	TAILS
E	$0	Prospect B
F	$0	Prospect C

If a head is flipped there is nothing to choose between E and F. However, if tails comes up, E offers prospect B which is preferred to prospect C, the prize if F had been chosen. A decision maker who discovers that his intuitive ranking of uncertain prospects violates this axiom, might be persuaded that he should follow the axiom, and that he should adjust his ranking accordingly. If he wishes to follow all of the Von Neumann-Morgenstern axioms, it can be shown that he must make his choices consistent with the expected utility procedure outlined above.

Many violations of the VN-M prescription occur when the lotteries involve extreme probabilities. Such lotteries, offering small but positive probabilities of disastrous outcomes, often crop up in public policy problems. The reader can test his own consistency with the VN-M axioms by answering the following questions:

What certain prize would you give up for each of the following lotteries?

Table 2-15

Lottery	Prize	Probability That It Is Received	Your Answer (The certain prize you would give up)
(1)	$0	.01	
	$10,000	.99	_____
(2)	$0	.02	
	$10,000	.98	_____
(3)	$0	.01	
	your answer for (1)	.99	_____

If your answer for (3) is less than your answer for (2), you have made a choice inconsistent with maximization of expected utility. On an expected utility

52. Prospect E in essence offers a 50-50 chance to win $1. Prospect F gives one chance in twelve to win $6.06. A well-known example of a set of lotteries that leads many individuals to violate this axiom is known as the Allais Paradox. See Savage pp. 100–104 for a discussion of this example.

basis, lottery (3) is equivalent to a lottery offering $0 with probability .0199 and $10,000 with probability .9801, a lottery which would be preferred to lottery (2).[53]

One final question: Now that this inconsistency has been pointed out, would you wish to adjust your valuations?

Risk Versus Uncertainty

So far we have been blithely talking about probabilities as if they were as easily calculated and generally accepted as probabilities involving the tossing of a die. Many years ago Frank Knight drew the distinction between situations where probabilities are known (and ordinary insurance principles apply), which he called situations of *risk* and situations in which probabilities are not known, which he called situations of *uncertainty*. The reason we abandoned the umbrella example temporarily is that it is a case of uncertainty, in this sense; just what the probability of rain is on a given day is not at all clear.

Many competing criteria have been suggested for situations in which the probabilities are not known; among the more popular candidates are the maximin criterion and the minimax regret criterion. The maximin criterion directs the decision maker to select that course of action which offers the highest security level. For purposes of illustration, we return to the umbrella problem for which the following VN-M utilities have been assigned.

Table 2-16

| | STATE OF NATURE | |
ACTION	Sun	Rain
Carry umbrella	3	5
Leave umbrella	8	1

If the man works on the assumption that no matter what action he takes, the worst outcome for that action will occur—sun if he carries the umbrella, rain if he leaves it behind—he should always carry his umbrella, because that action will guarantee him a payoff at least equal to three. Such a Milquetoast

53. Let $X represent your answer for (1). Lottery (3) offers a .01 chance of $0 and a .99 chance of $X. By the VN-M axiom we have just discussed, you are indifferent between the prize $X and a prize which offers the lottery with .01 chance of $0 and a .99 chance of $10,000. For you, lottery (3) should be equivalent to the following lottery:

prob. of $0	prob. of $X	$X equivalent	lottery 3 equivalent
		.01 chance of $0	.0199 chance of $0
.01 +	.99 ×	.99 chance of $10,000 =	.9801 chance of $10,000

this lottery is clearly inferior to lottery (2) which offers .02 chance of $0 and a .98 chance of $10,000.

approach would not be justified unless it were assumed that Nature was a malicious opponent (her every gain was his every loss) who always knew the man's choice before making her own.

If Nature is not omniscient in this fashion, the man would find it beneficial to mix his actions; sometimes carry the umbrella, sometimes not. For example, if he carried the umbrella three quarters of the time he would achieve an expected payoff of 4 if it rained or 4 1/4 if the sun shone. The reader with a mathematical bent might wish to demonstrate that his maximin strategy is to carry the umbrella 7/9 of the time. This strategy gives him an expected payoff of 4 1/9 against either strategy selected by nature.[54]

The minimax regret criterion focuses attention on the opportunity loss of an incorrect decision. This loss is measured by the difference between an achieved payoff and the payoff which could have been obtained if the decision maker had known what the state of Nature would be. The regret for carrying an umbrella when the sun is shining, (5), is the difference between the payoff for not carrying one, (8), which would have been the subject's choice if he had known that it would be sunny, and the payoff actually received, (3). Table 2-17 gives the regret for the other possible outcomes, according to the VN-M utilities given in Table 2-16.

Table 2-17

ACTION	STATE OF NATURE	
	Sun	*Rain*
Carry umbrella	$8-3 = 5$	$5-5 = 0$
Leave umbrella	$8-8 = 0$	$5-1 = 4$

The minimax regret criterion says that one should choose the course of action which minimizes the maximum possible expected regret for any strategy selection by Nature. In this case the prescription is to carry the umbrella 4/9 of the time. This procedure would yield an expected regret of 2 2/9.

Two specific objections may be raised against the use of this criterion. (1) This criterion is not independent of irrelevant alternatives; that is, the introduction of a new alternative may alter the choice among the original

54. The two payoff matrices below show a zero-sum game. Whatever strategies are chosen by the players, Ralph's gain is Henry's loss and vice versa (e.g., if Ralph chooses *A* and Henry selects II, Ralph pays 6 to Henry).

	Payoff to Henry, Ralph Chooses			Payoff to Ralph, Ralph Chooses	
	A	*B*		*A*	*B*
Henry I	7	−1	Henry I	−7	1
Chooses II	6	3	Chooses II	−6	−3

(The maximin strategy for Henry is II, it guarantees him a payoff of 3—the maximin strategy for Ralph is *B*, it guarantees him a payoff of −3.)

alternatives even though the new alternative is not chosen.[55] (2) There is no assurance that differences between VN-M utility values are in any sense an accurate measure of regret.

Personal Probability

The weakness of these criteria as aids for decision making under uncertainty is that they look only at the outcomes with no consideration of how likely the corresponding states of nature are. A wildly remote possibility might be the determining factor when these criteria are applied. The school of Bayesian decision theory, which has grown up in recent years, does take account of the likelihood of the various outcomes by using explicitly the personal judgment of the decision maker as to the probabilities of the various outcomes.

Bayesian analysis of uncertain prospects has the same simple structure as the Von Neumann-Morgenstern approach we discussed above. As before, the first step is to attach VN-M utilities to the possible outcomes. Inasmuch as there are no longer clearly defined probabilities with which to calculate expected utility, the second step is to quantify the decision maker's personal probabilities. We do this by asking him to compare a gamble involving a state of nature whose probability is unknown with gambles involving known probabilities. If he turns out to be indifferent between a lottery that offers him a valuable prize if the state of nature S occurs and a lottery that offers him the same prize if he draws a red ball from an urn containing thirty-five red balls and sixty-five black balls,[56] then we say, by definition, that he attaches a personal probability of 0.35 to the state of nature S. These personal probabilities are then used to calculate the expected utility of each alternative, and the alternative that offers the highest expected utility is selected.

Following this procedure, the decision maker in our umbrella example reveals that his personal probability for rain as the state of nature is equal to 0.35. Using the following analysis, he decides not to carry an umbrella.

$$\text{Expected Utility Carry} = (1-0.35)(3)+(0.35)(5) = 3.7$$
$$\text{Expected Utility Leave} = (1-0.35)(8)+(0.35)(1) = 5.55.$$

55. There will of course be cases in which new, unchosen alternatives will not be irrelevant. For example, you are visiting a friend in a small town, and he offers you a choice between bowling and the local symphony for evening entertainment. You decide to go bowling because you think that there is a good chance that the local symphony will be of very mediocre caliber. At this juncture your friend remembers that the local opera group will be performing that evening. It happens that you do not like the opera, but you might alter your original choice to the symphony. Any town that is sufficiently culturally oriented to support an opera group is likely to have a pretty fair symphony orchestra.

56. See Pratt, Raiffa, and Schlaifer for further discussion of this method of measuring personal probabilities.

This is merely a formal approach to the intuitive method that we outlined in our introduction to decision making under uncertainty, "A sensible decision maker estimates the probability of rain, and carries his umbrella if he judges this probability to be above some crucial level." The reader who wishes to test his understanding of our discussion should show that this crucial probability is equal to 5/9.[57]

Many of the most important decisions made in the sphere of public policy must be made with information so limited as to make all probability estimates uncertain. It is thus a matter of importance that some people do not believe probabilities unless they are objectively defined. Tell a cancer patient that he has a 25 percent chance of dying unless you cut off his leg. His decision may not depend upon his relative utilities for death and losing a leg, but rather upon his decision as to whether he will die or not. The cancer patient will not think that his chances of dying are 5 percent, 25 percent, or 95 percent. They are 0 or 100 percent. Decision makers might refuse to make the probabilistic judgments which would be necessary to their own decision problems. Of some persuasive value are the axioms that Savage has provided; if a decision maker accepts these axioms, he can find a consistent set of probabilities to guide his behavior.

The Bayesian approach simplifies the decision maker's problem by (1) drawing up a utility function that describes the decision maker's attitude toward gambling with the possible outcomes and (2) utilizing the decision maker's personal estimate of the probabilities of the relevant states of nature. This second step may have to be altered if the decision maker's knowledge of the probabilities of the possible consequences of his actions is not very good. In this case it is the technical expert's considered judgment on probabilities that we would want to combine with the decision maker's VN-M utilities.

Optimization over Time—
Evaluating Future Decisions

Our discussion thus far has proceeded on the assumption that the complete impact of any decision would be felt immediately. But we know that many decisions that are made today will have repercussions for many years into the future. When we decide to devote part of the national budget to a manned moon probe project we are committing ourselves to future expenditures and hopefully to future successes. When we decide to construct the Kennedy Library we know that our children and our children's children will

---

57. If the reader has become lazy, we reproduce the verifying calculations below:

Expected Utility Carry $(1-5/9)(3)+(5/9)(5) = 37/9$
Expected Utility Leave $(1-5/9)(8)+(5/9)(1) = 37/9$

If we increase the 5/9 to let us say 2/3, the expected utility of carry will exceed the expected utility of leave.

benefit just as they will suffer from the current spoilage of areas of natural beauty. Decisions with long-term implications are especially important in the public policy area, because the government as a continuing institution has been cast in the role of guardian of the nation's future; as we shall see below, investment for the future may be a special case of a public good.

The naïve questioner might ask, of what matter the time pattern of costs and benefits? In response, we quote from Herman Kahn's discussion of nuclear fallout and genetic deaths:

> If asked to choose among four situations—one in which 100% of the people were killed immediately, another in which 10% of each generation died prematurely for ten generations, another in which one per cent of each generation died prematurely for a hundred generations, or finally, one in which a tenth of a per cent of each generation died prematurely for the next thousand generations, there is no question which situation most people would prefer. Yet the total number of individuals killed is exactly the same.[58]

Whether or not we agree with Kahn's ultimate conclusions with respect to nuclear policy, we would probably go along with his contention that you have "done something very useful . . . if you can spread the genetic damage over tens of thousands of years." A death in the year 10,000 is not so significant as a death now, and on a less macabre level, a dollar benefit (or cost) in the distant future is of less import than a dollar benefit received today.

If we are to make the difficult choices between actions that yield streams of benefits and costs stretching into future years, we must extend the model of choice to enable us to make systematic comparisons between costs and benefits that are incurred and realized at different stages in time. The introduction of a dynamic element in decision making adds two major complications to our problem of choice.

1. Decisions and actions which we take in one time period may affect our ability to make future decisions, or to undertake certain actions in later time periods. We cannot treat independently all decisions made in different time periods.

2. We may not know the exact future effects of any decision or course of action. Indeed, we should expect that as we carry our estimates further into the future, our degree of uncertainty should increase. This factor is very evident in the numerous research-and-development decisions which must be made in our private as well as our public sectors. The role of uncertainty has come to dominate many studies of optimal R & D procedures.

Although they present no need for new conceptual schemes, the last two mentioned difficulties greatly increase the complexity of the decision-making process. The least tractable problems might come about when these two difficulties are encountered in the same problem. For example, a decision

58. Kahn, p. 48.

maker with a fixed outside budget must choose between alternative policies that will affect his future returns. It will not be possible for him to engage in a straightforward evaluation of the effect of any decision on future opportunities, because he is not certain how the decision will affect his future returns. In general, it will not be satisfactory for these purposes to replace an uncertain return by its expected value or even its certainty equivalent (the certainty equivalent to an uncertain prospect is the sum, expected with certainty, such that the decision maker is indifferent between it and the uncertain prospect). However, new developments in stochastic and dynamic programming, and in multistage decision theory have given us an increased ability to deal with the related difficulties of intertemporal interdependence and uncertainty.[59]

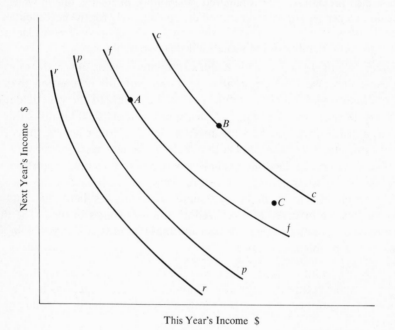

This Year's Income $

FIGURE 2-14

These techniques are more in the nature of solution aids than they are methods for attacking the problem directly. Even if we had methods for dynamic optimization readily available, we would not be in a position to make decisions that were in any sense optimal unless we knew which functions to optimize. We will touch only briefly on the mechanical details of the optimization process; we are primarily concerned with what it is trying to do, not how it is doing it.

59. See the pioneering efforts in this field by Bellman and Dreyfus.

As we indicated above, the decision maker would like to have a systematic method by which he could compare alternative time streams of returns and costs. In principle, Irving Fisher's classic work on the theory of interest gave us such a method. The approach is the by now familiar indifference-map analysis. The decision maker works with a n-dimensional indifference map, each dimension measuring his revenue or income in one of the n years in which his decision will have repercussions. A new project will be undertaken (that action will be selected) if it brings the decision maker to a higher in-difference curve than the one on which he is functioning at present. Figure 2-14, a diagram for a two-period model might clarify this procedure.

The decision maker will choose project B, that project which moves him to the highest indifference curve. Unfortunately, it may be quite as difficult for a decision maker to conjure up his intertemporal indifference map as it is for him to evaluate alternative time streams directly. Marginal evaluations of the type we discussed in connection with our elementary model of choice are of little assistance. It is the rare human mind that can think in terms of marginal trade-off rates between current income and let us say income in 1990, in the same way that it can think in terms of trade-off's between apples and oranges. Alert to this problem, economic theorists set about devising some short cuts, some rules of thumb that would enable the decision maker to evaluate alternative time streams without engaging in Herculean mental efforts.

Discounting

One such method relies on the simple arithmetic of compound interest. If the interest rate between year 0 and year I is r, then \$1 in year 0 can be converted to $1 + r$ dollars in year I. In a similar fashion a dollar return in year I can be exchanged for $1/(1 + r)$ dollars in year 0. This relationship leads to the idea of discounting future costs and return; the present value of a dollar in year n is $\$1/(1 + r)^n$ (because only $\$1/(1 + r)^n$ need be invested now in order to yield \$1 in year n). Why should a dollar today be worth more than a dollar one year from today? Because we have the option of investing the present dollar and obtaining a positive return during the year in which we would have to wait for the other dollar.[60] Economists have been greatly intrigued by the possibility of zero or negative rates of interest,[61] but positive interest rates are the rule in the economy, and governments like individuals must borrow and

60. This is much like the bundle of goods example (page 25) which was used to illustrate the choice criterion. Having a dollar today gives us all the same opportunities as having the dollar tomorrow. However, the converse is not true.

61. Imaginative economists cite the case of shipwreck victims adrift in a life raft with a large stock of disintegrating hardtack. The victims are likely to be trading their shares of the hardtack among themselves so as to reflect a negative interest rate— that is a pound today will be traded for the rights to less than a pound tomorrow. Zero-interest rates are less difficult to imagine. In the well-known stationary state of classical economics, there may or may not be a zero-interest rate.

lend in markets in which these positive rates prevail. (Whether the government should discount income streams at the market rate of interest is in fact a moot point. See our discussion below of the social rate of discount.)

Most projects will yield costs and returns in numerous future years. We apply the discounting procedure to each of these to derive their present values. The present value of the project is the sum of the discounted values of its future costs and returns. Consider the following time stream $(R_0, R_1, R_2, \ldots, R_n; C_0, C_1, C_2, \ldots, C_n)$ where R_t is the return in year t and C_t is the cost in that year. The present value of the stream (PV) is

$$PV = \left[R_0 + \frac{R_n}{1+r} + \frac{R_2}{(1+r)^2} + \ldots + \frac{R_n}{(1+r)^n} \right]$$
$$- \left[C_0 + \frac{C_1}{1+r} + \frac{C_2}{(1+r)^2} + \ldots + \frac{C_n}{(1+r)^n} \right]$$

which can be simplified to

$$R_0 - C_0 + \frac{R_1 - C_1}{1+r} \quad \frac{R_2 - C_2}{(1+r)^2} + \ldots + \frac{R_n - C_n}{(1+r)^n}.$$

The present value criterion says that a project should be undertaken if the sum of future returns minus costs, discounted back to the present, is positive—that is, if the present value is greater than zero.

Some readers may be familiar with an alternative criterion which employs the scientific sounding concept of the *internal rate of return*. It asserts that a project should be undertaken if that interest rate which would make its present value equal to zero is greater than the appropriate interest rate. This criterion is based on the intuitively appealing assumption that projects should be undertaken if they offer a rate of return greater than the rate at which money can be borrowed, or another base rate which the decision maker wishes to choose.

After a debate of appropriate length, economists came to realize that the two criteria will lead to the rejection and undertaking of the same projects if (1) there are no budgetary limitations, (2) if the appropriate rate of interest can be defined, and (3) projects do not preclude each other. Unfortunately, most public policy decisions must be made in the face of some budgetary constraint. The government planner cannot simply float another bond issue or increase taxes every time he discovers a new project which should be undertaken according to some criterion. What is needed is a method to choose among competing projects, to select those projects that are most desirable. Both the present value and internal rate of return methods are readily convertible to a priority approach. The present value decision rule is equivalent to the following rule taken from the "Green Book" for economic analysis of water resource projects.

> Rank all projects in descending order of the ratio of annual benefits (assuming that the benefit stream is constant) to annual amortized costs. Proceed down this rank list including as may projects as the budget for this year permits.[62]

It is implied that the procedure is repeated in future years. The internal rate of return method would substitute the words "internal rate of return" for "ratio of . . . amortized costs," but in other respects would be the same. There may not be full agreement between the rankings of these two criteria, but since both criteria have serious deficiencies it is not desirable to debate the matter here.[63]

The primary deficiencies of this approach are three in number:

1. This priority list approach may lead to inefficiency if the projects are indivisible and the budget constraint is not exactly satisfied.[64]

2. The procedure optimizes for only one year at a time, and fails to consider the costs incurred by delaying projects for future inception. Some projects may be better suited to present needs; others can be profitably delayed if, for example, their construction costs are falling. Consider the following numerical illustration involving three projects each of which costs $1.

Table 2-18

Net PRESENT VALUE
(BUDGETARY CONSTRAINT $1 EACH YEAR)

PROJECT	Year I	Year II	Cost of Delay
A	$2.00	$1.80	$0.20
B	1.80	1.10	0.70
C	1.20	1.15	0.05

The near-sighted Green Book procedure would lead us to choose project *A* in Year I and *C* in Year II, whereas it is clearly optimal to choose *B* in Year I and *A* in Year II.

3. There is no reason to assume that budgetary constraints will be absent in future years. Future budgets may be significantly affected by projects undertaken in this year. We can not make our decisions in a vacuum, as though this will be the last time that we will ever invest.[65]

There is a second, more empirically oriented, area of difficulty associated

62. See Marglin, p. 185.   63. Alchian.
64. Refer to our previous section on benefit-cost analysis.
65. Some business firms use a payoff period approach to investment problems. Projects are ranked on the length of time it takes for them to pay back their original investment. Such a ranking scheme is not completely without merit, especially as part of a more elaborate analysis.

with any attempt to employ these criteria.[66] We referred to the "appropriate rate of interest," but it is by no means clear what the appropriate rate might be for discounting public projects. Neoclassical economic theory tells us that the interest rate in a perfect capital market equals the marginal rate of time preference (the marginal rate of substitution of income in two consecutive time periods) for all decision-making units, and hence it is the appropriate rate of discount.

The Social Rate of Discount

In imperfect capital markets of our economy, there are many different interest rates, depending on who is the borrower and who is the lender. It has been proposed that the appropriate rate of discount for the government is the rate at which it can borrow. Against this it has been argued that the alternative to certain public expenditures may not be a reduction in government borrowing but a reduction in taxes; the discount rate that is proposed is the rate of interest faced by the recipients of the most likely tax cut. Both of these attempts to find a rate of discount which measures the opportunity cost of public investment neglect the fact that investment for the future may be a special case of a public good.

> The individual as a citizen, having his share of local pride, may desire an improvement in the general future state of welfare of the community. If, however, he alone directs his activities in a manner conducive to it, the effects of his action may be quite negligible. . . . Neither private interest nor altruism (except if he has grounds for assurance that others, too will act in a manner designed to promote the future welfare of the community) can rationally lead him to invest for the future, and particularly the far distant future to an extent appropriate from the point of view of the community as a whole . . . improvement in the future state of the community as a whole is one that must serve a group demand and not just the demand of isolated individuals.[67]

66. Jorgensen presents a rather sophisticated criticism with respect to the generality of Marglin's ambitious attempt to deal with dynamic investment problems.

> The crucial assumption implicit in Marglin's procedure is that an appropriate rate of discount for the evaluation of individual projects (or, for that matter, for devising an optimal dynamic plan for an individual project) can be taken as given independently of the construction budgets available in each of the construction periods. There is one set of circumstances in which this assumption is inconsistent with selection of an optimal path for community consumption. This is that *none* of the budget constraints is "effective", that is, that funds provided by the construction budget for each period are greater than or exactly equal to the construction outlays for that period which would be optimal *in the absence* of budget constraints.

At present there is no convenient way to overcome the difficulty that Jorgensen cites. How should we discount in the face of budget constraints?
67. Baumol, p. 92.

Just as an individual may be willing to fit his car with an anti-smog device if this is the price he must pay to get others to follow suit, he may be equally willing to invest for the future at a rate below the market rate of interest if he is assured that other individuals will be investing in like projects.

This rate is called the social rate of discount. In practice we hope to obtain the rate of discount for public investment by analyzing the preferences of a responsible decision maker. But it is not clear to what extent the "true" social discount rate, the rate at which individuals will bind themselves to invest, will be reflected in the decision maker's indifference curves between present and future income.[68]

Public Versus Private Investment

Even if we could adequately define the social rate of discount, and even if there were no budgetary constraints, we should not routinely apply this rate and undertake those projects in the public sector which satisfy the present value criterion (the internal rate of return criterion). The social rate of discount may be lower than the market rate of interest which governs private investment decision. The government does not have sufficient control over private investment to insure that all socially desirable investments in the private sector are undertaken.[69]

> The optimal solution, undertaking all investment that has a positive present value at the social rate of discount is precluded by the institutional structure, and we are consequently faced with the necessity of choosing the best of inferior combinations of public and private investment. Clearly, the goal in planning public investment should be to avoid displacing "better" opportunities in the private sector.[70]

Some elements in our society attach great importance to the concept of private ownership. Even if we adopt the modest goal that in our imperfect world we would like the private/public investment ratio to be the same as it would be in an optimal world, we will be forced to give further consideration

68. Maurice Allais, a French economist, recognized the possible conflict between optimal resource allocations that would arise if the self-interested actions of private consumers were allowed to determine this allocation. He introduced the concept of Allais optimality to deal with intertemporal situations. Allais optimality is weaker than Pareto optimality. In some sense it is equivalent to Pareto optimality within each time period, but not across time periods. "It [Allais optimality] amounts to accepting consumer preferences in the sphere of temporal allocation, but not in the sphere of intertemporal allocation; this would be the case under a system of forced savings in an otherwise competitive economy." Jacques H. Dreze, "Postwar Contributions of French Economists," *American Economic Review*, **LIV**: 4, Part 2, (June 1964), p. 39.

69. The government does have the tools of fiscal and monetary policy to give it some influence over private investment.

70. Marglin, 275–276.

to the methods that we have discussed above. In recent years economists have been devoting considerable thought to matters such as these, especially with respect to water-resource development. Nevertheless, these studies are only in their early formative stages, and some of the problems which are solvable in principle remain a long way from practical solution.

"Satisficing" Versus Maximizing

In recent years the concept of utility maximization as a norm for rational economic behavior has come under attack. The most severe blows have been dealt by psychologists and organization theorists; as a result some economists have incorrectly dismissed these analyses as behavioristic observations. What the attackers had in mind was

> . . . the replacement of the goal of maximizing with the goal of satisficing, of finding a course of action that is "good enough.". . . this substitution is an essential step in the application of the principle of bounded rationality.[71]

How have the advocates of the maximizing models of rational choice responded? Raiffa and Schlaifer state:

> We most emphatically do not believe that the objective of an optimizing analysis is to find the best of all possible courses of action; such a task is hopeless. . . . Only after a set of "reasonable contenders" has thus been defined does it become possible to apply formal procedures for choices among them. . . . "Satisficing" is as good a word as any to denote both the preliminary choice of contenders and the intuitive elimination of some of them.[72]

There are still areas of disagreement, but it is doubtful whether any analyst of rational choice procedures would claim that a decision maker should systematically investigate and evaluate all of the alternatives available to him. Such search is both time-consuming and costly, and an optimal decision procedure should take these factors into account. Enlightened advocates of the maximizing school accept this contention—they would agree that there is normative validity in the satisficing argument that the cost of decision making should be incorporated into the maximizing model. There may even be costs involved in formulating a decision model, or in making any attempts to be perfectly rational. The economist Lord Robbins refers us to the "marginal utility of not thinking about marginal utility." Robbins has a point. In most everyday decisions an informal evaluation of the most accessible and promising alternatives would be all that any maximizing model would require.

71. Simon (MM), pp. 204–205.　　　　　72. Raiffa and Schlaifer, p. viii.

As the price of his economizing on search and calculation, the decision maker may occasionally unknowingly eliminate from consideration his most promising alternative. But, as George Stigler says, "Ignorance is like subzero weather: by a sufficient expenditure its effects upon people can be kept within tolerable or even comfortable bounds, but it would be wholly uneconomic entirely to eliminate all its effects."[73]

The satisficers do not of course limit their attention to decision situations in which the consequences are relatively unimportant yet the alternatives difficult to evaluate. In fact, they have documented violations of "maximizing behavior" in situations where the consequences are weighty and the alternative actions relatively simple to investigate. In perhaps their best-known example individuals follow a course known as event matching, even though a more profitable alternative seems obvious. We will not discuss event matching here. Such failure to adopt an optimal decision which is easily discoverable belongs to the realm of descriptive decision theory.[74]

We repeat, the satisficing model does have normative validity if it is looked at as an attempt to incorporate the costs of information and decision making into the conventional maximizing model. In this light, satisficing behavior can be conveniently interpreted as a method by which a decision maker takes that course of action that he feels will yield him the highest expected utility. In order to see this, let us develop the satisficing theory of decision making a little further.

According to satisficing theory, the decision maker has an aspiration level; he accepts as satisfactory an alternative that promises a return at least as great as this aspiration level.[75] An aspiration level is a dynamic concept that can change as the decision maker proceeds to evaluate a series of alternatives. Herbert Simon, a founding father of the satisficing school of thought states:

> As the individual, in his exploration of alternatives, finds it easy to discover satisfactory alternatives, his aspiration level rises; as he finds it difficult to discover satisfactory alternatives, his aspiration level falls.[76]

Simon leaves us somewhat in the dark as to when the aspiration level is employed as a cutoff point. If the decision maker finds it easy to find satisfactory alternatives he raises his aspiration level so that they are no longer satisfactory. How hard must it be to discover a satisfactory alternative before we accept that alternative as really satisfactory?

A model of choice that attempts to maximize expected utility may in fact prescribe a cutoff level not unlike the aspiration level of satisficing theory. However, a maximizing economic model, unlike some satisficing models,

73. Stigler, p. 224.
74. See Simon (AER) for a discussion of event matching.
75. See Siegel.   76. Simon (MM), p. 253.

might attempt to arrive at such a cutoff point in a systematic fashion. The principle to be followed is simple. The decision maker should continue to evaluate new alternatives until the cost of this evaluation outweighs the expected gain should the new alternative prove superior to its predecessors.

The following laboratory example might clarify this procedure for the mathematically curious. Consider a decision maker who is faced with numerous alternatives which he can investigate and evaluate, but not without incurring the costs of carrying out such evaluations. A simplified version of his problem might be the following:

1. It costs $1 to evaluate an alternative.
2. Any alternative is equally likely to yield any integral value between $1 and $100.[77]
3. After as many evaluations as he wishes, he can choose one and only one alternative.

If the first alternative yielded $100 it would clearly be foolish for the decision maker to make any further evaluations, as he could not improve his outcome. Conversely, if his first alternative was evaluated as $1, further efforts would seem called for. There is some cutoff value between these two extremes with which he should be satisfied. The decision maker should continue to try out alternatives until the expected gain from trying out another alternative is outweighed by the $1 cost incurred in its evaluation.[78]

It can readily be established that the decision maker should continue to try out alternatives until he discovers one that yields at least $87, a value which might play the role of the decision maker's level of aspiration in a satisficing model. Table 2-19 shows how the $87 figure was established.

Table 2-19

$ Value of Next Alternative	1 2 ... 86 87 88 89 90 91 92 93 94 95 96 97 98 99 100
Gain If High is	
$86	0 0 ... 0 1 2 3 4 5 6 7 8 9 10 11 12 13 14
$87	0 0 ... 0 0 1 2 3 4 5 6 7 8 9 10 11 12 13
Probability of Occurrence	1/100 for all values
Expected Gain If High Is	
$86	= 1/100($1) +1/100($2) +1/100($3) + ... +1/100($14) = $ 1.05
$87	= 1/100($1) +1/100($2) +1/100($3) + ... +1/100($13) = $ 0.91

Thus the dollar cost of evaluating another alternative outweighs the expected gain if an evaluated alternative yields $87 or more.

For this problem the appropriate cutoff point was readily established. The

---

77. We are assuming that if, let us say, a $54 is drawn, the next draw is as likely to be a $54 as any other specific value. The reader familiar with urn-type problems may find it convenient to think of drawing with replacement.

78. We are assuming for purposes of simplicity that utility is linear with money— that we would put up $50 for a 1/2 chance to win $100.

process might not be so easy for more complex problems. In such cases it might not pay to set a cutoff point scientifically, but we would still want a systematic way of not being entirely systematic.

How can we account for the argument that a decision maker's aspiration level might change as he proceeds to evaluate alternatives? Let us say that we are drilling a potential oil field. If the first four holes are completely dry, it might be in accord with all rational principles to save our drilling expenses and try elsewhere. However, if we achieve moderate success on our early efforts, we might raise our aspiration level (cutoff point) and look for a first-class gusher. If the reader will indulge another example, we can present this principle in somewhat more analytic fashion. Let us complicate our original laboratory example by assuming that there are two possible states of the world: one favorable, the other unfavorable. It will no longer be the case that each alternative is equally likely to assume any integral value between $1 and $100. Rather we will assume that the values of the alternatives are distributed in the fashion suggested in Figure 2-15.

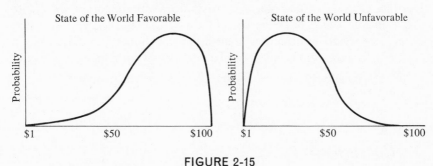

FIGURE 2-15

It might be wise for the decision maker to stop trying further alternatives if his first four evaluations yield $26, $18, $29, $47, but to continue in his evaluations if the evaluated alternatives yielded instead $89, $78, $83, $90. If the state of the world seems favorable he should raise his cutoff point, but he should lower it if his preliminary results indicated an unfavorable situation. One of the most important elements in any decision procedure is to know when we should stop searching; to this both the satisficers and maximizers would undoubtedly agree.

George Bernard Shaw appears to have summed up this argument pretty well:

> The open mind never acts: when we have done our utmost to arrive at a reasonable conclusion, we still, when we can reason and investigate no more, must close our minds for the moment with a snap, and act dogmatically on our conclusions. The man who waits to make an entirely reasonable will dies intestate.[79]

79. Bernard Shaw, "Androcles and the Lion," preface. Volume V, p. 421, of *Complete Plays with Prefaces* (New York: Dodd, Mead & Company, 1963).

and we might add "having spent a great deal on his effort to draw up an entirely reasonable will."

There may be costs involved in delaying a decision while additional information is being gathered. In a similar vein there may be a price to be paid for flexibility—flexibility being some measure of the future adaptability of an initial course of action to the circumstances which come to light after it is originally undertaken. In the real world we should expect that policy makers will be vitally concerned with the flexibility of their decisions. It is remarkable that the literature of normative economics has all but ignored this vital concept. We should expect that the subject of flexibility in policy decisions should be a fertile one for investigation from both a theoretical and descriptive standpoint.

Economic theorists have not given sufficient attention to the problems involved with optimal choice procedures when there are costs involved in acquiring information and in evaluating alternatives. The development of the satisficing model pointed out this shortcoming, and hopefully economics will follow the lead of the decision theorists who readily embrace the limited search principle which is at the core of the satisficing theory.[80] A general economic theory of information acquisition and optimal decision making under imperfect conditions has yet to be developed. Without such a development the concept of an optimal choice can be defined in principle, but not always in practice.

Conclusion

In our introduction we asked, "Of what use is the economic model of choice to the decision maker? Is not the ability to make difficult choices among competing ends the very asset that has placed him in his policy-making position?" We have proceeded to outline the model of choice and to point out the inherent difficulties when we attempt to apply it to policy-making decisions. Our initial questions point out a profitable area of pursuit. It would seem that we could learn a great deal about the theory of decision making if we observe how successful policy makers go about making decisions. Just as a knowledge of the basic principles underlying the model of choice

80. Decision theorists are far from having solved all of the problems in this field. A current puzzler is affectionately called the two-armed-bandit problem. The decision maker is confronted with two slot machines that are governed by unknown payoff schemes. However, the decision maker does know the distribution of possible payoff schemes for each of the two machines. He has a finite number of trials, on each of which he can play either of the two machines. At what point should he cut off his "experimentation" with both machines and stick with the one that appears to give the higher payoff?

might help a decision maker, so too a knowledge of how complex decisions are made might help us to extend our analysis into those situations too complex or abstract for an immediate logical extension of the normative model. Our faith in natural selection and the trial and-error method of education should lead us to believe that decision makers have developed some techniques for dealing with complexities of this nature. A knowledge of descriptive decision theory can aid us in developing a normative theory. Furthermore, if we are aware of the inadequacies in current policy-making techniques, we can better direct our theoretical attention in this area. What is needed is a greater feedback between the theory and the problems to which it has been or will be applied.

BIBLIOGRAPHY

Alchian, Armen, "The Meaning of Utility Measurement," *The American Economic Review*, **XLIII**, No. 1 (March 1953), pp. 26–50.

Arrow, Kenneth J., *Social Choice and Individual Values*, Cowles Foundation Monograph, No. 12, 2nd ed. (New York: John Wiley, 1963).

Banfield, Edward Christie, *Political Influence* (New York: Free Press, 1961).

Bator, Francis M., "The Simple Analytics of Welfare Maximization," *The American Economic Review*, **XLII**, No. 1 (March 1957), pp. 22–49.

Baumol, William J., *Economic Theory and Operations Analysis* (Englewood Cliffs, N.J.: Prentice-Hall, 1961).

—— *Welfare Economics and the Theory of the State* (Cambridge, Mass.: Harvard University Press, 1952).

Bellman, Richard E., *Dynamic Programming* (Santa Monica, Calif.: The RAND Corporation, 1956).

—— and Stuart E. Dreyfus, *Applied Dynamic Programming* (Santa Monica, Calif.: The RAND Corporation, 1962).

Bergson (Burk), Abram, "A Reformulation of Certain Aspects of Welfare Economics," *The Quarterly Journal of Economics*, **LII**, No. 2 (February 1938), pp. 310–334.

Buchanan, James M., and Gordon Tullock, *The Calculus of Consent* (Ann Arbor, Mich.: University of Michigan Press, 1962).

Chipman, John S., "The Foundations of Utility," *Econometrica*, **28**, No. 2 (April 1960), pp. 193–224.

Colm, Gerhard, "Economic Planning in the United States," *Weltwirtschaftliches Archiv*, **62**, No. 1 (1964), pp. 31–56.

Dean, Joel, and Joel Dean Associates, *Managerial Economics* (Englewood Cliffs, N.J.: Prentice-Hall, 1951).

Diesing, Paul, *Reason in Society: Five Types of Decisions and Their Social Conditions* (Urbana, Ill.: University of Illinois Press, 1962).

Dorfman, Robert, "Operations Research," *The American Economic Review*, **L**, No. 4 (September 1960), pp. 575–623.

Dorfman, Robert, *The Price System* (Englewood Cliffs, N.J.: Prentice-Hall, 1964).
—— Paul A. Samuelson, and Robert M. Solow, *Linear Programming and Economic Analysis* (New York: McGraw-Hill 1958).
Duesenberry, James S., *Income, Saving, and the Theory of Consumer Behavior* (Cambridge, Mass.: Harvard University Press, 1949).
Eckstein, Otto, "A Survey of the Theory of Public Expenditure Criteria" in *Public Finances: Needs, Sources, and Utilization* (Princeton, N.J.: Princeton University Press, 1961), pp. 439–494.
—— *Public Finance* (Englewood Cliffs, N.J.: Prentice-Hall, 1964).
Ellsberg, Daniel, "Classic and Current Notions of 'Measurable' Utility," *The Economic Journal*, LXIV, No. 255 (September 1954), pp. 528–556.
—— "Risk, Ambiguity, and the Savage Axioms," *The Quarterly Journal of Economics*, LXXV, No. 4 (November 1961), pp. 643–669.
Enthoven, Alain, and Henry Rowen, "Defense Planning and Organization" in *Public Finances: Needs, Sources, and Utilization* (Princeton, N.J.: Princeton University Press, 1961), pp. 365–417.
Fisher, Franklin M., "Income Distribution, Value Judgments, and Welfare," *The Quarterly Journal of Economics*, LXX (August 1965), pp. 380–424.
—— and Jerome Rothenberg, "How Income Ought to be Distributed: Paradox Enow," *Journal of Political Economics*, LXX (February 1962), pp. 88–93.
—— "How Income Ought to Be Distributed: Paradox Lost," *Journal of Political Economics*, LXIX (April 1961), pp. 162–180.
Fisher, Irving, *The Theory of Interest* (New York: Macmillan, 1930).
Galbraith, John Kenneth, *The Affluent Society* (Boston: Houghton-Mifflin, 1958).
Graaff, J. de V., *Theoretical Welfare Economics* (New York: Cambridge University Press, 1957).
Henderson, James M., and Richard E. Quandt, *Microeconomic Theory* (New York: McGraw-Hill, 1958).
Hicks, John R., "The Rehabilitation of Consumer Surplus," *The Review of Economic Studies*, VIII, No. 2 (February 1941), pp. 108–116.
Hicks, J. R., *Value and Capital*, 2nd ed. (New York: Oxford University Press, 1962).
Hitch, Charles J., and Roland N. McKean, *The Economics of Defense in the Nuclear Age* (Cambridge, Mass.: Harvard University Press, 1961).
Kahn, Herman, *On Thermonuclear War*, 2nd ed. (Princeton, N.J.: Princeton University Press, 1961).
Knight, Frank Hyneman, *Risk, Uncertainty, and Profit* (Boston: Houghton Mifflin, 1921).
Koopmans, Tjalling C., *Three Essays on the States of Economic Science* (New York: McGraw-Hill, 1957).
Krutilla, John V., "Welfare Aspects of Benefit-Cost Analysis," *Journal of Political Economy*, LXIX (June 1961), pp. 226–335.
Lampman, Robert J., "Making Utility Predictions Verifiable," *The Southern Economic Journal*, XXII (January 1956), pp. 360–366.
Lancaster, Kelvin, and R. G. Lipsey, "The General Theory of Second Best," *The Review of Economic Studies*, XXIV (1), No. 63 (1956–57), pp. 11–32.

Levine, Robert A., *The Arms Debate* (Cambridge, Mass.: Harvard University Press, 1963).

Little, I. M. D., *A Critique of Welfare Economics*, 2nd ed. (London: Oxford University Press, 1960).

Luce, R. Duncan, and Howard Raiffa, *Games and Decisions* (New York: John Wiley, 1958).

Maass, Arthur, *et al.*, *Design of Water-Resource Systems* (Cambridge, Mass.: Harvard University Press, 1962).

Marglin, Stephen A., "Economic Factors Affecting System Design" in Maass *et al.*, *Design of Water-Resource Systems* (Cambridge, Mass.: Harvard University Press, 1962), pp. 159–225.

———— "The Opportunity Costs of Public Investment," *The Quarterly Journal of Economics*, LXXVII, No. 2 (May 1963), pp. 274–289.

———— "The Social Rate of Discount and the Optimal Rate of Investment," *The Quarterly Journal of Economics*, LXXVII, No. 1 (February 1963), pp. 95–111.

Mishan, E. J., "A Survey of Welfare Economics, 1939–1959," *The Economic Journal*, LXX, No. 278 (June 1960), pp. 197–265.

Morse, Philip M., and George E. Kimball, *Methods of Operations Research*, 1st ed. rev. (New York: The Technology Press and John Wiley, 1958).

Musgrave, Richard A., *The Theory of Public Finance* (New York: McGraw-Hill, 1959).

Nath, S. K., "Are Formal Welfare Criteria Required?" *Economic Journal*, LXXIV (September 1964), pp. 548–578.

Novick, David, *Efficiency and Economy in Government through New Budgeting and Accounting Procedures* (Santa Monica, Calif.: The RAND Corporation, 1954).

Olson, Mancur, Jr., and Richard Zeckhauser, "An Economic Theory of Alliances," *The Review of Economics and Statistics*, XLVIII, No. 3 (August 1966), pp. 266–279.

Peck, Merton J., and Frederick M. Scherer, *The Weapons Acquisition Process* (Boston: Division of Research, Graduate School of Business Administration, Harvard University, 1962).

Pratt, John W., Howard Raiffa, and Robert Schlaifer, "The Foundations of Decision Under Uncertainty: An Elementary Exposition," *Journal of the American Statistical Association*, **59**, No. 306 (June 1964), pp. 353–375.

Raiffa, Howard, "Risk, Ambiguity, and the Savage Axioms: Comment," *The Quarterly Journal of Economics*, LXXV, No. 4 (November 1961), pp. 690–694.

———— and Robert Schlaifer, *Applied Statistical Decision Theory* (Boston: Division of Research, Graduate School of Business Administration, Harvard University, 1961).

Robertson, D. H., *Utility and All That* (New York: Macmillan, 1952).

Rothenberg, Jerome, *The Measurement of Social Welfare* (Englewood Cliffs, N.J.: Prentice-Hall, 1961).

Samuelson, Paul A., "Diagrammatic Exposition of a Theory of Public Expenditure," *The Review of Economics and Statistics*, XXXVII, No. 4 (November 1955), pp. 350–356.

———— "Evaluation of Real National Income," *Oxford Economic Papers*, New Series, **2**, No. 1 (January 1950), pp. 1–40.

Samuelson, Paul A., *The Foundations of Economic Analysis* (Cambridge, Mass.: Harvard University Press, 1947).

—— "The Pure Theory of Public Expendture," *The Review of Economics and Statistics*, **XXXVI**, No. 4 (November 1954), pp. 387–389.

—— "Social Indifference Curves," *The Quarterly Journal of Economics*, **LXX** (February 1956), pp. 1–22.

Savage, Leonard J., *The Foundations of Statistics* (New York: John Wiley, 1954).

Schelling, Thomas C., *The Strategy of Conflict* (Cambridge, Mass.: Harvard University Press, 1960).

Scitovsky, Tibor, "Note on Welfare Propositions in Economics," *The Review of Economic Studies*, **IX**, No. 1 (November 1941), pp. 77–88.

Sen, Amartya Kumar, "On Optimizing the Rate of Saving," *The Economic Journal*, **LXXI**, No. 283 (September 1961), pp. 479–496.

Siegel, Sidney, "Level of Aspiration and Decision Making," *Psychological Review*, **64**, No. 4 (July 1957), pp. 253–262.

—— with Alberta E. Siegel and Julia Andrews, *Choice, Strategy, and Utility* (New York: McGraw-Hill, 1964).

Simon, Herbert A., *Models of Man* (New York: John Wiley, 1957).

—— "Theories of Decision-Making in Economics and Behavioral Science," *The American Economic Review*, **XLIX**, No. 3 (June 1959), pp. 253–283.

Steiner, Peter O., "Choosing Among Alternative Public Investments in the Water Resource Field," *The American Economic Review*, **XLIX,** No. 5 (December 1959), pp. 893–916.

Stigler, George J., "The Economics of Information," *The Journal of Political Economy*, **LXIX**, No. 3 (June 1961), pp. 213–225.

Strotz, Robert H., "How Income Ought to Be Distributed: A Paradox in Distributive Ethics," *The Journal of Political Economy*, LXVI (June 1958), pp. 189–205.

—— "How Income Ought to Be Distributed: Paradox Regained," *The Journal of Political Economy*, **LXIX** (June 1961), pp. 271–278.

—— "Myiopia and Inconsistency in Dynamic Utility Maximization," *The Review of Economic Studies*, **XXIII** (3), No. 62 (1955–56), pp. 165–180.

Theil, H., *Economic Forecasts and Policy* (Amsterdam: North-Holland Publishing Company).

—— "Econometric Models and Welfare Maximization," *Weltwirtschaftliches Archiv*, **72,** No. 1 (1954), pp. 60–83.

Thomas, Harold A., Jr., "The Animal Farm: A Mathematical Model for the Discussion of Social Standards for Control of the Environment," *The Quarterly Journal of Economics*, **LXXVII**, No. 1 (February 1963), pp. 143–148.

Tinbergen, J., *Economic Policy: Principles and Design* (Amsterdam: North-Holland Publishing Company, 1956).

Valavanis, Stefan, "Traffic Safety from an Economist's Point of View," *The Quarterly Journal of Economics*, **LXXII**, No. 4 (November 1958), pp. 477–484.

van Eyk, C. J., and J. Sandee, "Quantitative Determination of an Optimum Economic Policy," *Econometrica*, **27,** No. 1 (January 1959), pp. 1–13.

von Neumann, John, and Oskar Morgenstern, *The Theory of Games and Economic Behavior*, 3rd ed. (Princeton, N.J.: Princeton University Press, 1953).

Weckstein, Richard S, "Welfare Criteria and Changing Tastes," *The American Economic Review*, **LII** (March 1962), pp. 133–153.

Wildavsky, Aaron, *The Politics of the Budgetary Process* (Boston: Little, Brown and Company, 1964).

de Wolff, P., "Central Economic Planning in The Netherlands," *Weltwirtschaftliches Archiv*, **62,** No. 1 (1964), pp. 181–207.

Chapter 3

JOSEPH L. BOWER

Descriptive Decision Theory from the "Administrative" Viewpoint

Introduction

MOTIVATION

The large-scale organization is the characteristic mechanism that men have chosen for ordering their joint efforts in order to accomplish objectives in contemporary industrial society. For this reason social scientists have long been interested in the operating characteristics of such organizations and the collective decision-making process. They have tried to discover generalizable traits of organizations that would permit the construction of a theory.

Generally speaking, they have attempted two sorts of theories. The first is concerned with what decision an organization *ought* to make. The second group is concerned with the way in which organizations actually go about making decisions. The problems that motivate this chapter involve the behaviour of organizations. We are interested in the process as well as the product of administration. For this reason, our focus is on the second class of theory.

Because the postwar decades have shown that the useful application of theory to practical problems is not limited to the physical sciences, it is widely recognized that a theory of large-scale organization would be extremely valuable to the administrators of these institutions. What is needed is a theory (1) that provides a simple picture of how an organization works, and (2) that provides a basis for improving the performance of organizations.

The objective of this chapter is to survey the literature of theories about organization to find one that will meet these two criteria. It does not spoil the punch line to note at this point that a satisfactory theory has not been found. In many cases those who developed theories of organization were uninterested in the problem of improving performance. Others found that the restrictions imposed by their methodology rendered them incapable of coping with the complexity of the large organization. They resolved their difficulty by finding a smaller problem that was tractable within the constraints imposed by their tools. A final group focused on the real problem but failed to produce a theory that could be tested.

The failure of organization theory to meet our tests would be preordained if these tests were stated in the traditional manner. The problems of social organisms are so complex that, given the present state of knowledge, a successful empirical test of rigorous theory is virtually impossible. For this reason, a secondary but important objective of the chapter is to develop a set of realistic criteria for use in evaluating theory. We give up our right to claim possession of a rigorous and tested theory, as those attributes are classically defined, and focus instead on the ability to improve performance. We seek a way of knowing when a theory can be demonstrated to permit improvement in the consequences of administrative action.

The remainder of this introduction is devoted to achieving the second objective and charting the course of the chapter. The following section analyzes the classical definitions of theory and testing. Then we may examine the existing concept of performance-oriented theory and establish the criteria used in the survey. The remainder of the chapter is devoted to the first objective: a survey of the theories of organization.

DESCRIPTIVE AND NORMATIVE THEORY

Theory may be usefully separated according to the purpose that motivated its construction. Meaningful theory consists of a set of logically consistent propositions that imply an empirical result that could conceivably be refuted by an experiment, even if only under ideal conditions. All meaningful theory is either "normative" or "descriptive." Its objective is either to provide rules that will improve the consequences that result from action, or to describe the patterns of behavior that characterize action.

A simplified example from the experience of World War II should help make the distinction clear. Fighter pilots in the Pacific typically encountered situations requiring incendiary shells one third of the time and armor shells two thirds of the time. It was observed that when left to their own devices pilots armed themselves with incendiary and armor piercing shells in the proportion of 1 to 2. The result was that in a given situation the odds on having the appropriate shells were $1/3 \times 1/3 + 2/3 \times 2/3 = 5/9$. Of course, had the pilots always carried armor-piercing shells, they could have improved results by being appropriately armed two thirds of the time: $1/3 \times 0 + 2/3 \times 1 = 2/3$.

A normative theory of arming would characterize the occurrence of the two types of situations as a random process with stable state probabilities, and prescribe the permanent choice of armor-piercing shells. A descriptive theory might characterize the pilots' choice mechanisms as "event matching" and predict that the proportion of each type of shell chosen would match the proportion of the time it would be the appropriate shell. Each theory would be potentially useful, but note: It would be coincidental if the normative theory provided insight into the choice mechanism of the pilot or if the descriptive theory provided a basis for improving the consequences of a pilot's choice.

Each model, if well formulated, might satisfy a number of the criteria for good theory. The causative argument is well identified; the assumptions underlying the models are consistent, minimal, and simple, and in each case the prescription or prediction that can be deduced rigorously from these assumptions can be confronted with a true empirical test.

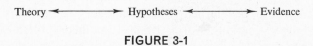

Theory ◄────────► Hypotheses ◄────────► Evidence

FIGURE 3-1

It is important to note that the tests are different. The confirmation of a descriptive theory is, in principle, an impossible task. It is not merely sufficient that the assumptions of the theory support hypotheses that are confirmed by evidence. The empirical confirmation of a descriptive theory demands that the evidence also imply the hypotheses and the hypotheses imply the assumptions, a situation our philosophers tell us cannot exist. The arrows in Figure 3-1, denoting deducible implications, must point both ways. When we speak of the empirical validation of descriptive theory, we mean merely that the theory is demonstrated to be not incorrect. Confirmation in this latter case is only possible if all alternative theories are rejected.

The confirmation of normative theory is somewhat simpler. It is necessary to show only that (1) the results using the models are superior to those without it according to a prespecified measure and (2) that the improvement observed bears a causative relation to the change in action prescribed.[1] In

---

1. The second step does not necessarily involve validation of a descriptive model. (a) Causation may be deducible; or (b) it may be observed, though not understood. Recipes, as they are used by most women, are normative theories that fall into the second category: causation is neither proved nor argued, it is accepted as a black-box phenomenon.

that subclass of normative theory in which the foundation assumptions of a deduced prescription consist solely of and totally embody the valued objectives of action, the second step is unnecessary: the relationship of prescription to assumption is that of theorem to axiom. Axiomatic decision theory may be totally devoid of descriptive content.

In summary, because normative and descriptive theories serve different purposes their tests are different. It should not be surprising, therefore, to find that, in fact, versions of both theories presented in the example above have been validated in the sense that (1) results improved when the normative prescription was followed, and (2) the behavior predicted by an "event-matching" model was not contradicted by the behavior observed.

DECISION THEORY

The genre decision theory obviously includes both descriptive and normative theories of decision making. The former subclass is vast, including theories at many levels of abstraction and concerning choice by all conceivable decision-making units. We survey these theories in the body of this paper. In this section and the one that follows, we investigate the purely normative decision theory, that subclass which is at least potentially devoid of descriptive content. Our goal is to discover whether normative decision-making theory provides a prescriptive guide to decision making in the large organization.

Schlaifer has described normative decision theory as the theory of rational choice in complex situations. Normative decision theory, often called statistical decision theory, has demonstrated that (1) if one can order the consequences associated with action, (2) if the ordering is transitive, and (3) if one can make certain simple kinds of choices in uncertain situations in a consistent and transitive fashion, then one should use the calculus of expected utility in order to make choices.[2]

The conceptual core of statistical decision theory, in its applied form, is a meticulous analysis of the relationships among valued consequences, events, and alternative choices and an explicit statement of subjective attitudes concerning the uncertainties that characterize these relationships, that is, a descriptive model.

The contribution of these two concepts should not be underestimated. Before the work of the statistical decision theorists, the theory of rational use of information was developed without reference to the costs associated with

2. The specific requirements underlying expected utility have been stated many times. An early treatment was that of Von Neumann and Morgenstern [53]; a particularly simple exposition is given in Luce and Raiffa [32], and a most elegant one in Pratt, Raiffa, and Schlaifer [40]. In addition to these names, Savage, Wald, Blackwell, Girshik, Neyman, Pearson, and Jeffreys have played leading roles in the development of decision theory. Numbers in brackets refer to position of reference in bibliography at the end of the chapter.

error or the evaluation of uncertainty where information was subjective rather than objective, that is, in the form of a real or hypothetical frequency distribution.

Rigorous statistical decision theory has been usefully applied to a number of problems ranging from weapons design to the selection of securities for investment portfolios. There are two common characteristics of tractable problems: they involve an individual decision maker, and value is unidimensional and functionally expressible in dollars. Neither of these characteristics is associated with the large complex organizations in which we are interested.

In the first place, the consequences that follow from a choice conditional upon events are usually multidimensional. For example, alternative water-resource-development programs have different capital costs, different operating costs, involve different sponsoring groups, have different benefits, and distribute these benefits in differing ways among the various groups in the population. In practice, these differences are incomparable. In the firm, alternative investment programs not only imply major differences in the mix of products, sales, profits, growth rate, and risk, but also class of customer, employee relations, form of organization, and style of leadership. For an intermediate manufacturer, vertical integration toward the customers implies the acquisition of a set of skills very different from that implied by integration back to production of raw materials. It is often exceedingly difficult to order such multidimensional lists of consequences. Where the alternatives are as complicated as new product divisions or hydroelectric dams the ordering required by normative theory can never be constructed.

The second reason organizational choice does not meet the conditions of the normative model has its origin in the definition of value. Because our subject is a group we must ask "Value according to whom?" In fact, the principal normative theory of group decisions is a set of negative results demonstrating that as yet it is impossible to construct from conflicting notions of individual value a single ordering that will permit group organizational choice.[3]

Moreover, depending upon the source of conflicting individual notions of values, the problem may be even worse. Conflict may not only be a disagreement among individuals as to what is best for the group. Within a group there may be subgroups, each of which has its own defined objectives. These need not be informal, socially oriented subgroups. More often they will be formally defined parts of a carefully designed organization. For example, in the Air Force organization, the Logistics Command is responsible for the "maintainability" of aircraft; the Systems Command is responsible for the "reliability" of an aircraft; the Operating Command is concerned with performance and

3. A discussion of the normative group-decision literature can be found in Bower [7].

availability; the Assistant Secretary of Financial Management is concerned with cost. It is rare when the separate missions of the four commands do not bring them into conflict.

THE NEED FOR A PRESCRIPTIVE THEORY

The failure of present normative theory to provide a solution to the group problem means that we must seek elsewhere for the systematic guidance of organizational choices. What we need is a theory of organization that will support the prescription of policy. We require as a foundation a model of organizational choice sufficiently well identified to uphold a causative argument relating prescription to results. The model may take either of two forms. It may be a set of axioms or conclusions capable of both (1) satisfaction by organizations and (2) supporting the deduction of a prescription; or it may be a descriptive model providing sufficient insight into the decision-making process to permit a relative improvement of the process. In either case, we require descriptive theory as a basis for progress. It is to a survey of the existing body of descriptive theory that we now turn.

DESCRIPTIVE THEORIES OF DECISION MAKING

The literature of descriptive decision theory embraces many disciplines. Economists, psychologists, sociologists of various kinds, political scientists, statisticians, mathematicians, and students of public and business administration have all made contributions. The variety of disciplines involved makes classifying and arranging the various theories difficult. The lack of attention traditionally paid to the distinction between normative and descriptive propositions aggravates the problem. Theory concerned with the proper choice of organizational objectives, and the associated choice of administrative tools to achieve those objectives, often contain many partial descriptive models as part of the normative framework. Macroeconomic theory is based on a whole series of partial descriptive models of the various decision units in the economy. Welfare economics has an equally conglomerate nature. Our treatment of this quasi-descriptive policy oriented theory shall be cursory at best. Chapter 2 provides a systematic survey of that literature.

Returning to theory with a descriptive focus, we find that attitudes toward aggregation further confuse matters. For example, the economists' theory of the firm sounds as if it refers to exactly the sort of organization we have in mind. In fact, it is a theory of individual choice and a very abstract one at that. Even so, it is used as a component sub-theory by econometricians building aggregate models of choice by the total business sector and by the national economy. On the other hand, some models of individual problem solving are used at a more aggregate level to explain group behavior.

To provide some order in our presentation we have divided the literature along substantive lines into theories of individual choice and theories of collective choice. We include the former group in the survey both because future theory of groups may be based on existing models of individual decision processes, and because many existing theories of group choice are best understood in terms of their sources in models of individual choice.

Theories of Individual Choice

THE CLASSICAL THEORY OF THE FIRM

The basic question to which economists have addressed themselves is the optimal allocation of resources in the national economy. In the pursuit of this goal a model of the productive unit was developed. In its traditional form this model has come to be called "the classical theory of the firm."

This model envisions the firm as a single decision maker using a series of inputs—labor, capital, and raw materials—to produce a series of salable outputs. It is assumed that the decision maker—economic man in his role as producer—desires only to maximize his profits, defined as the residual of sales revenue after costs are subtracted. Both costs and revenues of a given product are assumed to be monotonically increasing functions of the level output. Technology (the functional relation of inputs to outputs) is assumed determined, as is the price at which all combinations of the several outputs can be sold. These assumptions permit one to deduce the levels of output of the several products which will maximize the firm's profit.[4]

When profit is maximized—at the so-called equilibrium level of output—two sets of mathematical conditions are satisfied. The first is subject to economic interpretation: at equilibrium, incremental cost (for positive or negative increments) is equal to incremental revenue. The second condition concerns the rates of change in cost and revenue at the optimum.

Despite its simplicity, the model has been an extremely fruitful source of successful applications. In fact the quantitative tools of contemporary "sophisticated" business administration are simply extensions of the marginal calculus to specific business situations. Nonetheless, large organizations sometimes found that modern technologies and the constraints of limited processes and resources rendered the classical model overly restricted.

Recently some of these restrictions have been overcome. The exploitation of postwar developments in linear and nonlinear mathematics, for example,

4. The complete statement of the optimality conditions was not achieved until the absorption of the calculus of constrained maximization into economic theory. Samuelson [44] provides a good discussion of the proof. The treatment by Henderson and Quandt [27] is a fine introductory presentation. Both require knowledge of the calculus.

linear programming, has permitted considerable extension of the theory of the firm. Much of what is called operations research falls into this category. The success of this type of applied theory is largely determined by the extent to which the model is descriptive of the full problem requiring solution.

If we return to the descriptive foundation of the classical theory—economic man in his role as producer—we can see that from the broad point of view of our interest in policy, even the neoclassical model of the firm is quite limited. The "firm" is really a production manager looking *inside* his own organization, and concerned only with dollars.[5] He need not look elsewhere because his information about his markets is complete, and his organization responds with mechanical precision to his wishes.

THE THEORY OF CONSUMER DEMAND

In order to complete their model of an economy, economists required a model describing the sources of demand. The theory of consumer demand is their response.

The theory is based on economic man as a consumer. It is assumed that the chooser can order alternative bundles of commodities and services. If the ordering is transitive and complete, it is sufficient to determine that mix of consumption which will maximize satisfaction. At that point the marginal rate of substitution between any two products will equal the ratio of product price (price is the marginal cost).

In fact, the meaningful or testable portion of this theory is limited to the so-called theory of revealed preference. That theory asserts that if the model of consumption is correct, a comparison of consumption and prices in two periods will always reveal the following, given that income remains constant:

> If the sum of the products of prices in the previous period and the change in consumption of these products between periods is negative, then the sum of the products of prices in the current period and the change in consumption of these products is also negative. Or, if past consumption exceeded present consumption valued at past prices, then it must also exceed present consumption at present prices, indicating that present consumption is less satisfactory.[6]

5. The introduction into the theory of an awareness of competitive interdependence in the product market extends the usefulness of the model by permitting its incorporation into models of market behavior, but does not change its limitations as a descriptive model of the firm's decision process. Cournot [12], Edgeworth [18], Pareto [39], and Chamberlain [9], are the prominent names associated with the development of the "theory of imperfect markets," (markets in which interdependence is recognized).

6. If a consumer has the same amount to spend in two periods, and if an item-by-item comparison indicates that he bought less in the second period, when the items are valued at the prices of the first, then we know that prices must have changed so as to lessen the satisfaction he derives from consumption. Otherwise, he could have bought more in the previous period. In another setting this notion would be presented as an

It may be surprising to the noneconomist that revealed preference theory underlies the theory of index numbers, utility analysis, and the analysis of demand functions. Nevertheless, it is only as a conceptual precedent that it has an interest for us.

UTILITY THEORY

The limitations of the theory of the firm, particularly as a description of decisions under conditions of uncertainty, and the meagre meaningful conclusions supported by the theory of consumer choice, leave unsatisfied the desire for a rich theory of individual choice. It is not surprising, then, that the normative model has been explored as a descriptive theory.

To be sure, no one believes that individuals usually go through the mechanics of constructing a utility function and using the subjective-probability calculus in order to make their decisions. Visual observation of ourselves and our colleagues is evidence enough that no such process takes place. Still, it is worth inquiring whether people behave *as if* they made choices so as to maximize utility. If such is the case, and if we can reproduce people's utility functions, then we have a powerful device for predicting behavior.

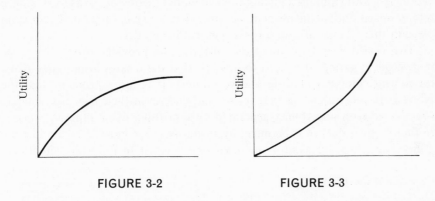

FIGURE 3-2   FIGURE 3-3

An early attempt to construct a utility function experimentally was made by Mosteller and Nogee (35) in 1951. Working with Harvard College undergraduates and with Massachusetts National Guardsmen, they discovered that in the context of a gambling situation in which choices were made between pairs of bets, the utility of incremental gains for Harvard students was decreasing (Figure 3-2) while that for Guardsmen was increasing (Figure 3-3). As a predictive device, the estimated utility functions were found highly imperfect but still superior to a naïve model that used simple monetary value.

---

implication of the principle of dominance which simply states that a man does not choose a less preferable alternative, if he can get a more preferable one without giving up anything.

Other experiments, particularly those by psychologists, have produced results that apparently contradict utility maximization as a descriptive hypothesis. These are the event-matching studies referred to above. In a trivial gambling situation—the equivalent of guessing correctly the result of sequential flips of a biased coin—subjects do not bet so as to win the most money (or any non-decreasing function of money such as utility), but rather they try to outguess the coin and end up event matching.

In a posthumously published study, Sidney Siegel [47] reports a series of experiments testing a utility-maximizing hypothesis in a slightly modified version. Siegel suggests that utility in such situations is two dimensional: the subject is concerned with the relative interest of what he is doing as well as with money earnings. This proposition was tested in an elegant experiment which varied the intellectual challenge of the experimental situation. Prediction using two-dimensional utility was extraordinarily accurate and event matching decreased as the task content was increased.

The result is really more discouraging than helpful, however. If it is correct, i.e., if the laboratory results are subject to generalization, then we are lost, for in rich and complicated situations, utility is likely to be a function of numerous uncontrollable variables and, therefore, not subject to estimation. We are left with Homans' [28] tautological model: people act so as to maximize return on emotional investment because that is what they do. There is no place in this scheme of things for a prescriptive model.

The World War II pilots of our introduction provide grounds for hope that Siegel is wrong. It is hard to imagine that the task of arming one plane for mortal combat lacks substantive interest. It is more probable that the pilots were not trained so that they could choose in their own best interest when faced with uncertainty generated by something like a random process. In fact, a great deal of experimentation suggests that most of us are like the pilots—we often act against our own best interest in uncertain situations.

PSYCHOLOGISTS

The Michigan School

The extent to which a literature exists documenting discrepancies between the assumptions of the utility model and the vagaries of human behavior is due in large measure to the efforts of Ward Edwards and Clyde Coombs, both psychologists at the University of Michigan.[7] In a series of elegant experiments it has been demonstrated that individuals have preferences for certain probabilities, for certain prizes, and for combinations of probabilities and prizes. The result undermines the efforts of others, e.g. Mosteller and Nogee, to construct utility functions. In the case of subjective probability (the explicit quantification of subjective feeling concerning relative likelihood of events),

7. See for example Coombs [11], and Edwards [19] and [20].

it was found that individuals overestimate the probability of unlikely events, underestimate the probability of likely events, and underestimate the information content of small samples.

Current experiments are exploring further the *relative* predictive power of expected monetary value, expected utility, subjective expected monetary value, and subjective expected utility as models of individual choice.[8] For our purposes the question is relatively uninteresting. Siegel demonstrated that even in an extremely barren choice situation multidimensional utility is required for predictive accuracy, and Edwards has shown the unidimensional model to have grave shortcomings as an approximation in only slightly richer situations.

Of more interest is the further methodological difficulty highlighted by the experiment. Coombs has derived a clever set of questions that simultaneously explores subjective attitudes toward the relative likelihood of events and the relative preferability of rewards. Patterns of choice can be identified *a priori* with each of the models. The difficulty arises when we turn to the task of prediction.

In order to construct a utility function it is necessary to elicit responses to questions concerning the relative preferability of simple gambles with different prizes. On the other hand, the construction of a subjective probability distribution requires a set of answers to questions concerning the relative preferability of simple gambles based on different events. Each set of questions involves both prizes and events. It is vital for the integrity of the results that the responses to the two sets of questions be independent. The individual's attitudes toward risk must not be allowed to confuse the reflection of his preference for rewards under certainty, and vice versa. The difficulty of achieving this interdependence is described in the next section. However, it should be apparent from introspection that one's attitudes toward likelihood and preference are typically interrelated. National shock at the assassination of President Kennedy certainly reflected preferences rather than the historical frequency of assassination in this country, at that time a frequency of one in seven. National driving and smoking habits reflect a similar distortion in the choice process.

A SUBJECTIVE EXPECTED UTILITY EXPERIMENT

In a 1954 experiment, Davidson, Suppes, and Siegel [14] tried to overcome the problems of interdependence above. It is theoretically possible to do so if an event can be found such that its occurrence and nonoccurrence are regarded equally probable. The difficulty in finding a neutral event is evident in the following quotation.

> A coin was tried and the subject given the opportunity to bet on heads (E) or tails ($\tilde{E}$); a die was used with odd numbers as E and even numbers as $\tilde{E}$;

8. The experiments are being conducted by Coombs.

and other equally simple or more complex games were tried. In every case most subjects showed a preference for either E or $\tilde{E}$. Finally an event was found which satisfied the conditions. This event was produced by means of a specially made die. On three faces of the die, the nonsense syllable "*ZOJ*" was engraved, on the other three faces "*ZEJ*."[9]

The authors found their results promising and the model successful "at least for alternatives consisting of losing or winning small (15¢) sums of money." Because such alternatives are orders of magnitude away from the ones we have in mind, it is probably fair to conclude that the utility model has limited use as a descriptive model for our purposes.

Stochastic Choice

The inconsistencies apparent in human choice behavior have also led psychologists (including many of the men already mentioned) to proceed on the basis of a somewhat novel presupposition concerning choice behaviour. Choice is described as probabilistic rather than algebraic. Luce, the principal exponent of the probabilistic hypothesis as a theory of choice, argues in his now classic *Individual Choice Behavior*, [31]

> At any instant when a person reaches a decision between, say, a and b we will assume that there is a probability $P(a, b)$ that the choice will be a rather than b. These probabilities will generally be different from 0 and 1, . . . The alternative is to suppose that the probabilities are always 0 and 1 and that the observed choices tell us which it is; . . .
> The decision between these two approaches does not seem to be empirical in nature. Various sorts of data—intransitivities of choices and inconsistencies when the same choices are offered several times—suggest the probabilistic model, but they are far from conclusive. Both of these phenomena can be explained within an algebraic framework provided that choice pattern is allowed to change over time, either because of learning or because of other changes in the internal state of the organism.[10]

Luce demonstrates the theoretical compatibility of perfect discrimination among consequences under certainty with stochastic choice in uncertain situations, and is able to axiomatize a descriptive utility theory based on stochastic choice. He regards the theory as a superior explanation of choice behavior.

We are not in a position here to argue the question. Instead, we reject as intuitively improbable (intolerable) the implication that a pragmatic norma-

9. See Davidson [14].

10. Luce, [31] p. 2. Instability of preference, referred to in the last sentence, is a problem we have not yet considered. It is notorious but true that peoples' preferences do change radically over time. From our point of view, instability is merely another problem with the utility model. We consider it in more detail when discussing alternate models.

tive theory can be constructed based on the assumption of stochastic preference. It is too much to expect a theory of policy prescription if policy objectives are subject to change, even if the change can be described by a probabilistic model.

OTHER BEHAVIORAL THEORIES

The Carnegie School

The theory and experiments described thus far have in common a concern with man as a unit of choice. The economist's model views man from the perspective of a vast market in which as either producer or consumer, he is a mere atomistic component.[11] The psychologists have viewed decision making as a special case, admittedly complicated, of the highly mechanistic Stimulus-Response (S-R) theory. A decision is a nearly mechanical response to a set of stimuli, and utility is a problem in scaling entirely analogous to those explored in the study of other fields of psychological perception.[12]

We have digressed to note this conceptual heritage because the theory we consider in this section is different in its origin. It was developed for the precise purpose of describing the very organizational administrators with whom we are concerned. The model of man it posits is, in certain senses, a good deal simpler than "economic man" and in its most elegant and recent formulations relies heavily on S-R theory. However, the man mapped by the theory is a warm-blooded, human decision maker—attempting to make rational decisions in the complex world of today's modern organizations.

Herbert Simon's Administrative Man

The man largely responsible for the theory of administrative man is Herbert Simon. Working from his initial model as it is described in *Administrative Behavior* [50], Simon and his colleagues at the Carnegie Institute of Technology have developed an elegant theory of choice in a complex world. The central concept of Simon's original model is the limited, or more precisely, the bounded rationality of the administrator. He says,

> It is impossible for the behavior of a single, isolated individual to reach any high degree of rationality. The number of alternatives he must explore is so great, the information he would need to evaluate them so vast that even an approximation to objective rationality is hard to conceive.[13]

11. It is entirely appropriate, given this conceptual inheritance, that the most recent breakthrough on the frontier of economic theory came when the insignificance of each single decision unit in the market was ultimately and precisely expressed by defining the decision maker as one point on the infinitely decomposable map of mathematically continuous space.

12. See, for example, Luce [31], p. 2.

13. Simon [50], p. 79.

He argues further that knowledge of the consequences that follow from each alternative act under consideration is fragmentary, that evaluation of future consequences is highly imperfect, and that the range of alternatives considered is limited.[14]

In order to function in his complicated and uncertain world, administrative man restructures the choice-requiring problems that he faces. First, he eliminates the scaling problem we have discussed in earlier theories above by reformulating multivalued goals into single-valued constraints. Instead of trying to maximize profit, the businessman chooses the first project he finds will satisfy his profit requirement or, as Simon would say, his aspiration in the profit dimension. Second, he vastly simplifies the range of choice he faces by ignoring all relationships but the most evident. The result is that the constraints upon his choices are few and clear cut. He is able to routinize the choice activity and express general solutions to recurring categories of problems as "rules of thumb."

The model that emerges, "satisficing," is a sharp contrast to those we have considered before, all of which are based on presupposition of maximizing behavior. Another contrast exists, which is evident if we examine further developments of Simon's model.

Because the functional relationship of events, acts, and consequences of the objective-maximizing problem is reformulated by the individual decision maker, the structure of the problem as well as the scale of value becomes subjective. For the model of decision making to be complete, it must include this subjective process of problem definition above and beyond a description of the act of choice. In fact, this requirement has been recognized. Over a period of time, emphasis in Simon's work has shifted from the deterministic relation of aspiration level and choice to the complete decision process that he has labeled "problem solving." In this evolution the motivational overtones of the theory have been reduced almost completely and the structure of a complete and tested model of the cognitive process has emerged. The model is summarized in the next section.

Aspiration and Problem Solving

The necessity for choice arises when more than one alternative courses of action present themselves to the individual. The differences among alternatives are reflected in terms of summary measures along those primary dimensions with which value is associated in the choice situation. An individual formulates his problem of choice in terms of finding an alternative that

14. The full force of the argument can be appreciated if we attempt to reconstruct the thinking of French generals in the opening days of World War II who, despite the enormous evidence to the effect, would not conceive that the Germans were in the process of flanking their army. They simply hadn't defined the war with Germany as including the alternative.

satisfies his level of aspiration along each dimension. The aspiration level is a budget,[15] a forecast, a criterion for survival, a traditional level of accomplishment, or a desired expectation which has been internalized as a goal.[16]

In all cases, it is that point at which the rate of change in value attributed to consequences is greatest. It is at the aspiration level that an expected outcome is deemed satisfactory and is accepted. If an alternative is below the aspiration level, the individual examines the next alternative or searches for new ones. If no alternative can be found that satisfies the individual's aspiration, he lowers his aspiration.[17] Over time, if one can always satisfy one's aspiration, its level rises.

It should be clear that the theory has considerable behavioral content. It describes a thought process and can support a prediction, both of a given decision and of a sequence of decisions over time. Simon's original justification of the theory was a series of assertive passages throughout *Administrative Behavior* which claimed that the theory satisfied the test of common sense and contradicted neither observation nor the psychological literature.[18] Since then the theory has been formalized and tested by Simon and others.

The General Problem Solver

The theory of choice developed above is at once simple and complex. It is simple because (1) it takes a restricted view of the chooser's environment, and (2) choice is simply a process of sequential search for a satisfactory alternative. It is complicated because until the 1950's there was no compact way of stating such a theory in a complete and rigorous fashion. The only language for models available prior to that time was mathematics, and the notation of that language does not easily encompass ideas such as conditional sequential processing or conditional specification based on tests for relative magnitude.

The language of computer programs is ideally suited for such statements, however, and in 1958 Simon, together with Newell and Shaw presented the "Elements of a Theory of Human Problem Solving,"[19] based on a computer program that solved problems in symbolic logic. Later they produced the General Problem Solver,[20] a program that solves a more general class of problems. The model postulates (1) a memory containing lists of the objects

15. Socialization of individual behavior takes place when an organization imposes constraints on individual choice. A budget is a primitive example of such socialization.

16. It is important to distinguish aspiration from expectation. The former reflects value, the latter relative likelihood.

17. Those who add motivational content to the theory describe the disappointment of aspiration as frustration and the behavior exhibited by the frustrated decision maker as demonstrating anxiety.

18. Simon [50] *passim*.

19. Newell, Shaw, and Simon [36].

20. Newell, Shaw, and Simon [37] and Newell and Simon [38].

involved in the problem being solved as well as relevant lists of attributes associated with the objects; (2) a set of "search and selection procedures that perform the tasks of searching the lists of information stores in memory, selecting those items that have the [desired] attributes, regrouping the selected items of information into new lists, and performing [logical] operations when necessary";[21] and, (3) "A set of rules or criteria that guide the [problem solving process] by stipulating when and how each decision process is to be used."[22] As is true with most programs, the lists are processed sequentially and recursively.

What is surprising is the enormous success the model has had with certain cases of well-structured problems. The model is tested by presenting it and a human with the same problem. The human output and a record of the human thinking process are translated into the same language as that of the computer. If an expert cannot distinguish which record was produced by the computer and which by the human, the model is deemed successful.

Simon and his colleagues have simulated a number of the classical experiments with very good results. These include the learning of nonsense syllables, and the event-matching experiments described above.[23] Equally intriguing is the success of the program as applied to chess. Problems eight moves deep, i.e. "white to mate in eight moves," have been solved by a simple list-processing program.[24]

It is worth digressing to note that a by-product of this work is the skill that has been developed in recording the "protocols" of the human problem-solving process. A microphone is hung under the chin of the subject being studied. He is asked to continually describe what he is doing. The result is a stream of comments such as "I am looking at my current position, (e.g., chess). I am trying to figure out what I want. I am looking at the moves available to me to see if any meet the tests I have, e.g., (a) the value in points of piece exchanges up to three deep is greater than zero, (b) my king is not left unprotected. . . ." This protocol provides a picture of the human thought process in terms of lists, search procedures, and decision rules, which can be represented in terms of a formal model.

Geoffrey Clarkson [10] performed what is probably the most startling problem-solving simulation in 1960. He studied by the method of protocol analysis the decision processes of an investment trust officer and using the problem-solving model, described these activities in a list-processing computer program. He then took four new trust accounts and recorded (1) the sum of money available for investment and (2) attributes, e.g., age, wealth, and ~~(2) attributes, e.g., age, wealth, and~~ attitudes, of the beneficiaries recorded on a three-valued scale, "high," "medium," and "low." This information was

21. Cyert and March [13], p. 255.   22. *Ibid.*
23. See, for example, Feigenbaum [21] and Feldman [22].
24. Simon and Simon [51].

given to the model, portfolios were selected and the movement of the stock market assimilated. Six months later the actual and simulated portfolios were compared. The least successful simulation is shown in Table 3-1.[25]

Table 3-1   Funds Available for Investment: $37,500

The Program Selected	The Trust Officer Selected
100 American Can	100 American Can
100 Continental Insurance	100 Continental Insurance
100 Equitable Gas	100 Equitable Gas
100 Duquesne Light	100 General Public Utilities
100 Libby Owens Ford	100 Libby Owens Ford
100 International Harvester	50 National Lead
100 Philadelphia Electric	100 Philadelphia Electric
100 Phillips Petroleum	100 Phillips Petroleum
100 Socony Mobil	100 Socony Mobil

It is hard to argue with the descriptive power of a model that provides so successful a simulation in so rich an environment. We must recognize, however, that the model *in and of itself* cannot support prescription. A normative model is required to provide a standard against which actual behavior can be compared. We have made progress, however; for, used together, the two models will enable us to deduce how behavior may be changed, i.e., what search procedures or decision rules could be changed so that, relative to current practice, improvements can be made in performance.

Another approach is to recognize that operationality for the descriptive model cannot be achieved until there exists an *a priori* means of determining the height of the aspiration level. Currently, we must observe behavior and from it deduce the level of aspiration. In fact, the simulation of the cognitive process does not require an explanation of the level at which aspirations settle and, therefore, it would be inelegant to use one. The result is a closed model that cannot predict the change in goals resulting from change outside the problem content. In this sense a trust adviser provides a relatively barren decision situation. More importantly, work in psychology indicates that a motivational model is required to relate extra-problem factors to choice for predictive purposes or purposes of indicating what external factors influence aspiration in a specifiable manner. For this reason, if it is desired to describe goal setting, the cognitive model is insufficient for a meaningful test. Others have attempted inductive models based on independent evidence.

Siegel: Aspiration and Utility United

In 1957, Sidney Siegel [47] hypothesized that for a discrete set of outcomes:

The level of aspiration of an individual is a point in the positive regions of his utility scale of an achievement variable. It is at the least upper bound of that chord (connecting two goals) which has maximum slope; i.e., the level

25. Clarkson [10].

of aspiration is associated with the higher of the two goals between which the rate of change of the utility function is a maximum.[26]

If there is a set of rewards, ordered by increasing preference, and if we examine the increment of utility as we move stepwise up the ordering, the level of aspiration is that point on the utility scale corresponding to that reward which involves the greatest increment in utility.

In the example shown in Figure 3-4, C is the aspiration level. An experiment performed by Siegel involving students gambling for grades provided data supporting the hypothesis.[27]

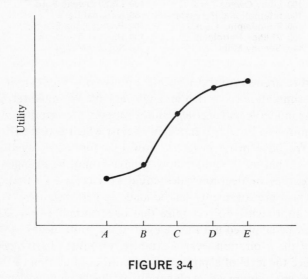

FIGURE 3-4

The importance of the experiment is twofold. First, it provides an empirical method for determining the level of aspiration. Second, if the utility function is continuous, the aspiration level corresponds to the inflection point of a rising function. This point does not change when the function is transformed by order preserving linear operators with the result that the aspiration level constitutes a point on an individual utility with extensive behavioral significance which may be compared meaningfully across individuals.[28]

In contrast, the level of aspiration is a unique point. As long as changes in utility functions are confined to the two categories described above (multiplication by a con-

26. Siegel [48], p. 257.　　27. Becker and Siegel [4].

28. It is hard to express the idea in nonmathematical terms: The problem of comparability originates with the fact that the decisions made by an expected utility maximizer will remain the same—the relative preferability of acts is unchanged— even if the function which converts rewards to utilities is multiplied by a positive constant. Nor is there a change if a constant is added everywhere. In short, the units by which utility is measured have no particular significance for the individual let alone comparisons across individuals.

stant or addition of a constant), the level of aspiration determined by seeking the point where the rate of change in utility is greatest stays the same. It is always meaningful to ask "Is A's level of aspiration higher than B's?" If the levels are known, the question means, "Will A be frustrated by a reward that satisfies B?" Siegel's result enables one to determine empirically levels of aspiration and then use them to analyze a situation involving more than one individual.

Theories of Collective Choice

THE ECONOMETRICIANS

Having discarded the theory of the firm as a prescriptive model of actual business organizations, we begin this section by resurrecting it for use at a far more aggregate level in the analysis of the production sector of the economy. The simple theory of the firm has provided econometricians the theoretical motivation for the study of collective decisions by the business sector. The econometric models which have been produced and the forecasts resulting from their use have supported a good deal of the analysis underlying contemporary Federal economic policy.[29] With very few exceptions, however, econometricians have been concerned with forecasting national aggregates, and confirming or rejecting hypothesized relationships among national aggregates. They are concerned with patterns of variation in the aggregate of decisions that are made, rather than the way in which these decisions are made. In terms of the distinction made in the introductory paragraphs they focus on *what* decisions are made, not *how* they are made. It is because econometric models of firms in aggregate have supported policy prescriptions and *not* because they have been proven good descriptions of the individual firm that we consider them here.

The methodology of the econometrician policy maker is simple. A variable exists which some agent desires to change. Let us say that the U.S. Government wishes to increase the level of private investment. The econometrician studies the investment process and discovers a set of economic variables that influence the level of investment. These are the so-called explanatory variables. Some of these variables he can control, others he cannot. His problem is to determine how to manipulate the controllable variables so as to increase investment. He collects data describing the level of these variables over time (time series statistics) or, where this is not possible, he finds "proxy variables" that reflect the same basic forces as the unobservable variables. An approximate statistical technique, usually linear regression, is used to estimate the quantitative relationship among the variables over time (i.e., the parameters and form of the equation, Investment $= f(x_1, x_2, x_3, \ldots, x_n)$.

29. Meyer and Glauber [34] provide an excellent survey of this field.

Assuming the explanatory variables are independent, the policy maker then knows how much investment will vary, if, say, the interest rate is lowered.

One problem with this approach lies in the data available for use by econometricians in the estimation process. Nature typically runs very uninteresting experiments. Many of the variables in the model, which in fact are independent, will have never varied independently. Profits, for example, will seldom behave differently from some function of sales in the preceding periods. A more important source of difficulty is the extensive interdependence that exists among most variables in the economy.

One approach to handling this problem involves the construction of an econometric model of the entire economy, based on sets of simultaneous equations.[30] Staggering statistical problems are involved, however, and to date, such models have had limited use in the generation of policy. The policy maker more commonly has recourse to theory when his data give out. Keynes and later aggregate economists have developed an elaborate theory describing the pattern of interdependence among the major variables in the economy. It is far too extensive a literature to be surveyed here. For our purposes it is relevant that (1) the model of economic man used and reused for business, consumers, and labor, has supported testable aggregate theory which over time has enabled policy makers to take an analytic approach to their job; and, (2) the theory does not provide any model of the goal setting or choice processes of an organization at any level of aggregation in non-economic dimensions, or any model of choice in the economic dimension at the disaggregate level of the modern firm.

HARVARD BUSINESS SCHOOL

One response to the failure of economists to describe the firm is institutionalized in the Harvard Graduate School of Business Administration. Over a period of five decades its faculty and research staff have collected thousands of case histories of individual businesses in operation. At first the research consisted largely of after-the-fact description of events provided by the individual managers who had been involved. Over a period of time it was recognized that a bias was introduced when information was obtained in this manner, and therefore effort was devoted to record events as they happened. A great deal of research has permitted some generalization. The bureaucratic model of the firm, a natural management-oriented evolution of Max Weber and Frederick Taylor, had replaced the economists' simple profit-maximizing model as the core of the organization theory, but the new research provided information that contradicted the basic assumption of the bureaucratic model. Instead of responding in simple and direct ways to

30. Classic examples of such models are Klein and Goldberger [30], and Duesenberry, Eckstein, and Fromm [17]. An enormous model was recently constructed under the sponsorship of the Social Science Research Council.

monetary incentives and changes in the physical environment, individuals were found to exhibit complex motivations and unsuspected forces, e.g., the norms of a work group, were found to have a powerful influence on behavior. The evolution of theory of the business organization dates from research on work groups prior to World War II,[31] but a model of the modern organization is only beginning to emerge and there are many candidate theories. These tend to be very complicated. One example is summarized in the following set of propositions, paraphrased from a doctoral dissertation:[32]

1. For the purposes of corporate strategic planning, a large modern firm cannot usefully be regarded as a single economic unit. Each subunit of such a company has independent goals of its own, some of which are in conflict with corporate interests.

2. Strategic planning at the corporate level is conceptually a more complex activity than planning at lower levels of the same company. Top management's problem is not simply a portfolio problem of selecting attractive individual proposals.

3. Strategic planning involves, to an extent, trading current resources for future benefits and, therefore, is intimately involved with the level of current operations.

4. Strategic planning is a behavioral as well as an economic process involving the whole company.

An example of the contrast between the empirical basis of the new theory and the observable reflection of the old is most available in the area of capital budgeting—the process of allocating investment dollars which motivates that subclass of economics called "capital theory."

The traditional model assumes that corporate management must decide in which portfolio of investment projects (present and expected future) it should invest a limited pool of capital. In line with this model, most large firms have established a procedure whereby investment projects are described in a standardized format, their attractiveness is summarized in one or two financial measures, and a set of criteria is used to screen projects. A committee of top management is established to approve proposals and weigh critically the advisability of marginal projects.

What happens in fact is quite different. First, given the general standards of project acceptability prevailing in industry today, most firms have more capital than they can invest. The problem then is really not one of rationing capital, but an unaccustomed problem of deciding which project the firm wants. Traditional finance answers the question, "Which wants do I satisfy when my resources are limited?" The contemporary firm faces the embarrassment of riches, "What do I want? My resources are not limited." Second, organizational life being what it is, executives soon learn that it is bad to have

31. See, for example Roethlisberger and Dixon [42].   32. Berg [5].

one's proposal turned down.[33] They learn that it is better for oneself to kill a project than to have it neglected by superiors. Third, the uncertainties of future markets are so great that any financial standards can be met, or missed, by changing slightly the degree of optimism incorporated into the forecasts upon which a proposal is based. Finally, engineering and financial staffs are usually busy. It takes time to analyze an idea and prepare a proposal. Analytical time almost always is the resource of a corporation that is subject to rationing. Furthermore, given common—as opposed to rational—thinking concerning sunk costs, it becomes increasingly hard to reject a proposal as it absorbs analytical hours. The net result is that the capital-investment decision is effectively made by that middle manager who authorizes the study and writing needed for a project proposal. It is that system of costs and benefits to which he responds—not necessarily those affecting the company's stock price—that determines the shape of the corporate investment process.

It is disturbing, perhaps, but true that most capital budgeting systems do nothing to insure that the sum of projects accepted will be a meaningful consistent set of activities. To the contrary, given that subgoals exist and are important, most systems serve to focus residual energy on the time consuming game of writing the proposal for a desired project so that the corporate financial tests are met. It would be far more useful if executives' time were used to test projects against the objectives of corporate strategy and to seek alternative approaches to an idea when the test is not met.

Current thinking at HBS has accepted these facts of organizational life. Research in both the Finance and Business Policy area is focusing on the interrelated problems of policy formulation and organizational choice. Recent work has built upon the work of the institutionalists discussed in the following section. Beyond the somewhat informal descriptive postulates, represented by those paraphrased above, the theoretical product of new research has been exceedingly limited. Andrews' exposition [1] of the business policy area's concept of strategy is a single exception which comes to mind.

THE INSTITUTIONALISTS

The same prewar research that stimulated new thinking at Harvard also influenced the ideas of Barnard, Selznick, and Thompson, the first of whom preceded Simon in the introduction of an administrative theory of organization.

Chester Barnard

In contrast with the authors we have considered up to this point, Chester Barnard theorized about administrative man on the basis of personal experience. A professional manager of a large organization, he wrote because

33. A common adage of corporate life, "Saying 'no' gets to be a habit," reflects this fact.

Nothing of which I knew treated organization in a way which seemed to me to correspond either to my experience or to the understanding implicit in conduct of those recognized to be adept in executive practice or in the leadership of organizations. Some excellent work has been done in describing and analyzing the superficial characteristics of organizations. It is important, but like descriptive geography with physics, chemistry, geology and biology missing.[34]

In his classic *The Functions of the Executive*,[35] Barnard begins by seeking the origins of organization in the limited effectiveness of individual choice. "The narrow limitations within which choice is a possibility are those which are imposed jointly by physical, biological and social factors."[36] Individuals choose whether or not to cooperate in a specific instance. "This choice will be made on the basis of (1) purposes, desires, impulses of the moment, and (2) the alternatives external to the individual recognized by him as available. *Organization results from the modification of the action of the individual through control of or influence upon one of these categories.*"[37]

By explicitly focusing on functional choice and activity, Barnard builds the basis for a prescriptive theory while making essentially descriptive statements. He distinguishes randomly cooperative behavior from that represented by his subject: formal organizations are defined

... *as a system of consciously coordinated activities or forces of two or more persons.* ... Systems of cooperation which we call organizations I regard as social creatures, "alive," just as I regard an individual human being, who himself is a complex of partial systems .. as different from the sum of these constituent systems—if, indeed, the word "sum" has any meaning in this connection. ... An organization comes into being when (1) there are persons able to communicate with each other and (2) who are willing to contribute action, (3) to accomplish a common purpose.[38]

Barnard goes on to develop the concept of informal organization—"the aggregate of ... personal contacts and interactions and associated groupings of people."[39] He suggests that informal organizations would be random in origin were it not that formal organization substantially structures the pattern of interaction among organization members. The informal structure that develops is necessary to formal organization as a means of communication, a source of cohesion, and a means of protecting the integrity of the individual.

Two standards, "effectiveness" and "efficiency" and the concept of "economy of incentives" complete the essential structure of Barnard's model. Effectiveness is the quasi-physical standard that measures an organization's success in carrying out whatever generalized purpose provides a rationale for its existence. He defines "efficiency of effort in the fundamental

34. Barnard [3], p. viii. 35. Barnard [3].
36. *Ibid.*, p. 15. 37. *Ibid.*, p. 17.
38. *Ibid.*, pp. 13, 79, 80, and 82. 39. *Ibid.*, p. 115.

sense [as] efficiency relative to the securing of necessary personal contributions to the cooperative system."[40]

These two standards permit Barnard to develop an exchange theory of organization.

> In every type of organization, for whatever purpose, several incentives are necessary, and some degree of persuasion likewise, in order to secure and maintain the contributions to the organization that are required. . . . Excepting in rare instances, the difficulties of securing the means of offering incentives, of avoiding conflict of incentives, and of making effective persuasive efforts, are inherently great. . . . Incentives represent the final residue of all conflicting forces in organization. . . .[41]

Because of the changing nature of the environment and human motives, the nature and strength of these forces change. Only by use of incentives are these forces balanced. "Economy of incentives" is the phrase Barnard uses to describe the use of incentives to achieve a *dynamic stability* in the exchange of benefits for cooperative effort. If we use the firm as an example and include stockholders as members of the organization (as they are by Barnard's definition), economy is a problem in dividing a shifting set of material and psychic rewards among competing individuals and groups.

Following a discussion of authority and the decision maker's environment, Barnard turns to a normative discussion of the functions of the executive: defining purpose, facilitating communication in the organization, and establishing an economy of incentives. Barnard's prescriptions are consistent with his theory, but they are not deduced from the theory.

A more important problem with the model Barnard offers is its point of view regarding the question we have been considering thus far—organizational choice. It is not necessarily true that a theory of organization for executives should focus on the executive as a source of purpose, particularly when the discussion of organizational origins and informal organization indicates that the formation of common purpose is a very complicated matter. Barnard notes that "it is an entire executive organization that formulates, redefines, breaks into details, and decides on the innumerable simultaneous and progressive actions that are the stream of syntheses constituting purpose or action."[42] Yet he does not really provide us with a model of how these forces are resolved and purpose clarified. An exchange theory is a very simple model of conflict resolution and before we can accept it, it would have to be tested. Barnard's theory is not a testable one; rather, it is a tautology which, in the context of the full treatment, has normative content.

Most of the work that followed Barnard has in one way or another replaced the asymmetric concept of economy. Selznick and Thompson, conceptual descendants of Barnard, both emphasize other concepts. It is worth noting that Barnard recognized (p. 154) that this part of his theory was borrowed

40. Barnard, p. 92.   41. *Ibid.*, pp. 158, 159.   42. *Ibid.*, p. 231.

from economics. The parallel between the recently developed theory of dynamic equilibrium and Barnard's "economy" is striking. It is more interesting to note that there were other theories of exchange for Barnard to draw upon, not obviously inferior for his purposes—descriptive or normative. The social-contract theories emerging from Rousseau and Locke, and the modern theory of bargaining beginning with Carnot, are directly to the point.

For our purposes, recent developments, particularly in bargaining theory and in political science are more attractive. The theoretical problem is our old one of multi-dimensional exchange and as we note below, some progress has been made in this area.

Philip Selznick

In the previous section, we noted that the complicated problem of conflict resolution in the organization seemed inappropriately described by Barnard with a neoclassical economic exchange model. Philip Selznick's book, *Leadership in Administration*[43] is essentially an alternative normative model of the conflict resolution process. Selznick begins by distinguishing from Barnard's tool-like "formal organization," the concept of the institution, "a natural product of social needs and pressures—a responsive, adaptive organism."[44]

> An institution has a history and interacts with the total social environment. When an enterprise begins to be more profoundly aware of dependence on outside forces, its very conception of itself may change. . . . As a business, a college, or a government agency develops a distinctive clientele, the enterprise gains the stability that comes with a secure source of support, an easy channel of communication. At the same time, it loses flexibility. The process of institutionalization has set in.[45]

Selznick includes Barnard's "informal" structure as one of the institutional aspects of the organization. The formal system draws upon spontaneous human behavior for strength.

> . . . It will in its turn be subordinated to personal and group egotism. . . . The unity of persons breaks through the neat confines of rational organization and procedure; it creates new strivings primarily for the protection of group integrity of individuals for place and preferment, in rivalry among units within the organization, and in commitment to ingrained ways of behaving. These are universal features of organizational life, and the problems they raise are perennial ones.

> Of these problems, organizational rivalry may be the most important[46]

Selznick introduces a normative content into his argument when he examines the decision-making process and isolates "critical" decisions which are leadership's responsibility. One of these critical decisions is the definition

43. Selznick [46].   44. *Ibid.*, p. 5.
45. *Ibid.*, p. 7.   46. *Ibid.*, pp. 8 and 9.

of organizational mission or purpose. Selznick argues for the need to structure the interaction of the organization and its environment. He caps his argument by developing the concept of "institutional embodiment of purpose" as the optimal approach to the resolution of organizational rivalry. "Beyond the definition of mission and role lies the task of building purpose into the social structure of the enterprise, or, [to use another phrase,] of transforming a neutral body of men into a committed polity."[47]

By building purpose into the entire structure of the organization through its institutional aspects—by shaping an institution's overall objectives— lower-level activity proceeds within an environment so structured as to limit dysfunctional individual and group behavior. By using the norms of social existence to channel activity rather than the formal rules of the organization, basic commitment to organizational objectives is reinforced by the very spontaneous forces that otherwise might prove divisive.

Selznick's argument is based on empirical evidence provided by his work with the TVA and his analysis of the International Communist Party. It is a rich and insightful discussion of leadership and organization. The realism and perception that characterize its view of organizational rivalry lend persuasiveness to the argument for institutional embodiment of purpose. And yet, Selznick's theory is largely analytic. It reports no test and no meaningful propositions. Moreover, it does not help us to answer the descriptive question "How do organizations choose?" Selznick argues that "critical decisions are made by management," yet we know that management does not always define critical questions for itself and that there is extensive evidence that indicates that the alternatives from which management chooses are generated in a series of routine decisions which in their aggregate may leave leadership very little choice.

Moreover, while the model presented prescribes that the critical activities of perception, analysis, and choice at the level of strategy be centred in the leader's hands, it is not obvious that the management is capable of performing these cerebral activities by itself. Organization is often required for analysis and choice if the scope of a problem is large, (as is the case with problems facing institutional giants). In short, while Selznick makes a valuable contribution in recognizing (1) that we must be principally concerned with the institutional aspects of organization and (2) that good leaders have their principal influence on the course of organizational life by shaping the institution, these two propositions are not nearly all that we need in order to describe and predict organizational behavior.

Victor Thompson

The problem of organizational rivalry is restated elegantly in a contemporary setting by Victor Thompson in *Modern Organization*.[48] Working from

47. Selznick, p. 90.   48. Thompson [52].

a Weberian model of organization (he speaks of "bureau-pathology"[49]), Thompson argues that "the most symptomatic characteristic of modern bureaucracy is the growing imbalance between ability and authority."[50] The source of this imbalance is the rapid pace of scientific and technological development that increasingly gives subordinates the skills to solve problems and their less well-trained superiors the power to command.

The pace of change has also greatly increased the complexity of the problems that the firm must resolve. Thompson suggests that organizations as problem-solving mechanisms depend on a factoring of the general good into subgoals. Individuals accept subgoals and become attached to them until at times there is an inversion of ends and means. The result is a rivalry among groups which greatly hampers solving those complex problems in which there is a great deal of technological interdependence.

Thompson believes that dysfunctional conflict among subunits of an organization cannot be resolved within the context of a strict hierarchy of authority. He argues instead for the cooperation among specialists that comes from "recognized and accepted mutual interdependence."[51] He prescribes decision making by groups of specialists in a highly decentralized unstructured organization.[52]

Although Thompson provides a powerful and suggestive analysis of the operation of a technically oriented organization, he seems to miss both the dynamic nature of the problems facing organizations (Selznick's "critical" problems are seldom well structured) and the critical role of leadership in generating a strategic purpose that will channel the institutional aspect of the organization as it tries to cope with a changing environment. In a sense Thompson is prescribing an organization for the simplified and static world of Simon's satisficers. The weakness of Simon's model for descriptive purpose is damning when it shows up in the normative context of Thompson's theory. The satisficing model cannot predict the impact of events on behavior unless they are included in the programmed model, and it does not incorporate a motivational view of aspiration. Similarly, Thompson's specialists can work out solutions to problems that constitute an organization's on-going task, but they do not have the general skills required to decide which sets of problems the organization should attack, nor how the style of solution should change as the environment shifts.

CARNEGIE

Three criticisms have been leveled at the work of one or more of the institutionalist authors that have been discussed thus far.

49. *Ibid.*, p. 152.   50. *Ibid.*, p. 6.   51. *Ibid.*, p. 189.
52. Otherwise "what appears to be a frank, open, rational, group problem-solving process is very often actually a bargaining or political process." *Ibid.*, p. 189.

1. Their models did not fully take into account organizational rivalry (Barnard).

2. Their models were not operational. No assumptions or conclusions were stated as testable propositions (Barnard, Selznick, and Thompson).

3. The normative prescription was vague, even relative to the informal character of the theoretical argument (Barnard, but especially Thompson).

The work at Carnegie by Cyert, March, and Simon[53]—an outgrowth of Simon's *Administrative Behavior* and his study of the problem-solving process in the individual—has been conducted specifically with the aim of improving on the first two aspects of organization theory. The third problem, weak prescriptive results, is *explicitly ignored* in the search for a behavioral theory of organization.

The first step in the evolution of the behavioral theory was *Organization*, an awesomely complete survey of the pre-1958 literature of organizations. The conclusions that it reports are the descriptive hypotheses that resulted from analytical as well as empirical studies of groups and organizations conducted, in almost all cases, at the middle-management or lower-management echelons of organization. Each finding is summarized in one or more statements of causal relation of the following form:

> The strength of the motivation to reduce conflict (and thus the rate of search) depends upon the *availability of bland alternatives* and the *time pressure.*
> The greater the use of *acceptable-level decision rules* and the less the *complexity of the environment*, the greater the use of *local changes in programs.*[54]

The propositions as stated are not easily testable. The concepts, such as "complexity of the environment," have not yet been made operational by measurement systems. However, chains of these statements together provide the outline for theory which shows up in later work. March and Simon examine the same interaction of individual motivation and formal organizational structure as did Barnard and Selznick, but in a substantially more systematic fashion.

Following the lead of Barnard, they focus on the decision of an individual to participate in the organization and, based on an exchange argument, postulate that "increases in the *balance of inducement utilities over contribution utilities* decrease the *propensity of the individual participant to leave* the organization, whereas decreases in that balance have an opposite effect." A number of partial analyses of the interaction among pairs of factors which influence this balance are reported.

Examination of what happens when there is dissatisfaction with the balance motivates a discussion of conflict in organizations. Some of the

53. March and Simon [33] and Cyert and March [13] are classic citations.
54. March and Simon [33] pp. 116 and 176 respectively.

descriptive propositions contained in their discussion are among the core propositions of the behavioral theory.

1. "Organizations functioning in a benign environment can satisfy their explicit objectives with less than a complete expenditure of organizational 'energy.' As a result, a substantial portion of activities in the organization is directed toward satisfying individual or sub-group goals. The organizational slack thus generated has several consequences. . . ."

2. "When resources are relatively unlimited, organizations need not resolve the relative merits of sub-group claims."[55] Conflicting activity may go on unchecked!

Because the remainder of their discussion is more easily summarized in the language of a problem-solving model, we turn to Cyert and March's summary effort, *A Behavioral Theory of the Firm*,[56] which treats the firm as a problem-solving organization.

Cyert and March begin by discarding the institutionalist view of an organization that implicitly or explicitly adopts the top manager, or the peak of an authority hierarchy, as the appropriate point from which to begin the analysis of an organization. In the process they implicitly reject the March and Simon distinction between inducements and contribution as well. In fact the traditional asymmetric exchange model is abandoned and the notion of a symmetrical coalition substituted in its place.

> Let us view the organization as a coalition. It is a coalition of individuals, some of them organized into subcoalitions. In a business organization the coalition members include managers, workers, stockholders, suppliers, customers, lawyers, tax collectors, regulatory agencies, etc.

> . . . Drawing the boundaries of an organizational coalition once and for all is impossible. Instead, we simplify the conception by focusing on the participants in a particular "region"—either temporal or functional. That is, over a specified (relatively brief) period of time we can identify the major coalition members; or, for a particular decision we can identify the major coalition members.[57]

Members of a coalition participate together because they share a number of goals. There is always conflict, however, both concerning unshared goals and concerning the division of the benefits of joint action. In one sense, it does not make sense to speak of the goals of an organization. In contrast to organic theories of groups, Cyert and March do not believe that groups have goals. Rather, there are "organizational goals" which represent some sort of conjunction of the active goals of the individual members of a coalition. The goals of coalition change as new participants enter or old ones leave. For a

55. *Ibid.*, p. 126.   56. Cyert and March [13].
57. *Ibid.*, [13], p. 27.

particular decision, the goals of the coalitions are the goals of that sub-coalition which can make the decision. Goals thus are responsive to changes in the "rules of the game" as well as changes in the complexion of the coalition.

Cyert and March turn to the Carnegie model of the individual and aspiration theory to motivate their concept of goals. Goals are evoked by the dimension of a problem and are determined by aspiration levels.[58] Choice takes place in response to a problem when an alternative is found which satisfies aspirations among all goal dimensions. "The variables that affect choice are those that influence the definition of a problem within the organization, those that influence the standard decision rules [used to make the choice], and those that affect the order of consideration of alternatives."[59]

Given this framework, four concepts, one a restatement of the two points above, constitute the core of the behavioral theory of organization.

1. To begin with, Cyert and March do not believe that organizations resolve conflict; i.e., they do not make compromise choices which necessitate all parties revising their aspirations. Rather, they "assume that an organization factors its decision problems into subproblems and assigns the subproblems to subunits [sub-coalitions] in the organization]. . . . The importance of such local rationality is the tendency for the individual subunits to deal with a limited set of problems and a limited set of goals,"[60] Because of organizational slack, it is possible for independent subunits to make choices that are internally inconsistent when viewed from the overall point of view of the total coalition. The point is that the coalition does not structure itself in a way that permits looking at a problem from the total point of view. In fact, slack is not the only factor that facilitates independent decision making by subunits. "Organizations resolve conflict among goals, in part by attending to different goals at different times.]. . . The resulting time buffer between goals permits the organization to solve one problem at a time, attending to one goal at a time."[61] This normatively imperfect process of resolving conflict is defined as the "quasi-resolution of conflict."

2. Cyert and March go on to argue that organizations avoid uncertainty. They operate so as to provide short-run reactions to short run feedback

58. Those familiar with game theory will recognize that the conceptual debt of this model to the game theorists is heavy. If one tried to construct a descriptive model of an organization in game theoretic terms it would look very much like the coalition above, particularly if the motivating problem permitted one to phrase the decision problem in the format of a game of fair division.

59. Cyert and March, p. 116. 60. *Ibid.*, p. 117.

61. *Ibid.*, p. 118. Although the behavior described by the authors may strike some as highly irrational, that issue is not in question. Descriptions of independent behavior by interdependent subunits in the Air Force organization may be found in Deavers and McCall [15], and other case studies describing the same pathology.

rather than face the uncertainty of long-range planning. They avoid the uncertainties of those upon whom they depend by negotiating arrangements, both explicit and implicit, with suppliers, competitors, and customers.

3. They further argue that "search" is motivated by problems. Organizations do not analyze their environment or seek to create new alternatives unless they are faced with a specific problem that cannot be solved with existing alternatives.

The search process itself is mechanical—it is a list-scanning process in which the order of alternatives is crucial—and it is simple minded. The search for a solution begins in the neighborhood of the "old" solution to that "old" problem that most closely resembles the existing one and proceeds outwards by simply modifying steps along traditional paths.

4. Finally, organizations learn. Cyert and March argue the notion as a separate proposition but it should be obvious, given their definition of an organization, that as the individual members of the coalition and its sub-coalitions learn, revise aspirations and decision rules, the organization will also *appear* to "learn."[62]

These four propositions (1) the quasi-resolution of conflict, (2) uncertainty avoidance, (3) problem-motivated search, and (4) organizational learning, permit the construction of a model of problem solving by an organization. The basic model in abstract form is shown in the flow chart in Figure 3-5. Note the branching and the feedback that are characteristic of computer programs. In fact, the model in its applied forms is very similar to a computer program, a necessity, since simulation is the only form of test that can be devised.

Interestingly enough, the Cyert and March model has not been tested as a total model of organizational problem solving. Rather, the principal field study reported describes a subcoalition with a single goal—a sales department's pricing behavior is modeled with success. Furthermore, the inputs to the model in this case are measures over the subcoalition. No attempt was made to construct goals from the individual aspirations of coalition members. For this reason the model tested was really the model of individual problem solving used by Clarkson. The fact that the behavioral model is not yet tested does not detract from the intuitive appeal of the descriptive propositions on which it is based. Quasi-resolution of conflict is a wonderful way of characterizing a good deal of the pathological behavior exhibited by organizations.

More important, however, are the insight the model offers into the process of organizational goal setting and choice, and the ability of the model or one like it to provide structure for the more informal theories of the same phenomena emerging from the field research of Harvard Business School.

62. The word "appear" is crucial. Given the Cyert and March concept of an organization as a set of coalitions, the organization cannot learn any more than it can have goals. Any other interpretation is internally inconsistent.

Moreover, the systematic approach taken by the authors in constructing their theory provides grounds for hope that some sort of test of certain key

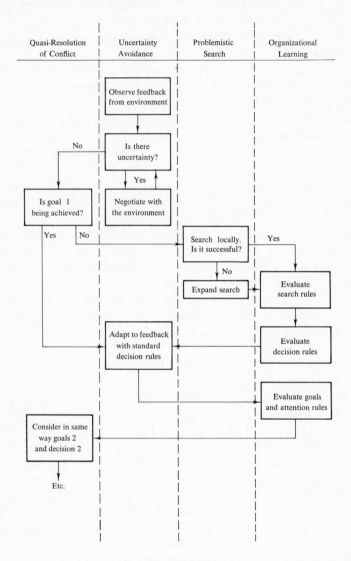

FIGURE 3-5

Source: Richard M. Cyert and James G. March, *A Behavioral Theory of the Firm*, p. 126. © 1963. Reprinted by permission of Prentice-Hall, Inc., Englewood Cliffs, N.J.

propositions is possible. Such partial tests could be crucial, however, for the normative implications of the theory derive principally from the first and fourth of the core propositions. (Note that these are implications and not prescriptions. The theory has no normative content.)

The first implies that truly major changes in the choice process of an organization necessitate reorganization of the coalition. If, for example, it is desired that more than one goal dimension be taken into account when a resource is allocated among competing claims for its use, it is necessary that the subcoalition which can make the decision include enough individuals interested in all the relevant dimensions to produce conflict within the group. Then the group can search for a solution—a set of acceptable claims consistent with the resources available—in which frustration of aspirations along the various goal dimensions is compromised in some purposeful fashion. The reorganization of the procurement program of the Air Force was based on precisely such an analysis. Program offices were created with responsibility for all dimensions of the program, replacing the specialist groups which previously existed. The trend in the business world the past few years away from extreme forms of decentralization reflects the same forces at work.

The fourth proposition, organizational learning, has implications of a similar nature. Changes in behavior within a subcoalition can be brought about by changing search procedures and decision rules, as well as goals. It is often easier to change means as opposed to ends. It is probable, for example, that progress in our political system will come fastest through expanded and revised search procedures. The institution called the Federal Government is at best a coalition and the one point on which there is a degree of national consensus is that individuals and subcoalitions shall be free to disagree as long as that conflict which exists can be absorbed by the abundance of our economic system or resolved by the set of decision rules called Constitutional process. Efficient use of resources may well come sooner if attention is focused on finding programs that will achieve a set of somewhat inconsistent goals economically, than if much energy is expended on the attempt to change goals so that they are consistent. In fact, if Cyert and March are correct, the latter approach is futile, because a change in goals would require a restructuring of all the subcoalitions in the nation.

At the more mundane level of our initial concern, we should recognize that the behavioral theory represents considerable progress. If it is ever tested successfully, it can serve as the descriptive model we desire to use in conjunction with already existing normative models. If only parts of the model can be tested these can be incorporated into a new prescriptive model.

Until the full model is tested (chains of Figure 3-6), quasi-resolution of conflict remains one of the strongest and most arbitrary of independence assumptions yet introduced into the theory of the firm. Analysis of the tractable case of a single subcoalition with a single goal can only be justified if it is *in fact* true that slack and sequential attention to goals permit subcoalitions to act as if the reality of the interdependence of their decisions does not exist.

THE SCIENTIFIC POLITICAL SCIENTISTS

It is somewhat ironic that as the Carnegie school's thinking shifted away from the simple model of economic maximization, students of political science turned their attention toward the economic model in the search for testable theory. Three landmark efforts in the field are Anthony Downs' *An Economic Theory of Democracy*, Buchanan and Tullock's *The Calculus of Consent*, and Theodore Riker's *The Theory of Political Coalitions*.[63] Interestingly enough, though each is an attempt to construct a deductive model of the political process, each focuses on a different aspect of that process.

Downs analyzes party strategy based on the assumptions that every government attempts to maximize political support and that every citizen is rational. Using these primitive notions of individual and group rationality he is able to develop a construct which supports meaningful theorems such as

A.1 Party members have as their chief motivation the desire to obtain the intrinsic rewards of holding office; therefore they formulate policies as means to holding office rather than seeking office in order to carry out preconceived policies.

or,

B.1 The citizens who are best informed on any specific issue are those whose income is directly affected by it, . . .[64]

Downs' objective is a model of politics equal in simplicity and power to the theory of consumer demand. He demonstrates that the maximizing principle in politics—political man as it were—is a very useful axiom, but his theory lacks descriptive power to the extent that the maximization of party support is an oversimplification.

Riker, for example, assumes a weaker degree of rationality:

Given social situations within certain kinds of decision-making institutions (of which parlor games, the market, elections, and warfare are notable examples) and in which exist two alternative courses of action with differing outcomes in money, power or success, some participants will choose the alternative leading to the larger payoff. Such choice is rational behavior and it will be accepted as definitive while the behavior of participants who do not so choose will not necessarily be so accepted.[65]

Riker then uses a game theoretic argument to deduce from this definition of rationality what he calls the "size principle":

In social situations similar to n-person, zero-sum games with side-payments, [gains of winners equal losses of losers with side compensation among players permitted] participants create coalitions just as large as they believe will ensure winning and no larger.[66]

63. Downs [16], Buchanan and Tullock [8], and Riker [41].
64. Downs [16] pp. 296 and 299 respectively.
65. Riker [41], p. 23.   66. *Ibid.*, pp. 32 and 33.

World history and especially American history are used to demonstrate the validity of the size principle as the determinant of the size of winning coalitions. From Riker's point of view, for example, the Southern Democrats are no accident. They are a result of the Democratic Party's being an excessively large winning coalition. The Northern and Western parts of the party constitute a minimum winning coalition under most circumstances. When they do not, the Southern Democrats assume the role of a "blocking" coalition, with a disproportionate power to affect the position of the total coalition. Riker also uses his model to argue persuasively the relative weakness of the U.S.A. and the U.S.S.R. in world affairs. Except in military conflict, neither constitutes a winning coalition by itself. As the military situation becomes stabilized neutral nations can demand a higher price for their alliance. They become the Dixiecrats of world affairs.

Because Riker does not have the equipment in his model for predicting the membership of the winning coalition, his model is more successful as an explanatory device than as a tool for prediction. If one is concerned with issues, the model alone cannot guide the forecaster or the policy maker. On the other hand, in conjunction with Fouraker's work, reported later, the model has very great promise.

Buchanan and Tullock are concerned with voter strategy rather than with party behavior. They ask the question, "which constitution is the best one from the point of a given individual?" In an interesting discussion they argue that in a situation where a sequence of votes is taken and where side-payments are the practice if not the rule, devices such as log-rolling serve the function of reflecting intensity of preference. The discussion relies on a formal analysis that focuses both on the opportunity cost of noncollective action and/or the direct cost to the individual of agreeing to work within a political framework in order to take collective action. The trouble is that the models used are not complete. A cost function must have a zero point which in the case of the opportunity cost of noncollective action is undefined. The optimum, the divergence from which determines opportunity cost, can only be defined by some benefit measuring social welfare function—which the authors proudly eschew—or by a set of rules that indicate for each individual his share of benefits to be distributed. (In the latter case the individual can choose his own optimum.) Such a set of rules is not included in the model. Finally as Rothenberg [43] points out, the authors' definition of rationality breaks down in their discussion of majority rule and this substantially weakens their results.

The importance of the book is that it does demonstrate that the so-called pathologies of formal organizational systems, payoffs, log-rolling, and so forth, have a rationale in that they permit intensity of feeling to be reflected in systems which, for ethical reasons, give one man one vote. Other research, some of which is reported here, indicates that it is important to recognize the beneficial aspects of internal market systems when they develop within the context of a formal organization. In fact, it may well be that the informal organization of Barnard is much more fruitfully analyzed with sophisticated economic models than with social models.

THE EXPERIMENTAL ECONOMISTS

It is a measure of the extent to which there has been progress in the field of organization theory that work carried on in an entirely separate area of the field by experimental methods produced results identical to Riker's. In another instance, a set of experiments conducted for the purpose of exploring the behavior of decision-making groups produced results concerning decision rules that have been interpreted along lines that parallel part of Buchanan and Tullock's argument. The experiments were conducted by economists who turned to the laboratory, more or less in desperation, in an attempt to discriminate once and for all the relative usefulness of the many contradictory models of group conflict that exist in economics. Fouraker[67] has provided a good summary of this literature, and we will focus here on his own work and an experiment by Bower.

Fouraker and Siegel

During 1958 Sidney Siegel's interest in the use of economic theory for the purpose of modeling human choice behavior, and Lawrence Fouraker's concern with the conflicting hypotheses existing side-by-side in the literature of oligopoly theory, led to a very fruitful collaboration. The rigorous methodology of experimental psychology was used to test the elegant theory of oligopoly in two series of bargaining experiments.[68]

The initial experiments are of limited interest for our purposes except insofar as the methodology was found to be a powerful tool for exploring the behavior of economic decision-making groups. We have already discarded oligopoly theory as a descriptive model of conflict between firms because it uses as its principal elements the oversimple traditional theory of the firm. As a test of models of interpersonal behavior the results are suspect when generalized beyond the experiments because no experimental test was made of the assumptions underlying the model of economic man. The alternate hypotheses tested were deduced from theory, but other theories based on other assumptions concerning behavior could generate the same hypotheses. In fact, somewhat ironically, while Siegel and Fouraker find the models based on economic man inferior to Schelling's [45] and Fellner's [23] more descriptive theory, a replication of their experiment by Zeckhauser [54], in which explicit steps were taken to break down the behavioral norms of ex-

---

67. Fouraker [24].
68. Siegel and Fouraker [49] and Fouraker and Siegel [26].

perimental sessions, produced results confirming the traditional theory.[69]

More interesting to the policy maker is the explanatory hypothesis generated in the same series of experiments and tested in more recent work.[70] Fouraker and Siegel noted that their results from conflict experiments with two persons of equal strength (in the experimental bargaining situation) could be explained very well by a level-of-aspiration model if each of the bargainers had an equal share of the reward as his aspiration. The aspiration-level model was again found useful in experiments with three person bargaining and in experiments where strength was unequal. Finally, Fouraker formulated an aspiration model of group decision making.[71]

The problem the group faces is to divide a set of benefits earned by working together as a coalition. As noted above this is an aspect of almost all group-decision problems even if it is seldom the whole problem. Fouraker begins by assuming that there is some decision rule, for example, majority rule, by which the coalition is able to make its decision. Then two possible states characterize all permutations of such "games of division". Either the reward to the coalition is large enough to satisfy the aspirations of a winning subcoalition or it is not. In the latter case Fouraker would expect to find a revision of aspiration by some individuals after some frustration had been experienced in trying to reach a decision, or alternatively there might be a complete failure to reach an agreement. Where the reward is large enough, however, Fouraker hypothesizes (1) that the winning coalition will be the smallest winning coalition (Riker!) and, (2) that the members of the winning subcoalition will be those individuals in the group with the minimum aspiration.

A simple example should make the point clear. Suppose a three-man group dividing $10 has aspirations of $3, $3, and $5. Fouraker hypothesizes that the group will divide the money $5, $5, $0. The third man cannot make a counteroffer to either of the first two that will both satisfy his own aspiration and improve the position of the man to whom he is making the counter-offer. The same is true even if there is slack and the reward to be divided is $15. Fouraker's hypotheses were supported by a series of experiments in 1962.[72]

Despite the obvious oversimplicity of the experimental situation, there

69. Siegel and Fouraker are quick to acknowledge the extent to which any particular set of results is a product of a given set of experimental conditions. In particular their results shift according to their hypotheses as they manipulate the completeness of information available to their subjects. Also in Fouraker and Siegel [26] pages 205–207, the limitations of the experiments are discussed.

70. It should be noted in passing that this is the power of experimental research. It produces real data on a limited number of interacting variables. It may be that nothing is proved by the data, but knowledge about human behavior is increased and new hypotheses are generated.

71. Fouraker [25].

72. Within the context of his experiments where a "leader" was established, Fouraker hypothesized a solution in which the "leader" would obtain $4.99 by offering the other low-aspiration member $5.01.

are intuitive, appealing implications of the results for the real organizations with which we are concerned. Furthermore, they could be incorporated in extensions of the behavioral model of Cyert and March. Let us suppose that the decision-making coalition with which we are concerned is an executive committee which sets policy for a large organization and which is faced with a choice among alternate strategies. Obviously value in such a situation is multidimensional, so there will be more than one "goal dimension" along which aspirations are relevant. Fouraker has suggested that the committee can be represented by points on a coordinate system. Figure 3-6 is an example

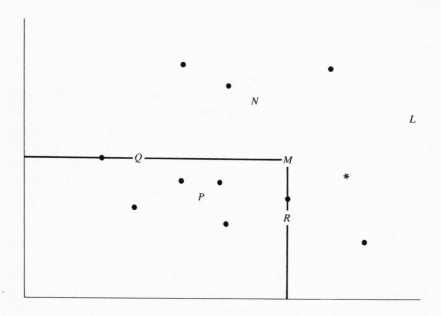

FIGURE 3-6

in two-goal dimensions. Each point represents the interaction of the level of aspiration of an individual along the goal dimensions. He will not vote for an alternative below and/or to the left of the point. The capital letters denote alternatives. Assuming majority rule decides, point *M* is the alternative that will be chosen by the minimum winning coalition. If the group leader (*) believes that it is important for the organization to adopt a strategy with higher goals along a given dimension his job is to work at raising the aspirations of those members of the winning minimal subcoalition with the highest aspirations along the dimension with which he is concerned.

The graph also enables one to see the value of disparate points of view in an on-going organization. To change the course of the group fairly radically, the leader above needs move only one or two men, and moreover, he can count on the help of one or two strong partisans to help him. A committee without diversity is one where the points representing individuals all fall fairly close to a straight line from the origin. In such an instance should change be desirable it may be impossible to bring about. Many individuals must be moved and there are no dissidents to whom power can be shifted.

It should be clear, as we extend Fouraker's results, that he and Riker have the same model of organization behavior in mind. Fouraker goes further than Riker by specifying in terms of aspiration level, the composition of the minimal coalition. In both cases, however, it is the desire of the winners to divide the group reward among as small a group as possible that provides stability for the winning coalition.

The Role of Conflict in Group Decisions

Virtually every theory of group behavior discussed thus far shares the common assumption that interpersonal conflict has a debilitating effect on group decision making. A series of experiments conducted during 1961 explored the interrelationship among the information structure characterizing a a group (specialized or overlapping), the decision rule used by the group, and the relationship between individual goals and the group goal within the context of an economic decision-making committee. The "experimental results [showed interpersonal] conflict to be an important factor motivating constructive thought and analysis—as well as acrimony."[73] Conflict was found to stimulate group search by motivating the individual to present all the information at his disposal in order to support his position. Similarly, conflict was also found to motivate more intensive analysis of the information at hand. In fact, "data suggest that it may be fruitful to examine bargaining as an information pricing process." On the other hand, "data . . . indicate that the probability of reaching agreement decreases as interpersonal conflict increases."[74] The role of the decision rule is interesting for it was found to act in a nearly independent fashion; a simple, easy-to-use rule offset the debilitating effect of interpersonal conflict on group choice without substantially affecting the quality of choice measured against a group standard.

These results cannot be generalized any more than can Fouraker's. Though the domain was more realistic, the link between data and theory less rigorous, still they suggest that a good deal more can be learned about formal organization (for that is what a decision rule is) than is already known, and furthermore, that improvements in formal organization can radically affect the quality of group decisions.

THE GAME THEORIES

Before concluding this survey it is necessary for completeness sake to describe the normative decision theoretical work concerning groups, which as

73. Bower [7], p. 17.   74. *Ibid.*, p. 20.

a literature is commonly referred to as game theory. Because the literature is extensive and our space is limited, we confine our comments to a short discussion of the role played by game theory in the overall development of organization theory, rather than attempt a survey of substantive content. Very little of the game theory literature is actually applicable to the class of problem we have been considering, but the models used have such intuitive appeal and descriptive power that in nonrigorous formulations they are often used to describe a variety of complicated decision problems under uncertainty.[75] An excellent survey of the literature, both broad and deep, can be found in Luce and Raiffa's *Games and Decisions*.[76]

The basic question to which the literature is addressed is the mathematical construction of a theory of rational economic decision making in a social setting under uncertainty. The uncertainty may result from the acts of others upon whose behavior one's own welfare depends. For certain special cases, for example, the two-person zero-sum game, the problem has been solved in the sense that a unique strategy can be devised which optimally satisfies a set of prespecified criteria.[77] The trouble with game theory is that its ability to cope with *n*-person cooperative games (such as those we have been considering in all the literature discussed above) is extremely limited. At best, a set (not necessarily small) of possible strategies can be described as dominating all others, but generally speaking even such weak conclusions require the introduction of a more stringent and arbitrary set of assumptions.

The contribution made by game theory is important, nonetheless. Only through axiomatic analysis is it possible to learn the precise relationship between conclusions concerning social behavior and the assumptions one is willing to make. Arrow [2], for example, proved that an apparently innocuous set of constraints upon a group-decision rule was inconsistent, in the sense that no rule for mapping individual preferences into a group act could be devised which would not violate one of the constraints. From his analysis, considerable insight was obtained into the sources of stability in many of our social institutions, both private and public. From our point of view, the normative literature of group decisions would have contributed more to the science of policy formulation had effort been directed at exploring these sources of stability rather than at circumventing Arrow's mathematical result. The search for weaker axioms with descriptive content is one alternative

75. For example, one often hears a course of action described as a "minimax" strategy. Most of the time, this will be a very loose use of the word. Still, when used as a more specific form of the adjective "conservative," the term *minimax* communicates a great deal to the listener concerning the approach represented by the strategy so described.

76. Luce and Raiffa [32].

77. A two-person zero-sum game is a bargaining problem in the assignment of a reward between two persons in which one must lose what the other wins (and thus the sum of the rewards is zero).

and the traditional study of welfare economics is another. Welfare economics is the problem of counseling the member of a coalition, *or* for that matter the coalition itself, as to "the economic aspects of social states," *given* "the ethical values which one would take as data." Most progress in the former area is likely to come from the experimental economists, and in the latter from the scientific political scientists.

Conclusions

THE NEED FOR A SYNTHESIS

We have surveyed a great body of literature in a very short space. In doing so, we have generally complained of inadequacies of one sort or another in the material covered. Before we go on to summarize and categorize these inadequacies it is worth recalling that almost all our criticism was preceded by the phrase "for our purposes." This is important, for our interest was almost never the objective that motivated the research in question.

It is not surprising, therefore, that we were unable to find a theory of organizational decision making which provided rigorous support for prescription. In every case, we were faced with one of two problems. Either the theory was rigorous in construction but was based on nonoperational assumptions, or it was descriptive but devoid of normative content and could not be used alone to support prescription. It was also true that the models which encompassed the full normative problem of choice in the modern institution did not constitute testable theory, and that the meaningful theories did not encompass all of the first-order problems of organizational choice that were described in the empirical literature.

In short, the theory of organizations is still in an infant stage as far as the policy maker is concerned. To some extent we know what is needed, however, and it is thus possible that effort can be usefully invested in accelerating and guiding the maturation process. There must be a synthesis of normative and descriptive theory. As noted in the first section both normative and descriptive content are prerequisites for prescription. The problem is that from the point of view of those doing the research in either area, there are substantial costs involved in attempting the synthesis. For the normative theorist there appears to be an inevitable sacrifice in rigor involved in any attempt to incorporate the staggering complexity of the modern institution into his model. For the descriptive theorist, a sacrifice in his ability to describe the primitive state of management practice seems to be implied by an attempt to introduce normative premises into the analysis. Each is probably correct in his analysis.

Even so, we would argue that the sacrifice should be made. If we look at federal economic policy, for example, the major benefits we enjoy today are the results of theoretical contributions made during the 1920's and 1930's, particularly Keynes' *General Theory*.[78] Keynes is brilliant and filled with insight, but by contemporary standards not especially rigorous. Turning to the firm, we can note that while operations research has contributed to the efficiency of operations, the real quantum jump in performance came in the 1920's when General Motors and DuPont applied Marshallian marginal analysis to inventory control and financial management. Again, by modern standards of theoretical rigor, some of Marshall's arguments are both incomplete and/or flawed.

The lesson we can draw is clear. Where it has progressed and contributed to the solution of major economic problems in either the public or private sector, economics has been *problem* oriented rather than methodologically oriented. Furthermore, it has focused on critical problems. In the tradition of the political economists of the eighteenth and nineteenth centuries, economists have used theory to increase and communicate a profound understanding of the real world. Adam Smith sensed, described, and demonstrated in his argument the workings and benefits of a freely competitive price system two centuries before mathematical topologists proved the theorems which permitted someone else to show that Smith was correct. It was the *Wealth of Nations*, however, and not Wald's demonstration, that competitive equilibrium existed, that helped to discredit and end mercantilist economic policy.[79] In contrast to the political economists, all but a very few of the behavioral-decision theorists have ignored the critical decisions of the organization: they have rejected as "unstructured" those nonroutine decisions that shape policy and provide a framework for the most static internal organizational system. The field research of Harvard Business School and Barnard's and Selznick's theories are the principal exceptions to this categorization.

This will continue to be the case as long as research looks to past research or theory for its principal focus. We must learn that our use of past triumphs of theory and method needs to be constrained and conditioned by the nature of our present problems. If they do not work we must learn to discard them, whatever theoretical or methodological discontinuity is involved. What is needed in organization theory is problem-oriented understanding of organizations used as a basis for a theory that clarifies and extends understanding. The literature that develops should have as its reference locus the problems of organizations rather than the structure of preceding theory or the values of a particular methodology. Descriptive research which does not focus on prob-

78. Keynes [29].

79. Historically it is certainly true that empirical research or empirical concern underlies virtually all progress in science. We are arguing a bit more, however; we believe problem-oriented empirical research to be the fastest route to the solution of problems in social science.

lems is as limited an approach to the solution of problems as normative theory which has no descriptive basis.

METHODOLOGICAL DIFFICULTIES

Having argued without qualification for a synthesis of normative and descriptive work, it is only fair to note that the achievement of such a synthesis is no small matter. The tools of the social scientist for the observation and measurement of organizational behavior and choice are primitive. The language available for describing his observations in a meaningful form is only beginning to emerge with the elaboration of programming language. And as we have noted already, the subject of the proposed observation, measurement, and description is very complex.

Despite the magnitude of the problem facing students of organization, certain points are evident from our survey. First, there is no substitute for field research. If our object is to prescribe for capital budgeters in large corporations, we have to observe how, in fact, capital is allocated in the organization. It will do no good to read the formal procedure or seek a description from the man in charge. Moreover, if our goal is a general prescription, we will have to observe many organizations. Comparative studies should be undertaken. Once the practice of observing organizations and recording these observations in a systematic fashion becomes common practice, there may in effect be published data. Until then, new field research is in order.

Second, experimental methodology should be extended. At this time, it is the only form of empirical research in social science that permits controlled observations. That is, only in the laboratory is one able to screen out or randomize variables not being studied, *and* control all other variables. Progress by experimental economists has been steady, but slow. Results with implications for modern institutions await more ambitious forms of experimentation. It may well be that large payoffs await small sacrifices in the controlled quality of data. Organizations should be encouraged to conduct experiments of their own. Firms already spend fortunes for market research and it should not be too hard to interest them in research *if* they are shown how they can profit from what they learn.

Finally, and far more controversial than the foregoing, it appears that a strong theoretical background complements empirical research. The proposition is considered obvious in most of the sciences, but is often rejected precisely in those institutions where the ability to carry on good empirical work is concentrated. Advocates of a theoretical background argue that it is necessary to provide training in the art of building theory and to provide the conceptual metaphors that constitute the building blocks of theory. Certainly our survey indicates that those models of the modern institution that were most complete were based on the understanding of field observation or experience, but were also the weakest models structurally.

BIBLIOGRAPHY

1. Andrews, Kenneth R., *A Concept of Corporate Strategy*, BP 795 (Cambridge, Mass.: Harvard Business School, 1964).
2. Arrow, Kenneth, *Social Choice and Individual Values* (New York: John Wiley, 1951).
3. Barnard, Chester, *The Functions of the Executive* (Cambridge, Mass.: Harvard University Press, 1938).
4. Becker and Siegel, "Utility of Grades: Level of Aspirations in a Decision Theory Context," *Journal of Experimental Psychology*, **48** (1954), pp. 303–312.
5. Berg, Norman, *The Allocation of Strategic Funds in a Large Diversified Company*, unpublished dissertation (Harvard Graduate School of Business Administration, 1963).
6. Bergson, Abram, "On the Concept of Social Welfare," *Quarterly Journal of Economics*, **68** (1954), pp. 233–252.
7. Bower, Joseph L., "The Role of Conflict in Economic Decision Making Groups," *Quarterly Journal of Economics* (May 1965).
8. Buchanan, James M., and Gordon Tullock, *The Calculus of Consent* (Ann Arbor: University of Michigan Press, 1962).
9. Chamberlin, Edward H., *The Theory of Monopolistic Competition*, 6th ed. (Cambridge, Mass.: Harvard University Press, 1950).
10. Clarkson, Geoffrey P. E., *Portfolio Selection—A Simulation of Trust Investment* (Englewood Cliffs, N.J.: Prentice-Hall, 1962).
11. Coombs, C. H., and S. S. Komouta, "Measuring Utility of Money Through Decisions," *American Journal of Psychology*, **71** (1958), pp. 383–389.
12. Cournot, A., *Researches into the Mathematical Principles of the Theory of Wealth* (New York: Macmillan, 1897).
13. Cyert, Richard M., and James March, *A Behavioral Theory of the Firm* (Englewood Cliffs, N.J.: Prentice-Hall, 1963).
14. Davidson D., P. Suppes, and S. Siegel, *Decision Making: An Experimental Approach* (Stanford, Calif.: Stanford University Press, 1957).
15. Deavers, K., and J. McCall, *An Analysis of Procurement and Product Improvement Decisions* (Santa Monica, Calif.: RAND RM-3859, 1963).
16. Downs, Anthony, *An Economic Theory of Democracy* (New York: Harper & Row, 1957).
17. Duesenberry, James S., O. Eckstein, and Gary Fromm, "A Simulation of the U.S. Economy in Recession," *Econometrica*, **28** (1960), pp. 749–809.
18. Edgeworth, F. Y., *Mathematical Psychics* (London: Paul, 1881).
19. Edwards, Ward, "Probability Preferences in Gambling," *American Journal of Psychology*, **66** (1954), pp. 349–364.
20. ———, "Reward Probability, Amount, and Information As Determiners of

Sequential Two Alternative Decisions," *Journal of Experimental Psychology*, **52** (1956), 177–187.

21. Feigenbaum, E., "The Simulation of Verbal Learning Behavior," *Proceedings Western Joint Computer Conference*, 1961.

22. Feldman, J., "Simulation of Behavior in the Binary Choice Experiment," *Proceedings Western Joint Computer Conference*, 1961.

23. Fellner, William J., *Competition Among the Few* (New York: Alfred A. Knopf, 1949).

24. Fouraker, Lawrence E., "A Survey of Some Recent Experimental Games," *Recent Advances in Game Theory* (Princeton, N.J.: Princeton University Press, 1962).

25. ———, "Level of Aspiration and Group Decision Making," in Messick and Brayfield, eds., *Decision and Choice: Contributions of Sidney Siegel* (New York, McGraw-Hill, 1964).

26. ——— and S. Siegel, *Bargaining Behavior* (New York: McGraw-Hill, 1963).

27. Henderson, James, and Richard Quandt, *Microeconomic Theory* (New York: McGraw-Hill, 1958).

28. Homans, George, *Social Behavior—Its Elementary Forms* (New York: Harcourt, Brace and World, 1961).

29. Keynes, J. M., *The General Theory of Employment, Interest and Money* (New York: Harcourt, Brace and Company, 1936).

30. Klein, L. R., and A. S. Goldberger, *An Econometric Model of the U.S., 1929–1952* (Amsterdam: North-Holland Publishing Company, 1955).

31. Luce, Duncan, *Individual Choice Behavior* (New York: John Wiley, 1959).

32. ——— and Howard Raiffa, *Games and Decisions* (New York: John Wiley, 1957).

33. March, James, and Herbert Simon, *Organizations* (New York: John Wiley, 1958).

34. Meyer, John, and Robert Glauber, *Investment Decisions, Economic Forecasting and Public Policy* (Cambridge, Mass.: Harvard University Graduate School of Business Administration, Division of Research, 1964).

35. Mosteller, Frederick, and Philip Nogee, "An Experimental Measurement of Utility," *Journal of Political Economy*, **59** (1951), pp. 371–404.

36. Newell, Allan, J. C. Shaw, and H. A. Simon, "Elements of a Theory of Human Problem Solving," *Psychological Review*, (1958), pp. 151–166.

37. ———, ———, and ———, *A Variety of Intelligent Learning in a General Problem Solver* (Santa Monica, Calif.: RAND P-1742, 1959).

38. ———, and H. A. Simon, *GPS, A Program That Simulates Human Thought* (Santa Monica, Calif.: RAND P-2257, 1961).

39. Pareto, V., *Manuel d'Économie Politique* (Paris: M. Giard, 1909).

40. Pratt, J. W., H. Raiffa, and R. Schlaifer, "The Foundations of Decision Under Uncertainty, An Elementary Exposition," *The Journal of the American Statistical Association* (June 1964).

41. Riker, Theodore, *The Theory of Political Coalitions* (New Haven: Yale University Press, 1962).

42. Roethlisberger, Fritz, and W. Dickson, *Management and the Worker* (Cambridge, Mass.: Harvard University Press, 1939).

43. Rothenberg, Jerome, "Review of the Calculus of Consent," *Econometrica* (July 1964).
44. Samuelson, Paul, *The Foundations of Economic Analysis* (Cambridge, Mass.: Harvard University Press, 1947).
45. Schelling, T. C., "Bargaining, Communication and Limited War," *Journal of Conflict Resolution*, **1** (1957), pp. 19–36.
46. Selznick, Philip, *Leadership and Administration* (New York: Harper & Row, 1957).
47. Siegel, Sidney, with Alberta E. Siegel and Julia Andrews, *Choice, Strategy, and Utility* (New York: McGraw-Hill, 1964).
48. ———, "Level of Aspiration and Decision Making," *Psychological Review*, **64**, pp. 253–262.
49. ——— and L. E. Fouraker, *Bargaining and Group Decision Making* (New York: McGraw-Hill, 1959).
50. Simon, H. A., *Administrative Behavior* (New York: Macmillan, 1945).
51. ——— and P. A. Simon, "Trial and Error Search in Solving Difficult Problems," *Behavioral Science*, 1962.
52. Thompson, Victor A., *Modern Organization* (New York: Alfred A. Knopf, 1961).
53. Von Neumann, J., and O. Morgenstern, *The Theory of Games and Economic Behavior* (Princeton, N.J.: Princeton University Press, 1944).
54. Zeckhauser, Richard, *Collaboration and Composite Games*, unpublished honors thesis (Harvard College, 1962).

Chapter 4

ENID CURTIS BOK SCHOETTLE

The State of the Art in Policy Studies

In the twentieth century, the social sciences have become increasingly "aware of the policy process as a suitable object of study in its own right, primarily in the hope of improving the rationality of the flow of decisions."[1] Recently, there has emerged a broad body of theory consistent in its orientation toward identifying the conditions under which numerous individuals can maximize attainment of agreed-upon goals through the use of social mechanisms.[2] This shared orientation—emerging out of each of the separate disciplines of the social sciences—would have been impossible fifty years ago.[3] Since World War I, however, American social scientists have been called on to deal with certain social problems arising in a period of protracted international conflict and economic change. The involvement of this group of disciplines with major issues of social choice required an understanding of how the social system which affected policy outcomes operated.[4] As the

1. H. Lasswell and D. Lerner (eds.), *The Policy Sciences* (Stanford, Calif.: Stanford University Press, 1951), p. 3.
2. R. A. Dahl and C. E. Lindblom, *Politics, Economics, and Welfare* (New York: Harper & Row, 1953), pp. xxi-xxii.
3. *Ibid.*, Chapter 1.
4. See Lasswell and Lerner, *op. cit.*; see also, D. Lerner (ed.), *The Human Meaning of the Social Sciences* (New York: Meridian Books, 1959).

techniques of the social sciences became increasingly equipped to handle a number of variables, the model of the policy process became increasingly complex, and tended to stress patterns of behavior rather than idiosyncratic incidents of behavior.

This chapter will be concerned with a description of how contemporary social science theory analyzes the processes of policy formulation and execution. We assume there is utility in estimating as accurately as possible the political future of policy ideas, which necessitates knowing what kinds of policy issues, recommendations or procedures will engender inhibiting consequences and which will produce rapid consensus.

Our analysis will proceed on two levels, concentrating first upon the participant in the policy-making process, and second, upon the system of policy formulation. Raymond Bauer has asserted that any political system engaged in policy-making activity has a series of leverage points: actors, roles, institutions, processes, and so on, which can be acted on to affect the output of the system.[5] Methods of analyzing these individual points will comprise the first section of the chapter. Second, we shall be concerned with how the process of policy-making interacts with the larger political system so that patterned interaction among relevant participants occurs to promote policy objectives.

This dual emphasis on the individual engaged in the policy-making process and on the systemic properties of the process itself reflects what we see as the shared orientation of the social sciences in contemporary analyses of policy-making problems. The works of Lasswell and Lerner, Dahl and Lindblom, and Braybrooke and Lindblom are perhaps the broadest formulations of this shared orientation that exist in the literature.[6] These authors are jointly concerned with providing a basis for improving rational, efficient methods of policy formulation in order to maximize the outputs of public policy in accordance with the values of democratic society. In doing so, they tend to concentrate on how the *individual policy maker* operates within an ongoing *political system*, and it is this dual focus which we have adopted throughout this chapter.

More specifically, we have adopted Braybrooke and Lindblom's "strategy of disjointed incrementalism" as the most useful description of how the policy-making process operates in a democratic political system, notably, in the United States. In stressing the parameters of individual choice, the authors assume a political system which necessitates a continuous, gradualist approach to policy problems. With this assumption in mind, it may be useful to outline their argument.

5. R. Bauer, "Establishing Priorities for Data Gathering" (mimeograph, Boston, Mass.: Harvard Business School, July 6, 1964), p. 1.

6. Lasswell and Lerner, *op. cit.*; Dahl and Lindblom, *op. cit.*; D. Braybrooke and C. E. Lindblom, *A Strategy of Decision* (New York: Free Press, 1963).

The strategy of disjointed incrementalism, as outlined in Chapter 5 of Braybrooke and Lindblom's *A Strategy of Decision*, consists of eight inter-related attributes that provide a systematic strategy for problem solving.

1. Choices are made in a given political universe, at the margin of the status quo.
2. A restricted variety of policy alternatives is considered, and these alternatives are incremental, or small, changes in the status quo.
3. A restricted number of consequences are considered for any given policy.
4. Adjustments are made in the objectives of policy in order to conform to given means of policy, implying a reciprocal relationship between ends and means.
5. Problems are reconstructed, or transformed, in the course of exploring relevant data.
6. Analysis and evaluation occur sequentially, with the result that policy consists of a long chain of amended choices.
7. Analysis and evaluation are oriented toward remedying a negatively perceived situation, rather than toward reaching a preconceived goal.
8. Analysis and evaluation are undertaken throughout society, that is, the locus of these activities is fragmented or disjointed.

The utility of the formulation for our purposes is that it provides three basic criteria for any theoretical approach to the policy-making process. First, it demands that any theory about the process stress attributes of the individual policy maker and the system in which he operates. Second, it requires that the theory relate variables which intervene between the individual and the system, such as interest group behavior, role-playing, and so on, to the operation of these two basic variables. Third, it focuses attention on how to change or improve the policy product. The bodies of theory which we shall analyze in this paper will be discussed in terms of how well they meet these criteria.

The Participant in the Policy-Making Process: Theoretical Approaches

"The focus of our concern is first of all to understand the behavior of the individual—or if not the individual, the smallest meaningful unit of analysis—confronted with manifestations of public policy problems."[7] In the literature of the social sciences, there are a number of theoretical concepts which emphasize various characteristic behaviors and reactions of political actors. The approaches we have chosen to discuss are not an exhaustive listing; rather,

7. R. Bauer, "Position Papers for NPA Information Project" (mimeograph, Boston, Mass.: Harvard Business School, June 1, 1964).

they appear to be the most useful ones for the purpose of explaining individual behavior in the policy-making process.

INDIVIDUAL MOTIVATION AND ASPECTS OF THE SOCIALIZATION PROCESS: THE POLITICAL ORIENTATION OF POLICY MAKERS

Sociologists, psychologists and political scientists have all studied the linkages between personality and opinion formation, and the effects of resultant political orientations on political behavior. The classification of types of political orientation set forth by Parsons and Shils has been widely adapted by other behavioral scientists, notably Angus Campbell and M. Brewster Smith, Jerome Bruner and Robert White, and we shall use it here. Orientation, in Parsonian terms, refers to "the internalized aspects of objects and relationships" and includes "(1) *cognitive orientation*, or knowledge of and belief about the political system, its roles and the incumbents of these roles, its inputs and outputs; (2) *affective orientation* or feelings about the political system, its roles, personnel and performance; and (3) *evaluational orientation*, the judgments and opinions about political objects that typically involve the combination of value standards and criteria with information and feelings."[8]

Smith argues that such orientations, when focused on a particular issue about which the individual forms an opinion, serve three functions for the individual. *Object appraisal* tests reality to assess the relevance of his opinion to his ongoing concerns. *Social adjustment* is the mechanism by which the opinion facilitates, maintains or disrupts the individual's relations with significant others. *Externalization* enables the opinion to serve as a personal response to an external event in a manner affected by the individual's unresolved problems.[9] These three approaches, treated respectively by writers stressing the classical rational calculus in political opinion, theorists of group influence, and Lasswell and his students, together form a pluralistic schema which, in Smith's view, is more useful than "simpler views of the functions of opinion."[10] More important, the three functions of object appraisal, social adjustment, and externalization may have divergent consequences for individuals holding a given opinion.[11] Opinions founded on object appraisal might well be influenced by new information; those based on

8. G. A. Almond and S. Verba, *The Civic Culture* (Princeton, N.J.: Princeton University Press, 1963), p. 15; see also Almond, "Comparative Political Systems," *Journal of Politics*, **XVIII** (1956); see also T. Parsons and E. A. Shils (eds.), *Toward a General Theory of Action* (Cambridge, Mass.: Harvard University Press, 1959), pp. 53ff.

9. M. B. Smith, "Opinions, Personality and Political Behavior," *APSR*, **LII** (March 1958), p. 10; see also M. B. Smith, J. S. Bruner and R. W. White, *Opinions and Personality* (New York: John Wiley, 1956).

10. Smith, *ibid.*, p. 11.

11. *Ibid.*

social adjustment could be more easily altered by the opinions of relevant reference groups; those serving the function of externalization could perhaps be changed only by a form of "conversion."[12]

Thus, a single policy conclusion may reflect a wide range of personal opinions and attitude structures among those who reach it. A given opinion or policy stand camouflages "the much subtler distinctions often drawn in the attitudinal object as privately construed, and in the person's orientation toward it."[13] For this reason, Smith feels it inefficient to study a publicly expressed policy stand as the end product of its advocates' political orientations. He finds it more profitable to look at a given policy as a "phenomenon of social consensus (which may best be described in categories of sociological theory)" such as cross-pressure analysis.[14] Where shifts in opinion, policy initiatives, or strategies of influences are the object of scrutiny, however, he suggests there is utility in more intensive appraisals of, for example "the personal values and interests . . . which a particular topic engages, in a defined public, or of the degree to which the attitudes prevalent on a topic in a defined population serve one or another of [the] three functions."[15] In such a manner, one could tap the functional and motivational aspects of a policy maker's behavior and his susceptibility to different strategies of argument or information. For a defined political group this research procedure is conceivable; Lucian Pye, for example, has attempted to explain the behavior of classes of policy makers in Burma in this fashion.[16] Robert Lane has also applied this orientational analysis to fifteen "common men" in New Haven, to find the sources of their political ideology.[17]

Other scholars have applied a more generalized analysis to political personality and political culture, in order to identify the motivational aspects of certain classes of political actors. Lasswell, for example, intensively scrutinized the life histories of different types of political actors: agitators, administrators, and theorists, in order to draw a developmental profile of classes of role incumbents and to test their capacity to play given specialized or composite roles.[18]

Using the concept of political culture as a point of departure, Almond and Verba have attempted to identify the content of democratic culture by examining a sample of attitudes in a number of democratic systems.[19] The concept of "political culture" discriminates between political and nonpolitical attitudes and developmental patterns, stressing the psychological orientation

12. *Ibid.*, p. 12.   13. *Ibid.*, p. 1.
14. *Ibid.*, p. 17.   15. *Ibid.*, p. 16.
16. See L. Pye, *Politics, Personality and Nation Building* (New Haven: Yale University Press, 1962).
17. See R. E. Lane, *Political Ideology* (New York: Free Press, 1962).
18. See H. Lasswell, *Psychopathology and Politics* (New York: Viking Press, 1960).
19. Almond and Verba, *op. cit.*, p. 12.

toward social objects as they relate to the political system. In so doing, the concept emphasizes the process of induction or socialization into the political system which individuals undergo in a given society and evaluates the political system as it is internalized in the cognitions, feelings, and evaluations of its population.[20] In this framework, Gabriel Almond has characterized the Anglo-American political system as a homogeneous, secular, political culture which promotes multivalued, rational, calculating, and bargaining behavior on the part of political participants. Politics in such a system is viewed as a pragmatic game in which the stakes are not too high, because the great majority of the population is agreed upon the ultimate social goals.[21] One can hypothesize that the modal political orientation of political actors within the American political system will complement these cultural characteristics.

THE SELF-INTEREST OF THE POLICY MAKER: SATISFICING BEHAVIOR

Current students of the policy-making process accept Herbert A. Simon's finding that in complex situations in which there may be multiple goals or internal goal conflict within an uncertain environment, individuals engage in satisficing rather than maximizing behavior.[22] Such behavior is, in Simon's terms, adaptive, and consists of searching for new alternatives of action when performance falls short of the level of aspiration, while "at the same time, the level of aspiration begins to adjust itself downward until goals reach levels that are practically attainable."[23] Should these two mechanisms operate too slowly "to adapt aspirations to performance, emotional behavior will replace rational, adaptive behavior."[24] In this formulation, man is not confronted with fixed and known alternatives which have known consequences when he maximizes his valued goals, as the classical theory of choice suggests.[25] Instead, goals can be both vague and inconsistent; alternatives "are not given but must be sought, and determining what consequences will follow on each alternative becomes an arduous task."[26] Theoretically, the substitution of adaptive man for economic man involves the recognition that man must engage in costly processes of acquiring knowledge about his environment, and that in any case his knowledge will be incomplete and his perception of

20. Almond and Verba, *op. cit.*, pp. 13–14.   21. Almond, *op. cit.*

22. See H. Simon, "Theories of Decision-Making in Economic and Behavioral Science," *American Economic Review*, **XLIX** (June 1959), pp. 255–257; see also D. Braybrooke and C. Lindblom, *A Strategy of Decision*, Part II, for an alternative formulation of Simon's findings.

23. Simon, *ibid.*, p. 263.   24. *Ibid.*

25. H. Simon, "Decision-Making and Administrative Organization," *Public Administration Review*, **IV** (Winter 1944), p. 19.

26. See Simon, "Theories of Decision-Making . . . ," *op. cit.*, p. 272.

his environment distorted.[27] In short, "perception and cognition intervene between the decision-maker and his objective environment."[28]

In stressing that individuals engage in satisficing behavior, pay attention to only a very small segment of their environment, and filter information through their prior orientations to their environment, Simon suggests a mode of analysis for the policy-making process. Banfield, Wildavsky, and Bauer, Pool, and Dexter have used the assumption of satisficing behavior as a basis for studying individuals' pursuit of their self-interest in policy formation.[29] For example, Bauer, Pool, and Dexter make two related points: first, that the policy maker utilizes strategies, rules of decision, and styles of role playing to compensate for his limited informational and computational capacities; and second, that most people are not clearly aware of their self-interest. The authors find that the small businessman in their sample engages in pure satisficing behavior in that he calculates "self-interest on the assumption that basically all he can do is what he is now doing, but . . . a little better."[30]

That men pursue their own self-interest, given their identification of a value with their self-interest, is tautological. However, three aspects of the formal concept of self-interest give rise to interesting questions about policy making: who is the self under consideration, what value is he pursuing, and over what time period.[31] In the absence of complete information about these dimensions of self-interest, the policy maker is forced to adopt strategies, or rules of decision, which can be altered, within limits, by new information. Clearly, the habitual strategies, the information sources, and the perceived self-interest of relevant policy makers, in addition to their political orientations, are crucial determinants of the behavior of individual participants in the policy-making process.

ROLES IN THE POLICY-MAKING PROCESS

Heinz Eulau has said that the concept of role is the theoretical "coin of the realm in the social sciences."[32] Roles concentrate "attention on the inter-relatedness and interdependence of human beings in various systems of action" by creating mutual expectations about the attitudes or behaviors of significant others in the course of social relations, and by regularizing human action.[33] Thus, a role is a "social prescription of some, but not all, of the

27. *Ibid.*, p. 269.   28. *Ibid.*, p. 272.

29. See Edward C. Banfield, "The Decision-Making Schema," *Public Administration Review*, **XVIII** (Autumn 1957); Edward C. Banfield, *Political Influence* (New York: Free Press, 1961); R. Bauer, I. Pool, and L. Dexter, *American Business and Public Policy* (New York: Atherton Press, 1963); and, A. Wildavsky, *The Politics of the Budgetary Process* (Boston: Little, Brown and Company, 1964).

30. Bauer, Pool, and Dexter, *ibid.*, p. 129.   31. *Ibid.*, p. 474.

32. H. Eulau, *Journeys in Politics* (New York: Bobbs-Merrill, 1964), p. 256.

33. *Ibid.*

premises that enter into an individual's choice of behavior," and as such is an obvious focus for empirical research.[34]

At the outset, however, it is important to stress two systematic approaches typified by Almond's work on political culture and Neil Smelser's study of structural-functionalism.[35] These will help emphasize the significance of role playing in the political system.

First, Almond conceives of the political system as a group of interacting roles, or a structure of roles, which pattern social interaction. His characterization of the Anglo-American political system includes a description of its role structure, which he sees as highly differentiated, directed toward specific functions, manifestly organized and bureaucratized, and with a high degree of stability of function.[36] Such a prototype serves, as did his analysis of the democratic political culture, as a point of departure for more specific investigations of role playing in a democratic policy-making process.

Smelser, using Parsonian analysis, identifies social change as a sequence of structural, or role, differentiation.[37] As society becomes more complex and specialized, social organization and role differentiation will become more complex and specialized as well. In isolating manifest, specialized roles as a crucial characteristic of modern societies, he emphasizes Almond's point about the structure of roles in modern democratic societies.

In addition, however, Smelser stresses that systematic relationships among subsystems of the social system provide the major basis for interaction among specialized roles. Thus, boundaries exist between subsystems because of role specialization, and boundary interchanges themselves must be handled by specialized roles within each subsystem so that performances and sanctions generated in each subsystem become predictable.[38] Multifunctional roles—particularly those at the boundaries of various subsystems—thus contribute crucially to boundary maintenance and hence to the stability of the social system. Smelser's emphasis on multifunctional roles is a useful insight into role playing in the policy-making process.

Turning to the study of individual role playing, the individual role player is both oriented to others in the system and is himself an object of orientation. Both orientations constitute his role.[39] In the analysis of any individual role, it is necessary to consider three theoretical problems: the degree of consensus which exists in any given policy-making process on the role definition; the conformity of the role incumbent to expectations about his behavior; and, methods of resolving role conflict.[40] Exploration of these three issues will

34. H. Simon, "Theories of Decision-Making . . . ," *op. cit.*, p. 274.

35. See G. Almond, "Comparative Political Systems," *op. cit.*, and N. J. Smelser, *Social Change in the Industrial Revolution* (London: Routledge & Kegan Paul, 1959).

36. See Almond, *ibid.*   37. Smelser, *op. cit.*, p. 1.

38. *Ibid.*, p. 14.   39. *Ibid.*, p. 13.

40. See N. Gross, W. S. Mason, A. McEachern, *Explorations in Role Analysis* (New York: John Wiley, 1958).

both account for varying behavior of incumbents of the same position, and elucidate the functioning of the policy-making process.[41]

Gross and his associates consider the problem of consensus about role definition an important variable which significantly affects the functioning of social systems. Furthermore, the role incumbent's "perception of the degree of consensus on expectations held by significant others (and) on evaluative standards applicable to his position" affects, in the opinion of Gross, his role behavior.[42] In other words, the degree of role consensus is a function of two variables: actual sharedness of value orientations throughout the system about the roles in the system, and the motivational orientation or commitment of the incumbent to some degree of shared expectations about his role.[43] These two variables should be investigated as a major aspect of any analysis of political role playing.

Turning to the conformity of role incumbents to expected behavior, Gross defines expectations empirically as a description of how incumbents should or do interact, according to both the role incumbent and significant others.[44] Because the incumbent's behavior is a form of group behavior, influenced both by expectations he holds for himself and by expectations others hold, investigation of his conformity should proceed along two lines: the degree of agreement (or consensus) between his expectations and the expectations of others; and the degree of conformity between his motivations, attitudes, and personality and the demands of the role. Again, Gross emphasizes that "the different expectations held for incumbents' behavior and attributes are crucial for an understanding of their different behaviors and characteristics."[45] Furthermore, these expectations are subject to change over time, and additional inputs of information.[46]

Finally, methods of role conflict resolution must be analyzed. One can differentiate conceptually between intra-role and inter-role conflict: the first being that caused by multiple and conflicting role occupancy; the second, by incongruent expectations about the rights or obligations of two or more interdependent roles.[47] Role conflicts can also be differentiated if one articulates the "conceptual distinction between expectations that are perceived as legitimate and those perceived as illegitimate" by various role definers.[48] In both instances, one must concentrate on various role definers. In both instances, one must also concentrate on various differing sets of expectations held by different political actors.

The extensive literature on role playing in contemporary American politics can be culled for hypotheses concerning consensus on roles, fulfillment of expectations, and role conflict, which at the same time stress the

41. *Ibid.*
43. *Ibid.*, pp. 37–40.
45. *Ibid.*, p. 321.
47. *Ibid.*, p. 5.

42. *Ibid.*, p. 37.
44. *Ibid.*, p. 58.
46. *Ibid.*, p. 323.
48. *Ibid.*, p. 324.

interactive qualities of role structures. To cite only one example, Wildavsky's qualitative description of the budgetary process stresses the dependence of this ongoing process upon a division of labor among the participants. Their roles represent patterns of expected behaviors: the agencies advocate programs; the Bureau of the Budget protects the President's interest by limiting the advocated programs; the House Appropriations Committee guards public funds by further restricting the advocated programs; and finally, the Senate Appropriations Committee serves as a responsible appeals court for unsatisfied claimants. Consensus upon these roles and their fulfillment create stable patterns of mutual expectations which reduce the costs of policy making and the likelihood of role conflict.[49]

DESCRIPTIVE DECISION-MAKING THEORY

In his analysis of the decision process, Harold Lasswell stipulates seven functions performed in the making of any decision.

These include the intelligence function, i.e., the gathering of information which may include either information which suggests a problem for policy-makers' attention or information for the formulation of alternatives. A second function is the recommendation of one or more possible policy alternatives. A third is the prescription or enactment of one among several proposed alternative solutions. A fourth is the invocation of the adopted alternative, and a fifth is its application in specific situations by executive or enforcement officers. A sixth stage of the decision process is the appraisal of the effectiveness of the prescribed alternative, and the seventh is the termination of the original policy.[50]

In the later stages of the process, the policy makers may utilize new information in order to alter the original policy, thus initiating the decision process again. It is this ongoing character of the decision process in a broad political context which most contemporary students of decision making utilize.

In Herbert Simon's discussion of choice, the author dissects decisions into their component premises, and then seeks to discover where the premises originate.[51] He stresses, as we noted, an important restriction upon decision makers: that the information gathering necessary to reduce uncertainty is costly,[52] and that consequently "the decision-maker's model of the world encompasses only a minute fraction of all the relevant characteristics of the real environment, and his inferences extract only a minute fraction of all the

49. Wildavsky, *op. cit.*, pp. 160–161.

50. As discussed in J. Robinson, *Congress and Foreign Policy-Making* (Homewood, Ill.: Dorsey Press, 1962), p. 6.

51. See Simon, "Decision-Making and Administrative Organization," *op. cit.*; and also "Theories of Decision-Making . . . ," *op. cit.*

52. Simon, "Theories of Decision-Making . . . ," *ibid.*, pp. 269–272.

information that is present even in his model."[53] Thus, he concludes, decisions are inferred from a finite number of values and facts which makes it necessary to take "the individual decision premise as a unit of description, (and) hence to deal with the whole interwoven fabric of influences that bear on a single decision."[54]

This focus upon the decision premise and the environment which influences the decision is more productive, in our opinion, than the use of the authoritative decision itself as a focal point of analysis, as Richard Snyder advocates. In Snyder's formulation, the seven steps in the decision process which Lasswell outlines are considered as a single dynamic social action, resulting in and sustaining a decision taken by authoritative, that is, official, decision makers. The main elements in the schema are the behavior of the *actors*, through crucial political *structures*, in a *situation*, and the prime analytic objective is "the recreation of the social world of the decision-makers as they view it."[55]

Within the context of actors operating through structures in a given situation, Snyder incorporates many of the variables necessary in analyzing policy formulation. For example, his analysis of *actors* is based on the assumption that the behavior of official decision makers reflects nonauthoritative action by interest groups and others. He also treats the actors as products of varying patterns of socialization and recruitment. In the case of *behavior within organizational structures*, he includes as variables the decision maker's perceptions, strategies, priorities of choice, goals, and expectations, as well as the rules flowing from the organizational context.[56] Finally, in analyzing the *situation*, he includes the environmental conditions impinging upon the decision maker such as the pressure to act, the cruciality of the decision, and the time dimension of the problem, as well as the decision maker's perception of these environmental conditions—the value and priority the decision maker imputes to the problem and his interpretation of it.

In dealing with decision making from the fundamental perspectives of the properties of the system and the characteristics of the actors, Snyder approaches policy making in accepted contemporary fashion. However, he submerges the relevant findings of communications theory, role theory, personality and socialization theory, pressure group theory, and so forth, in a two-step flow which appears to us to be more an artifact of organizational neatness than a theoretical insight of heuristic value.

In addition, concentrating upon the authoritative decision as a focus of analysis fails to accommodate two other types of decisional activity. The first is

53. *Ibid.*, p. 272.   54. *Ibid.*, p. 273.
55. Richard Snyder, "A Decision-Making Approach to the Study of Political Phenomena," in Roland Young (ed.), *Approaches to the Study of Politics* (Evanston, Ill.: Northwestern University Press, 1958), p. 17.
56. *Ibid.*, pp. 16–17.

the situation of a "decision paradox," that is, a situation in which there is a policy without a decision by any unit under analysis.[57] As Bauer, Pool, and Dexter have argued, actors become committed to decisions through various influences and processes, within various contexts, along a range of issues.[58] In their words, decisions are "not necessarily taken in a social group between the time that an issue is recognized and the time that one or more persons are committed to a course of action."[59] This approach stresses the fact that often "decisions" are merely phases of an ongoing controversy, in contrast to Snyder's view that they are analytically discrete entities.

In the second case, emphasizing decisions which can be identified fails to account for a "non-decision-making situation." This situation occurs "when the dominant values, the accepted rules of the game, the existing power relations among groups, and the instruments of force, singly or in combination, effectively prevent certain grievances from developing into full-fledged issues which call for decisions. . . ."[60] As Schattschneider has pointed out, "all forms of political organization have a bias in favor of the exploitation of some kinds of conflict and the suppression of others because *organization is the mobilization of bias*."[61] In order to identify which latent issues might be prevented from gaining access into the decision-making process, it is necessary to analyze the dominant values and procedures of the political system. In ascertaining what "the rules of the game" operative in a given political system are, one can determine which groups they favor and the dynamics by which these status quo–oriented groups influence community values and institutions.

These two deviant cases of decisional activity reemphasize our continuing concern that any analysis of the decision-making process recognize two factors. Decision making is, first, an ongoing process and, second, it cannot be isolated from its contextual setting. Such a perspective will illuminate the process of policy formation, rather than reifying its end product.

GROUP THEORY: THE GROUP AS THE SMALLEST MEANINGFUL UNIT IN POLICY MAKING

Group theory in political science originated with the work of Arthur Bentley and has been carried on by David Truman, Charles B. Hagan, Earl

57. See Robinson, *op. cit.*, p. 3.

58. Bauer, Pool, and Dexter, *op. cit.*, p. 482; see also R. Bauer, "Problem Solving Behavior in Organizations," in Hargrove, Harrison, and Swearingen (eds.), *Business Policy Cases with Behavioral Science Implications* (Homewood, Ill.: Richard D. Irwin, Inc., 1963).

59. *Ibid.*, p. 482.

60. Bachrach and Baratz, "Decisions and Non-Decisions," *APSR*, LVII, No. 3 (September 1963), p. 641.

61. E. E. Schattschneider, *The Semi-Sovereign People* (New York: Holt, Rinehart and Winston, 1960), p. 71; see also, Bachrach and Baratz, "Two Faces of Power," *APSR*, LVII, No. 4 (December 1962), p. 949.

Latham, and others.[62] Before criticizing the theory, it may be useful to outline the major, agreed-upon tenets of these theorists who see groups as the ultimate "real" of politics.[63] To use Truman's terminology, these theorists identify a *group* as any interacting plurality of individuals which may, on the basis of a shared interest, make claims on other social groups. A *potential group* is a collection of individuals with common attitudes who will interact to form a group if other groups threaten their interests. Finally, *social equilibrium* is achieved when patterns of group interaction are characterized by a high degree of stability.[64]

Three basic propositions follow. First, since society constitutes a plurality of interacting groups, the political process can be viewed as groups competing for power over the allocation of resources. Second, group interaction is the primary source of an individual's attitudes. Third, interaction tends toward equilibrium, since potential groups establish rules of the game under which various groups compete, and hence any breach of these rules will produce counteraction by some newly mobilized group.[65]

Earl Latham moves beyond Truman's position to a view of the government as a group comparable to other nonofficial groups, since all act as channels for the exercise of power.[66] In addition, Latham argues, the state at any given time "represents the consensus by which the groups exist in mutual relationships," thereby establishing and enforcing norms of group behavior. Thus, group interaction "generates the rules by which the community is to be governed and ... public policy ... formulated."[67]

Finally, Charles Hagan generalizes these arguments so that the concept of group, as the true expression of social activity, incorporates the significance of the individual, the institution, and the idea (or ideological premise) in the political system.[68] In his view, the individual acts only as a representative of an interest or group; an institution is the collective action of those supporting it—that is, groups; and an idea is an abstract expression which only gains meaning from group interests.[69] In this manner, Hagan obeys the injunction of Bentley that when groups are adequately stated, everything is stated.[70]

62. See Arthur Bentley, *The Process of Government* (Chicago: University of Chicago Press, 1908).

63. H. Eckstein, *Pressure Group Politics* (London: G. Allen, 1960), p. 153.

64. See D. Truman, *The Governmental Process* (New York: Knopf, 1951), Chapters 2 and 16.

65. See S. Rothman, "Systematic Political Theory," *APSR*, **LIV**, No. 1 (March 1960), pp. 18–20.

66. See E. Latham, *The Group Basis of Politics* (Ithaca: Cornell University Press, 1952), p. 12.   67. *Ibid.*, p. 27.

68. See C. Hagan, "The Group in a Political Science," in R. Young (ed.), *Approaches to the Study of Politics, op. cit.*

69. *Ibid.*, pp. 46–47.

70. See P. Odegard, "A Group Basis of Politics," *The Western Political Quarterly*, **XI**, No. 3 (September 1958), p. 690.

The major criticism of group theory revolves precisely around this attempt to banish the individual, roles, institutional structures, and ideas or attitudes from the political process. To try to explain politics on the basis of group competition without giving attention to these other variables is fruitless; to submerge these other variables in the concept of groups is both misleading and inefficient. Harry Eckstein, in examining the utility of the group approach to politics, has concluded that pressure-group politics are a function of three main variables: the attitudes of individuals and of the society at large, the structure of governmental decision making, and the patterns of policy making in the political system.[71] We shall briefly analyze group theory in these terms.

Individual values, perceptions, and orientations, as we have seen, are functions of the individual's personality and socialization, on the one hand, and information level and role on the other. Thus, these are significant analytic variables, and should be explored directly, rather than assumed to be a function of group membership as the group theorists assert. Indeed, Truman has recognized that groups undertake purposive action, which suggests that individuals perceive some common interest prior to their action through groups, although Truman does not push his argument that far.[72] His concept of potential group membership also suggests that perceived self-interests and certain attitudes toward the rules of the game in society precede the formation of groups, thus contradicting his argument that groups are the source of individual attitudes.[73]

On a systematic level, an analysis of socialization processes and political culture may do more to explain the degree of consensus in the political system than the assertion that group competition tends toward an equilibrium governed by certain rules of the game. Legitimation of and consensus about group activity, in other words, is founded in "the fundamental political ethos of a society," rather than by the groups themselves.[74]

The structure of governmental decision making also independently determines the political behavior of groups. Almond and Coleman, in their outline of political functions, argue that the character of groups engaged in the function of "interest articulation" is determined by the social structure of the given political system.[75] The channels of participation open to interest groups are not determined by the interest groups themselves. Instead, the structure of government influences both groups' expectations of political effectiveness and the possible scope and intensity of their political activity.[76]

Related to the influence of governmental structure on group behavior is

71. See Eckstein, *op. cit.*, Chapter 1.   72. See Rothman, *op. cit.*, pp. 25–26.
73. *Ibid.*, p. 23.   74. *Ibid.*, p. 28.
75. G. Almond and J. Coleman, *The Politics of the Developing Areas* (Princeton: Princeton University Press, 1960), Introduction.
76. Eckstein, *op. cit.*, p. 30.

the influence of governmental policy itself. "Policy," in Eckstein's view, "creates politically active groups."[77] The welfare state, for example, has generated a plethora of interest-oriented groups which bargain with the government over policy alternatives. Thus, policy serves as a situational element in the political system "which selects among the objective attributes of groups, those which are of special political account."[78] Indeed, Eckstein argues that pressure group politics are most intense when the issues involved are narrowly delimited, technical, and professional—issues which attract little public interest and which neither challenge the ultimate right of the government to make policy, nor threaten to replace those who wield such governmental authority.[79] This view of interest-group behavior, substantiated by observers of the role of government in scientific affairs, is far removed from pure group theory which asserts that government *is* the competition between groups in an equilibrium state.

In concluding this section on the role of groups in the policy-making process, we restress that group behavior is a function of attitudes held both by group members and by the society at large, of the structure of governmental decision making, and of the composition of governmental policy. All of these variables are subject to empirical analysis. Groups, in modern political systems, do not substitute for government. As a meaningful unit of political analysis, groups engage in "an intermediate level of activity between the political and the apolitical."[80] If decision-making theory lays too much stress upon the authoritative locus of the allocation of values in the political system, group theory lays too little. Policy making occurs in an intermediate range, where communications between the governing and the governed takes place.

ELITE THEORY: POLICY MAKING AS AN ELITE OCCUPATION

Much attention of modern political science has been focused on elites: their socio-economic characteristics; patterns of political recruitment; communication patterns and circulation; the effect of the social system, such as social stratification, upon their composition; and, particularly in community studies, patterns of decision making.[81] This outpouring of work can contribute to a powerful general model of policy making only if it is made dynamic, that is, if motivational and strategic factors are added to what we know about elite composition. In the words of Dwaine Marvick:

> Relatively little attention has been given to such matters as the self-image of political leaders, the opinions they hold of one another, their awareness of the processes in which they participate, or their concern with the groups

77. *Ibid.*, p. 27.   78. *Ibid.*, p. 36.
79. *Ibid.*, pp. 155–157.   80. *Ibid.*, p. 26.
81. For a review of this literature see S. I. Keller, *Beyond the Ruling Class* (New York: Random House, 1963).

whose life circumstances are affected by their performance. Virtually nothing is known of the differences in commitment to the "rules of the game" which regardless of the route to power, may be found generally to characterize leaders of middle-class origins. . . . Still less is known of the differences in skill and ability introduced by the selective workings of political-recruitment ladders. Little is available that highlights the process by which political leaders become "professionalized" either in the sense of acquiring a distinctive kind of "know how" or in the sense of achieving a degree of psychological detachment from the merits of a public policy, seen in terms of the public and group interests.[82]

Thus, it is the exploration of elites' perceptions of their own and others' political behavior, and identification of various kinds of elite strategies and skills across a wide range of issues that will go far toward explaining society's commitment to various policy alternatives.

Harold Lasswell, in his concept of "developmental constructs," has stressed the idea that elites are transformed in periods of social change. The values they seek to maximize, their expectations about events which will affect their value positions and influence the groups with which they identify, and the political premises they draw from these varying perspectives are ultimately a function of the objective context in which they operate: a garrison state, a highly technical society, and so on.[83] Given an understanding of this context, Lasswell argues, one can evolve maps of elite expectations and thus predict what values elites will pursue at what costs.[84] In any dynamic analysis of elite behavior, this outside parameter of level of development must be stated.

Given such a contextual setting, Robert Dahl has outlined what are perhaps the most rigorous theoretical requirements for an elite model. He argues that to defend successfully the proposition that an elite does in fact authoritatively allocate values in society, one must identify "a controlling group, less than a majority in size, that is not a pure artifact of democratic rules; . . . a minority of individuals whose preferences regularly prevail in cases of differences in preferences on key political issues."[85] One must assume that the political effectiveness of an elite meeting these requirements is a function both of its potential for control and its potential for unity on policy alternatives.[86] The hypothesis of an existence of a ruling elite is strictly tested only if three conditions hold: the hypothetical ruling elite is a well-defined group; there is a fair sample of key political decisions in which preferences of the

82. D. Marvick, "Political Decision-Makers in Contrasting Milieus," in D. Marvick (ed.), *Political Decision-Makers* (New York: Free Press, 1961), p. 15.

83. See H. Lasswell, "Agenda for the Study of Political Elites," *ibid.*, pp. 264–287.

84. *Ibid.*, p. 278.

85. R. Dahl, "Critique of the Ruling Elite Model," *APSR*, **LII**, No. 2 (June 1958), p. 464.

86. *Ibid.*, p. 465.

hypothetical ruling elite prevail against those of other groups; and, in such cases elite preferences regularly prevail. The burden of such proof lies with those who assert that such an elite group exists.

We cannot digress into a discussion of the methodological problems of community power analysis. Suffice it to say that in both local community studies such as Floyd Hunter's *Community Power Structure*, and national community studies such as C. Wright Mills' *The Power Elite*, the assertion that an elite power structure exists is not proved in Dahl's terms. Two major assumptions are unwarranted: that elites could be identified solely by associational role or socio-economic status, and that these elites could exert power over a variety of policy issues. What is necessary to test such assumptions is an exploration of the *actual behavior of potential elite members* (whom we know to be individuals of certain socio-economic status and occupants of certain social roles) *within a given policy-making process, across a variety of policy issues.*

Several recent analyses of elite behavior on different political issues offer useful hypotheses for exploring the role of elites in policy formulation. These findings and hypotheses, it will become apparent, traverse several of the pitfalls noted earlier in decision-making and group explanations of the policy-making process. They place primary emphasis on the *individual*: his background and personality structure, his strategies of behavior, and his social role. Moreover, in moving between official and nonofficial individuals, and in concentrating on how these worlds communicate with and activate each other, these studies present a dynamic view of policy formation in which informational and communication inputs are major factors.

In the most general sense, the elite "subculture consists of whatever shared norms, expectations and interpretations leaders employ as a basis for responding to each other."[87] This leadership is founded on a "functional interdependence between its public and private segments,"[88] and on any given issue consists of governmental leaders and private opinion makers whose roles foster their participation in forming policy about that particular issue. The term *opinion makers*, proposed by Rosenau, means those individuals who have access to impersonal channels of communication, a prerequisite for wielding influence. To this extent, a potential pool of elite individuals is identified functionally. However, it must be added that very many American citizens *could* have access to impersonal communications— that is to say, they could write letters to Congressmen, to newspapers, to leaders of organizations, and so forth.

Thus, stating that elite participation in a given policy decision consists of governmental leaders and involved private decision makers who have access

87. See J. N. Rosenau, *National Leadership and Foreign Policy* (Princeton: Princeton University Press, 1963), p. 35.
88. *Ibid.*, p. 8.

to impersonal communications channels tells us little until we define the elite behaviorally. We assume that leadership behavior on an issue will emerge from those occupants of social roles who perceive some self-interest in the resolution of the issue. Bauer, Pool, and Dexter, and Rosenau have substantiated this relationship between amount of communications activity undertaken by members of the elite, and the kind of self-interest they perceive in foreign trade and foreign aid policies, respectively. This relationship can be tested on other policy issues, as can its corollary: that as an individual, through acquisition of new information, increasingly recognizes that his self-interest is involved in an issue, he will increase his political activity on behalf of the given issue.

The distribution of influence in society is skewed in favor of an elite highly involved in the political subculture, comparatively more active, calculating, rational, informed, and communicative than other segments of the population, and motivated to action through perceived self-interest. These facts in themselves, however, do not explain how influence will be distributed.[89] In the first place, political leaders are constrained by the necessity to maintain political support; thus to a certain degree they make policy choices which they perceive will win them support. An election, in other words is a great indirect source of influence on policy. Yet leaders "do not merely respond to believed preferences of constituents; they also shape them."[90] Thus, the leaders' differing attitudes toward and power over various issue areas are crucial variables in elite policy-making behavior.

Bauer, Pool, and Dexter, Dahl, and Rosenau all substantiate the view that various leaders with different combinations of political resources exert differential amounts of power in different issues.[91] Leadership is specialized among various sectors of public policy; in Dahl's study of policy making in New Haven, for example, only three political leaders exerted direct influence in more than one issue area, and two of these were mayors of the city. Rosenau found that only a few leaders expressed opinions about several issues; most opinion makers in his sample were specialists who limited themselves to matters of their own functional expertise.

Several critics of this theory of pluralistic elite structure have argued that elites may be united in the areas of "non-decision making," that is, the elite as an entity may dominate the organizational "mobilization of bias" so that certain latent issues are never considered.[92] However, the discovery of

89. See R. A. Dahl, *Who Governs?* (New Haven: Yale University Press, 1961), pp. 90–102; see also P. Bachrach, "Elite Consensus and Democracy," *The Journal of Politics* 24 (1962), pp. 439–452.

90. Dahl, *ibid.*, p. 164.

91. *Ibid.*, p. 228. See also *infra*, Chapter I, section II.

92. See Bachrach and Baratz, "Decisions and Non-Decisions," *op. cit.*, and J. L. Walker, "A Critique of the Elite Theory of Democracy," *APSR*, LX, No. 2 (June 1966), pp. 285–295.

pluralism in elite decision making, that is, the finding that different members of the elite subculture are activated by different issues does, at least, apply to positive policy decisions in which political elites are active.

That the elite subculture is pluralistic across issue areas is best explained by the distribution of political resources throughout the elite groups.[93] All citizens do not have an equal share of resources; on the other hand, resources are fragmented among potential elite members. Those who have access to one major resource, such as money, often do not have access to others. There are many kinds of political resources, such as money, prestige, access to media, skills, and so on, which are available to different citizens according to their functional specialities. No one type of resource dominates all others in all or even in most key decisions; with some exceptions, a resource is influential only in some issue areas. Finally, virtually no fairly large group completely lacks some resources with which to influence behavior.[94]

These propositions help explain the phenomenon of specialized elite activity over issue areas and bring out a crucial distinction often overlooked in elite studies: the difference between actual and potential influence. Even though a given elite individual may have access to considerable political resources, and thus be potentially influential, there are other variables that may affect the amount of actual influence he exerts. He is presented with differing alternative opportunities for using his resources in different issue areas. He may differentially estimate the value of a successful effort. Finally, he may, over his life cycle and over the course of political events, expend or amass resources at different rates.[95] These factors all serve as constraints on his ability to influence events. It is, therefore, likely that in order to maximize his scarce resources he will specialize in an issue area relevant to his own self-interest and reflecting his specialized function.

Thus we have seen that the mobilization of a given elite individual on a given issue is a function of several factors: his functional role, his perceived self-interest, his amount and kind of political resources, and his willingness to invest these resources in a given phase of political activity. All four factors are subject to manipulation; indeed, information about a policy maker's role, self-interests, political resources and environmental pressures may be crucial if changes in policy are to be effected. Again, we return to the main findings of these sections on the individual in the policy-making process. We must define behavior in terms of a policy maker's perceptions of political goals made under conditions of little information, pre-occupation, and personal motivation.[96]

93. Dahl, *op. cit.*, Chapter 19.
94. *Ibid.*, p. 228.
95. *Ibid.*, pp. 273–274.
96. See Bauer, Pool, and Dexter, *op. cit.*, p. 485.

Policy Making in a
Political System

The second major purpose of this chapter is to elucidate policy making as a characteristic process of a given political system. We shall deal, therefore, with several concepts common to the social sciences which stress the regular interaction of a number of variables. Inasmuch as these concepts are so inter-related, we shall not divide the discussion into discrete sections. After re-viewing the concept of a *system*, and in particular, a *political system*, we shall discuss *consensus* as a necessary condition of any political system. We shall further analyze consensus formation and maintenance in terms of the *role structures* and *rules of the game* characterizing the political system. In addition, we shall assert that the operative role structures and rules of the game in a given political system serve most generally as the policy-making process within that political system. Finally, we shall briefly discuss two crucial activities of any policy-making process: the *allocation of priorities* and the reception and handling of *feedback* concerning the consequences of policy acts. These two functions were selected as representing two of the most generalized mechanisms by which the policy-making process, and the indi-viduals comprising it, interact with the environment in the larger social system.

A *system* is said to exist when certain properties or their interrelationships vary interdependently and vary within definable limits.[97] Influences within a system counteract each other in characteristic forms of interdependence; when they cease to do so, the system no longer exists. Thus, the justification for asserting that a system exists depends on evidence of interdependent influences, which are brought into action by various stimuli.[98]

Any system, according to Parsonian action theory, is characterized by action, or behavior, that is oriented toward specific goals. Collective action is organized around relationships among several actors, creating a social sys-tem with shared value orientations. Since these relations are not random, they consist of a network of roles. Two conditions must be fulfilled in order for the system to remain stable: the actors must in some degree remain com-mitted to their shared value orientations, and their role-playing activity must be in sufficient conformity with the norms of interaction so that action is possible within the framework of the system.[99] Thus, value orientations, specific goals, and regularized patterns of role playing are all functional to a system; they are also analytic variables that must be identified in order to understand the functioning of a system.

97. See T. M. Newcomb, "Communicative Behavior," in Roland Young (ed.), *op. cit.*

98. *Ibid.*

99. T. Parsons, "Some Highlights of the General Theory of Action," in Roland Young (ed.), *ibid.*, p. 286.

The *political system*, a subsystem of the social system, consists of all actions related to making the authoritative allocation of values for society.[100] It is the social subsystem peculiarly responsible for goal attainment in the society as a whole.[101] As David Easton has outlined, the *inputs* into the political system from the environment consist of *demands* for scarce resources, and popular *support* both for the political system's right to make decisions and for specific decisions previously demanded.[102]

Demands may arise externally, elsewhere in the social system, as major issues of conflict which members of the political system construe as important. Or they may arise internally in the political system, through alteration of the political relationships of members. *Support* provides the political system with the resources for conflict resolution. Conversely, the political system can generate further support, either through providing solutions that meet demands generated in the social system, or through politicizing nonpolitical groups within the social system into the norms and rules of the political system. Thus, inputs provide dynamism in terms of information and energy for the political system.

The *outputs* of the political system are the *decisions* and *actions* of the authoritative political system which to some extent satisfy the demands of the social system. It is the conversion of inputs, through the application of resources within the system, into outputs that approximates a specific act of policy making.[103] Having produced outputs, the authoritative policy makers can expect the members of the social system at large to respond to them. Information concerning this response is then communicated to the authorities who in turn may respond with further policy outputs. It is this continuing, never-ending flow of policy, dependent upon feedback, between the authoritative political system and the society which approximates the policy-making process.[104]

This systematic view of the policy-making process identifies the peculiarly "political" aspects of the social system: the structures and processes which generate and allocate power. The specific relationships involved are the institutional patterns and roles which are recognized by the social system as responsible for goal attainment in that society. The support given the government by the society legitimates its exercise of responsibility; conversely, the government is enabled to act with real power in order to win further support.

100. See D. Easton, "An Approach to the Analysis of Political Systems," *World Politics* (Winter 1956); see also D. Easton, *A Systems Analysis of Political Life* (New York: John Wiley, 1965), Chapters 1 and 2.

101. T. Parsons, *op. cit.*, p. 298.

102. The following discussion follows the line of argument in D. Easton, *op. cit.*, and T. Parsons, "Power, Party, and System" in S. S. Ulmer (ed.), *Introductory Readings in Political Behavior* (Chicago: Rand, McNally, 1961).

103. See Easton, *A Systems Analysis of Political Life, op. cit.*, pp. 31, 349.

104. *Ibid.*, pp. 28–29.

Within the system, conflicts are resolved on three levels: through norms shared by the political community; through established rules of the game by which the community regularly settles disputes; and, through the government's negotiation of a specific controversial issue. On a generalized level, both support and conflict resolution reflect political consensus. On a specific level, support and conflict resolution express an acceptance both of the bargaining process involved in policy formulation and of its outputs.

In diagrammatic form, the relationship between the social system, or the public, and the political system, or the polity which authoritatively allocates values, can be seen in this way:

POLITY   PUBLIC

<---- Generalized Support
       Effective Leadership ---->
<---- Advocacy of Policies
       Binding Decisions ---->

These boundary interchanges depict the set of processes by which power is allocated, major policies agreed upon, and public attitudes toward them influenced and brought to bear.[105]

It is within this functional context of the political system that we shall view the process of policy making. We shall discard out of hand four theoretical formulations of the policy-making process: decision-making theory, group theory, elite theory, and institutionalism. As we have seen in the first section, decision-making theory is an inefficient way of organizing the complex of variables which impinge on the policy-making process. Group theory is a form of "reductionism" which does not even adequately explain the functioning of individuals in the political system; it cannot, therefore, explain the interactive processes that form the system. Elite theory, while isolating important analytic variables such as the roles, perceptions, and decision-making patterns of elite individuals, must be tied to dynamic, process variables in order to gain explanatory power. Elite theorists such as Floyd Hunter and C. Wright Mills who assert that elite behavior actually determines the outputs of the policy-making process do not, in our estimation, prove their case. Finally, institutional and legal descriptions of the policy-making process were found wanting by early twentieth-century political scientists, notably Lord Bryce and Arthur Bentley. Few political scientists today would consider a description of the constitutional and institutional prescriptions for policy making an adequate explanation of that process.

We do not imply that decision-making processes, political groups, elites, and institutional frameworks are insignificant factors in politics. On the contrary, we consider them important variables, necessary in any systematic formulation of the policy-making process, but not sufficiently powerful as

105. T. Parsons, "Power, Party and System," *op. cit.*, p. 130.

organizing principles or theoretical constructs to provide a model of the policy-making process.

Instead, we choose to view the policy-making process as the process of transformation which turns political inputs into political outputs.[106] This transformation presupposes a degree of political consensus: in Parsonian terms, a shared value orientation which governs goal-oriented action in any social system. As we have seen, such consensus is a source of support for the legitimacy of the political system; it enables the authoritative individuals in the system to resolve conflicts and exercise power in the allocation of resources.

Within this consensus, individual actors with various perceptions of their self-interest and external environment, operate in fairly specialized roles according to the accepted rules of the political game. Both the style of the role playing and the degree of adherence to the rules vary with the perceptions of the individuals operating within them. However, the roles and the rules do limit the range of behaviors of those individuals, and by so doing, maintain stability in the political system. Thus we focus on role structures and the rules of the game as the major determinants of the policy-making process. These roles and rules are manifestations of the political consensus within society and thereby functional to the political subsystem of the social system. They also act as limits on varying perceptions, goal-oriented behaviors, and strategies of individuals who act in the political system.

Robert Dahl has emphasized the relationship between the role structures and rules of the game operative in the political system, on the one hand, and consensus formation and consensus maintenance, on the other, in his finding that the elite minority, which comprises the political stratum, is more sensitive and committed to the norms of the political system than the public at large.[107] This commitment is not sufficient, however, to explain the persistence of consensus. Consensus, in Dahl's mind, is a "recurring process of interaction" among members of the political stratum and the apolitical population. The process conforms to the following assumptions and pattern:

1. Over time, the population at large believes in the democratic creed.

2. Most Americans believe the American political system is consistent with that creed.

3. Socialization engrains this belief in the identity between the democratic creed and the American political system.

4. Since the creed is vague, citizens frequently disagree on its derivative "rules of the game" and specific policy applications.

106. See Easton, *A Systems Analysis of Political Life, op. cit.*; see also R. C. Wood, "The Contributions of Political Science to Urban Form," in W. Z. Hirsch (ed.), *Urban Life and Form* (New York: Holt & Company, 1963).

107. This enumerated argument follows R. Dahl, *op. cit.*, pp. 315–324; see also J. S. Coleman, *Community Conflict*, (New York: Free Press, 1957) for an analogous analysis of conflict generation and resolution.

5. The political stratum is more familiar with and committed to the democratic creed than the rest of the population and, as such, collectively serve as democratic "legitimists."

6. The political stratum has greater access to political resources, and greater political skill than the rest of the population, and hence can usually defend the norms of the democratic creed against critics.

7. When disagreements over application of the prevailing norms occur within the political stratum, settlement tends to emerge through negotiations among that stratum.

8. The political stratum is strongly committed to rules and procedures which specify certain roles and prescribe means to settle disputes.

9. Ordinarily, then, it is not difficult for a stable system of rights and privileges to exist that, at least in important details, does not have widespread public support and occasionally even lacks majority approval. As long as the matter is not a salient public issue—and whether it is or not depends partly on how the political stratum handles it—the question is substantially determined within the political stratum itself. When disagreements arise, these are adjudicated by officials who share the beliefs of the political stratum rather than those of the populace; and even when these officials adopt positions that do not command the undivided support of the political stratum, members of the political stratum, and particularly the professionals, tend to accept a decision as binding until and unless it can be changed through the accepted procedures. This is the essence of their code of democratic legitimism.[108]

10. If a significant segment of the political stratum desires policies, or changes in the rules of the game, which it doubts can be effected through accepted procedures internal to the political stratum, it may shift strategies and attempt to arouse public support for its proposals. In this fashion it hopes to utilize popular support in order to force other members of the elite to accept its position. In this case, the other members of the elite might make counterappeals to the public. Both sets of appeals will be couched in terms of the democratic creed and will tend to become increasingly emotional and irrational.

11. Ordinary citizens must then react: by withdrawing into apathy; deciding on the basis of partisan loyalty; or looking for cues from organizations or acquaintances.

12. The appeal to the populace may terminate in various ways: the issue can decline in public interest or a compromise can be effected.

Thus, the ordinary citizen's attitudes are relevant to the policy-making process only when the political stratum intensively appeals to them. "Even then, the actual outcome of the appeal does not necessarily reflect majority attitudes. . . . These are not always known; they are guessed at in a variety of

108. R. Dahl, *ibid.*, p. 321.

inaccurate ways; and they have to be filtered through the tighter mesh of the political stratum . . . before they can become public policy."[109]

Yet Dahl stresses that elite consensus on the democratic creed supports a democratic system in three important ways. First, the elite tends to operate within the creed. Second, the creed makes occasional appeals to the public virtually inevitable, since appeals are legitimated by it. Third, the creed limits the character and course of an appeal, since the creed itself requires that the appeal be couched in terms of the creed and permits a dispute which cannot be resolved by the political stratum to be handled in a manner sufficiently orderly so as not to disrupt the system.[110] Thus, while the elite normally exerts great influence and uses its disproportionate amount of political resources to gain its ends, there are enough "slack" resources among potential counterelites and the public at large to limit the extent of the elite's influence.[111] This factor operates to maintain the value orientations of the polity—the political consensus.

Thus the roles which individuals fill in the political system and the rules by which they play the political game are ultimately determined by the imperatives of the political consensus. No policy decision can be so final that it absolutely forecloses the possibility of counteraction by some major groupings in opposition to it. Political solutions, therefore, are provisional actions that permit debate to continue, although the framework adopted may definitely favor one or another side. This provisional bias, however, reflects another manifestation of political consensus: that all parties to debate want some action to be taken.[112] Within this broad limit of political consensus, policy making occurs.

In this fashion, the policy-making process can be explored in terms of a transactional model "which views all the actors in the situation as exerting continuous influence on each other."[113] In addition, it can be said that the role structures and rules of the game comprise the policy-making process, since it is through them that the "actors in the situation [exert] continuous influence on each other." As intervening factors between the individual political actor and the generalized norms of the political system, these roles and rules have certain distinctive attributes, and comprise an important part of the policy maker's environment. One must examine, therefore, all major arenas or subsystems of the political system dealing with different segments of the allocative process: interest groups, skill groups, Congress, the Executive and its administrative subdivisions, and so on, in order to identify their

109. *Ibid.*, p. 324.   110. *Ibid.*, p. 324–325

111. It is in this sense that the possibility of a social movement arising outside the current elite consensus is allowed for in Dahl's system. See J. L. Walker, *op. cit.*, and R. Dahl, "Further Reflections on 'The Elitist Theory of Democracy'," *APSR*, **LX,** No. 2 (June 1966), pp. 285–305.

112. Bauer, Pool, and Dexter, *op. cit.*, pp. 36, 79.

113. *Ibid.*, p. 456.

unique role structures and operating rules. As we have seen in the first section of this chapter, individuals vary in terms of attitudes, values, cognition, role expectations and role behavior. Within any given political arena, however, the variations may be patterned to conform to the particular role structure and rules of that subsystem.[114]

Role structures and rules of the game do not, however, vary only among different political subsystems. A major finding of several recent policy studies is that role playing and rules of the game vary across policy issues as well. For example, in analyzing Congress, Bauer, Pool, and Dexter point out that some issues are utterly crucial for their advocates while creating no cross-pressure for other Congressmen; post office raises, patronage, highway contracts, and so on, will thus be supported by Congressmen so as to build up good will.[115] (Logrolling, in fact, reflects quite staunch adherence to the rules of the game in Congress.) On other issues in which local interests are perceived by Congressmen as antagonistic to national interests, cross-pressures and hence divisiveness will increase. Similarly, Rosenau argues that issues lie on a continuum that runs from issues which permit the development of consensus to those which divide the political elite and the public. Issues such as foreign aid, for example, require tangible sacrifice for intangible objectives and thus lie at the divisive end.[116]

Perhaps the most sophisticated attempt to discriminate among the roles and rules relevant to different policy issues has been that of Theodore Lowi.[117] He argues that since individuals' interrelationships are a function of their expectations, and that in politics, expectations are determined by governmental outputs, political relationships will therefore be determined by the type of policy issue at stake. He goes on to assert that for every distinctive type of policy, there will be distinctive kinds of political interrelationships, with characteristic role structures, elite groups, and rules of interaction. The three classes of policy which he outlines—distributive policies, regulatory policies, and redistributive policies—have corresponding policy-making processes closely conforming to the models of logrolling or consensual politics; political bargaining among interest groups; and conflicts between elites

---

114. It is now possible to specify with some degree of accuracy the role structures and ongoing rules of the game in various political subsystems on certain policy issues. This is not the place to give even a brief review of these "many partial theories of political allocation," as Easton terms them. (See Easton, *A Systems Analysis of Political Life, op. cit.*, p. 474.) For an exemplary discussion of the role structures and ongoing rules of certain political subsystems, notably Congress and various interest groups involved in American foreign trade policy, see Bauer, Pool, and Dexter, *American Business and Public Policy, op. cit.*

115. Bauer, Pool, and Dexter, *op. cit.*, p. 433.

116. Rosenau, *op. cit.*, p. 359.

117. T. J. Lowi, "American Business, Public Policy, Case-Studies, and Political Theory," *World Politics*, XVI, No. 4 (July 1964), pp. 677–715.

and counterelites, respectively. These three classes also lie on a consensus/ divisive continuum.

Regardless of the political subsystem or the policy issue involved, however, each act of policy making involves the allocation of policy priorities and the handling of feedback concerning various policy outputs. On an individual level, it is through such general functions as these that participants in the policy-making process interact with each other and elements within the larger political and social systems. It is also through these two functions that the policy-making process, on a systematic level, performs the authoritative allocation of values for the social system at large.

The fate of any given policy issue is largely determined by its level of priority in the minds of individuals who will influence its outcome. "Where a given issue stands in priority affects not only the fight for resources but also the whole manner of its handling".[118] The emergence of a political issue in the transactional flow of mutual influence offers opportunities for various individuals to build political resources. Some may, for example, support issues which they perceive to be of low priority in order to win support for their higher priority issues. Moreover, the pressures of time, scarce resources, and the need to maintain effective social relationships within the political system are such that an individual can choose to push only a very few issues of highest priority to him. Thus, one can predict an individual's behavior on a given issue only with reference to the entire map of competing issues with which he is dealing, and with due recognition that he will act in sufficiently predictable manners so that others on whom he must depend will continue to maintain mutually supportive relations with him.[119] Thus, in addition to the goals of individual policy makers, continuing expectations about role-playing behavior and adherence to the rules of the ongoing political game on the part of all involved influentials will largely determine the priority of a given policy issue.[120]

The dependence of priority allocation upon the systematic attributes of the policy-making process is well illustrated by the controversy over the introduction of program budgeting into the operating procedures of administrative agencies in the United States Government. The argument chiefly revolves around the question of whether or not the process of budget making—which is indistinguishable, by assumption, from policy making since it concerns in concrete terms the authoritative allocation of resources to implement values—can be "rational" in the sense that the new techniques of program budgeting and systems analysis suggest.

In order to elucidate this controversy, it is necessary to briefly review the

118. Bauer, Pool, and Dexter, *op. cit.*, p. 480.
119. *Ibid.*, pp. 480–481; see also, Easton, *A Systems Analysis of Political Life*, *op. cit.*, pp. 444, 448.
120. Rosenau, *op. cit.*, p. 33.

component elements and objectives of program budgeting.[121] First, program budgeting is composed of the following three elements: structural considerations, analytical process considerations, and information system considerations.

The *structural* aspects of program budgeting are concerned with establishing a set of categories oriented primarily toward "end-product" or "end-objective" activities that are meaningful from a long-range-planning point of view. . . .

Analytical process considerations pertain to various study activities conducted as an integral part of the program budgeting process. The primary objective of this type of analytical effort is to systematically examine alternative courses of action in terms of utility and cost, with a view to clarifying the relevant choices (and their implications) open to the decision-makers in a certain problem area.

Information system considerations are aimed at support of the first two items. There are several senses in which this is important, the primary ones being (1) progress reporting and control and (2) providing data and information to serve as a basis for the analytical process—especially to facilitate the development of estimating relationships that will permit making estimates of benefits and costs of alternative future courses of action.[122]

Second, the objective of program budgeting is to identify and choose the ultimate goals of the federal government through the measurement of the costs and benefits of concurrent programs which may fulfill these goals. The process of budgeting involves the planning, comparison, and coordination of government programs in such a way that, assuming scarce resources and a highly uncertain future, the goals of the government may be implemented most efficiently.[123] These goals represent the political, philosophical, and administrative assumptions of the government. Arthur Smithies has described this process of maximizing desirable goals efficiently as consisting of the following five steps:

1. Appraisals and comparisons of various government activities in terms of their contributions to national objectives.

2. Determination of how given objectives can be attained with minimum expenditure of resources.

3. Projection of government activities over an adequate time horizon.

4. Comparison of the relative contribution of private and public activities to national objectives.

121. See D. Novick (ed.), *Program Budgeting: Program Analysis and the Federal Budget* (Cambridge, Mass.: Harvard University Press, 1965), *passim*.

122. G. H. Fisher, "The Role of Cost-Utility Analysis in Program Budgeting," in *ibid.*, p. 61.

123. See A. Smithies, "Conceptual Framework for the Program Budget," in *ibid.*, pp. 18, 26.

5. Revisions of objectives, programs and budgets in the light of experience and changing circumstances.[124]

Several difficulties must necessarily arise in the course of this process. Costs may be fairly effectively measured, since they can be reduced to a shared dollar metric, although problems associated with such calculations should not be underestimated. Yet benefits are infinitely more difficult to measure than costs. To a greater or lesser degree, benefits can be measured only on the basis of the policy maker's personal judgment and intuition, since there is currently no way to solve the problem of interpersonal comparison of utilities, and hence no agreed-upon means of evaluating the merits of different programs for different people with differing kinds and intensities of preference, except through the policy-making process.[125] In addition, both costs and benefits must be extrapolated into an uncertain future to be useful. Finally, once programs are articulated in terms of long-range costs and benefits, it is necessary, in a democratic system, to win a consensus among policy makers that these programs are advisable and useful.

In contrast to formal program budgeting, the budget-making and appropriations process currently operative in the American political system circumvents most of these difficulties. First, it treats budgets as if they were non-programmatic, that is, as "marginal monetary adjustments to existing programs so that the question of the ultimate desirability of most programs arises only once in a while."[126] The existing level of expenditures is largely taken for granted, and usually only incremental changes are considered. In Wildavsky's view, this situation is caused by the need of the policy-making process for consensus. He argues that "the mitigation of conflict is a widely shared value in our society, and [that] . . . program budgeting is likely to affect that value" by focusing on the inevitably controversial programmatic content of budgetary choices.[127] Furthermore, Wildavsky claims that the process of incremental change is as rational as program budgeting, since various participants, exercising their own partial views of the policy-making process, will ultimately take into account more consequences of a given program than a comprehensive review of its costs and benefits.[128] In Wildavsky's words, "a partial adversary system in which the various interests compete for control of policy (under agreed-upon rules) seems more likely to result in reasonable decisions—that is, decisions that take account of the multiplicity of values involved—than one in which the best policy is assumed

124. *Ibid.*, pp. 26–27.

125. See *ibid.*, p. 48; see also Davis, Dempster, and Wildavsky, "A Theory of the Budgetary Process," *APSR*, **LX**, No. 3 (September 1966), p. 529.

126. Wildavsky, *op. cit.*, p. 60.

127. *Ibid.*, p. 138. For extended discussion, see *ibid.*, pp. 135–138.

128. *Ibid.*, p. 156; see also C. E. Lindblom, "The Science of 'Muddling Through'," *Public Administration Review*, **19** (Spring 1959), pp. 79–88.

to be discoverable by a well-intentioned search for the public interest for all by everyone."[129]

In summary, this incremental interpretation of the budgetary process and its resultant allocation of priorities reflect the findings of Braybrooke and Lindblom and of Simon discussed earlier. In the solution of complex problems, policy makers necessarily develop *ad hoc* decision rules, or aids to calculation, in order to find solutions that will win the widest possible consensus while still partially satisfying the participants' self-interest.[130]

A policy-making function closely related to this process of priority allocation is the handling of feedback concerning various policy outputs. Raymond Bauer, in a provocative argument, has noted that the dichotomy between planning and not planning has virtually disappeared, largely because of the introduction of a "dynamic model of guidance that has come explicitly or implicitly from modern technology," notably, feedback.[131] Cybernetics, Bauer asserts, is based on the assumption that error is inherent in all natural, physical, and social systems.

> One can set goals and make plans but the cybernetic model demands an active information system with sensors to determine the consequences of actions. In addition, it demands provision for feeding this information back to decision centers and readiness to change one's behavior in response to signals of errors being committed. Thus a sophisticated approach to planning shares some of the characteristic features of "muddling through," which has long been regarded as the extreme of not planning.[132]

Bauer particularly stresses that this doctrine of "muddling through," or, in our terms, incremental policy making

> is based on elaborate concern for second-order consequences of actions. It assumes that social systems and processes are very complex phenomena, and that it is impossible to determine in advance exactly what results will be created by one's actions or what difficulties will be encountered. However, the doctrine of muddling through has a contemporary look in its sensitivity to feedback from the environment, and its disposition to change tactics when the data fed back suggest that the results produced differ from those intended.[133]

The feedback process involves four phases, as Easton has emphasized: outputs as stimuli, the feedback response, the information feedback about the response, and the output reaction to the feedback response.[134]

129. Wildavsky, *ibid.*, p. 167.

130. See Davis, Dempster, and Wildavsky, *op. cit.*, p. 543.

131. R. Bauer, "Detection and Anticipation of Impact: The Nature of the Task," in R. Bauer (ed.), *Social Indicators* (Cambridge, Mass.: M. I. T. Press, 1966), p. 8.

132. *Ibid.*, p. 8.   133. *Ibid.*, p. 7; see also, Lindblom, *op. cit.*

134. Easton, *A Systems Analysis of Political Life, op. cit.*, p. 381.

If we begin with the outputs and their outcomes, we shall find that these provide the stimuli for the members of the system, the behaving units whom they may affect or may be perceived to affect. . . . These members may then respond to the stimuli by modifying their demands and varying their support for one or more of the basic political objects. We shall discover that it is here that outputs and inputs of both demands and support become dynamically interrelated. In continuation of the feedback flow, directly or indirectly the members communicate their sentiments to the authorities, another set of behaving units who were initially responsible for the outputs or who choose to do something further about these outputs. Finally, these authorities may then react to the response by follow-up outputs and this reaction may be considered the start of another cycle in the flow of effects and information along the systematic feedback loop.[135]

Thus the political system must be equipped with facilities for providing policy makers with information about the state of the political and social systems, and the impact upon them of any policy action taken.[136]

A specific illustration of the operation of this systemic feedback loop is the operation of the budgetary process. The feedback of data concerning the impact of programs, including special events, crises or technological developments that may influence programs, are quickly reflected "in the formal feedback mechanisms—the actions of the departments, the Bureau of the Budget and [the] Congress—to which they are directed."[137] The utilization of such feedback by the policy makers makes the policy process "highly interrelated, cumulative, and consistent": in short, incremental in the same way as does the process by which priorities are allocated.[138]

The view of the policy-making process as a succession of strategies of disjointed incrementalism, seems to fail to account for new policy departures: dramatic breaks with the past such as the atomic bomb or the space program. However, such events can be treated as random disturbances in the otherwise stable and incremental policy-making process, only momentarily producing a fluctuation in the old patterns of policy making which quickly reassert themselves.

135. *Ibid.*, pp. 380–381.
136. See *ibid.*, Chapter 23, for a general discussion of this problem.
137. David, Dempster, and Wildavsky, *op. cit.*, p. 531.
138. See Easton, *A Systems Analysis of Political Life, op. cit.*, p. 369.

Chapter 5

KENNETH J. GERGEN

*A*ssessing the Leverage Points in the Process of Policy Formation

Introduction to the
Problem

Tracing the process of public policy formation in a social system may often be an arduous task. The complex web of social interaction from which policy emanates, has long remained recalcitrant to analysis in depth. One major fact facilitating investigation in this area is that all members of a society are not equally implicated in the decision-making process. The typical analyst has successfully been able to focus on a delimited number of persons whose roles in the process are central. However, the success of such an approach fully depends on one's capacity to identify this core group of persons. It is toward the development of an adequate methodology for identifying such persons that this chapter is directed.

In exploring the question of methodology a number of traditional areas of study become relevant. The host of studies dealing with the notion of power in society is of course quite pertinent. A thorough treatment of methodology should ideally take into account the conceptual subtleties found in the more theoretical treatments of the subject (for example, Merriman, 1934; Russell, 1938; Lasswell and Kaplan, 1961; Schermerhorn, 1961) as well as the lessons to be learned from the many empirical ventures in the area (such as Hunter, 1953; Schulze and Blumberg, 1957; Miller, 1958; Dahl, 1961). Closely related and equally important are examinations of public leadership (Lowe and McCormick, 1957; Wilson, 1960; Bell, Hill, and Wright, 1961) and social or political influence (Lazarsfeld, Berelson, and Gaudet, 1944; Banfield, 1961; Patchen, 1963). Indeed, an analysis of methodology involved with the recognition of participants in public policy formation could be couched in the terminology of any of these respective areas. Fruitful distinctions have also been made between such concepts as power and influence (cf. Parsons, 1963). However, to avoid the surplus meanings often attached to such terms as "power" and "influence," and to facilitate a more general analysis of methodology, this chapter will utilize the notion of *leverage points*.

The implications of the term *leverage point* can be understood by considering any social system constituted by a set of interacting subunits. If the social system is taken to be an entire society, the subunits at one level might be the institutions or organizations within the society. At a more microlevel the individual members of the society might be the focal subunits. The present paper will avoid commitment to any one system level; in one instance the entire society may be considered and in another a single community may be the subject of interest. In other words, it is hoped that the analytic schema presented here will be sufficiently broad that it may have relevance regardless of the exact nature of the social system chosen for study. On the other hand, the analysis will assume in each case that the subunits of greatest importance are individual persons rather than organizations or institutions, and that a thorough understanding of public policy will ultimately depend on knowledge of individual participants.

The further assumption can be made that one major source of change in a social system is the entry of new information into the system. When new information becomes available it can further be assumed that modification of the system will depend to a large extent on the configuration of subunits. The modification of some subunits will be largely dependent on the state of other subunits with which they are functionally related, while other subunits may be less functionally dependent and thus more autonomous. On an empirical level, this might mean that in a patriarchal family the decision to buy a new car will depend primarily on the father, or that urban renewal might await the approval of the mayor of a city. To say that the modification of the system depends to a greater extent on the initial state of some subunits rather than others is to say that subunits vary in their degree of leverage in the system. Individual persons can thus be considered leverage points for the system as a whole, and the question of how these leverage points may be isolated for study is the central focus of this chapter.

The remainder of the chapter will be organized into two major sections. In the first a model will be developed that will attempt to spell out some of the important parameters of the problem. Using the model as a heuristic device, the second section will examine a number of the major methods used to identify those occupying primary positions of leverage.

A Three-Dimensional Model for the Identification of Leverage Points

As a methodological issue, the identification of influentials has been a lively one. Methods have been criticized variously for making spurious assumptions as to the nature of power structures, their lack of correlation with other measures of the same phenomenon, their instability over time, etc. Perhaps the most prevalent criticism used in this internecine conflict is that certain methods do not account for the many subtleties encountered in the social milieu. This criticism has taken various forms, from noting that one method mistakenly lumps together all forms of power or influence to pointing out that another does not do justice to the subrosa or latent power faction in society.

Any model designed as an abstract representation of reality must necessarily fail to account for all the nuances of real life. The present attempt, however, is to provide a schema that will specify at least a minimal set of parameters to be considered in assessing leverage points, while at the same time avoiding the major criticisms of oversimplification. The resultant model thus isolates several dimensions of leverage rather than concentrating on technical problems of mensuration. Specific methods of measurement will be the subject of the final section of the chapter.

To return to the discussion concerning societal subunits, the present model assumes that any individual in a society can be compared along three dimensions relevant to the concept of leverage. These dimensions are issue relevance, subphase resources, and personal efficacy. Explication of each of these separate dimensions follows.

ISSUE RELEVANCE. Persons vary greatly in their relationships to a given public issue, and different issues may impinge on a person in varying degrees (cf. Jennings, 1963, discussion of "issue involvement"; and Danzger, 1964, on "salience"). One can thus speak of the relevance of a given issue for a given person, and compare the relevance of a single issue for different people. It might be conjectured that issue relevance reflects the degree to which public policy on the issue can alter the customary behavior patterns of the individual. An issue will be relevant to an individual to the extent that for him it can potentially modify the *status quo*. For example, changes in urban mass transportation would be of less relevance to the farmer than to the urban department-store owner or commuter. In a similar manner, the issue would be of greater relevance to the governmental representative of the latter group than the former.

With respect to leverage, the further assumption is made that the greater the relevance of an issue to a person the stronger will be his attempt to exert leverage. This is to say that the greater the potential effect of a public policy on an individual's life, the more likely he is to be motivated in affecting the outcome of this policy. In a quasi-democratic society the degree of relevance should thus also bear a direct relationship with the amount of actual leverage. Given the freedom to vote, to state his position publicly, to communicate with his governmental representative, and the like, a person who is deeply affected by a public issue will have more to do with its ultimate disposition than one who is unaffected. For the public official this would mean that the greater the relevance of the issue to his constituents or to himself, the greater the resources he might muster in defense or support of it.

Figure 5-1 displays a graphic form of the three-dimensional model. As can be seen, the vertical dimension represents the variable of issue relevance. In terms of three-dimensional space, the greater the relevance of a given issue to a person, the closer to the top of the diagram he would be placed. It is important to note, however, that the issue-relevance dimension has been subdivided and each subsection represents a separate public issue. It follows from the preceding statement that separate issues may be varyingly relevant for a given individual and that relevance of one issue may be quite unrelated to relevance of another.

There is a second important reason for this latter modification of the model. One of the more controversial topics in the literature on power elites has to do with whether such influentials possess generalized or circumscribed power with regard to public issues. The earlier assumption (cf. Hunter, 1953) was that those belonging to the power elite in a given community influenced most public policy decisions for this community. Merton (1957) later advanced this issue by distinguishing between *polymorphic* and *monomorphic* spheres of influence. He found that local or provincial leaders in a community tended to have more generalized or polymorphic influence, while the cosmopolitans in the community tended only to influence specific issue outcomes. More recent inquiries have raised serious doubts about the initial assumptions (cf. Polsby, 1959; Wolfinger, 1960; Dahl, 1961), and have indicated that the more accurate assumption is that there are only a few influentials involved with any single issue and that for the most part their influence is relegated to a small cluster of related issues. Using different methods for identifying influentials, both Dahl (1960) and D'Antonio and Erickson (1962) have reported results that confirm the more recent and pluralistic view of American politics. The implication is that when assessing leverage points, the more precise and more accurate approach will differentiate among issues and their degree of relevance for specific individuals.

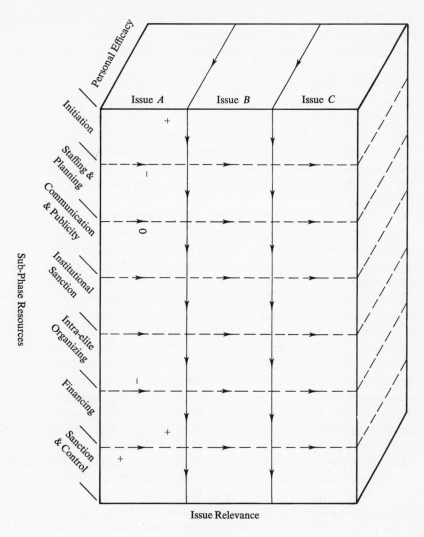

FIGURE 5-1

SUBPHASE RESOURCES. In addition to questioning the assumption of leverage across substantive issues, one might also raise doubts about leadership across time with regard to a single issue. The formation of public policy is seldom, if ever, a single-state process taking place at a single point in time. Between the inception of an idea and its ultimate implementation many events transpire. These events may be conceptualized as overlapping temporal stages, each of which may affect the final outcome of a given issue.

Within any stage it is possible to envision a set of resources that would give a person leverage in that stage (cf. Blau, 1964). These resources may be highly varied in nature. Some may accrue to an individual as a result of a particular public office that he holds; others may be in the form of financial holdings, ownership of mass media, and even the respect or admiration of others. At the outset it would seem quite unwise to assume that any single individual will possess a great number of resources at all stages, or in some instances, even more than one. In other words, for any given issue there may be several important leverage points depending on the number of stages. In Figure 5-1 each of these stages is represented by a subsection along the horizontal axis of the model. For each stage an individual could have a varying number of resources. The greater the resources possessed by a person at any stage, the further to the right of the subsection would he be represented in the diagram.

At this juncture, specification of the stages of public policy formation may be somewhat conjectural. However, an early formulation by an exceptionally well-qualified student of the area (Stouffer, 1958) provides an excellent point of departure. With the aid of Stouffer's analysis, the following stages can be distinguished:

Initiation. It is often difficult to determine the exact source of an idea that eventuates in public policy. However, given the existence of an idea, it does seem safe to say that there are some persons who occupy more optimal positions for initiation. In many communities, for example, the role of initiator may be institutional and thus delegated to public officeholders such as mayor, city manager, or city councilman. On the other hand, there may be noninstitutional positions, the occupants of which may initiate ideas with high probabilities of making an impact. For example, the industrial magnate, "resident expert" on a given topic, or newspaper editor may often function in this capacity.

As indicated by Figure 5-1, it is exceedingly important to take into account specific public issues when specifying the occupant of the initiator role. The position of industrial leader may be of little importance, for example, when considering the issue of public health. At the outset one might hypothesize that the public official may be able to initiate more effectively over a wider variety of issues than persons in noninstitutional positions of authority. This latter group may become effective only for specific areas in which they are considered to have expertise. Along these same lines, one might question the efficacy of some national policy-making groups in initiating policy on the local level. It could well be that the national policy stance may be perceived as irrelevant or even alien to the locale. The racial integration battle is a case in point.

It is also important to note that the role of initiator is considered independently of his capacity to present his ideas effectively. The capacity to "package" an idea should be considered an aspect of the person's personality or personal efficacy and will be discussed further on under a separate heading.

Staffing and planning. Although an idea may be effectively initiated, it may function as an empty "campaign promise" until specific plans have been laid out by qualified persons. For example, the staff that developed the specific details of President Johnson's actions to overcome poverty certainly played a crucial role in the ultimate acceptance of the idea. The leverage of such persons is often far greater than would meet the public eye. Such persons often have access to a far greater amount of relevant information than anyone else. Decisions under such circumstances often become arbitrary and it is difficult for anyone less familiar with the information to question them. In terms of the diagram, it would seem that staffing and planning are largely issue-specific.

Communication and publicity. Seldom considered by the majority of studies of power structure is the degree to which an individual has access to the general public. Although a plan may be well developed and effectively staged, in many instances subsequent action may be completely stifled if it is opposed by the general public. Persons controlling the mass media thus gain a considerable degree of leverage over issues of public policy. However, such leverage may by no means be confined to newspaper editors, television and radio commentators, and the like. Persons of high rank or station are often considered newsworthy in themselves and thus gain almost automatic access to the mass media.

Institutional sanction. Once a specific issue has been developed and publicized, its fate may largely depend on sanctions provided by existing social institutions. In most instances where far-reaching policies are being implemented, governmental bodies (whether local, state, or national) are in a position either to enhance or thwart such implementation. However, leverage in this area is hardly limited to formal governing bodies. Other organized institutions including businesses, unions, chambers of commerce, and many and varied interest groups may also be in a position to bring weight to bear on an issue. Although in most such organizations the amount of leverage might be roughly assessed by means of organizational diagrams or through knowledge of the hierarchy, such may not always be the case. In the United States Senate, for example, there are distinctions made between junior and senior senators, and the potentially enhanced leverage of the senior senators would not be indicated on any formal organizational chart. Also contributing to differential leverage among such persons would be matters of personal efficacy, charisma, ability to organize those around them, and other characteristics.

Intra-elite organizing. At one time the predominant image of community power structure was that of a single pyramid with a small, elite oligarchy at the top and the remainder of the community relegated to lower levels. More recent investigations have found numerous communities, particularly urban centers, in which the early conception is found to be lacking (cf. Scoble and Janowitz, 1960; Schulze, 1961; Pelligren and Coates, 1956). The more widespread form of power structure seems to be one in which there are a number of pyramid-like influence groups, the heads of which are not all public officials. Community decisions thus seem to be affected by the way in which coalitions are established among the leaders of the various influence groups.

With this latter conception in mind, it becomes important to consider the process of coalition formation itself. The person capable of bringing about agreements and compromise among the top influentials in various areas would have considerable leverage in most issues of public policy. In some instances this role may be a function of the individual's personality. However, independent of personality, there may be certain positions that would be more optimally suited for this function than others. Specifically it would seem that the greater number of relationships of functional reciprocity that a person has within this group, the more capable he will be of forming coalitions. The person who interacts with the majority of the key influentials in such a way that there are joint payoffs of considerable magnitude should be in an optimal position for coalition formation. For example, the industrialist who depends on, and is depended on by, financial leaders, tax officials, the chamber of commerce, and the mayor may be in a better position to effect solidarity among this group than any single other.

This discussion need not be confined to the community alone. In Congress, for example, the capacity to organize key figures in support of a bill may be a crucial function in the passage of legislation. The congressman who can coordinate various factions or interest groups can be said to have considerable leverage in that body.

Financing. Bringing almost any public policy into fruition requires financial resources. Possession or control of these resources thus gives an individual considerable leverage. For example, in a study of Battle Creek, Michigan, (cf. Smuckler and Belknap, 1956) it was found that the director of the city's major bank was involved with almost all major community decisions requiring fund raising. However, as Stouffer (1958) has pointed out, there may be cases in which the financial role may not so easily be designated. In many instances both public and private financing may be involved, and some of these sources may reside outside the community.

Sanction and control. Even though a policy decision may imply large-scale modification of the social system, whether the behavior of the populace will actually be altered by the decision is yet another matter. As an instance, the Supreme Court's 1954 ruling on civil rights has resulted in successful action in all of the phases discussed before. However, the control of public conduct remains an issue of the first magnitude. Until public behavior is actually affected, it is not proper to speak of public policy formation.

At a national level this function may reside in such positions as the presidency or attorney general, while on a local level it may be in the hands of various law enforcement officials. In terms of positive sanctions, however, public behavior may be more affected by the mass media and thus a double role in the process of policy formation may be indicated for persons possessing leverage in the area of communications and publicity.

Thus far, two dimensions of leverage have been considered: issue relevance and subphase resources. The third major dimension, that of personal efficacy, can now be added to the model.

Personal Efficacy

Both dimensions of issue relevance and subphase resources tacitly assume that individuals are substitutable across positions. If any two persons were highly involved in an issue and possessed an equal number of resources, the above formulation would imply equal degrees of leverage for both. However, common experience tells us that the efficacy of any two such individuals may be highly disparate. One may attract less public attention, communicate less effectively, or get along with others less well, and these factors may seriously hamper his influence in any situation. It would seem, then, that there may be a certain personality constellation or set of social capacities that may be highly correlated with a person's effective leverage.

Although such a personality dimension is seldom reflected directly in standard measures of power or influence, the literature on the personal characteristics of leaders is extensive. For example, Lasswell (1948) has speculated on the psychodynamics of persons in power. Empirical studies have found that such factors as intelligence (Cattell and Stice, 1953), self-confidence (Drake, 1944), sociability (Newcomb, 1943), height (Gowin, 1915), level of aspiration (Hunnwalt, Hamilton, and Morris, 1943) and dominance (Richardson and Hunnwalt, 1943) may all be related to leadership capacities. Mann's (1959) review of the literature concludes that leaders consistently tend to be better adjusted, more dominant, more extroverted, more masculine, less conservative, and more interpersonally sensitive than nonleaders. Studies of communicator characteristics most effective in the process of attitude change (cf. Hovland and Weiss, 1951; Tannenbaum, 1956) would also be relevant. Gibb (1954) has noted, however, that the majority of the above studies have failed to take into account the possibility that differing situations may demand different personalities for effective leadership. It is also apparent that there is great need for empirical research dealing with public leaders as opposed to leaders of small groups or formal organizations.

Even though such studies as those cited would allow one to speculate meaningfully about the personal characteristics related to degree of leverage, there is certainly room for further research in this area. Suffice it to say at this point that research into a set of "crucial" characteristics could be extremely useful in the final development of a sensitive measure of leverage.

To summarize, the discussion thus far has attempted to develop a model to represent the most significant aspects of leverage in public decision making.

The model suggests that any individual can be placed in at least one point in three-dimensional space with regard to leverage. This point would indicate the degree of leverage that could be attributed to the person with respect to a single issue. (In graphic terms, a person occupying the uppermost point with respect to any issue, the right-hand-most point with regard to the phase of policy formation, and the forward-most point in terms of personal efficacy, would be said to have the greatest amount of leverage.) This model would also suggest the incorporation of the notions of power and influence. Although these terms are often used in very imprecise and value-laden ways, it might be possible to speak of power in terms of a point in three-dimensional space, and to orient each of the dimensions operationally.

On the other hand, the model remains somewhat oversimplified. There are certainly further characteristics to consider. The present attempt thus represents an arbitrary set of decisions, although decisions based on a number of pervasive themes in the relevant literature. However, a number of further distinctions can be incorporated with the addition of a number of dynamic properties to the model.

The Dynamic Characteristics of the Model

The model has thus far provided for the categorization of persons along certain dimensions. Although categorization is a necessary first step, the ultimate aim is, of course, to predict the course of events. It is with the consideration of some dynamic properties that the emphasis shifts from classification to prediction.

ISSUE EVALUATION. It first seems clear that the process of policy formation does not derive from the simple specification of the positions of leverage alone. For persons occupying each of these positions, a policy issue is evaluatively loaded, and it is this evaluative component that may largely determine the way in which leverage will be used. Persons tend to be "for" or "against" an issue outcome and this basic attitude may largely determine their behavior toward the issue. With this in mind it is possible to speak of any point as having an evaluative component. This component will fall along a continuum, and the polarities may be indicated by a plus $(+)$ or minus $(-)$ depending on whether the person feels positively or negatively about a given issue outcome. Intermediate points between the extremes may be indicated by using signs of varying sizes, and a zero (0) to indicate neutrality or ambivalence.

POTENTIAL AND ACTUAL LEVERAGE. The addition of the evaluative dimension allows consideration of three additional issues. The first involves a distinction between *potential* and *actual* leverage (cf. Bierstedt, 1950; Danzger, 1964). Although occupying a strong position of leverage, there is no guarantee that a person will actually attempt to utilize his capacities in a particular instance. A governor may be in an optimal position to affect public morality but remain essentially dissociated from the issue. His leverage remains in potential form, and in a sense, might not be considered leverage at all.

Returning to the notion of evaluative loadings, it seems safe to assume that the more polarized a person's position with respect to a given issue, the more likely his leverage will be activated rather than potential. If a public official feels strongly about civil rights he is more likely to use his powers to make strides in this area. This is also to say that a greater degree of leverage can be attributed to persons who maintain polar positions (although it is also possible that persons who are extremely polarized on an issue may lose leverage as a result of their being stigmatized as extremist, or irrationally one-sided). Such assumptions are also quite consistent with the literature on social attitudes which seems to indicate that the stronger a person feels about an issue, the more likely he is to behave consistently with his feelings (cf. Campbell, 1963).

LEVERAGE CONFIGURATION. A second derivation from the above has to do with the configuration of leverage. Up to this point it has simply been assumed that the sum of the individual leverage points provides an adequate characterization of the system. However, considering the total configuration yields additional information and suggests a number of empirical questions. To take an example, one can consider persons *a*, *b*, and *c*, each of whom is highly involved with initiation of policy on a given issue. Further, *a* has greater leverage than either *b* or *c*. The question can immediately be raised whether the combined leverage of *b* and *c* may not be greater than that of *a*. Such a question has interesting research implications, but in terms of predicting the behavior of the persons involved, a consideration of the evaluative loadings is crucial. Knowing the sign of the loadings, one could predict what coalitions would form, and thus what points of leverage might be neutralized. Knowing the intensity of these loadings, one could speculate meaningfully about the strength and impact of a given coalition. In the example given, if *b* and *c* both felt intensely about the issue they might easily neutralize the leverage of a less intense *a*.

This discussion can be broadened to include the entire configuration of leverage points in the matrix. Conceivably, if one could specify the evaluative properties of all leverage points in the matrix, predictions could be made about the success or failure of a given policy. For example, the predominance of highly positive points in optimal positions of leverage should lead to an enactment of a given policy. The degree of predominance and the intensity of the evaluative loadings would of course be significant variables. One might also give some thought to identifying which stages are of most importance in carrying through or blocking action. One might thus predict the failure of a policy if, at a particular phase of the process, there were a high predominance of negative leverage points. Coalition formation across subphase would also be a relevant concern.

PROCESS THROUGH TIME. A third issue relevant to the evaluative loadings has to do with the process of policy formation through time. It would seem that the configuration of leverage seldom remains static, and that the formation of public policy might best be characterized as process with continuously changing features. A consideration of evaluative loadings would seem central in determining the nature of such changes. To be more specific, that persons in positions of leverage do interact with each other on a relatively intimate basis seems indicated in a variety of instances (cf. Hunter, 1954; Mills, 1956). In addition, it is clear from the literature on attitude change that the interaction of two persons of dissimilar viewpoints will produce marked changes (including both convergence and polarization). One might thus expect a constantly changing set of evaluative loadings in the leverage matrix over time.

As a result of such shifts an investigator might not be able to make extremely accurate predictions of the course of policy from a single assessment of leverage points. This problem could potentially be alleviated in at least two ways. If channels of communication among persons occupying positions of leverage could be gauged, it would be possible to make predictions regarding the course of change over time. In addition, one might bring to bear what is known about the process of social influence. Particularly relevant would be those studies dealing with the influence process in situations where power differentials exist (cf. Jones, Gergen, and Jones, 1963; Blau, 1964).

In summary, by adding the evaluative dimension to the model, the focus has shifted from categorization to prediction. This modification has also allowed for a closer look at the system of leverage. However, before going on to consider available methods as they relate to the model, it becomes necessary to discuss several factors that may greatly modify the system of leverage.

VARIABLES INFLUENCING THE MODEL

The previously mentioned model was intended to be broad enough to include both community and national decision-making processes. However, there are several additional variables that appear to affect or modify major components of the model.

SYSTEM SIZE. The majority of studies of public power and influence have confined themselves to cities and small communities. Although a variety of techniques has been used to identify influentials in these studies, one fact that does emerge consistently is that of a general positive relationship between the size of the city or community and the number of influentials. (Although Hunter's study of national power (1959) appears to contradict this trend, his contention is that the major decisions in the United States depend primarily on only 300 persons!)

The implication that the number of leverage points will depend on the size of the social system has considerable significance. When considering smaller communities there would, in effect, be a collapsing of at least two dimensions of the model. First, because there would be fewer influentials, the leverage points for one issue should be much the same as for any other. Thus, the specification of leverage points in such a community should potentially generalize across a large number of issues. Additionally, in smaller communities individual influentials should have leverage in more than one subphase of the policy formation process. Rather than collapsing the phases, each person could be represented by more than one point on the model. This would mean that a person's degree of leverage would be increased by the number of times he was represented in the various subphases. In predicting the outcome of an issue, such a person would thus be given greater weight.

Finally, it seems quite likely that in very large systems, the capacity of any single person to identify all those having leverage in the system would be limited. It is probably the case, however, that all those involved primarily in one subphase have a more accurate picture of the configuration of leverage in that subphase than anyone else. Thus, if reputation becomes important in establishing leverage, the most optimal way in which to assess this reputation would be to approach those persons initially identified in a given subphase.

ISSUE IMPACT. Earlier the notion of issue relevance was advanced and used primarily to highlight the importance of the individual's relationship to any given issue. It was said that the more likely an issue was to alter the status quo for an individual, the more relevant it would be. Broadening this scope, it can also be seen that there are some issues that affect entire societies, while others may be of importance to only a limited segment. In this sense, one can speak of *issue impact* to refer to the number of persons who will potentially be affected or for whom an issue will have relevance. (It is also possible to distinguish between objective and perceived impact. The mass media can be particularly important in modifying people's perceptions of the relevancy of an issue.) The implications of the concept of issue impact are several.

First, the number of persons for whom leverage points should be specified may be directly related to issue impact. The greater the impact, the more people who will be seeking active engagement in the decision-making process. Second, there may also be a relationship between issue impact and the degree of polarity on the valuational dimension discussed above. People live in networks of affective ties. If a person realizes that an issue will affect not only himself but all those to whom he is personally tied, his reaction to the issue may be much more extreme. The norms of his subgroup will justify him; his empathy with this group will buttress him. As indicated before, there should also be a relationship between the degree of polarization and actual as opposed to potential leverage. One might speculate that the greater the issue impact, the greater the number of persons actually attempting to exert leverage.

Thus far a model for representing the various dimensions of leverage in a social system has been developed. It is now possible to examine a number of methods that have been used to study power and influence and to evaluate them in terms of the foregoing discussion.

Procedures for Assessing
Leverage Points

THE REPUTATIONAL APPROACH. Perhaps the most widely used and most controversial method of identifying the powerful or influential members of a social system is the reputational approach. First used by Hunter (1953), this method normally entails asking various "knowledgeable" persons in a community to nominate persons whom they feel to be the most influential. (In some instances, this list may be compiled from names appearing in newspapers or from the investigator's own judgments.) Although this initial list may vary greatly in size from one study to another, it generally includes a sizable proportion of formal or institutional leaders. In many studies this initial list may be submitted to a panel of "experts" who vote on persons they feel to be the "most influential." Although the results of this procedure may be applied directly, an added feature for many studies has been to interview the top influentials (as determined by the foregoing procedure) in order to obtain additional nominations. These interviews (cf. Hunter, 1953; Tumin and Rotberg, 1957; Miller, 1958) serve to validate the initial nominations and to add to the list a number who may not be publicly known.

This general approach has had numerous critics (cf. Dahl, 1961; Polsby, 1959; Wolfinger, 1960, 1962). It has been argued, for example, that the validity of the approach depends on the nominator's ability to identify the powerful or influential. Not only is there no guarantee that the nominators occupy a privileged vantage point in this respect, but the relationship between *perceived* and *actual* influence has received little close attention. Questions have also been raised about the way in which nominations have been obtained. In many instances the respondent is simply asked to identify persons in the community who are the most "powerful," "influential," or "important." Such questions are highly ambiguous and subject to individual interpretation. The answers to such questions may also be unduly influenced by recent issues or happenings in the community. Difficulties have also been pointed out in establishing a cutoff point for nominations. The decision as to how many votes it takes before a person can be included in the "power elite" is often arbitrary and proves little about the number of persons who may actually form the power nucleus. Finally, it has been pointed out that the method itself yields what appears to be a static power structure, without regard to the actual nature of the power complex.

The reputational approach is also subject to several criticisms when examined from the standpoint of the described model. As it is often used, the method fails to distinguish among issues. The hidden assumption in many such studies has been one of polymorphic influence, whether or not such influence exists. The method also fails to distinguish among the various stages of the policy formation process. As a result, those stages that have high public visibility are probably overrepresented. Persons involved with staffing and planning or with inter-elite organizing may seldom be included. Personal efficacy is also not specifically accounted for by the reputational approach. However, it would seem that those who have personal capacities to lead are more likely to have reputations for being influential. The valuational position of the various nominees on various issues is also unaccounted for with the reputational approach. This is an important shortcoming when considering the power configuration in a community or society. As Wolfinger (1960) has pointed out, the reputational approach does not yield a precise "description of a city's political system because it does not indicate whether they are allies or enemies. To establish the existence of a ruling elite, one must show . . . that those who have the most influence are united so as to act in concert rather than in opposition."

In spite of these many shortcomings, the reputational approach does have a number of valuable attributes relevant to operationalizing the above model. First, it is relatively easy to administer. There are no complex scoring systems, and it can provide a set of likely candidates in a short period of time. Second, if used properly it can reveal the identity of influential persons not holding formal positions of leadership. In addition, the reputational approach allows for familiarity with the thoughts and opinions of persons actually engaged in the process of public policy formation. It is a relatively nonartificial and direct method of assessment. Thus, although it would seem unwise to adopt the method as a direct operational representation of the model, some of its characteristics might be retained in developing an adequate method.

THE POSITIONAL APPROACH. Certainly one obvious way of locating influentials in a society is simply to select those who occupy formal positions of public leadership. In a business organization, for example, one might well assume that the configuration of power is largely reflected in the formal diagram of the organization. Similarly, in a society one might simply choose elected or appointed public officials who occupy leading positions.

This general approach has been widely used as a point of departure for studying such groups as elected political leaders (Matthews, 1960; Wakely, 1957), civil servants (Bernstein, 1958; David and Pollock, 1957), business leaders (Warner and Abegglen, 1955; Newcomer, 1959), military officers (Davis, 1948) and officeholders in voluntary associations (Stouffer, 1955). However, the majority of studies in this vein have been devoted to discussing the characteristics of persons in these various positions rather than the configuration of power.

In terms of the leverage model, the major difficulty with this approach is in deciding what formal positions are most central. There are certainly two or three crucial leverage positions in any community, city, and such, but there might be wide disagreement in adding further positions to this list. Should both the chairman of the local charity fund and the newspaper editor be added to the list, for example, and if so, to which should be attributed the greater degree of leverage? There would seem to be no adequate a priori solution to this problem, although one might obtain rankings of the influence of various positions by the occupants of many other similar positions.

It is also the case that many influential persons in a community may not hold formal positions of leadership. Ex-officeholders, distinguished citizens, the extremely wealthy, or the informal opinion leaders may all possess a considerable degree of leverage and yet not be represented by the positional method.

In terms of this model, it seems that formal positions could be discovered that would represent most of the phases of policy formation. However, there would yet remain the difficulty of representing informal leaders in the various phases. In basic form the positional approach would not discriminate among issues or issue relevance, but such a difficulty could be obviated by obtaining ratings along such dimensions from the various occupants. Nor does the positional approach account for the valuational positions of the persons involved. Again, the method could be slightly modified to meet this objection. With respect to the model, perhaps the major shortcoming of the positional approach is its failure to account for the dimension of personal efficacy. The positional approach rests on the assumption that it is the position alone that forms the basis of leverage, and not the particular capacities of the occupant.

A number of the better aspects of both the reputational and positional approaches have been combined in what Polsby (1959) has termed the "leadership pool" approach. This method, actually used in Dahl's (1961) study of New Haven, requires that the researcher initially specify the issue areas of interest, for example, urban redevelopment, mass transportation, and the like. After determining the issue area, all persons holding formal positions of authority with respect to the issue are listed. This can be done in conjunction with a group of knowledgeables in the area. For example, when dealing with public education, Dahl's list included the members of the Board of Education, the Superintendent of Schools, his staff, school principals, and so forth. Intensive interviews are then conducted with each of the members of the leadership pool, and during these interviews key issues in the area are identified as well as additional persons who might play an active role in determining policy. As can be seen, this approach is sensitive to issue specificity, avoids premature closure on the list of influentials, and could potentially reflect the various phases of policy formation. More will be said regarding this approach later.

THE SOCIAL PARTICIPATION APPROACH. A third method relevant to assessing leverage has centered on the degree to which an individual participates in various aspects of public life. Supposedly a person who is more politically active in a community is more influential in matters of public interest. Although such a correlation seems tenable, the majority of the studies in this area have tended not to focus on the top echelons of power. For example, Foskett (1955) developed a social-participation scale specifically relevant to the policy-formation process. Items on this scale dealt with such activities as voting, political discussion with friends and family, attendance at meetings, and the like. Although such items might discriminate among influentials at a grass-roots level, it would seem rather insensitive at the upper levels of influence. Most of the studies in this area (cf. Agger and Omstrum, 1956; Sills, 1957; Wright and Hyman, 1958) have similarly been involved with participation at the general population level.

Although this method seems only remotely sensitive to the various dimensions of the described model, it does have an advantage worth considering in the development of a final measure. Rather than relying on the opinions of others about a person's reputation or on the behavior a person *should* engage in if holding a public position, the social-participation approach relies heavily on the observable behavior of the individual. A measure of actual behavior seems particularly appropriate when assessing the degree of relevance of an issue to an individual. As noted, an issue that will affect the person's life should potentially motivate him toward greater action.

THE OPINION-LEADERSHIP APPROACH. An additional approach to leverage has concentrated on persons who seem to influence the opinions of those about them. The prototypical study in this area is that of Lazarsfeld, Berelson, and Gaudet (1944) in which it was found that the most significant factor producing opinion change in a panel of voters was discussion with others. Persons who were more likely to influence the opinions of those about them were termed "opinion leaders." In the many further studies in this area (cf. Merton, 1949; Katz and Lazarsfeld, 1955; Agger, 1956; Rogers and Beal, 1958) such subjects as the issue-specificity of opinion leadership and the characteristics of opinion leaders have been considered. The large majority of such studies have used members of the general population to designate opinion leaders. As a result, designated leaders have not generally been major officeholders or had quite the status of persons selected with either the reputational or positional approaches.

Although the opinion-leadership approach might be of some aid in determining leverage in the area of communication and publicity, it would be of little general utility in terms of the model. However, the method does suggest an interesting area for research. One is often tempted to think of top-level influentials as being autonomous individuals whose primary function is to mold the thoughts and lives of those about them. On the other hand, such persons are themselves subject to processes of social influence. Social reality is no less an important factor in determining their opinions than the opinions of the man on the street. This point was foreshadowed by the previous discussion on communication and influence among those having leverage. As an empirical issue, the question might be one of identifying the major sources of opinion change among the top influentials. With regard to the predictive aspects of the model, it seems that those nominated as opinion leaders among this group would have much to do with the final outcome of the public issue.

A DEMOGRAPHIC APPROACH. In many studies involving the identification of a power elite, the demographic characteristics of the final nominees have been examined. Bell, Hill, and Wright (1961) have reviewed a host of such studies and have discussed a number of demographic characteristics that seem to persist regardless of specific techniques. Regardless of the method used, for example, the vast majority of influentials in the United States are males, between the ages of forty and sixty, white, business or professional, born in the United States, and Protestant. For certain purposes such information could be very valuable. As an instance, if one were interested in assessing the effects of an information campaign concerning a specific issue, and the information was primarily intended for those in positions of leverage, a lengthy procedure for identifying such persons might be unnecessary. Rather, one might assume that regardless of the specific issue, the majority of those possessing leverage would fall in a group with the above mentioned characteristics. Thus, if the information were funneled to all those falling into this group, the likelihood would be great of reaching the desired recipients and the cost of the venture relatively small.

A PROPOSED TECHNIQUE FOR ASSESSING LEVERAGE. As a result of this discussion it is now possible to spell out a technique that would represent all aspects of the three-dimensional model. This technique combines certain aspects of a number of the described approaches, and its various advantages can be discussed with the enumeration of each step of the approach.

This technique involves two stages. The first is the identification of issues of interest and the individuals involved in formal positions of leadership. Initial interviews might be conducted with as many of these persons as possible in order to obtain information regarding key subissues, individuals involved in the issue areas, and ratings of all nominees on relevant policy phases.

The second stage would build on the information so gathered. Subissues would be more specifically delineated, a complete list of actors having leverage compiled, and extensive interviews conducted with each person in the final sample.

The technique is described in more detail below:

Stage I: The initial step would be to determine a specific set of issues of interest. The assumption of polymorphic influence seems untenable except in a minority of instances. Thus, as in the "pooled-leadership" approach, it seems wise to determine a set of general issues at the outset.

As a second step, two or three knowledgeable persons in the area might be interviewed. Each of these individuals would be used to indicate the formal positions of leadership involved in policy decisions in the specific area. In essence, this step would take advantage of the positional approach to leverage discussed before.

An initial interview might then be conducted with as many of the persons thus named as possible. During these initial interviews, the following information might be obtained:

1. *Information concerning key issues.* Within a given area of interest, there might be several key issues or important policies in question. In the case of foreign aid, for example, there are questions concerning the recipients as well as the amounts to be allocated and the form of allocation. Different individuals may be important in making decisions in different areas. Sharp delineation of issues is thus important.

2. *Information concerning other individuals involved in the issue area.* Here the attempt might be to broaden the initial list to include specifically those who might not occupy formal positions of leadership. This step would utilize certain advantages of the reputational approach to leverage.

3. *Ratings of all nominees on relevant policy phase.* Each respondent might be asked to sort a certain number of individuals on the initial list and all those mentioned in inquiry 2 on the basis of the policy formation subphase in which they were most active.

Stage II: On the basis of the information collected (see the first paragraph of Stage I), the next step would be to sharpen the focus on a set of more specifically delineated subissues within the general topic area. For example, in the area of mass transportation, subissues might center around the needs of a given area or the desirability of certain types of transportation.

Based on the information obtained (see paragraphs 2 and 3 of Stage I), a complete list could be compiled of all those mentioned as having leverage according to their relevant subphase. From this list a final sample might be selected. It would include a significant proportion of those from each of the subphases.

Extensive interviews could then be conducted with each person in the final sample. (This would of course mean a second interview for a significant percentage of the population.) During this interview the following information would be obtained:

1. Each respondent could rate the degree to which each person in his

own subphase possessed resources sufficient to determine public policy for each subissue. For example, any individual involved in financing would rate the degree to which all others previously identified with this function would be instrumental with regard to the financial aspects of each relevant subissue.

2. Each respondent could indicate the degree to which each subissue was relevant to him. He could indicate the degree of importance to him of any policy decisions made in the area.

3. Respondents could be questioned as to their own positions on the various subissues and the intensity with which they held their views.

4. Each respondent could rate all those within his subphase on a series of dimensions relevant to the notions of personal efficacy discussed earlier.

Additional information about the persons with whom the respondent was most likely to interact might also be useful in predicting likely patterns of communication and influence.

As can be seen, this general technique attempts to reflect each of the major dimensions of the model. It first of all takes into account issue specificity, and if multiple issues were utilized, a measure of polymorphic leverage could easily be generated. It then centers on the formal or positional system of leverage, and uses this system to generate information concerning persons capable of exerting leverage in an informal sense, and to designate at which leverage subphase each candidate might be placed. This latter step also takes into account multiple modes of leverage and is thus an advantage over the earlier assumption that power or influence is unidimensional in nature. Assessments of resources within leverage subphases and ratings of personal efficacy are obtained for any individual only from those persons most likely to be acquainted with the area. Such a step maximizes the likelihood of obtaining assessments from persons who are, in each instance, knowledgeable. Finally, assessments of issue relevance are obtained from the individuals themselves. Taking account of relevance is in itself an advantage over earlier systems. The technique may not be quite so easily administered as some of those more often used, but it would potentially be more precise and useful as a predictive device. The utility of the approach would of course depend to a large extent on the capacity of the interviewers to obtain candid and unbiased responses from the respondents.

In summary, the preceding discussion has attempted to develop a model of social leverage. The various aspects of the model were then used in analyzing available methods for the actual assessment of leverage. Finally, a sketch of a method that might take full advantage of the various aspects of the model was discussed. The ultimate utility of this discussion to the process of public policy formation is, of course, subject to empirical evaluation. Such evaluation is currently being undertaken.

BIBLIOGRAPHY

Agger, R. E., "Power Attributions in the Local Community: Theoretical and Research Considerations," *Social Forces*, **34** (1956), pp. 322–331.

—— and V. Ostrom, "The Political Structure of a Small Community," *Public Opinion Quarterly*, **20** (1956), pp. 81–89.

Banfield, E. C., *Political Influence* (New York: Free Press, 1961).

Bell, W., R. J. Hill, and C. Wright, *Public Leadership* (San Francisco: Chandler, 1961).

Berstein, M. H., *The Job of the Federal Executive* (Washington, D.C.: The Brookings Institution, 1958).

Bierstedt, R., "An Analysis of Social Power," *American Sociological Review*, **15** (1950), pp. 730–738.

Blau, P., *Exchange and Power in Social Life* (New York: John Wiley, 1964).

Campbell, D. T., "Social Attitudes and Other Acquired Behavioral Dispositions," in *Psychology: A Study of a Science*, Vol. 6, Koch, S., ed. (New York: McGraw-Hill, 1963).

Cattell, R. B., and G. E. Stice, *The Psychodynamics of Small Groups* (Urbana, Ill.: Laboratory of Personality Assessment and Group Behavior, University of Illinois, 1953).

Dahl, R. A., "Leadership in a Fragmented Political System: Notes for a Theory." Paper read at Social Science Research Council Conference on Metropolitan Leadership, Northwestern University, Evanston, Ill., April 1960.

—— *Modern Political Analysis* (New Haven: Yale University Press, 1961).

D'Antonio, W. V., and E. Erickson, "The Reputational Technique As a Measure of Community Power," *American Sociological Review*, **27** (1962), pp. 362–376.

Danzger, M. H., "Community Power Structures: Problems and Continuities," *American Sociological Review*, **29** (1964), pp. 707–717.

David, P. T., and R. Pollock, *Executives for Government* (Washington, D.C.: Central Issues of Federal Personnel Administration, The Brookings Institution, 1957).

Davis, A. K., "Bureaucratic Patterns in the Navy Officer Corps," *Social Forces*, **27** (1948), pp. 11–18.

Drake, R. M., "A Study of Leadership," *Character and Personality*, **12** (1944), pp. 285–289.

Foskett, J. M., "Social Structure and Social Participation," *American Sociological Review*, **20** (1955), pp. 431–438.

Gibb, C. A., "Leadership," in *Handbook of Social Psychology*, Vol. II, G. Lindzey, ed. (Reading, Mass.: Addison-Wesley, 1954).

Gowin, E. B., *The Executive and His Control of Men* (New York: Macmillan, 1915).

Hanawalt, N. G., C. E. Hamilton, and M. L. Morris, "Level of Aspiration in College Leaders and Non-Leaders," *Journal of Abnormal and Social Psychology*, **38** (1943), pp. 545–548.

Hovland, C. I., and W. Weiss, "The Influence of Source Credibility on Communication Effectiveness," *Public Opinion Quarterly*, **15** (1951), pp. 635–650.

Hunter, F., *Community Power Structure* (Chapel Hill, N.C.: University of North Carolina Press, 1953).

Hunter, F., *Top Leadership, U.S.A.* (Chapel Hill, N.C.: University of North Carolina Press, 1959).

Jennings, M. K., "Public Administrators and Community Decision Making," *Administrative Science Quarterly*, **8** (1963), pp. 18–43.

Jones, E. E., K. J. Gergen, and R. G. Jones, "Tactics of Ingratiation Among Leaders and Subordinates in a Status Hierarchy," *Psychological Monographs*, **77** (1963), No. 3 (Whole No. 566).

Katz, E., and P. F. Lazarsfeld, *Personal Influence* (New York: Free Press, 1955).

Lasswell, H. D., *Power and Personality* (New York: W. W. Norton, 1948).

―――― and A. Kaplan, *Power and Society* (New Haven: Yale University Press, 1961).

Lazarsfeld, P. F., B. Berelson, and H. Gaudet, *The People's Choice* (New York: Duell, Sloan, and Pearce, 1944).

Lowe, F., and T. C. McCormack, "A Study of the Influence of Formal and Informal Leaders in an Election Campaign," *Public Opinion Quarterly*, **20** (1957), pp. 651–662.

Mann, R. D., "A Review of the Relationships Between Personality and Performance in Small Groups," *Psychological Bulletin*, **56** (1959), pp. 241–270.

Matthews, D. R., *United States Senators and Their World* (Chapel Hill, N.C.: University of North Carolina Press, 1960).

Merriam, C. E., *Political Power* (New York: McGraw-Hill, 1934).

Merton, R. K., "Patterns of Influence," in *Communications Research 1948–1949*, P. F. Lazarsfeld, and F. N. Stanton, eds. (New York: Harper & Row, 1949).

―――― *Social Theory and Social Structure* (New York: Free Press, 1957).

Miller, D. C., "Decision-Making Cliques in Community Power Structures: A Comparative Study of an American and English City," *American Journal of Sociology*, **65** (1958), pp. 299–310.

Mills, C. W., *The Power Elite* (New York: Oxford University Press, 1956).

Newcomb, T. M., *Personality and Social Change* (New York: Dryden, 1943).

Newcomer, M., "The Big Business Executive," in *Industrial Man*, W. L. Warner and N. H. Martin, eds. (New York: Harper & Row, 1959).

Parsons, T., "On the Concept of Political Power," *Proceedings of the American Philosophical Society*, **107** (1963), pp. 233–262.

Patchen, M., "Alternative Questionnaire Approaches to the Measurement of Influence in Organizations," *American Journal of Sociology*, **69** (1963), pp. 41–52.

Pellegrin, R. J., and C. H. Coates, "Absentee-Owned Corporations and Community Power Structure," *American Journal of Sociology*, **61** (1956), pp. 413–419.

Polsby, N. W., "The Sociology of Community Power: A Reassessment," *Social Forces*, **37** (1959), pp. 232–236.

Richardson, H. M., and N. G. Hanawalt, "Leadership As Related to the Bernreuter Personality Measures," *Journal of Social Psychology*, **17** (1943), pp. 237–267.

Rogers, E. M., and G. M. Beal, "The Importance of Personal Influence in the Adoption of Technological Changes," *Social Forces*, **36** (1958), pp. 329–335.

Russell, B., *A New Social Analysis* (New York: W. W. Norton, 1938).

Schermerhorn, R. A., *Society and Power* (New York: Random House, 1961).

Schulze, R. O., "The Bifurcation of Power in a Satellite City," in *Community and Political Systems*, M. Janowitz, ed. (New York: Free Press, 1961).

Sills, D. L., *The Volunteers* (New York: Free Press, 1957).

Smuckler, R. H., and G. M. Belknap, *Leadership and Participation in Urban Political Affairs* (East Lansing, Mich.: Government Research Bureau, Michigan State University, 1956).

Stouffer, S. A., "A Research Program on Leadership and Decision-Making in Metropolitan Areas." Unpublished mimeograph, Department of Social Relations, Harvard University, 1958.

—— *Communism, Conformity, and Civil Liberties* (New York: Doubleday, 1955).

Tannenbaum, P. H., "Initial Attitude Toward Source and Concept As Factors in Attitude Change Through Communication," *Public Opinion Quarterly*, 20 (1956), pp. 413–425.

Tumin, M., and R. Rotberg, "Leaders, the Led, and the Law: A Case Study in Social Change," *Public Opinion Quarterly*, 21 (1957), pp. 355–370.

Wakely, R. E., "Selecting Leaders for Agricultural Programs," *Sociometry*, 10 (1957), pp. 384–295.

Warner, W. L., and J. C. Abegglen, *Occupational Mobility in American Business and Industry* (Minneapolis: University of Minnesota Press, 1955).

Wilson, J. Q., *Negro Politics* (New York: Free Press, 1960).

Wolfinger, R. E., "A Plea for a Decent Burial," *American Sociological Review*, 27 (1962), pp. 841–848.

—— "Reputation and Reality in the Study of 'Community Power'," *American Sociological Review*, 25 (1960), 636–644.

Wright, C. R., and H. H. Hyman, "Voluntary Association Memberships, of American Adults: Evidence from National Sample Surveys," *American Sociological Review*, 23 (1958), pp. 284–294.

Chapter 6

KENNETH J. GERGEN

Methodology in the Study of Policy Formation

Introduction to the
Problem

Building an adequate theory in any area of the social sciences depends ultimately on the availability of "real world" data. Without a substantial data base, the inductive process by which social science develops may give rise to spurious and misleading conceptual premises. Testing the validity of any theoretical premise would obviously rely on additional factual information. However, the development of such a data base inevitably relies upon the adequacy of the methods by which information is obtained. The present focus is thus on the methods used in the gathering of data concerning the formation of public policy.

Data concerning the processes of public policy formation are both spotty and unsystematic. There are several reasons for this empirical dearth. During the past decade one of the knottier methodological problems for persons interested in this area has been identifying the participants in the process. Who indeed are the persons significantly engaged in the formation of public policy? Much of the literature in this area has been reviewed in the preceding chapter. A second difficulty has to do with the lack of a sophisticated theory of public policy formation, theory that would orient the potential investigator to the significant issues and variables involved. The development of such theory is, of course, highly dependent on the availability of factual data. The development of theory may be equally hampered by the fact that the various arenas of public policy formation are not sufficiently similar to suggest concepts of a general nature. What are the conceptual similarities, for example, in the way in which foreign policy is formed, and the way in which members of a small midwestern community decide on the style of architecture they will permit in their community? A final difficulty, and one of major proportions, is that policy formation is normally historically bound. The persons and the situation yielding a decision in one given period of time are never replicable. The payoff of studying events under such conditions may, for social scientists interested predominantly in the cumulative aspects of science, be somewhat limited.

There is no better corrective for many of these difficulties than the availability of far-ranging data on public policy formation. This chapter is concerned with the methods of obtaining such data. Up to this point, what data exist are largely in the form of public records or cursory observation. The present approach departs from such methods in its orientation toward detailed analyses of decision makers at work. Rather than relying on public documents or secondhand reports, the present chapter hopes to outline a set of complementary methods by which data can be obtained concerning the decision maker's behavior, thoughts, perceptions, and feelings in the ongoing decision-making process. The chapter is composed of three sections. First, a brief sketch will be made of the system of events upon which the methods of assessment should focus. Second, a number of methodological issues of particular relevance to the measurement of policy formation will be discussed. Based on the discussion of these general issues, the third section will treat a number of specific methods of assessment that should be of the greatest utility in research on public policy formation.

The System of Assessment

In studying public policy formation, there are quite clearly multiple sources of data. One could spend a lifetime investigating policy formation at the international, national, or local level. Whereas one investigator might focus on the interrelationships of entire social systems, another might confine his analysis to communication in small groups of decision makers; still a third might concentrate intensively on the actions of a single individual. While one investigator might look only at those in top positions of leadership and assume that the remainder of society will follow their dictates, another might see the development of policy as a function of "grass roots" social movements. Each of these approaches would suggest a separate observation base, and there might be little overlap in data sources.

Because of time and space limitations, this chapter will focus on a circum-scribed set of topics. These topics center on the assessment of the individual decision maker in his relations with others. This focus follows from notions generated in the preceding chapter in which it was reasoned that in most societies the responsibility for the formation and execution of public policy is not equally distributed. Rather, persons differ in what is termed "leverage" (roughly synonymous with power or influence), and those with greater lever-age are felt to have greater potential for rendering change in society. This general approach suggests that one of the more fruitful ways of studying public policy formation would be to concentrate on those individuals with greater amounts of leverage.

In keeping with this orientation, there would seem to be three major sources of data of major methodological interest. Initially one would want to be able to specify those objective factors that impinge on individuals pos-sessing leverage. Such factors may be highly variegated, and might include not only information received by the person from various sources, but also the social influences to which he is subjected, the larger systems of which he is a member, and the role specifications in which he is enmeshed. Second, and much more complex from a methodological point of view, would be the psychological processes operating within the individual himself. How can one assess the perception the person has of his world, his attitudes and feelings, or the quasi-rational processes that yield decisions? Finally, one would certainly have an interest in an objective description of the resultant conduct of the individual. There is clearly not a one-to-one relationship between what a person feels or thinks and his subsequent behavior, and an emphasis on behavior patterns is thus made all the more salient. If we were interested solely in prediction, there is a sense in which knowledge of resultant behavior may be of more importance than knowing about those psychological processes that may give rise to this behavior. However, since we are interested also in increased understanding and possible influence of this behavior, we are con-cerned with both the person's internal state and with his behavior.

It is quite clear that this triple set of foci is restricted in scope. For example, the large-scale processes of decision making, dealing with the interrelation-ships of large bodies, receive little attention in this particular schema. It is felt that an understanding of the individual and his behavior within a specific context is basic, and that the interrelationships of social systems can best be analyzed once such understanding is achieved. In any case the systematic gathering of behavioral data, including the "internal state" of the relevant actors, is the crucial new ingredient in the study of policy, and such data must concentrate on individuals as the basic points of observation.

Selected Methodological Issues

There are a large number of methodological criteria and issues that are of potential concern to any investigator in the social sciences. However, although it may be a simple matter to pay lip service to such criteria, it is yet another matter to consider their specific implications for a given empirical study. Such criteria and issues normally remain at such an abstract level that it is all too easy to avoid the derivation to the concrete instance. The purpose of this section is thus to discuss a number of major methodological issues and their specific relationship to the three data sources described above. This discussion will by no means be a complete survey of issues. Rather a limited group has been selected on the basis of several criteria: (1) They have widespread applicability; (2) they lead to particular concrete steps that may be taken in research on policy formation; and, (3) their specific relevance to the study of policy formation has not elsewhere been discussed. Although of general importance, issues of scaling, numerical analysis, operational definitions, and generalizability will not receive attention here because they do not generally meet the preceding criteria. The problem of sampling will receive cursory attention, but this problem is covered to some extent in the discussion of leverage in Chapter 5. For broader discussions of methodology the reader may wish to consult other sources.[1]

VALIDITY. The validity of a measure is generally defined as the extent to which the observation chosen to reflect a characteristic of a situation or an individual reflects what is consensually felt to be the "true" characteristic. For example, observations may simply reflect random occurrence or occurrences unrelated to the chosen characteristic. It should be noted, however, that because a measure that aids in prediction is felt to be more valid than one that doesn't, this definition propels us headlong into consideration of utility. One function of policy study should be to develop models that will allow us to understand the process of policy formation in such a way that we can predict the effects of given inputs in a situation. In other words, the data should hopefully have utility in subsequent real life situations. Although it is controversial as to whether utility itself should be considered a criterion of validity (cf. Cattell, 1964; Wallace, 1965) we will find that the notion of utility permeates our consideration of the several ways that may be used to establish validity.

Among these various modes of establishing validity, one that has predominated in earlier attempts at dealing with policy formation is *face validity*.

---

1. See for example, Festinger and Katz (1953), Selltiz, Jahoda, Deutsch, and Cook (1960), and Kerlinger (1964). References cited appear in the bibliography at the end of the chapter.

In this case, one's observations may have a rather direct and intuitively obvious relationship with the characteristic being measured. For example, in attempting to measure the amount of publicity given to a certain program or person, face-valid procedures might include the amount of newspaper space devoted to the issue or person, the extensiveness of information campaigns devoted to it, and so on.

In other instances, measuring instruments may also gain validity through simple predictive means. In other words, the observations may be useful in predicting to some other behavior of the individual or characteristic of the environment. If a measure of community cohesiveness is highly useful in predicting the degree to which the community is split in voting over public issues, the measure can be said to have *predictive validity*. As can be seen, in this instance the notions of validity and utility are most thoroughly intertwined.

Finally, if the characteristic one is attempting to measure is internal to an individual (that is, a psychological construct), and the observation is thus only an indirect indicator, it becomes necessary to resort to what is termed *construct validity*. In this instance validity is obtained by correlating one's observations to other observations of the individual that should be rationally or theoretically related. In measuring isolationist attitudes in the study of foreign aid, for example, one might expect a conservative estimate of required aid to be associated with a person's favoring domestic development. The issue of utility again becomes relevant, because in certain instances one might infer from certain types of public behavior an attitude that can be used to predict a person's private position on a policy issue.

For at least two of the three data sources described above, face validity can be relied upon to a major extent. In assessing the objective environment of the individual and his overt behavior, primary reliance on face-valid measures would seem appropriate. However, two related problems deserve at least some mention. First and most obvious is the prime attention that must be given to the exact relationship between the variable presumably being measured and the datum. For example, the amount of time elapsing between the time a given executive receives a request and the time he acts upon it, may not reflect so much the priority assigned to the request as the difficulty of the task that it instigates. Second, and slightly more subtle, is the problem of obtaining a sufficient sample of observations to establish face validity. In trying to plot the proportion of time spent by a legislator in various activities, it is an important question as to the number of days on which observations should be made and the time span that should be considered. In part, such considerations will clearly depend on the amount of time and resources available for research. This issue will receive closer attention in the section on reliability.

For the third major data source, the internal processes of the individual, the notion of construct validity becomes salient. Measures of attitudes, opinions, values, motives, and perceptions would all be included. In the study of policy formulation, there seem to be two major ways of increasing construct validity. Attention might be given first to developing multiple measures of each construct. If interested in a respondent's attitude toward urban renewal, an interviewer might ask several different types of questions, each relevant to the problem but approaching it from a slightly different standpoint. The intercorrelation of responses on the various items would provide some indication of construct validity. A second alternative is to include measures of other constructs or behaviors that should theoretically be related. Scores on a political liberalism measure could be buttressed by measures of attitudes toward various minority groups, and perhaps to the way the individual had voted on related issues. Thus, as a general rule of thumb, in developing questionnaires or sets of questions for interviewing, prime attention should be given to the cross-relevance of the various items in the series.

In any case a single observation or an answer to a single question may seldom be adequate unless the construct is very simple (Which candidate is preferred in an election?), or one's theoretical model is sufficiently elaborate and firmly established that it demands a single, crucial piece of information (Which of two messages will reach a man first?). Instances of either of these types are exceptional.

RELIABILITY. With few exceptions, studies related to policy formation have relied on a single set of observations made over a relatively short period of time. A typical study is one based primarily on a single set of interviews with a number of persons in policy-making positions. Such studies are highly advantageous in the sense that large amounts of data can be obtained in areas about which little is initially known. In the early stages of research on a topic, a maximum amount of information can be generated in a minimum amount of time. Perhaps the major shortcoming of this approach has to do with the issue of reliability, or the degree of variation in behavior caused by inconsistencies in measurement. For the majority of such studies, there is no way of determining the extent to which observations reflect either simple inconsistencies in the measuring device or temporary and fluctuating behaviors on the part of the individual being studied. A respondent's answer to a specific question might often be difficult to code in a sufficiently precise fashion; many times such responses may only reflect temporary mood states, or the fact that until the interview the respondent may never have thought about the issues raised.

The question of reliability is closely linked to that of validity. If it were known that a given observation were perfectly valid, reliability would not be an issue. A perfectly valid measuring instrument should not be subject to random error or biased by temporary mood states. Likewise, an instrument that is highly unreliable cannot properly be said to possess great validity.

It would thus seem that if research is to represent an advancement in techniques, attention must be directed to the issue of reliability. There are two alternative procedures that might be followed in this regard, and neither generally proves to be expensive or time consuming. In measuring the objective environment of the individual or his behavior, it is normally not an excessive hindrance to obtain multiple observations at randomized intervals over a period of weeks or months. The reliability of the measure is thus said to be ascertained through its *stability*. A second possibility is to allow several different observers to assess the same phenomenon, and to establish reliability through comparing the results of the various raters. This is normally termed the *equivalence* method for determining reliability. Because the first method requires the training of only a single investigator, a convenient rule of thumb might be to use the stability criterion in all cases except those in which complex phenomena are being observed. In the latter instances, the estimates of a single judge or observer may well introduce systematic bias. For example, judgments of the number of attempts made by x to influence y, or the amount of "social" *vs.* "task-oriented" communication taking place, are highly subjective and may thus be highly biased by the estimates of a single observer. Thus one observer might classify a conversation at the water cooler as socializing, another classify it as maintenance work on channels of communication, and a third as an effort to get specific information by way of an indirect method. Such systematic biases may stem from the observer's model of the process he is observing and/or from his background knowledge of the specific events. Multiple judges would tend to reduce such bias.

Neither of these methods of increasing reliability is entirely adequate when attempting to assess the psychological processes of the individual. There are several reasons for this. The stability of a set of responses can first of all be influenced by the respondent's memory of his earlier answers to the questions. The situation may also be psychologically different for the respondent during the second testing. His interest and motivation may be lower, and resentment triggered as a result of being asked the same questions a second time. Using multiple investigators in the face-to-face situation has additional shortcomings. The presence of a third or fourth person in an interview may well bias the respondent's answers in unknown ways (cf. Taietz, 1962).

There are, however, two modifications of the equivalence method that could be useful. Reliability through equivalence may also be established, not with multiple observers, but with multiple measures administered during the same testing session. The majority of standard personality tests rely on such a method by simply including several indicators of the given trait or characteristic on the test battery. Thus, when assessing attitudes, values, or personality, a number of interrelated items are normally used. As a second alternative, certain aspects of the respondent's behavior can be recorded directly (for example, tape recording all interviews) with little added expense. In this way several judges may independently rate certain aspects of the behavior and thus establish reliability.

In conclusion, it is worth noting one aspect of the problem of reliability that is usually overlooked. The degree of difficulty one has in obtaining reliability may in itself be indication of the stability of the phenomenon being observed. For example, some attitudes are so clearly defined and stably held that virtually any method will provide the same answer, while other attitudes may be altered by the instruments used or the circumstance under which they are probed. The existence of this problem should always alert investigators to the fact that in many instances unstable and evanescent phenomena are possibly under consideration.

INVESTIGATOR BIAS. Within the past decade, major interest has centered on the effects of the investigator himself on what he studies. Hyman's (1954) summary of the literature on the effects of the interviewer on the information obtained in the survey interview is now a classic. More recently, the survey interview has been viewed as a game in which the respondent bargains with the interviewer in order to receive certain outcomes (Back and Gergen, 1963). A further series of studies (Gergen, 1965b; Gergen and Wishnov, 1965) demonstrated a number of characteristics of a person that may cause another to modify the information he presents about himself. An entire research program is being carried out by Rosenthal (cf. his 1964 summary) to explore the way in which an experimenter may unwittingly alter the results of his investigations.

Such biases may be exceedingly important in policy research. First, in studying the environment of the individual or his behavior patterns, the presence of the investigator may well cause subtle changes to take place in these phenomena. It is difficult to believe that when all members of an organization are aware that a participant observer is in their midst, their behavior continues as usual. An alternative to this form of participant observation might be to enlist the aid of someone already within the organization. Similarly, in obtaining an objective assessment of the behavior of a given individual, problems arise if the person is aware that he is being observed. Davis (1964) undertook a study of executive behavior patterns and obtained his major data by following the executives about during their daily round of activities. He notes that he was asked to leave on a number of occasions in which the executives felt that he would unduly inhibit free discussion. Some attention might be given to employing persons already occupying privileged and innocuous vantage points to record observations. For example, with the permission of her employer, a secretary might be paid to record a number of simple events or behavioral occurrences during the day. Her presence would at least be customary and noninterfering.

There is a second and different sense in which the investigator can introduce systematic bias in studying the above data sources. The experimental literature on social perception is rife with instances in which a person's perception of the environment is influenced by his feelings or motives (cf. Feshbach and Singer, 1957; Dearborn and Simon, 1958). In fact, the so-called *new look* in the psychology of perception is largely based on just such phenomena. The implication of this line of research for present purposes is clear: to the extent that the observer has an emotional investment in the outcome of his observations, there is a risk that his observations will not reflect what he actually observed. A possible concrete instance of this source of bias may serve to clarify. Persons who carry out the day-to-day task of observing and recording data from real life situations are often manifestly aware of the hypotheses and expectations of the senior investigator. The attempt to please the senior investigator by furnishing him confirming results may not cause the researcher to falsify his data, but research seems to indicate that he may be much more sensitized to confirming instances than to negative instances (cf. Rosenthal, 1964). In other words, the attitudinal dispositions of the researcher may cause him to scan his environment in a biased fashion.

A second type of perceptual bias arises from premature closure on research problems. It is of course impossible to record all happenings in the environment. The researcher must necessarily limit his observations to those aspects that are of theoretical relevance. However, if such limitations are introduced too early, subsequent observation may not be sensitive to highly relevant but initially unconsidered occurrences (cf. Hovland, 1957). The observer may simply not be sensitive to such occurrences and fail to take them into account.

These particular aspects of investigator bias suggest several possible steps that might be taken to minimize their effects. Although the researcher who does the day-to-day observation may need extensive training in carrying out his duties, consideration might be given to witholding the specific hypotheses of the study or the functional relationships of theoretical interest. Many investigators take just the opposite tack on the assumption that complete familiarity with the research will breed higher morale and greater dedication on the part of the low-level researcher. However valuable these latter objectives, they might be unduly costly in terms of the contribution to knowledge that might otherwise be made. Short-term dedication and high morale are also purchasable commodities.

Premature closure on the research problem can also be avoided. It is always beneficial if the investigator can gain as much first-hand experience of the research context as possible. As a result of this experience, measures can be developed in line with theoretical interests. It is then valuable to engage a group of consultants who are actively engaged in the organization or system being studied. These "participant consultants" can closely scrutinize the measures and perhaps suggest other possible sources of relevant data.

Thus far, investigator bias has been discussed only as it relates to the stages of measuring the environment and overt behavior. However, special problems of investigator bias arise when attempting to assess the psychological characteristics of the individual. Such characteristics must necessarily be inferred from external behavior. If a person says that he feels a certain way about a specific issue, his statement is normally considered *prima facie* evidence of his external state. However, there is no guarantee of complete correspondence between overt and covert levels of behavior. Research has indicated that the characteristics of the interrogator, the context of the interrogation, and the respondent's view of the purposes of the investigation may all significantly influence his overt responses.

If the face-to-face interview is to be relied on as a primary source of data, there is no ultimate solution to the problem of bias. There are, however, several ways of reducing bias arising from the social nature of the situation. For one, the respondent's anonymity can be guaranteed. If the respondent feels that his name will never be attached to what he says, more candid responses can well be anticipated (cf. Hyman, 1954). It is also important to consider how the study is represented to the respondent. Experience seems to indicate that the optimum tactic is to give the respondent as little relevant information as possible. That is, a study might be backed by a prestige name or by a statement sufficient to communicate the importance of the overall objectives. The respondent's opinions are thus made to seem as important as possible, but any information concerning the value judgments, hypotheses, or hopes of the study would be excluded. A final preventive measure would be to use multiple interviewers and assign them respondents randomly across the various strata of the sample. In this way, bias arising from the personal characteristics of the interviewer would be randomized throughout the study and no particular subsample would be systematically affected.

In addition to these various techniques of reducing bias arising from the presence of the investigator, there is a final alternative that avoids investigator effects almost entirely. Rather than reducing bias in the situation, it is also possible to obtain independent measures of the construct in question. In measuring a specific attitude, the investigator might not content himself with only the respondent's verbal report. Independent assessments of the attitude might be obtained with data from other aspects of the respondent's life. For example, if the investigator is interested in attitudes toward federal control of utilities, questions in the interview might be supplemented with checks made on the individual's voting behavior in relevant elections, his contributions to relevant campaigns, or the views of his associates concerning the position he has espoused. As can be seen, this method of avoiding bias dovetails closely with the earlier discussion of validity and reliability.

QUESTION BIAS. Although the sources of investigator bias are many, there are additional sources of bias which may occur regardless of the characteristics or behavior of the investigator. One of the most important of these sources has to do with the way in which questions are asked. Regardless of who may be doing the asking, a particular question may elicit responses determined by characteristics of the question itself rather than the "state of nature." It is clear that such bias will primarily be restricted to the face-to-face interview or questionnaire, and will be most relevant when assessing psychological processes or phenomena. Such processes or phenomena tend to demand more and better data for their assessment because of their inherent characteristics. They are inferred constructs not susceptible to direct observation.

There are several ways in which question bias can occur. One of them stems from a notion that has often been voiced by researchers in the area of public opinion. It has been ventured that many opinions expressed by respondents in the public-opinion interview may well be formulated for the first time in the interview itself. This may particularly be the case if the respondent has thought very little about the issues in question or if the issues have been of little relevance to him. In a sense, then, the question itself has a certain demand characteristic and may cause the respondent to attempt an answer regardless of qualification. Such instances create great difficulties in generalizing from a particular set of results. If 60 per cent of a sample feel that the Taft-Hartley Law should not be repealed, the investigator cannot be certain that the respondents either know what the law is or what its implications are. Generalizing to what the respondents might do if repeal were to become likely would be treacherous. In this sense, "spontaneous" opinions are unreliable and probably of little predictive value.

Certain precautionary measures can be taken to minimize this difficulty. The crucial component of the problem is that the questions are ones about which the respondent is *uninformed*. It is hardly likely that a chairman of a large corporation will provide an unconsidered answer to a question about the Taft-Hartley Law. It would thus seem that a useful research step would be to assess the relevancy of particular questions to individuals in a sample prior to the time of actual testing. For example, several representatives from the sample to be tested could be used for the preliminary screening of questions or items to be used. They could be asked not only about the particular form of the various questions, but also about their general relevance to the sample. In situations where such a plan proves unfeasible, it is possible to build in a check for respondent knowledge in the questioning itself. For instance, in the present example, respondents could first of all be asked about their understanding of the Taft-Hartley Law, and then later about their attitudes.

A highly related question has to do with the salience of issues to individuals. Questions can deal with issues about which the respondent is fully informed, but these issues may simply be of little relevance to him in his daily activities. It would thus be open to speculation as to what the individual's opinion or actions would be if the issue were later to become salient. And it is certainly clear that if an issue is not salient, it is not likely to form a significant determinant of the person's decision-making behavior.

There are steps that can be taken to alleviate this difficulty. The Bauer, Pool, and Dexter (1963) study of American business and public policy is instructive. These investigators present a number of survey findings indicating the view of businessmen toward tariffs. The investigators also obtained data indicating the relative salience of the tariff issue to the businessman. On the basis of these data more objective estimates could be made of the relationship between business opinion on the matter and the actions or decisions that one might anticipate from this group.

The placing of questions is also an important factor. If the major portion of the interview dealt with mass transportation, it would seem wise to include items concerning the salience of the issue in the early phase of questioning. As data from a study by Back and Gergen (1963) indicate, responses during an interview may be highly influenced by continued questioning on a single theme. In this instance, questions about mass transportation themselves may cause an artificial salience to be produced directly in the interview.

An additional alternative for estimating salience might be in the form of open-ended questioning. Under certain circumstances, the respondent may be asked to talk at length about some of the issues or factors that may have affected his decisions. One could then note either the amount of time taken before discussing a key issue or the number of other issues mentioned prior to one of key interest. A variant on this method is to devise a series of questions with increasingly narrow focus that enable the investigator to note at which stages in this funneling process the issue is mentioned.

Thus far, two highly related forms of question bias have been discussed. Two additional but unrelated forms also deserve attention. First, a considerable amount of research corroborates the fact of a high positive correlation between the degree to which a response is socially desirable and the likelihood of occurrence of that response (cf. Edwards, 1958). It is still an open question as to whether people in actuality hold socially desirable opinions or act in socially desirable ways. To some extent, responding in a socially desirable manner may result from the fact that interviewing is by nature social. Some precautionary steps dealing with this difficulty have been already indicated. There are also further steps that can be taken with regard to the particular form of the questions themselves. For example, the possibility of obtaining a representative group from a proposed sample to screen questions has been discussed. This group could also be used to examine the proposed items for instances in which social desirability might play a significant role. On the basis of this screening, items could be rewritten or response alternatives altered. In the Back and Gergen (1963) study it was found that continued questioning along a certain line seemed to suggest a more socially desirable way of responding to interview questions. An additional lesson to be learned here is that careful placement of items in an interview schedule may also serve to mitigate the effects of social desirability.

Finally, question bias may also arise from the particular response alternatives offered to respondents. Although questions that offer only a limited number of responses are efficient and lend themselves to quantification, they can be quite deficient in other respects. Response alternatives might not reflect the complexity of opinion on an issue or adequately cover the range of likely responses. In such instances the respondent may avoid a question by not committing himself to a response, or choose a response that does not actually reflect his feeling on the issue. Again, these difficulties can be overcome to a great extent through the use of a screening group.

RETROSPECTIVE BIAS. The issues of reliability and validity that have been raised are of wide-ranging familiarity to social scientists and have been of perennial concern to anyone interested in problems of measurement. Issues of investigator and question bias have begun to receive much systematic attention only within the past decade and are relevant to a more circumscribed set of measurement techniques. The issue of retrospective bias has yet to receive extensive attention except in limited areas,[2] and is primarily germane to those instances in which a respondent is asked to reconstruct events or happenings that occurred at some earlier time. Such instances have typically played an important role in the study of decision making. Particularly when little is known about the process of decision making in a given area, openended questions are often used that direct the respondent to reconstruct the past history of a problem and his relationship to it. The information gained by such means is often used to buttress the theoretical analysis of the decision-making process. The importance of retrospective bias in such instances is made very salient in two recent studies of decision making. In Culbertson's (1965) study of the role of businessmen in determining national policy regarding application of technology, it was found that the respondents' recollection of their behavior had only a tangential relationship with the public record of their activities. In the Bauer, Pool, and Dexter (1963) study of American businessmen and public policy, it was found that a number of those interviewed had actually forgotten the occurrence of reasonably important events until their memory was restored with relevant information. Because retrospective accounts are likely to play an extremely important part in any detailed study of policy formation, the focus of this section is on the accuracy of such reports and on ways in which distortions may be reduced.

2. For example, marketing studies have shown that persons overreport large purchases (e.g., an automobile) if the time period about which they are asked is quite long, such as a year. A person who bought an automobile 13, 14, or 15 months ago is likely to report it as bought within the year. On the other hand, if the purchase period is short, the number of purchases of small, regularly used items, such as loaves of bread, is likely to be underestimated.

As one surveys various areas of concern in the social sciences, a number of investigations can be found that relate to the problem of retrospective bias and each points to factors that may be important to consider. Perhaps the earliest contribution to our understanding of retrospective reconstruction is contained in the now classic studies of Ebbinghaus (1913) on memory. Although these studies were poorly controlled and Ebbinghaus himself served as the subject, it is clear that retention of various kinds of material is a negatively accelerated function of the amount of time elapsing between learning and subsequent testing for retention. Ebbinghaus' studies have since been repeated under more methodologically rigorous conditions. The literature in this area reveals a number of factors that may affect the amount of material retained. Luh (1922) has shown that if it is a simple matter of recognizing material that has been learned previously, people retain approximately 80 per cent of what has been learned several days earlier. If they are presented the learned materials in a scrambled order, they show approximately 50 per cent retention after several days. If, however, they are asked to reconstruct the material and no added stimuli are present, only 30 per cent of the material is retained. Others have found that the overlearning of material aids in recall (Kreuger, 1929) and that more meaningful material is remembered better (Guilford, 1952).

A variety of sources suggest a second factor as being extremely important in determining what is recalled in a situation: the degree of positive affect associated with an event. Early work in this area stemmed from that aspect of Freudian theory that dealt with the repression of unacceptable motives. A number of laboratory experiments seemed to provide good support for the Freudian notion by demonstrating that people would remember fewer events with emotionally negative associations than those associated with positive affect (cf. Zeigarnik, 1927; Marrow, 1938). Additional support for this general hypothesis came from studies on the learning and retention of material that was antagonistic to the values of a person. Such investigations consistently demonstrated that contravaluent material is learned less rapidly and forgotten more easily (Levine and Murphy, 1943; Alper and Korchin, 1952).

It also seems possible to interpret two more recent studies of a quite different vintage in terms of this general principle relating memory to affective associations. Robbins (1963) interviewed groups of parents who had participiated in a longitudinal study of child-rearing practices. The parents had been interviewed at a number of intervals during the development of their children. In the final interview, at which time the mean age of the children was approximately three years, the parents were asked to recall various practices used with their children during the preceding years (such as age of weaning, toilet training, occurrence of thumbsucking, and the like). Gross discrepancies between the retrospective account and the account given by parents during the early development of the children were discovered. Important for present purposes is the fact that these distortions were in the direction of the child-rearing procedures recommended by recent manuals of child training (especially that of Spock). In an additional study by Jones, Gergen, and Davis (1962), subjects presented themselves to an interviewer either in an attempt to make a good impression or to be as honest as possible. Subsequently they found that the interviewer either liked or disliked them. When asked how honest they had been in the interview, subjects who had found that the interviewer liked them indicated that they had presented a more honest self-picture than those who had met with disapproval. The indication is that people will distort their memory of their intentions in a situation, as a result of the later repercussions of their behavior. Both of these latter studies are particularly important for present purposes because they show that individuals will not only fail to remember unpleasant events, but will distort their recollection of the past in self-enhancing ways.

Given these various sources of distortion, the significant question is, of course, how to reduce their effects. Snyder and Paige (1962) provide several alternative approaches to this problem. They suggest, for example, that a chronology of various events associated with the decision issue be formulated prior to interviewing, and presented by the interviewer to the respondent at the interview. They suggest that such a chronology may aid the respondent to recall accurately his and other's behavior and increase the richness of his mental associations. Such a procedure would certainly seem appropriate in light of the Luh (1928) findings previously discussed. Snyder and Paige (1962) also suggest that close questioning of several respondents can allow the development of a list of "memory checks." This list may be used in subsequent interviews to remind respondents of various crucial factors or to assess the trustworthiness of various responses. If the decision issue could be specified in advance, it is also possible to have a variety of decision makers keep diaries concerning their actions and motives regarding the issue. Such a technique also reduces the amount of interviewing subsequently necessitated.

Selected Techniques
of Assessment

Now that a number of important methodological issues have been discussed, we can take a closer look at several specific techniques used to assess various aspects of the decision-making process. As will be recalled, three primary-data sources were designated. However, several of the techniques to be discussed in this section are applicable to the assessment of more than one of these sources. Participant observation, for example, may be used to collect information about all three areas. Thus, no attempt will be made to group various methods under specific areas of applicability. It is also to be understood that the following list of methods does not begin to exhaust all available possibilities. We have tried to include those most likely to be of use in analyzing public policy formation on an individual level, and several methods were excluded because of their lack of specific relevance to the above discussion of issues. The analyses of statistical records and personal documents are cases in point. Both might be of great utility for research in the area of public policy formation, but a slightly different set of issues from those discussed above is more relevant to these methods (cf. Allport, 1942; Gottschalk, Kluckhohn, and Angell, 1945).

PARTICIPANT OBSERVATION. One outstanding method of obtaining information concerning the environmental context of decision making and the behavior of those individuals involved is that of participant observation. Used skillfully, participant observation can also serve to obtain indications of relevant psychological processes. In extreme form, the method requires that the investigator play an active role in the social system of interest. Such systems are normally ones that are relatively closed to observation from without. For example, in this vein, researchers have joined adolescent gangs, had themselves committed to mental institutions, and participated in labor unions. At the same time he is participating in the social system, the researcher attempts to observe the happenings in his surroundings. He usually records his experiences after the event. Both observation and recording are accompanied by analysis and speculation concerning underlying structure and processes in the environment.

The major advantage of this approach is that it allows the observer to obtain information about life in areas where little may initially be known or where group entry is a major problem. A thorough and searching analysis by a participant can sensitize him to a host of issues and factors that could not have been discerned from a more remote position. However, there are major shortcomings to this approach. The lack of formal criteria of assessment, independent checks on observation, and recurrence of phenomena prevent the introduction of normal standards of validity and reliability. In addition, the fact that results depend only on the views of a single individual who may be emotionally involved with the phenomena being studied raises serious issues of investigator bias. The amount of time required and the financial investment in such methodology can also be high.

A number of these difficulties may be alleviated if the observer does not function as a complete participant in the situation. Various levels of involvement and the problems attached thereto have been discussed by Junker (1960). If group-entry problems are solved, the observer may make his presence completely known to the persons being studied and allocate himself completely to the role of observer in the situation.[3] For example, an observer may attach

3. The classic early example of this technique is Roethlisberger and Dixon, *Management and the Worker.*

himself to a governmental office or agency, sit in on council meetings, or even accompany a high-leverage individual on his daily round of activities. Even though the behavior he observes may be altered somewhat by his presence, procedures of observation can be formalized to some extent and minimal criteria of validity and reliability be established. Greater time can also be spent in the spontaneous analysis of the behavior being observed and thus sensitize the individual to specific kinds of behaviors as they occur. This less intensive form of participant observation would seem particularly valuable if coupled with systematic interviews with the individuals observed. In this way one might check out various hypotheses or gain fresh insights into the behavior being observed.

In instances in which the primary intent of the investigator is to gain information on the surroundings or environmental context of decision making, actual participation in the environment may be avoided altogether. For example, at much less cost it would be possible to gain the rapport of long-standing members of the system and to conduct intensive interviews. Such interviews might be structured only to the extent that the respondent would be asked open-end questions concerning his work environment, social contacts, daily routines, and such. The investigator could take on the role of spontaneous analyst and formulate additional questions as needed. If several persons from the same social setting were thus interviewed, such an approach might also lend itself to considerations of validity and reliability.

In summary, it would seem that complete participant observation should be used sparingly if at all. The more detached form of this method is used most successfully in studying a limited sample of persons and their environments. As an example, detached observation might be used to study the lives of a select group of persons having maximum leverage. Intensive study of the way such persons interact with their environment could be highly enlightening, and coupled with interviews of the same individuals, could do much to further understanding of policy formation during the introductory stages of research.

THE FACE-TO-FACE INTERVIEW. Probably the most widely used of all methods in research on policy formation is that of the face-to-face interview. The interview has the major advantage of a high information yield, with a relatively small financial investment. Information pertaining to all three of the data sources can be obtained through interviewing. The face-to-face interview also ensures that virtually all members of the chosen sample are eventually reached. In addition, the interview can be highly flexible and can facilitate the investigation of highly complex issues. As we have noted, difficulties of validity, reliability, question bias, and retrospective bias can be partially remedied. The major problem in the interview remains that of investigator bias, but as we have also pointed out, steps can be taken to reduce such bias to currently acceptable limits.

The literature dealing with the face-to-face interview is voluminous.

Although the present treatment is by necessity cursory, there are three types of interviewing procedures that might be of particular use in studying public policy formation. The first—and most widely used—is the standard survey interview. This type of procedure has been used with relative success by a number of researchers in the policy area (cf. Eulau, Buchanan, Ferguson, and Wahlke, 1959; Matthews, 1960; Clapp, 1963). Normally, questions for such interviews are standardized and asked of all respondents in the same manner. Although the questions may offer a fixed set of alternative responses, in cases where little is known about the respondent's attitudes, perceptions, and so forth, open-end questions have been the rule. Several differences between these types of questions have been previously described.

The standard survey interview is most appropriate during two stages of research on policy formation. In the introductory stages where little may be known, the interview can yield a rich volume of information to be used in formulating more specific hypotheses. In this stage of research, open-end questions are most appropriate (cf. Lazarsfeld, 1944), and less attention may be paid to standards of validity and reliability. Once clear theoretical formulation has been developed and a better understanding gained of appropriate response alternatives, a set of fixed alternative items can be developed, with prime consideration given to matters of validity and reliability, and these items subsequently administered to a sample sufficiently large that statistical procedures can be employed.

A less structured interviewing procedure has been termed by Merton and his associates "the focused interview" (cf. Merton and Kendall, 1946; Merton, Fiske, and Kendall, 1956). In this case, before he makes the interview, the investigator develops a series of hypotheses concerning the effects of the environment on the person. This entails, of course, that the investigator possess a prior working knowledge of his area of study. On the basis of these hypotheses, the investigator fashions an *interview guide* that contains a list of major areas of inquiry and the hypotheses. The guide serves to orient the interviewer to specific types of questions. However, unlike the standard interview, the guide does not list a specific set of questions to be asked of each respondent. Rather, the interviewer is allowed considerable freedom in the type of question he asks and when he asks it. In addition, he is allowed to probe more deeply whenever it appears desirable. In other words, the guide provides a set of foci for the interviewer, but the interviewer himself determines the exact form and structure of the interview as he best sees fit.

The focused interview can be advantageous in several ways. It allows for a much deeper probing of attitudes, motives, and such, than the standard interview, and is thus most useful when exploring psychological processes. It is also sensitive to unanticipated responses bearing on specific hypotheses, and such responses can be given further attention in the interview itself. However, the success of this method does depend in great measure on the familiarity of the interviewer with the environment of the respondent, and the interviewer's capacity for sensitive exploration. Extensive interviewer training is thus a necessity. Because the interviewer plays such an active role in the interview and has no standardized set of questions, the likelihood for contamination through both investigator and question bias is high. Also, standard checks of validity and reliability are somewhat difficult to include.

Even with its disadvantages, the focused interview may be highly advantageous during the phase of investigation between initial and final data gathering. That is, preliminary facts may be used to establish a set of working hypotheses. The focused interview may provide support for these hypotheses as well as a rich body of supplementary material. A final verification of hypotheses might be based on more rigorous methodology and a larger sample. Additionally, the focused interview may be especially advantageous with persons of high prominence. Such persons may well resent an overly structured interview, and, in addition, they may play such a sufficiently distinctive role in the policy-making process that greater flexibility in questioning may be desirable.

A final variation of the face-to-face interview has been termed the protocol method (cf. Clarkson and Pounds, 1963). In this instance individuals are asked to think or solve problems aloud, and tape recordings are made of all their responses. These recordings, or protocols, can then be used for a variety of purposes. As can be seen, this technique is not greatly dissimilar to the interview variation on participant observation discussed before. However, the emphasis in the present case is not so much on how the individual sees his environment, as it is on how he relates to it in special circumstances. The technique might thus be to ask a series of hypothetical questions concerning what courses of action the individual would take, and why, when he is faced with particular problems. This method can yield much information concerning psychological processes and resultant behavior at a relatively low cost and lends itself to considerations of reliability. It is also relatively uncontaminated by investigator and question bias. However, it does require that much forethought be given to how protocols may be coded (cf. Lazarsfeld and Barton, 1951), and to whether response frequencies in the various coding categories are sufficiently large to draw reliable conclusions.

EXPERIMENTAL FIELD METHODS. An implicit assumption in the discussion thus far has been that research should be directed towards establishing correlations in natural settings. The assumption is based on several factors: when studying processes such as public policy formation, the most relevant and highly generalizable context is that in which actual public decision makers are operating; insufficient data are available to provide either a good understanding of the important variables or of their exact functional relationships; and, when using natural settings it is normally very difficult, or unethical, to introduce systematic manipulations. However, as one's understanding of the policy process improves, a number of these factors may undergo change. It may well be that sufficient data to define a limited number of significant variables and their functional relationships can be obtained; in addition, it is possible that natural settings can be secured to offer the opportunity for some type of systematic manipulation. Such opportunities should be highly valued. Correlational studies do not as yet offer good evidence of causal relationships between variables, and it is often difficult to be sure of the important variables for lack of adequate controls. Studies utilizing natural manipulations, for example, observing the effects of an innovation in an otherwise stable system, are more advantageous but synchronizing the manipulation with one's various resources is normally very difficult. Data obtained through controlled experimentation are thus at a premium in the area of public decision making and could potentially contribute much to our understanding.

As examples of experimental approaches, types of information could be introduced into a social system at selected points. Brochures supporting a particular stand on an issue or simply attempting to increase the salience of an issue could be sent through the mail to an experimental sample. Community action on the issue, attitudes expressed during interviews, or the measured salience of the issue to the individual could all serve as dependent variables, and comparisons could be made with relevant control samples. If persons with high leverage were identified, it would be of interest to attempt to expose such persons to varying amounts of persuasive information and observe the effects in terms of action taken on an issue. Tracing the communication flow of various kinds of information within the upper echelons of the system would also be feasible through the use of experimental manipulation.

MEDIATED COMMUNICATION. There are various methods of gathering information that do not require face-to-face confrontation with the respondent. One method for obtaining information concerning any of the three data sources previously described is through questionnaires sent through the mail. Matters of validity, reliability, and question bias can be treated in several of the ways described in preceding sections, and investigator bias can be reduced to a minimum (cf. Hyman, 1954). This method is also the least expensive of those discussed thus far. The major problem with the method is, of course, that many people do not return questionnaires, and nonrandom processes are often at work to determine the composition of the final sample. Normally, if returns are obtained from as many as 50 percent of the initial sample a study can be considered relatively successful. However, biases toward return are normally in the direction of excluding those who travel a lot and including those who are more interested, more literate, and more partisan with respect to the issue at hand (cf. Parten, 1950).

This method seems particularly valuable in cases where a large amount of information about more superficial attitudes and behavior is needed within a relatively short time. A probe in depth or a search for new insights would be better facilitated through either the focused or protocol interview. When the person was fully conscious of his behavior or was known to hold attitudes about a particular topic, the mail-out questionnaire may be useful. This method can also be considered integral with two earlier suggestions. In Chapter 5, a demographic method for determining leverage was discussed. The basic notion was that persons possessing high leverage consistently fall into circumscribed demographic groupings. Although all persons in such groupings might not have high leverage, one could be assured that by far the greater percentage of those having high leverage fall into the groupings. Thus, if questionnaires were sent to all those in a community or city who possessed the appropriate demographic characteristics, statistically reliable data could be obtained with relative ease.

It was also suggested that experimentation would be a valuable adjunct in the present research. One procedure that may be very useful would be to choose several communities at random, and to subject high-leverage residents in them to influence attempts through information campaigns and such. Influence attempts could be centered around a single issue of national importance. Mail-out questionnaires could serve as a follow-up device to determine the impact of the information campaigns. Further questionnaires might be sent to persons of low leverage to observe the impact of information flow. Most interesting would be the instance in which some kind of legislation was in the balance. If the model developed in the leverage paper is correct, one should be able to predict the outcome of legislation by knowing the attitudes of those possessing maximum leverage in the various resource subphases.

Under certain specialized circumstances it is possible to gain useful information in a short period of time through telephone interviews. In spite of the fact that rapport is difficult to develop over the telephone, and because there are obvious limitations placed on the number and types of questions asked, such interviews may play an important role. In the sense that there is far less bias through sample loss, they may be more valuable than the mail-out questionnaires. In the section on validity it was noted that under conditions where one's theoretical constructs are sufficiently simple or well developed, minimal information may be required in any one instance. Situations in which questions offering only a limited range of alternative responses are employed may lend themselves to telephone questioning.

ROLE ANALYSIS. Each of the methods discussed can be used without commitment to particular theoretical concepts or delineated data sources. Role analysis, on the other hand, does orient one to a more circumscribed set of considerations. It is also the case that the analysis of social roles may be based on a composite use of several of the mentioned single methods. In essence, role analysis sensitizes the investigator to somewhat specific aspects of the data source, and carries with it a number of conceptual distinctions that have had widespread application. Role analysis itself is less a specific tool for the obtaining of this data.

The concept of social role has been found to have considerable utility in the understanding and predicting of social behavior (cf. Linton, 1936, 1945; Znaniecki, 1940; Cottrell, 1942; Komarovsky, 1946; Benne and Sheats, 1948; Newcomb, 1951; Parsons, 1951; Sargent, 1951; Sarbin, 1954; Slater, 1955; Merton, 1956; Rommetveit, 1955). Although it is true that not all theorists use the concept in a similar fashion, there does seem to be considerable consensus in applying the term to the more or less stable aspects of a person's behavior observed when he interacts with either another person or a delimited class of other persons. In the majority of instances role behavior is said to be integrally related to the system of expectations that others have about the particular person in question. Such expectations may give rise to positive reinforcement for in-role behavior and negative consequences for behavior that deviates from expectation. In that role behavior is generally stable and ensconced in the system of normative expectations, it is also apparent why the concept of role is often used in treating persons occupying certain positions or statuses within society. For a lesser number of investigators, role also implies functionality; by engaging in role behavior, the person is contributing in some way to the viability of the social system of which he is a member. Since this latter assumption has generally proved less fruitful in research than in theory, it will not receive major attention in the present analysis.

The concept of social role would also seem to have considerable utility in treating the formation of public policy. For example, in the earlier discussion of leverage (Chapter 5), it was ventured that there were several phases through which a decision must successfully pass before becoming activated. In each of these phases, it was suggested, there were persons possessing certain types of leverage. Whereas one person might largely serve to initiate policy matters, another might essentially have control of the purse strings. In addition, it was assumed that the process of policy formation was primarily social in character, and that the social interaction among high-leverage persons was of major importance. One could thus speak of a leverage system. As can be seen, the concept of social role can be a valuable adjunct in understanding system process. The social behavior of any person within the system may be highly patterned. Members of the system may variously develop expectations about the behavior of other members. These expectations may largely influence the type of behavior in which any member engages during the process of decision making.

In addition, each decision maker may be a member of a separate social system. Whereas the person who staffs and plans for a given decision issue may be a member of a government body, the financier may be an executive in a large bank or the head of a corporation. As Bauer, Pool, and Dexter (1963) have indicated, the role which such persons play in their respective social systems has a great impact on their decisions in any given instance. Any understanding of their relations within these systems could well be facilitated through role analysis.

Although the concept of social role has occupied a central position in theory, the attempts at operationalizing the concept have been far fewer. In their review of the literature on roles, Neiman and Hughes (1951) suggest that the term may be of very little utility, because it has generally failed to figure prominently in the development of empirical hypotheses. Although it is not clear why the scientific utility of a concept must always be measured against the yardstick of operationalism (cf. Carnap, 1955), there are numerous instances in which the concept has been put to good empirical use. A discussion of several of these instances may prove helpful with regard to developing suitable methods for the study of public policy formation.

One of the most historically significant lines of research related to social roles has centered around the work of Everett C. Hughes (1937, 1938, 1946, 1952, 1956, 1958). Although the concept of role has played less than a central function in the work of Hughes and his colleagues, their approach to occupations and work is clearly relevant. Their general approach to occupations initially involved the development of field-work techniques at a time when others were engaging almost solely in speculative accounts. The two major techniques fostered from a long series of investigations were the face-to-face interview in the occupational setting and participant observation. Among the occupations studied using these and other devices were the merchant seaman (Beattie, 1950), the public servant (Bendix, 1947), the flat janitor (Gold, 1950), the rabbi (Carlin and Mendlovitz, 1951), the school teacher (Harris, 1952), the aging industrial worker (Ireland, 1951), congressmen, (Mauksch, 1961), the police (Westley, 1951), and real-estate agents (Hughes, 1928). Methodologically, one of the more important legacies from these various studies is Junkers' (1960) monograph on field methods. The value of his book has already been commented on. For the present, it might be said that the major lesson that one may learn from this volume regarding role analysis is the importance of understanding a person's occupational behavior from the point of view of the person himself. In essence, for the investigator this means immersing himself in the context of the person being studied and making a determined effort to understand the way in which the subject conceptualizes the world about him.

In addition, however, the Hughes group has also highlighted several crucial considerations for the study of social roles. The first of these are the day-to-day small groups of which the individual is a member. The individual's conception of self and role may be influenced markedly by both formal and informal interaction in such groups. A second aspect of importance is the institutional setting in which the person is enmeshed. How does he perceive his relation with the larger institution? What is expected of him? What is sanctioned? What is rewarded? How does he function within the system? The third issue of relevance for role analysis has to do with the individual's relationship with his cultural context. His conception of his occupational role and his occupational behavior may be determined in large part by his perception of himself within the larger social context.

The general method of intensive interviewing and long-term presence of the investigator at the scene of investigation has been followed in a variety of more recent attempts at depicting the behavior of persons occupying certain social positions. For example, Buchanan, Eulau, Ferguson (1960) have studied the state legislator. The United States congressman (Dexter, 1957; Clapp, 1963) and the senator (Matthews, 1960, 1961) have received similar attention. Concern has also been given to such roles as the professional politician (Mitchell, 1958), the federal executive (Bernstein, 1958), and the small-city banker (Kimbrough, 1958). While each of these studies enriches our knowledge of the lives led by the various role incumbents, it is also true that this general line of investigation can only form a preliminary wedge into the problems of understanding policy formation. Such analyses do not usually result in specific operational definitions or quantifiable results. In order to test theoretical propositions relating two or more variables, more rigorous methodology is necessary.

A move toward more rigorous observation has been evidenced within the past decade. Concomitant with this move has been the development of many role-related variables and a series of studies attempting to specify the interrelationship of such variables. For example, the concept of *role clarity* has been used to refer to the person's perception of the degree of explicitness provided by others concerning what types of behavior are expected. Schwartz (1957) has examined the way in which lack of role clarity may produce frustration for the person in not providing clear-cut norms for behavior. Wardell (1952) has observed that the lack of role clarity may produce strain for the chiropractic physician in his practice. Closely related to the concept of role clarity is that of *role consensus*, or the degree to which others agree as to the type of behavior expected from a person occupying a certain position. In perhaps the most extensive analysis of any social role, Gross, Mason, and McEachern (1958) found that the degree of consensus felt by school superintendents concerning their roles was dependent upon the content of the specific role, the background similarity of the superintendents, and the size of the educational organization in which the superintendent was employed. These investigators further distinguish between *intraposition consensus*, or the degree to which persons occupying the same position agree as to the expectations applying to that position, and *interposition consensus* which refers to the agreement between what the role incumbents feel is expected and what those occupying other positions feel is expected. Thomas (1959), Hanson (1962), and Julian (1962) have continued this line of research by focusing on a number of additional variables (such as system size, amount of communication among occupants, amount of training, and the relationship of the person to other positions in the system) which affect degree of consensus.

Role conflict, or the degree to which the person finds himself confronted by opposing expectations, has also been a source of major concern among investigators in this area. Sources of role conflict among public officials (Mitchell, 1958), insurance agents (Wispe, 1955), school superintendents (Seeman, 1953; Gross, Mason, and McEachern, 1958), among chaplains (Burchard, 1954), and professional military officers (Bidwell, 1961) have all been studied. These and other investigations (cf. Merton, 1957; Toby, 1952; Bloombaum, 1961; Killian, 1952; Turner, 1962, Perry and Wynne, 1959) have also shed much light on general reactions of persons to conflicting roles. The body of evidence concerning the factors that predict the ways in which people will resolve role conflict (for example, legitimacy, personality, and social sanction) is of considerable relevance to the problem of predicting decision making in the policy area.

As can be seen, the various aspects of the social role that have been explored are quite varied, and each exploration sensitizes one to new dimensions of the problem. With this background, it is now possible to ask a number of more pointed questions concerning role analysis of high-leverage persons. As a précis of this discussion it may be useful to review briefly the most exhaustive and well known of the attempts to analyze a single social role. In 1958 Gross, Mason, and McEachern published their account of the role of the school superintendent. Although the results of this study are important in their own right, several of the procedures are of specific relevance to the present concern. It is first noted that all participants were interviewed by a senior investigator for a period of approximately eight hours. It was felt by the investigators that to obtain information in relatively sensitive domains required an extensive period of rapport building. More delicate questions were not introduced until the fifth or sixth hour of the interview. Although the lengthy interview was felt to be necessary as a result of pretest experience, for the role analysis of high-leverage persons such lengthy interviews may well not be practicable. The development of specialized techniques for building rapport would be highly useful.

It is also of interest that Gross, Mason, and McEachern chose to carry out interviewing in a location especially established for that purpose. As they note, it was extremely difficult to obtain the desired rapport and continuity when carrying out the interview in the respondent's office. In this manner, the interviewer was not forced to accommodate himself to the variety of interruptions that otherwise occurred. In addition, the independent location seemed to prompt more candid replies on the part of the respondent. Finally, it is noteworthy that Gross, Mason, and McEachern used a variety of interviewing techniques, including self-administered questionnaires, interviewer-administered questionnaires, and closed- and open-ended questions. By shifting methods of questioning it was found that fatigue was avoided. The greatest fatigue was found, interestingly enough, with the closed, self-administered questionnaires.

Although the Gross, Mason, and McEachern study provides some highly useful information concerning techniques of intensive role analysis, the question of analytic focus is another matter. For example, to what extent would data concerning role consensus, role clarity, or role conflict lend itself to an understanding of policy-making behavior? Since one pivotal aspect of these various concepts is that of social expectancy, the question may be rephrased in the following way: To what extent is the policy-making behavior of the high-leverage person determined or influenced by the expectations others have about his behavior? To what extent are major policy makers sensitive to the pressures of social expectancy? There is at least some evidence (cf. discussions by Homans and Riecken, 1954, and Hollander, 1958) indicating that those occupying senior positions in a status hierarchy maintain considerable independence from the system of social or institutional norms by which they are surrounded. In a study by Gergen and Gibbs (1965), it was further demonstrated that in a task setting, senior members of a status hierarchy would act in such a way as to *violate* the expectations of them held by lower-ranking persons.

On the other hand it does seem to be the case that elected public officials may be highly sensitive to the expectations of their electorate. It may also be that certain high-leverage persons may be more sensitized to the expectations of other high-leverage persons than to the expectancies of those within their respective formal organizations. For example, a person who wields great influence in the planning stages of policy making or who has control of mass media may be much more influenced by the expectations of other influentials than those of a planning board or the general public. This discussion raises two major empirical questions. For any high-leverage person, toward what groups is he sensitive in terms of responding to social expectation? Second, to what degree and under what circumstances will behavioral conformity to these expectations occur? Any light shed on these issues would have a three-pronged payoff: It would enrich our understanding of the determinants of the behavior of public policy influentials, it would point to potential sectors from which communications to the policy maker might have optimum impact, and finally it would expand the scope of role theory in the sorely needed direction of associating role-theory concepts to specific overt behavior.

As noted above, one pivotal aspect of most role-related concepts has to do with social expectancy. There is a second aspect that also deserves attention in this discussion of empirical focus. Role theory is largely concerned with relatively stable patterns of behavior in which a person may engage while occupying a certain institutional position. Clearly, if understanding is to be gained of the way in which the policy maker processes information in making decisions, it would be useful to know about his characteristic modes of behavior. Policy decisions are inextricably connected to the spheres of daily behavior in which the decision maker engages.

Of course, through long-term observation of single policy makers one might be able to conceptualize common behavior patterns. However, given limited resources and the need for extensive data, it again seems appropriate to develop interviewing methods. Here it is useful to return to the emphasis of Hughes and his coworkers on understanding occupational role through the eyes of the role incumbent himself. The empirical focus, then, is on the way in which the person himself defines his various roles.

Although such a focus seems simple enough at the outset, there are a number of subtleties that deserve final attention. Personal definition of role is never absolute. The age-old folk lesson of the carpenter asked about his activities is relevant here. Simultaneously, he is nailing a board, laying a foundation, constructing a building, and contributing to the beauty and betterment of the human race. In short, personal definitions of behavior are multiple, and each yields slightly differing information about the person's orientation toward his work. It may also be ventured that the nature of the definition yielded in a given instance will depend on the reference groups salient to the individual at that particular time. The occupational definitions that a person may provide to a close friend, a business associate, a competitor, and his wife may all be different and yet all equally believed by the person. Issues of question and interviewer bias again arise, for it could be speculated that the definition an interviewer receives may be quite dependent on the role that he is seen to occupy by the respondent and the way the questions are phrased.

In coming to grips with these issues, an appropriate procedure might include having the respondent first describe his occupation in very concrete and operational terms. More abstract definitions may be more useful in tapping underlying psychological properties, such as immediate goals, a reference group whose acceptance is important, or some life goal. Such sources of motivation may be of great importance in understanding any given behavioral instance. In order to explore these more abstract definitions, the respondent might be asked to define his actions a number of times, in each instance with a different reference group in mind. The respondent might be asked to comment on his work from the standpoint of himself as public officeholder, professional lawyer, possessor of influence, family head, or other position. Such a procedure lends itself also to asking about the person's role *vis-à-vis* a particular policy issue at stake in a given study. It would be of interest, for example, to know how the newspaper editor or bank president defined his role with regard to a specific issue such as mass transportation.

This emphasis on multiple role structuring has considerable implication for future research. Knowledge of the particular definition chosen by the person in a situation should reveal much about the decisions that he might make and the likelihood of certain behaviors occurring. With sufficient data, for any given role position one might construct a distribution of various role definitions. If behavior could be empirically associated with each type of definition, one could conceivably predict decision making in new situations for new populations of such persons. It is also probable that one's role definitions may be altered from one situation to another. The businessman who may essentially define himself as aggressively motivated in the service of financial gain may quite well redefine himself as a publicly responsible citizen when faced with certain public policy issues. Such situationally dependent role shifts would be worthy of special attention.

Overall Research
Strategy

The preceding review of methods of research suggests the possibility of an overall strategy in the study of public policy formation. One might think in terms of a strategy of interlocking research phases. During early stages, procedures more appropriate for gathering general information about the context of the decision maker and his behavior might be gathered through such devices as participant observation or mail-out questionnaires. As hypotheses and speculations about process and cause-and-effect relationships were developed, such methods as the focused or protocol interview might be employed for studies in depth. At this point some form of role analysis would also be appropriate. On the basis of the information obtained, a standardized interview might be developed for the more rigorous testing of hypotheses. In instances in which factors could be isolated and cause-and-effect relations specified, experimentation might serve as the final phase of research. Whenever possible, research methods might also be systematically varied as part of the research design. In this way, methodological advances might accompany more generalized advances in knowledge. Within this framework, however, it should constantly be remembered that policy formation is a continuing process, and it is almost impossible to freeze the process at any one point and gain an adequate conceptualization. Just as those persons involved with policy formation may be constantly altering their perception of issues and others about them, so must the researcher be continuously ready to alter research strategies.

In summary, this paper has discussed a number of the more important methodological issues and research methods relevant to the study of public policy formation. Although the treatment of neither issues nor methods was exhaustive, it is hoped that those issues most salient to the study of public policy formation were included. It should be concluded, however, that a chapter in methodology is never complete, and that each empirical study should hopefully augment our present understanding.

BIBLIOGRAPHY

Allport, Gordon, *The Use of Personal Documents in Psychological Science* (New York: Social Science Research Council, 1942).

Back, Kurt W., and Kenneth J. Gergen, "Idea Orientation and Ingratiation in the Interview: A Dynamic Model of Response Bias," *Proceedings American Statistical Association*, pp. 284–288, 1963.

Bauer, Raymond, Ithiel de Sola Pool, Lewis Anthony Dexter, *American Business and Public Policy* (New York: Atherton Press, 1963).

Beattie, Walter M., *The Merchant Seaman*. University of Chicago, M.A. thesis, 1950.

Bendix, Reinhard, *The Public Servant in a Democracy*. University of Chicago, Ph.D. dissertation, 1947.

Benne, K. D., and P. Sheats, "Functional Roles of Group Members," *Journal of Social Issues*, IV, No. 2 (1948), pp. 41–49.

Bernstein, Marver H., *The Job of the Federal Executive* (Washington, D.C.: The Brookings Institute, 1958).

Bidwell, C. E., "The Young Professional in the Army: A Study of Occupational Identity," *American Sociological Review*, 26 (1961), pp. 360–372.

Bloombaum, M., "Factors in the Resolution of Role Conflict." Paper read at American Sociological Association, St. Louis, August 1961.

Buchanan, W., H. Eulau, L. C. Ferguson, and J. C. Wahlke, "The Legislator As Specialist," *Western Political Quarterly*, XIII, No. 3 (September 1960), pp. 636–651.

Burchard, Waldo W., "Role Conflicts in Military Chaplains," *American Sociological Review*, XIX (1954), pp. 588–535.

Carlin, Jerome, and Saul Mendovitz, *The Rabbi, Sociological Study of a Religious Specialist*. University of Chicago, M.A. thesis, 1951.

Cattell, R. B., "Validity and Reliability: A Proposed More Basic Set of Concepts," *Journal of Educational Psychology*, 55 (1964), pp. 1–22.

Clapp, C. L., *The Congressman: His Work As He Sees It* (Washington, D.C.: The Brookings Institute, 1963).

Cottrell, Leonard S., Jr., "The Adjustment of the Individual to His Age and Sex Roles," *American Sociological Review*, VII (1942).

Culbertson, John, *The Role of Businessmen in the National Policy Determination of Commercial Applications of Communications Satellite Technology* (Boston: Harvard Business School, 1965).

Dearborn, C. DeWitt, and H. A. Simon, "Selective Perception: A Note on the Departmental Identification of Executives," *Sociometry*, 21 (1958), pp. 140–144.

Dexter, Louis Anthony: "The Representative and His District," *Human Organization*, XVI, No. 1, (Spring, 1957), pp. 2–13.

Ebbinghaus, H., *Memory: A Contribution to Experimental Psychology.* Translated by H. A. Ruger and C. E. Bussenius (New York: Columbia University Press, 1913).

Edwards, A. L., *The Social Desirability Variable in Personality Assessment and Research* (New York: Holt, Rinehart and Winston, 1957).

Eulau, H., W. Buchanan, L. Ferguson, and J. C. Wahlke, "The Political Socialization of American State Legislators," *Midwest Journal of Political Science*, **III**, No. 2 (May 1959), pp. 188–201.

Feshbach, S., and R. D. Singer, "The Effects of Fear Arousal and Suppression of Fear upon Social Perception," *Journal of Abnormal and Social Psychology*, **55** (1957), pp. 283–288.

Festinger, Leon, and Daniels Katz, *Research Methods in the Behavioral Sciences* (New York: Holt, Rinehart and Winston, 1953).

Gergen, Kenneth J., "Interaction Goals and Personalistic Feedback As Factors Affecting the Presentation of Self," *Journal of Personality and Social Psychology*, **1** (1965), pp. 626.

—— and B. Wishnov, "Others' Self Evaluations and Interaction Anticipation as Determinants of Self Presentation," *Journal of Personality and Social Psychology*, **2** (1965), pp. 348–358.

Gold, Ray, *The Chicago Flat Janitor*, University of Chicago, M.A. thesis, 1950.

Gottschalk, L., C. Kluckhohn, and R. Angell, "The Use of Personal Documents in History, Anthropology, and Sociology," *Bulletin* 53 (New York: Social Science Research Council, 1945).

Gross, Neal, Ward S. Mason, and Alexander W. McEachern, *Explorations in Role Analysis: Studies of the School Superintendency Role* (New York: John Wiley, 1958).

Guilford, J. P., *General Psychology* (Princeton, N.J.: D. Van Nostrand, 1952).

Hanson, R. C. "The Systematic Linkage Hypothesis and Role Consensus Patterns in Hospital-Community Relations," *American Sociological Review*, **27** (1962), pp. 304–313.

Harris, Barbara M., *The School Teacher in an Upper-Middle Class School.* University of Chicago, M.A. thesis, 1952.

Hollander, E. P., "Conformity, Status, and Idiosyncrasy Credit," *Psychological Review*, **65** (1958), pp. 117–127.

Homans, George C., and Henry W. Riecken, "Pyschological Aspects of Social Structure," in *Handbook of Social Psychology*, Vol. II, Gardner Lindzey, (ed.) (Cambridge, Mass.: Addison-Wesley, 1954).

Hovland, C. I. (ed.), *The Order of Presentation in Persuasion* (New Haven: Yale University Press, 1957).

Hughes, Everett C., "Institutional Office and the Person," *American Journal of Sociology*, **XLIII** (November 1937), pp. 404–413.

—— *Men and Their Work* (New York: Free Press, 1958).

—— "Position and Status in a Quebec Industrial Town," *American Sociological Review*, **III, 5** (October 1938), pp. 709–717.

—— "Social Institutions," in *New Outline of the Principles of Sociology*, Part V, pp. 223–282, N. A. Lee, (ed.) (New York: Barnes and Noble, 1946).

Hughes, Everett C., "The Sociological Study of Work," *American Journal of Sociology*, LVII (March 1952), pp. 423–426.

—— *A Study of a Secular Institution: The Chicago Real Estate Board*. Department of Anthropology, University of Chicago, Ph.D. dissertation; 1928.

Hyman, Herbert, *et al.*, *Interviewing in Social Research* (Chicago: University of Chicago Press, 1954).

Ireland, Ralph, *The Aging Industrial Worker: Retirement Plans and Preparation with Some Reference to the Meaning of Work*. University of Chicago, Ph.D. dissertation, 1951.

Jones, E. E., K. E. Davis, and K. J. Gergen, "Some Determinants of Reactions to Being Approved or Disapproved As a Person," *Psychological Monographs*, 76, No. 2, Whole No. 521 (1962).

Julian, J., "Some Determinants of Role Consensus Within and Between Organizational Strata," paper read at Pacific Sociological Association, Sacramento, April, 1962.

Junker, B. H., *Field Work: An Introduction to the Social Sciences* (Chicago: University of Chicago Press, 1960).

Kerlinger, Fred N., *Foundations of Behavioral Research* (New York: Holt, Rinehart and Winston, 1964).

Killian, L. M., "The Significance of Multiple-Group Membership in Disaster," *American Journal of Sociology*, 57 (1952), pp. 309–313.

Kimbrough, Emery, "The Role of the Banker in a Small City," *Social Forces*, 36, No. 4 (May 1958), pp. 316–322.

Komarovsky, Mirra, "Cultural Contradictions and Sex Roles," *American Journal of Sociology*, LII (1946), pp. 184–189.

Kreuger, W. C. F., "The Effect of Overlearning on Retention," *Journal Experimental Psychology*, 12 (1929), pp. 71–78.

Lazarsfeld, Paul F., "The Controversy over Detailed Interviews—An Offer for Negotiation," *Public Opinion Quarterly*, VIII (1944), pp. 38–60.

—— and Allen H. Barton, "Qualitative Measurement in the Social Sciences," in Daniel Lerner and H. Lasswell: *The Policy Sciences* (Stanford: Stanford University Press, 1951).

Levine, J. M., and G. Murphy, "The Learning and Forgetting of Controversial Material," *Journal of Abnormal and Social Psychology*, 38 (1943), pp. 507–517.

Linton, Ralph, *The Cultural Background of Personality* (New York: D. Appleton-Century Company, 1945).

—— *The Study of Man* (New York: D. Appleton-Century Company, 1936).

Luh, C. W., "The Conditions of Retention," *Psychological Monographs*, 31, No. 142 (1922).

Marrow, A. J., "Goal Tensions and Recall: I, II" *Journal of General Psychology*, 19 (1938), pp. 3–35 and 37–64.

Matthews, Donald R., *U.S. Senators and Their World* (Chapel Hill, N.C.: University of North Carolina Press, 1960).

Mauksch, Hans, *The Social and Political Background of the Members of the Seventy-sixth United States Congress*. University of Chicago, M.A. thesis, 1951.

Merton, Robert K., "The Role Set: Problems in Sociological Theory," *British Journal of Sociology*, VIII, No. 3 (June 1957), pp. 106–120.

―――― *Social Theory and Social Structure* (New York: Free Press, 1956).

―――― M. Fiske, and P. L. Kendall, *The Focused Interview* (New York: Free Press, 1956).

―――― and P. L. Kendall, "The Focused Interview," *American Journal of Sociology*, LI (1946), pp. 541–557.

Mitchell, William C., "Occupational Role Strains: The American Elective Official," *Administrative Science Quarterly*, III, No. 2, (September 1958), pp. 210–228.

Neiman, Lionel J., and James W. Hughes, "The Problem of the Concept of Role—A Re-survey of the Literature," *Social Forces*, XXX (1951), pp. 141–149.

Newcomb, Theodore M., *Social Psychology* (New York: Dryden Press, 1951).

Parsons, Talcott, *The Social System* (New York: Free Press, 1951).

Parten, Mildred Bernice, *Surveys, Polls, and Samples* (New York: Harper and Row, 1950).

Perry, S. E., and L. C. Wynne, "Role Conflict, Role Redefinition, and Social Change in a Clinical Research Organization," *Social Forces*, 38 (1959), pp. 62–65.

Robbins, Lillian Cukier, "The Accuracy of Parental Recall of Aspects of Child Development and of Child Rearing Practices," *Journal of Abnormal and Social Psychology*, 66, No. 3 (March 1963), pp. 261–270.

Roethlisberger, F. J., and W. J. Dickson, *Management and the Worker* (Cambridge, Mass.: Harvard University Press, 1943).

Rommetveit, Ragnar, *Social Norms and Roles: Explorations in the Psychology of Enduring Social Pressures* (Minneapolis: University of Minnesota Press, 1954–1955).

Rosenthal, Robert, "Experimenter Outcome-Orientation and the Results of the Psychological Experiment," *Psychological Bulletin*, No. 6, pp. 405–412, 1964.

Sarbin, Theodore, "Role Theory" in *Handbook of Social Psychology*, Vol. I, Gardner Lindzey, (ed.) (Cambridge, Mass.: Addison-Wesley, 1954), pp. 223–258.

Sargent, Standsfeld, "Concepts of Role and Ego in Contemporary Psychology," in *Social Psychology at the Crossroads*, John H. Rohrer and Muzafer Sherif, (ed.) (New York: Harper and Row, 1951).

Schwartz, Charlotte G., "Problems for Psychiatric Nurses in Playing a New Role in a Mental Hospital Ward," in *The Patient and the Mental Hospital*, M. Greenblatt, D. J. Levinson, and R. H. Williams, (ed.) (New York: Free Press, 1957).

Seeman, M.: "Role Conflict and Ambivalence in Leadership," *American Sociological Review*, 18 (1953), pp. 373–380.

Selltiz, Claire, Marie Jahoda, Morton Deutsch, and Stuart W. Cook, *Research Methods in Social Relations* (New York, Henry Holt, 1960).

Slater, Philip E., "Role Differentiation in Small Groups," in *Family, Socialization, and Interaction Process*, A. Paul Hare, Edgar F. Borgatta, Robert F. Bales, (ed.) (New York: Free Press, 1955).

Snyder, Richard C., and Glenn D. Paige, "The United States Decision to Resist Aggression in Korea: The Application of an Analytical Scheme," in *Foreign*

Policy Decision Making, Richard C. Snyder, H. W. Bruck, Burton Sapin, (eds.) (New York: Free Press, 1962), pp. 206–250.

Taietz, Philip, "Conflicting Group Norms and the 'Third' Person in the Interview," *American Journal of Sociology*, **68** (July 1962), pp. 97–104.

Thomas, E. J., "Role Conceptions and Organizational Size," *American Sociological Review*, **24** (1959), pp. 30–37.

Toby, Jackson, "Some Variables in Role Conflict Analysis," *Social Forces*, **XXX** (1952).

Turner, R. H., "Role-Taking Process versus Confirmity," in *Human Behavior and Social Processes: An Interactionist Approach*, A. Rose, (ed.) (Boston: Houghton-Mifflin, 1962).

Wahlke, J. C., W. Buchanan, H. Eulau, and L. C. Ferguson, "American State Legislators' Role Orientations Toward Pressure Groups," *Journal of Politics*, **XXII**, No. 2 (May 1960), pp. 203–227.

Wallace, S. Rains, "Criteria for What?" *American Psychologist*, **20,** No. 6 (June 1965), pp. 411–418.

Wardwell, W. A., "The Reduction of Strain in a Marginal Social Role," *American Journal of Sociology*, **61** (1952), pp. 16–24.

Westley, William, *The Police*. University of Chicago, Ph.D. dissertation, 1951.

Wispe, L. G. "A Sociometric Analysis of Conflicting Role Expectancies," *American Journal of Sociology*, **61** (1955), pp. 134–137.

Zeigarnik, B., "Über das Behalten von erledigten und unerledigten Handlungen," *Psychologie Forschrift*, **9,** pp. 1–85.

Znaniecki, Florian, *The Social Role of the Man of Knowledge* (New York: Columbia University Press, 1940).

Chapter 7

LEWIS M. SCHNEIDER

Urban Mass Transportation: A Survey of the Decision-Making Process*

Introduction

THE URBAN MASS TRANSPORTATION PROBLEM

This chapter will investigate the subject of urban mass transportation, certainly one of the more frustrating public policy questions confronting decision makers in our society. The urban transportation problem refers to the general task of moving persons and goods within urban areas by a variety of technologies including the automobile, truck, railroad, bus, rapid transit, and streetcar. The urban mass transportation dilemma can be thought of as one aspect of the general problem. For purposes of this chapter, mass transportation will refer specifically to the movement of people in urban areas by mass-transit companies (operating rapid transit, buses, and streetcars) and commuter railroads. Thus an investment in the highway system designed to facilitate private automobile transportation will not be considered an investment in urban mass transportation. On the other hand, highway construction obviously has a major impact on both the overall urban transportation picture and on individual urban mass-transportation companies.

* This chapter was prepared during the summer of 1964 and revised extensively during 1965. Minor changes were made during the fall of 1966, but the bulk of the substantive material was current as of 1965.

The urban mass transportation problem has different meanings for different people, yet, in the aggregate, it looms as a major source of discomfort and bewilderment to our nation. For example, the "senior citizen" residing in a small town and without access to an automobile sees the problem as the sudden termination of local bus service. In the mushrooming cities the crisis strikes the home-to-work commuter as a lethal mixture of sick transit companies and commuter railroads, each often characterized by declining demand (particularly during off-peak hours), uncomfortable and poor service, increasing fares and costs of operation, reduced or nonexistent profits, and the inability to secure capital funds for modernization and expansion. Although the few remaining commuter railroads operate as private enterprise, the adverse financial trends have forced most mass transit companies in our larger cities from private to public enterprise. Today, only three of the twelve largest cities in the United States (Washington D.C., Philadelphia, and Baltimore) are being served by private companies.[1] In the case of the last two, legislation has been passed to acquire the transit companies.

In both small towns and large cities the mass transportation crisis stems from the private automobile and changing land-use patterns. Each reinforces the other. The automobile has enabled residential, commercial, and industrial activities to flee from the core and central cities to the suburbs. In turn, the attractiveness of the suburbs has stimulated others left behind to purchase automobiles and join the exodus. These new land-use patterns have seriously hurt both urban mass transportation and the central cities. Mass transportation functions most efficiently when connecting high-density industrial, commercial, and residential activity in the central cities. The diffusion of economic activity into the suburbs has often produced travel patterns of relatively low volume (in terms of time and space) that cannot profitably be handled by mass transportation. As Vernon has pointed out: "Instead of wondering how to haul people to and from the central business district with comfort and dispatch, our prime question may well be how to move people from the dispersed homes in one suburb to the dispersed plants in another."[2]

Equally important as the changing land-use patterns has been the desire of people to use an automobile wherever possible. Ernest Dichter has explained this phenomenon in these words:

> The most important symbol of middle class development in the world

1. For a discussion of the different forms of public ownership and operation see Norman Kennedy and Wolfgang Homburger, *The Organization of Metropolitan Transit Agencies* (Berkeley: University of California Institute of Transportation and Traffic Engineering, 1961); City of Philadelphia, Mayor's Transit Task Force, *The Public Transit Authority—A Study of Five Cities* (Philadelphia: Published by the City, 1963); and Wilfred Owen, *The Metropolitan Transportation Problem* (Washington, D.C.: The Brookings Institution, 1956), 191ff.

2. Raymond Vernon, "The Economics and Finances of the Large Metropolis," *Daedalus*, XC (Winter 1961), p. 43.

today is the automobile. It is the automobile which represents achievement and personal freedom for the middle class. . . . The automobile is the symbol of mobility; the automobile has become the self mobile.[3]

The automobile has had its greatest effect on urban mass transportation patronage in the smaller towns where travel volumes are low and traffic congestion is minimized. The American Transit Association has reported that between 1954 and 1963, 194 transit companies abandoned operations in the United States. The overwhelming majority of these companies served small cities and towns. But even in the largest cities of our country, clogged expressways and parking lots have not deterred travelers from choosing the automobile in preference to urban mass transportation. Except during the peak home-to-work commuting hours, the vast majority of urban trips in our largest cities are made by private automobile.[4] This imbalance between peak and off-peak patronage has contributed substantially to the deteriorating financial position of existing urban mass transportation companies.

This chapter will confine itself to urban mass transportation in our larger cities. There are two reasons for this limitation. On the one hand, our nation is completing a transition from a rural to an urban society. The problems of the small towns and cities are receding; the major policy decisions during the next decades will concern our largest metropolitan areas. By the year 2000, 85 percent of our population is expected to live in urban areas with 107 million of them in ten super-metropolises ranging in size from 5 to 23 million people.[5]

At present there is a great deal of controversy over the land-use patterns in the future urban areas. If the central business districts and surrounding central cities are revitalized on the principle of relatively dense residential, commercial, and industrial activity, a strong urban mass transportation system would seem to be appropriate to insure circulation of persons. But others maintain that even though our urban areas will increase in population, the trend will be to greater dispersion and lower density activity. In such an environment, as noted earlier, urban mass transportation will not be able to function efficiently. In short, the major decisions on land use will necessarily dictate the nature of the urban transportation system.

3. Ernest Dichter, "The World Customer," *Harvard Business Review* (July-August 1962), pp. 118–119.

4. For statistics of urban trip patterns see Wilbur Smith & Associates, *Future Highways and Urban Growth* (New Haven: Wilbur Smith & Associates, 1961); J. R. Meyer, *et al.*, *The Urban Transportation Problem*, (Cambridge, Mass.: Harvard University Press, 1965); and U.S. Congress, Senate, Committee on Interstate and Foreign Commerce, Special Study Group on Transportation Policies in the United States, *National Transportation Policy: Preliminary Draft of a Report*, 87th Cong., 1st Sess. (1961), pp. 582–632. Hereafter cited under its popular title, *Doyle Report*.

5. Smith & Associates, *op. cit.* p. 10; and Jerome Pickard, *The Metropolitanization of the United States* quoted in the *Human Need for Rapid Transportation* (Mansfield, Ohio Press, 1960), p. 1.

A second reason for confining this chapter to the large city is that the urban mass transportation alternatives become more interesting (though complex and expensive) as the population of the urban area increases. For example, in a small town, urban mass transportation choices will be limited to low-capacity vehicles (buses, taxis, and the like). In the largest cities the choices seem limited only by the imagination of inventors. The public is daily bombarded with technological processes designed to solve urban congestion. These include electronic highways, automobile-trains, monorails, bilevel commuter rail cars, rapid transit, hydrofoils, and air-cushion vehicles.[6] By focusing on that sector of urban mass transportation involving a considerable variety of choices, it seems reasonable to expect that our understanding of the decision-making process will increase.

Until 1960 it could be stated with confidence that, except perhaps in the largest cities such as New York City and Chicago, the task of handling urban transportation would be given to the private automobile almost by default. As the financial crisis in the urban mass-transportation industry worsened, higher fares and poorer service drove patrons into their automobiles. Highway construction in urban areas was accelerated by the Federal Highway Act of 1956 which authorized the federal government to bear 90 percent of the costs of the interstate expressway network. Approximately $18 billion under this program was earmarked for urban highway construction. It is estimated that between 1956 and 1971 over $29 billion will be spent on urban roads and expressways under the interstate and federal primary and secondary road programs.[7] Local communities, which recoiled from aiding mass transportation, willingly financed downtown parking garages in a vain effort to transform the central business district into a kind of super-suburban shopping center.[8]

Within the past few years, however, major policy changes at all levels of government have caused predictions of a resurgence of urban mass transportation activity. Many cities are now trying to revitalize their central business

6. For surveys of technological developments see various issues of *Railway Age*, *Metropolitan Management, Transportation and Planning* and Institute for Rapid Transit, *Newsletter*. Three monographs on technology are Donald S. Berry, George W. Blomme, Paul W. Shuldiner, and John H. Jones, *The Technology of Urban Transportation* (Chicago: Northwestern University Press, 1963), A. Scheffer Lang and Richard Soberman, *Urban Rail Transit* (Cambridge, Mass.: Joint Center for Urban Studies of the Massachusetts Institute of Technology and Harvard University, 1964), and Herman S. Botzow, *Monorails* (New York: Simmons Boardman, 1960).

7. U.S. Congress, House, Committee on Ways and Means, *Final Report of the Highway Cost Allocation Study, Parts I–V*, 87th Cong. 1st Sess., 1961, H.R. 54, pp. 55–56.

8. For a critique of such strategy see Jane Jacobs, "Downtown Planning," *America Is Going Places*, R. L. Bowersox (ed.) (Erie, Penn.: General Electric, 1962), p. 12.

districts and have attempted to include modernized and/or expanded urban mass-transportation networks in their comprehensive plans. For example:

In 1962, the Port of New York Authority, which had historically concentrated its urban transportation efforts on highways, bridges, and tunnels, embarked on a $150 million program of purchasing, refurbishing, and operating the bankrupt Hudson & Manhattan rapid-transit system.

In 1962, New Jersey and Pennsylvania's Delaware River Port Authority approved a $62 million extension of its Philadelphia-Camden rapid-transit line into the New Jersey suburban area.

In 1962, the voters of the San Francisco Bay Area Rapid Transit approved a $792 million bond issue to finance the majority of a $1 billion rapid-transit system. The State of California has agreed to supply an additional $132.7 million from surplus Oakland Bay Bridge tolls.

In 1964, the Massachusetts legislature passed a bill providing for a $225 million program for urban mass transportation improvements throughout the state. It is anticipated that the financial assistance provided by the state (through an increase in the cigarette tax) will lead to the extension of Boston's rapid-transit system.

In 1965, Pennsylvania passed legislation authorizing $12.9 million for mass transit and operating subsidies.

In 1961, the federal government for the first time directly aided mass transportation through a program of loans and demonstration grants. In 1964, following an intensive campaign by pro-transit interests, the program was expanded to a $375 million combination of capital, demonstration, and research and demonstration projects. In 1966, the three-year program voted in 1964 was extended to include fiscal years 1968 and 1969 with $150 million being authorized for each of those years.

On the other hand, progress in most other large cities is at a standstill pending approval of specific projects and/or general methods of financing mass transportation investments.

In short, urban mass transportation stands at the proverbial crossroads. Together with the cities it serves, it may reverse past trends and enjoy a renaissance marked by modernization and growth. Or, as an alternative, it can continue to decline as a tax-supported public service, with a status (as one transit official has said to the writer) "one step below the sanitation department."

OBJECTIVES AND STRUCTURE OF THIS CHAPTER

The urban mass transportation industry's future will be determined by a host of decision makers. This chapter will attempt to spotlight these individuals, job titles, or institutions and their place in the mass transportation investment process. Unfortunately, this process is not easy to dissect for scientific analysis. It is a dynamic system, which refuses to hold still for scrutiny, with interfaces between a variety of interests including planners, businessmen, public servants, the press, the administrators of railroads and transit companies, and the general public. Further complicating the picture is the fact that activity is simultaneously carried on at the local, state, and federal levels.

These decision makers (or "leverage points") generate and are exposed to a barrage of information including facts and half-truths. The second objective of this chapter will be to examine the nature and sources of these varying

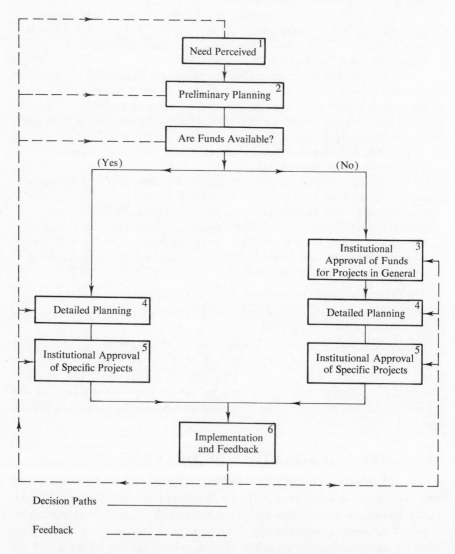

FIGURE 7-1. The Urban Mass Transportation Investment Process

kinds of information. The end result, hopefully, will be a better understanding of the urban mass-transportation investment process.

The author has identified six key steps in the approval and implementation of urban mass transportation projects. As shown in Figure 7-1, these include: (1) need perceived, (2) preliminary planning, (3) institutional approval of funds for projects in general, (4) detailed planning, (5) institutional approval of specific projects, and (6) implementation and feedback.

Figure 7-1 can be thought of as a reference chart for decisions arrived at in a logical sequence. But, in actuality, investment decisions need not conform to the sequence shown. A pool of funds (Box 3) may be sought before any specific needs are perceived (Box 1). Or Box 5 may be undertaken simultaneously with Box 3. In short, the flow chart is more normative than descriptive.

Each element in this model will be discussed in the following sections of this chapter, with primary attention being given to the identification of decision makers and the nature and sources of information. The chapter will close with a summary of the findings, a discussion of areas and specific cases for further study, and a treatment of some of the problems involved in carrying out future research in this field.

Need
Perceived

Urban mass-transportation projects do not just happen. Initially, a person, group, or institution believes strongly that its perception of the urban transportation problem requires the modernization or expansion of existing components of the urban mass transportation network, or the creation of a wholly new form of urban mass transportation. At the local, and to a lesser extent the state levels, this need is usually expressed in terms of a specific project or group of projects, such as, "It is imperative that the Milwaukee Avenue and State Street elevated-subways be extended out the median strips of the Northwest or South expressways." In the author's model, needs are perceived for specific projects normally at the local or state levels.

On the other hand, it has been pointed out that an increasing amount of activity with regard to investments in urban mass transportation is being carried on at the federal level. But this concern usually centers on establishing a pool of funds (Box 3 in the flow diagram) or approving (Box 5) transportation projects, in contrast to determining the needs for specific projects.

Mass transportation projects may originate from one or more of many sources including: (1) planners, consultants, and engineers; (2) transit company or railroad officials; (3) public officials; (4) the business community; (5) the press; and (6) other elements of the general public.

PLANNERS, CONSULTANTS, ENGINEERS

A major characteristic of the mass transportation investment process is the failure to assign responsibility for needs as perceived by planners to a central legitimatized group. The mass-transportation system functions as a part of an area's overall transportation network including highways, parking facilities, pedestrian walks, and plazas. Unfortunately the institutions for planning these facilities are as complex and uncoordinated as the investments themselves.

For example, transportation planning in a given urban community might be carried on simultaneously by the state department of public works (highways), city and suburban town planning commissions, autonomous parking and turnpike authorities, city and town highway departments, the academic community, private firms engaged in consulting activity for the various interest groups who perceive needs, in-house engineers working for transit companies or commuter railroads, and business groups. (The last two will be treated in following sections.) Although these groups often agree on the diagnosis of a community's urban mass transportation problem, they frequently have strong differences of opinion as to appropriate cures.

A recent significant trend in the urban mass transportation decision-making process is the promotion of coordinated planning by the federal government. The major stimulae have been the Housing Act of 1961 and the Urban Mass Transportation Act of 1964. Each has stated clearly that capital and demonstration grants to urban mass transportation will not be approved by the Housing and Home Finance Agency (HHFA)[9] unless the project in question conforms to a unified or officially coordinated urban transportation system that is part of the comprehensively planned development of the urban area. As of July 1, 1965, federally aided urban highways had to conform to such a plan.

Planning assistance is available to communities through federal highway-aid planning funds (1.5 percent of the highway construction apportionments to each state) and the so-called "701" funds for general community planning (including transportation planning). This planning assistance is conditional upon at least one-third matching by the state of local government, but the matching can be in service rather than money.

If, in actuality, future mass transportation projects stem from needs as perceived by such federal aid planning groups as the Chicago Area Transportation Study, it would be useful to digress on the problems of regional transportation and land-use planning. In the simplest terms, a general transportation plan attempts to forecast future volumes of trips between different sectors of an urban region within some time horizon, assign these trips to

9. The mass-transportation responsibilities of the HHFA were transferred to the Urban Transportation Administration of the Department of Housing and Urban Development (HUD), established in late 1965.

different modes of transportation, and recommend investments in transportation facilities that are necessary to handle the forecasted traffic volumes according to an objective criterion (minimize costs, maximize benefits, and so forth).

Some problems immediately arise. Why are trips taken? The studies attempt to answer this question by taking an inventory of existing trip patterns and economic and demographic indicators. In addition to detailed data on existing land-use patterns, population, employment, and the timing, routing and length of trips, information is collected pertaining to the triptaker including age, educational level, income, type of residence, type of occupation, automobile ownership, and the like. These descriptive statistics are then analyzed to yield functional statements such as total volume of trips as a function of income, employment levels, automobile ownership, and residential density.

The second problem is to take the static descriptive model of trip generation and extrapolate it to some future time. This is fraught with danger including the forecasting of the basic variables and the handling of feedback between transportation facilities, land-use activity, and trip volumes. Even if one could say with assurance that x volume of trips will be taken between zones i and j in the year 1980, what modes of transportation will be used? At this stage factors such as comfort, cost, convenience, and speed enter into the model. This question of consumer preference for different modes is hotly debated, for the end product is a recommendation of specific kinds of investments from the spectrum of automobiles, buses, rail rapid transit, hovercraft, moving sidewalks, and the like.

The existing state of the art in general urban transportation planning has been well summarized in three studies.[10] The California report notes that modal split is "perhaps the most inadequate phase of traffic analysis at the present."[11] The Lang and Soberman book emphasizes the short-comings of past traditional planning, but looks to the future with a certain amount of optimism:

> At best the demand for any type of passenger transportation is an extremely complex phenomenon and one subject to great uncertainty. . . . The demand for a transit system that will reach physical maturity in 15 or 20 years, moreover, depends upon a future market and a future set of competing transportation systems the character of which is extremely difficult to predict. The limited methodological capabilities of traditional planning and engineering

10. Richard M. Zettel and Richard R. Carll, *Summary Review of Major Metropolitan Area Transportation Studies in the United States* (Berkeley: University of California Institute of Transportation and Traffic Engineering, 1962); Lang and Soberman, *op. cit.*, pp. 99–105; and B. V. Martin, F. W. Memmott, and A. J. Bone, *Principles and Techniques of Predicting Future Demand for Urban Area Transportation* (Cambridge, Mass.: Massachusetts Institute of Technology, School of Engineering, 1963).

11. Zettel and Carll, *op. cit.*, p. 11.

have simply been unequal to this complexity. Fortunately, these methodological deficiencies are gradually being overcome.[12]

In addition to the methodological questions, another serious problem in the planning process warrants concern. Theoretically, the outputs of these transportation and land-use studies would constitute "normative statements of need perceived," for, as noted, they recommend facilities to meet forecasted travel needs according to objective criteria. Yet, it seems unrealistic to assert that these planning groups are immune from the pressures of other interest groups concerned with urban transportation and land use. To what extent do these pressures interact with the methodological questions to produce less than optimal decisions?

But, even if the recommendations were optimal (from a planning point of view), would they be acted upon? Here is a major question for further study: namely, the success of the major transportation studies in converting tables, formulae, equations, and maps into tangible investments in urban mass transportation. The California study interviewed planners in twelve cities on this question of implementation and reported that:

> . . . the general impression we received was a quiet confidence that the studies would exert a great influence on transportation development in the metropolitan area. And this would come about even though the study itself did not expect to become an authority or czar over transport development; nor would any other single "implementing agency" be created.[13]

On the other hand, the final conclusion of the California study was somewhat less than encouraging:

> Unfortunately, there is little factual evidence at present of the extent to which transportation planning and development can play a truly significant role in altering patterns of land-use development in view of all other forces at work. For that matter, there is little consensus as to the range within which land use patterns can be deliberately guided over the long run by general planning prescriptions acceptable to American political, social and economic concepts. Within this particular area, then, it must be said that the results of the major metropolitan transport studies remain highly speculative.[14]

It seems clear that any study of the mass transportation investment decision-making process must focus on the relationship between planners, particularly the legitimatized "Area Transportation Studies" and other "leverage points" at the need perceived and institutional approval stages of the model. Questions which warrant further study include: (1) To what extent does the product of an "Area Transportation Study Group" represent the pressure of other interested groups? (2) Inasmuch as there may be strong

12. Lang and Soberman, *op. cit.*, p. 85.
13. Zettel and Carll, *op. cit.*, p. 18.
14. *Ibid.*, p. 65.

differences of opinion between those working for an "Area Transportation Study Group" and other planners, how are these differences of opinion presented to the ultimate decision makers? (3) Most important perhaps, how do the ultimate decision makers view needs as perceived by planners in comparison to requests for specific projects by others in the community?

TRANSIT COMPANY OR RAILROAD OFFICIALS

Traditionally many urban mass transportation projects have emanated from institutions that would build and/or operate the facilities. In many instances, a project is viewed as a means of overcoming an existing operating problem. A good example is a program of rapid-transit platform lengthening to eliminate bottlenecks. In other cases, the company asks for aid to accommodate expected future patronage.

Most recently the decline in the financial fortunes of urban mass transportation has reduced the ability of private companies to afford in-house planners or engineers. At times private companies have hired consultants at the need-perceived level. Often this practice is intended to ward off competition from a publicly financed facility. Thus, the Chicago & North-western Railroad together with the Chicago Transit Authority retained a consultant in 1961 to analyze the relative merits of railroad commuter versus rapid-transit service in Chicago's northwestern transportation corridor.

On the other hand, the public urban mass transportation companies have often been extremely active at this stage. Sometimes this is the result of specific legislation. In other instances the public transit company takes the initiative without legislative impetus in proposing new projects. The Chicago Transit Authority submitted several transportation plans to the citizens during the decade 1954–1964. CTA's proposals were not always endorsed by all segments of the planning community. Witness this criticism by a study group at Northwestern University:

> It should suffice to say that the Authority, however competent it is to operate a bus and transit service, does not have the competence or authorization to assess or prescribe community benefits or needs, and that technical efficiencies in a free society, count for far less than individual choice.[15]

In short, the motives behind the proposals of the transit companies and railroad commuter lines are a mixture of community responsibility and a healthy dose of organizational self-interest. Investments in urban mass transportation from the transportation company's point of view obviously mean a healthier environment (in the financial sense) for the company's officials and workers.

An interesting research question would be to compare transportation

15. Northwestern University Transportation Center, *Basic Issues in Chicago Metropolitan Transportation* (Chicago: Northwestern University Press, 1958), p. 24.

company planners with the aforementioned traditional urban planners engaged in urban comprehensive transportation studies. How do they interact? Whose recommendations carry the greatest weight? Will transportation companies divest themselves of the planning function, preferring to build and/or operate projects conceived by others, or will they invest in personnel in an effort to become the "legitimate" urban mass transportation planners for a given community?

PUBLIC OFFICIALS

It is difficult to generalize as to the attitude of the public official toward urban mass transportation at the need-perceived stage. In conversations with newspaper reporters in five large cities the author received the impression that until very recently public officials appeared to gain voter support by fighting transportation companies rather than supporting them. There have been notable exceptions to be sure. For example, Richardson Dilworth as Mayor of Philadelphia strongly supported a program of subsidized railroad commuter service.

The attitude of a public official tends to reflect his office. Thus, the highway-oriented county engineer of Cuyahoga County favored strongly a highway system for handling Cleveland's urban transportation needs and successfully blocked construction of a downtown subway loop.[16] Public officials of suburban communities perceive the urban mass transportation problem differently from the mayors of central cities, particularly if solutions involve the imposition of new taxes on the suburbs.

But public officials in central cities are confronted and troubled by the paradox that they need to strengthen the core city by promoting urban mass transportation, yet they must face central city voter resistance to taxes that would finance transportation projects designed to make suburbia-central city transportation easier. By and large, it now appears that public officials in central cities are changing their attitudes at the need-perceived level. As they find the highways alone do not save the core cities, they are listening more to the "transit-oriented" planners and transportation officials, and turning (perhaps in desperation) to urban mass transportation as a part of a balanced transportation network.

THE BUSINESS COMMUNITY

In many respects the sentiments of the business community parallel those of public officials. Within a given urban region there will be a major split between those favoring the core city and those favoring businesses that

16. An excellent study of this struggle can be found in Dallas M. Young, *Twentieth Century Experience in Urban Transportation: A Study of Cleveland* (Cleveland: Western Reserve University Press, 1960).

have moved to suburbia. At present core-city activity is declining relative to the whole of the urban area. On the other hand, central city and core area renewal may bring about a reversal of this trend.

On the whole, the business community has vigorously promoted the automobile and highway system during the postwar period. In the suburbs the trademark of the shopping center is the sprawling blacktop parking area. In the core cities business has primarily relied upon free or partially subsidized parking facilities to lure customers and workers. In some cities retailer-transit cooperative plans have been instituted whereby a retailer gives the customer a transit token for a minimum amount of purchases. But the retailer-customer cooperative plans have been more successful in the reimbursement of auto-mobile parking fees.

In some cities the business community has promoted urban mass trans-portation. Despite the opposition to federal mass transportation aid by the United States Chamber of Commerce (to be discussed shortly), local Cham-bers of Commerce in large cities such as Boston have established transporta-tion committees, supported proposals for aid, and recommended specific projects. In Boston, a segment of the business community sponsored a research study of a recent rapid transit extension as an aid in planning more such facilities.[17] In the same city the top executive of a petroleum company published full-page advertisements in the local newspapers urging residents to ask their representatives to promote commuter rail service and rapid-transit lines.

THE PRESS

Generally speaking, the central city press favors strongly urban mass transportation as necessary for a healthy central city. (Another less obvious reason is that the transit rider is a newspaper purchaser, whereas the auto-mobile driver on the expressway gets his news and reports on traffic conges-tion via the radio.) The press serves a useful purpose in reporting the needs perceived by others, but does not normally initiate proposals for specific projects. On the other hand, at the stages of funding or specific project approval, press support can be important although not necessarily crucial.

THE GENERAL PUBLIC

The patient, long-suffering general public remains an enigma to urban mass transportation planners and doers. Until the late 1950's its travel habits were still a mystery. But, as noted in the earlier section on planning, we now have a better understanding of what kinds of trips are taken, although the

17. See Greater Boston Economic Study Committee, *A Study of Commuters on the Highland Branch* (Boston: Published by the Committee, 1960).

answers to the questions of why and by what mode still remain unclear.

The nature of urban trips can be represented on a multidimensional matrix whose axes represent kinds of persons, types of trips, and times of trips. Kinds of persons would include sex, age, occupation, place of residence, and so forth. The major types of trips would include work, shopping, recreation-social, and school. In the largest cities this kind of analysis shows that urban mass transportation is potentially most attractive to:

1. The young, old, and poor for all trips during all hours of the day, because they do not have access to an automobile.

2. The home-to-work trip during peak hours for all but the highest income groups, if highways are congested. The low- and moderate-income workers value the low cost of urban mass transportation, whereas the more affluent commuters will use mass transportation to avoid traffic congestion.

3. Central city shoppers of low- and moderate-income during off-peak hours because of cost. More affluent shoppers only when parking lots are filled to capacity.

4. School trips in central cities.

The first group can be highly influential through the political process in preserving a minimal amount of urban mass transportation. For example, subsidized bus service in small towns and money-losing surface routes in the large cities can be attributed to pressure from this sector. The third and fourth groups also can be instrumental in providing for somewhat higher levels of traditional surface bus service.

However, it would seem that favorable decisions for urban mass transportation projects on a large scale depend upon the support of the second group. The importance of this group lies in the *timing* of the trip. The highway system is capable of handling trips during off-peak periods, and parking facilities that are priced so as to encourage short-term, midday parkers versus all-day parkers could satisfy the demand by shoppers. The crisis develops in the largest cities when the home-to-work commuters jam the expressways and then preempt valuable core and central city land to store their vehicles during working hours.

The general public can perceive its needs through any of the aforementioned institutional channels and/or rely on such public interest groups as the League of Women Voters and neighborhood associations. In analyzing the role of the general public, relevant questions might be: (1) Does the public usually take an active role in the mass transportation investment process, or is it complacent? (2) If it acts, how does it communicate its needs to the ultimate decision makers? (3) What is the relationship between the general public and other need perceivers? and, (4) Do need perceivers in the general public conceive of their community's problem as unique, or is there an awareness of other communities' approaches to the same problem?

Preliminary
Planning

Preliminary planning might well be considered an integral part of the need-perceived stage rather than being separately identified. Quite often a statement of requirements will be accompanied by preliminary planning. The final report of a transportation study group will include recommended rapid-transit routes and rough estimates of construction and operating costs. Needs as perceived by political officials quite often include sketchy details of routes and costs.

The purpose of spotlighting this segment of the decision-making process is to emphasize the fact that information may arise at the need-perceived level that may not be completely accurate in the light of subsequent detailed planning. Yet decision makers may have access *only* to this preliminary information, particularly if the financing of detailed plans depends upon approval of the specific project. In such circumstances Box 5 would precede Box 4, in Figure 7-1, and the final cost of the project could substantially exceed the original preliminary estimates that led to project approval.

A relevant research question therefore could be the analysis of information flowing from these preliminary plans. Who develops the information initially? Are estimates based on rough averages or on more detailed studies of actual anticipated costs? Is better information subsequently developed? To what extent do the activities of different institutions result in duplication of effort at the preliminary planning stage? Does the quality of information in the preliminary planning stage have a measurable effect on the final decision?

Are Funds
Available?

In the author's model, action is the response to a specific need perceived. The need is refined and costed by preliminary planning. A critical question then arises for the ultimate decision maker. Are funds available? If the answer is affirmative, the mass transportation investment process is facilitated. For example, several railroads in the Chicago area have been able independently to finance new double-decked, air-conditioned, commuter railroad equipment, and thus were spared the fight for public funds.

As a result of the declining financial condition of urban mass transportation, most firms in this industry lack internal resources and are denied funds by traditional financial institutions. The total cash flow in 1961 for the nation's twelve largest mass-transit companies (representing 61 percent of the total industry's investment) was about $14 million. Yet, two recent estimates of the urban mass transportation industry's capital needs during the next two decades fell within a range of $9.8 to $10 billion.[18]

The problem thus becomes one of welfare economics, whereby costs and revenues as defined by the accountant are replaced by quantitative measures of social cost and benefits. Any deficiency between project revenues and project costs of socially desirable investments (where the social benefits would presumably have a ratio of at least 1.0 to the social costs) would be borne by the taxpayers. Before specific projects can be evaluated on a cost-benefit ratio basis, it is best to have institutional approval of the policy of public support of urban mass transportation. In this manner a pool of funds together with an administrative mechanism to judge projects can be established before effort is wasted on planning in detail projects for which there is no hope of financial approval.

Institutional Approval for Funds for Projects in General

LOCAL VERSUS STATE AND FEDERAL RESPONSIBILITY

A transit official once told the author, "There is nothing so local as local transit." Historically this statement well defined the financing of investments in urban mass transportation. Until the mid-1950's most public financing of urban mass transportation facilities was carried on at the local level. Even today several of our largest cities budget considerable funds for urban mass transportation.[19]

Recently there has been a major shift in this pattern. Local credit and taxes are being drained increasingly by the needs of schools, housing, police protection, and welfare. The urban mass transportation industry has had to turn to state legislatures and to the Congress for financial aid. Since 1962 the industry has made great strides in establishing pools of funds for mass transportation investments. An excellent illustration of this achievement was the successful campaign to obtain federal aid.

FEDERAL PROMOTION OF URBAN MASS TRANSPORTATION: 1955–1961

As recently as 1955 a government report sanctioned the historical policy of federal disinterest in urban mass transportation, by indicating that the issue was a local or state problem. But by 1960 pressure from the urban areas

18. Lewis M. Schneider, *Marketing Urban Mass Transit: A Comparative Study of Management Strategies* (Boston: Division of Research, Graduate School of Business Administration, Harvard University, 1965), pp. 25–26.

19. *Ibid.*, pp. 51–52.

on the federal government had reached the point where the Senate passed a bill authorizing $100 million in loans for mass transportation and broadening the use of federal urban-planning grants to include mass-transportation planning. The House failed to pass the measure.

In 1961, the cities, railroads, and transit companies again went to the federal government for aid and returned partially victorious. The Housing Act of 1961 authorized a $50 million loan fund, the use of federal funds for mass-transportation planning (the so-called 701 funds), and $25 million in grants to cover two thirds of the cost of demonstration projects. (Subsequently a combined appropriation of $42.5 million was made for loans and demonstration grants.) The demonstration grants and planning funds were administered by the Housing and Home Finance Agency (now part of HUD. See footnote 9). These grants could not be used for capital projects. During the first year of the program, $8.3 million of a total of $10.97 million in demonstration grants went to finance improved railroad commuter service. In 1963 the pattern changed as $11.5 of $18.9 million went to mass-transit companies primarily for the development of new kinds of rapid-transit equipment.[20]

But the mass-transportation industry still lacked federal aid for capital projects.

FEDERAL AID FOR CAPITAL PROJECTS FOR URBAN MASS TRANSPORTATION

In 1962, following the Transportation Message of President Kennedy, a $500 million capital-aid program for urban mass transportation was introduced into the Senate and House. Hearings were held in 1962 and 1963 and the Senate passed a $375 million measure in April 1963. In that same month the House Banking and Currency Committee reported favorably a similar bill. But the Democratic leadership made no effort to have the Rules Committee report the measure for fear that Republican opposition combined with anti-federal-spending elements in the Democratic party would defeat the measure. In January 1964 President Johnson voiced his support for the urban mass transportation bill. On June 25, 1964, the House passed the measure, and the Urban Mass Transportation Act of 1964 was signed into law on July 9.[21]

Several groups normally active at the need-perceived stage also supported efforts to obtain a pool of funds for urban mass transportation. They were joined by others who supported the general policy of strengthening urban

20. *Ibid.*, pp. 58–59.
21. For more detailed discussions of the passage of the Urban Mass Transportation Act of 1964 see *Congressional Quarterly 1963 Almanac*, p. 556; *1962 Almanac*, p. 561; *Weekly Report* (week ending July 3, 1964), p. 1338; and George M. Smerk, *Urban Transportation: The Federal Role* (Bloomington: Indiana University Press, 1965), pp. 171–177.

areas or urban mass transportation through federal aid. A partial list of those testifying during the 1962 and 1963 hearings indicates the diversity of interests and the number of groups involved: representatives of the Housing and Home Finance Agency and Bureau of Public Roads; individual Senators and Representatives; individual mayors; officials of transit companies and railroads; Amalgamated Association of Street, Electric Railway & Motor Coach Employees of America; American Farm Bureau; AFL-CIO; American Municipal Association; Chamber of Commerce of the United States and members of individual chambers; Institute for Rapid Transit; National Housing Conference; Railway Progress Institute; and the U.S. Conference of Mayors. Letters, statements, reports, and the like, were submitted by the Comptroller General, Treasury, Justice Department, American Institute of Architects, American Institute of Planners, National Association of Home Builders, Association of American Railroads, and American Road Builders Association. The positions of some of these groups will be discussed below.

URBAN TRANSIT COMPANIES. Urban transit companies constitute the major part of the urban mass transportation industry.[22] As defined by the American Transit Association (ATA), the urban mass-transit industry comprises "all organized local passenger transportation agencies except taxicab and suburban railroads, sightseeing buses, and school buses."[23] It includes companies operating buses, streetcars, subways, and elevated railroads. The ATA represents about 85 percent of the urban mass-transit companies. The organization had mixed feelings concerning programs of federal aid. On the one hand, the largest companies, most of which were publicly owned, strongly supported measures that would permit them to finance new rapid-transit routes. On the other hand, the overwhelming majority of the membership represented local bus companies, many of which were quite small. This segment of the association saw federal aid as the prelude to public ownership of their companies. There was a strong fear that publicly financed rapid-transit extensions could divert riders from private transit companies and accelerate financial disaster.[24] Therefore the representative of the ATA testified in favor of the aid program, but asked for safeguards to prevent the use of public funds to destroy private enterprise. One vocal member of the ATA, the president of the D.C. Transit System, questioned the extension of federal power and demanded that grants be made directly to private transit

22. For example, in 1965 railroad commutation passengers and revenues were $192.6 million and $136.4 million respectively. The comparable statistics for the mass transit component of mass transportation as reported by the American Transit Association were 6.8 billion revenue passengers and 1.5 billion dollars.

23. American Transit Association, *Transit Fact Book 1963 Edition* (New York: American Transit Association), p. i.

24. For an example of one such instance see Lewis M. Schneider, "Impact of Rapid Transit Extensions on Surburban Bus Companies," *Traffic Quarterly*, XV (January 1961), pp. 135–152.

companies. (Both the Housing Act of 1961 and the proposed Urban Mass Transportation Acts of 1962 and 1963 provided that the HHFA would administer funds through local public agencies. These agencies could then negotiate with private companies on questions of equipment, service, and the like. It was anticipated that private companies could benefit from the aid by leasing equipment from local public agencies.) Another member of the ATA resigned from the association saying,

> The federal government gets its funds by coercion from people who live, work and are taxed in all parts of the nation. To force people in Blue Bump, Mississippi, to pay, in their taxes, for the failures of transit to break even or make a profit in Chicago, Milwaukee, Los Angeles, New York or else-where . . . is immoral legalized robbery.[25]

The ATA, beset by internal differences of opinion and extremely sympathetic to the demands of its private company members, avoided strong statements favoring publicly financed rapid-transit systems, but preferred to stress the poor financial condition of the industry, inequitable tax policies by states and municipalities, and the need to include mass transportation in area highway planning. Its major research contribution was the aforementioned study of the number of transit companies sold or abandoned during the previous decade. By stressing the inability of transit to service smaller communities, the Association was able to broaden the base of Congressional support from the "rush hour congestion-oriented representatives" of the largest cities to the "senior citizen-those who cannot drive-conscious representatives" of all urban areas.

The plea by the ATA for protection of private companies carried great weight, for it appealed to those members of Congress who viewed with suspicion the extension of federal power into local areas. The enacted Urban Mass Transportation Act of 1964 barred federal assistance to acquire private transit firms or to establish services that would compete with existing private firms unless the HHFA administrator determined that financial assistance was essential to the development of a coordinated urban mass-transportation system. If private companies were purchased, the law required that adequate compensation be made and that employee rights be protected.

In view of the failure of the American Transit Association to take a strong stand in favor of rapid transit, a separate organization was formed representing large transit companies operating rapid-transit routes, industry suppliers, and other interested parties. This Institute for Rapid Transit proved to be quite active in preparing and disseminating information. Its representatives testified at all hearings, and stressed the efficiency of rapid transit in solving the problems of rush-hour congestion. (Of course, this message mattered little to the smaller

25. Paul Ditmar, "Letter to the Editor," *Metropolitan Transportation*, **LVIII** (February 1962), p. 11.

towns.) The Institute published a quarterly newsletter of accurate descriptive information on rapid-transit systems. In 1964, during the final months of debate on the capital aid program, the Institute sent out weekly news bulletins to those they believed might support investments in rapid transit. Perhaps the most important function of the Institute was its stimulation of support from industry suppliers. This point will be amplified in a later section.

Representatives of individual transit companies also testified. At one extreme was the testimony by one of the directors of the San Francisco Bay Area Rapid Transit District. He described the aforementioned successful 1962 referendum, but was quick to note that federal aid could shorten the construction timetable significantly, thereby saving interest costs. (The strategy of the SFBARTD, culminating in voter approval of the project, will be discussed in more detail under the heading of specific project approval.)

More common was the testimony from representatives of systems that had not succeeded in obtaining local funds. Their tendency was to stress the the greater efficiency of mass transportation compared to automobiles ("the Congress Street rapid-transit line at less than one-third capacity handles more riders during the peak hour than the paralleling expressway") thus justifying the expenditure of federal funds to ease traffic congestion.

Although the transit officials included in their testimony lists of specific projects, the overall tone of the testimony was to have Congress establish a general pool of funds for the nation as a whole. (An interesting comparison would be the specific rivers and harbors "pork barrel" projects submitted annually to Congress.) Thus, the chairman of the Chicago Transit Authority said:

> It is extremely gratifying to those of us who carry the responsibility for transit operations to know that the important role of transit in the Nation's economy is being accorded proper recognition at the highest level of government, and that the appropriations now proposed are sufficient in amount to launch the revitalization of the transit industry on a broad scale.[26]

In short, the transit industry, though far from united in philosophy, generally supported efforts at the national level hoping that federal aid might trigger support for transit at the state and local levels, much as the Federal Highway Aid Act of 1956 gave a strong impetus to highway construction.

COMMUTER RAILROADS. The commuter railroads were also split on the issue of federal aid. The relatively prosperous Chicago roads, with a long history of "don't expand the federal involvement in business" were conspicuous by their absence from the hearings. The eastern railroads, however, blamed much of their financial troubles on their commuter operations. Officials of the major eastern commuter railroads (New Haven, New York

26. U.S. Congress, Senate, Committee on Banking and Currency, *Hearings, Urban Mass Transportation*, 87th Cong., 2nd Sess. (1962), p. 465.

Central, Erie, and others) asked the American Municipal Association to document the sad status of the commuter railroad operations. Their study, *The Collapse of Commuter Service*,[27] was reproduced in the Congressional Hearings and often cited. In particular, the estimate of $31 billion to replace existing commuter railroad lines with highways was stressed. As noted, the commuter railroads took the initiative in getting demonstration grant funds under the provisions of the Housing Act of 1961.

It is reasonable to assume that top railroad managements particularly in the East, would be happy to abandon commuter operations or turn the facilities over to public agencies. In this respect, their attitudes differ sharply from the "have nots" in the urban mass-transit industry. The railroads can survive on freight traffic (and in fact would probably increase their earnings by eliminating their passenger operations), but the transit industry will benefit only if investments are made in rapid transit.

CITIES. The largest cities, in common with the transit companies serving them, also appeared to support urban mass transportation legislation. Although some mayors testified on behalf of their own cities, the strongest impact was made by two associations, the American Municipal Association (representing 13,500 municipal governments) and the United States Conference of Mayors. The AMA's position stressed the need for fixed rail-transportation facilities, in keeping with their study *The Collapse of Commuter Service*, whereas the Conference's resolution supported the policy of balancing mass transportation against the automobile without special reference to communter railroads.

THE CHIEF EXECUTIVE. President Kennedy strongly recommended mass-transportation aid in his Transportation Message of 1962. His successor, President Johnson, reaffirmed the Executive Branch's policy on this subject in the State of the Union Message of 1964. Shortly before passage of the Act, he stated,

> Now we need a major national effort to solve the problems of rapid transit and we are determined to make that effort. . . . Both Democrats and Republicans are supporting [the Urban Mass Transportation Act] because transportation is a bi-partisan problem. It is also national in scope.[28]

It is reasonable to conclude that the Democratic Administration's support of urban mass transportation aid was consistent with its overall policy of extending federal aid to urban areas when local resources were insufficient. On the other hand, a Republican Administration would most likely favor self-help at the local level. It seems likely that the Urban Mass Transportation

27. American Municipal Association, *The Collapse of Commuter Service* (Washington, D.C.: American Municipal Association, 1959).

28. Speech at the dedication ceremonies for the San Francisco Bay Area Rapid Transit System in Concord, California, on June 19, 1964. Reproduced in *Passenger Transport*, June 26, 1964, p. 5.

Act of 1964 would not have been passed under a Republican Administration, despite the alleged bipartisan support.

CONGRESSIONAL SUPPORT. Urban mass transportation legislation was most closely identified with Democratic Senator Harrison Williams of New Jersey. His interest in the problem was logical inasmuch as he represented a state that was deeply involved in a continuing railroad commuter and mass-transit crisis. The House floor manager of the 1964 Bill, Representative Albert Rains (D. Ala.), set the stage for support from smaller communities. One of his statements reflected the effective lobbying of the American Transit Association:

> Traffic congestion has become a major problem in most cities and transit service has been reduced or discontinued in many places. In fact, more than 100 localities have lost transit service entirely since 1954, primarily in communities of 50,000 or less. This emphasizes the fact that this is not just a big city bill but is needed just as much by smaller towns. In any community there is always a part of the people who are not able to rely on the private automobile to meet their transportation needs. Either their incomes are too low or they are too old or too young or have some infirmity so that they have to rely on buses or other rapid transit. For these people a reduction or loss of transit service is a serious blow.[29]

Congressional opposition to the bill was typified by the testimony of Senator Lausche (D. Ohio). Lausche agreed that there was a mass-transportation problem, but emphasized that federal aid would encourage communities to delay their projects in the hopes of getting large federal subsidies. He stated that federal aid would lead to "federalized ownership of railroads, [and] municipal and county ownership of your local transportation system,"[30] and asked that the states and communities solve their own mass transportation problems.

He also put into the record the results of research undertaken by Professor Moses of Northwestern University. Moses concluded that to divert 37 per cent of the automobile drivers to the Chicago transit system, it would be necessary to offer more than free transportation; it would be necessary to pay each driver twenty cents per trip. By citing Moses' discussion of his findings, Lausche implied that the demonstration grant program would be costly and not solve basic problems.

The urban mass transportation aid proposals did not exactly receive overwhelming support.[31] The senate passed the measure in April 1963 by a

29. Urban Passenger Transportation Association, *Weekly Report of Mass Transportation Legislation* (No. 11), p. 1.

30. U.S. Congress, Senate, Committee on Banking and Currency, *Urban Mass Transportation Act of 1963*, 88th Cong., 1st Sess. (1963), p. 458.

31. In part this followed from a lack of "grass-roots" support. For example in the Fall of 1963, Senator Harrison Williams was quoted: "If every commuter whose train was broken down and if every bus rider who has waited 20 or 30 minutes

52–41 vote. The affirmative House vote in June 1964 was only 212–189, and the Senate vote on the amended House version passed 47–36.

HOUSING AND HOME FINANCE AGENCY. The Housing and Home Finance Agency, which would administer mass-transportation aid, was naturally a major proponent of the legislation. The HHFA supported its stand with a study made by the Institute of Public Administration which advocated the mass-transportation demonstration and capital-grant programs. (The study also estimated the $9.8 billion need cited earlier.) The administrator of the HHFA was careful to emphasize that the aim of the programs was to assist local governments in solving their transportation problems, not to dictate policies. As information began to emerge from the demonstration programs, HHFA representatives transmitted the data to Congress. They stressed that the demonstration programs had succeeded in increasing urban mass transportation patronage.

OTHER EXECUTIVE AGENCIES AND DEPARTMENTS. The existence of support from the Chief Executive and Department of Commerce (HHFA) did not guarantee approval from other sectors of the Executive Branch. The most serious change resulting from objections from the Executive Branch was the deletion of a provision that would have permitted the federal government to guarantee up to $375 million of revenue bonds issued by local government agencies to finance mass-transportation programs. This provision had been inserted at the request of autonomous transit authorities which did not have the power to raise the one-third local contribution necessary for federal aid. The ultimate deletion stemmed from the strong objections of the Treasury Department which stated that the supporting of tax-exempt government bonds could impair the management of the overall government debt structure.

Another government agency in the Executive Branch with a major interest in urban mass transportation was the Bureau of Public Roads. Clearly, the BPR was walking a tightrope. If mass-transportation aid succeeded in diverting automobile drivers, it could result in a cutback of the urban highway-construction program. On the other hand, the Chief Executive had made it clear that there would have to be better coordination between mass transportation and highway planning, implying that the highways and private automobiles alone would not always be sufficient to meet urban transportation needs. The BPR's statement tried to resolve this dilemma by emphasizing the importance of buses versus rail rapid transit and called for the inclusion of special bus lanes in urban expressways:

> Some of the older and larger cities, particularly in the eastern part of our Nation, have developed around rail rapid transit systems and it seems certain that they will continue to be dependent on these systems. Possibly

for the bus to come by had written their Congressman, we would have had the legislation passed by now." *Passenger Transport* (October 11, 1963), p. 1.

comprehensive transportation planning studies will indicate the desirability and practicability of constructing rail rapid transit systems in other cities. . . . Without minimizing the importance of rail rapid transit in particular cases, we believe that the flexibility offered by the rubber-tired bus operating over the broad and inclusive networks of streets and highways offers untapped opportunity for attractive public transportation.[32]

This question of rail transit versus bus operation could have had serious repercussions had it been debated during the fight to get federal aid. Had there been a split between the "rubber tire" and the rail interests the common front would have been broken with the result being a complete loss of aid. This question of technology was not emphasized in actuality, and the Urban Mass Transportation Act of 1964 gave no preference to highway or rail transportation. But, it can be expected that major differences of opinion will arise at the specific project approval state (Box 5 of Figure 7-1) as to the use of buses or fixed-rail facilities.

PRO-AUTOMOBILE INTEREST GROUPS. Automobile interest groups such as the Automobile Manufacturers Association (AMA) and American Automobile Association were relatively silent during the three-year fight. Letters from the American Automobile Association and American Road Builders Association to the Senate subcommittee asked that work on the interstate and other highway programs not be cut back because of investments in mass transportation.

The Automobile Manufacturers Association was quite active on other fronts. Its strategy was to sponsor research and to create a broad climate of opinion within the planning and government communities promoting buses and automobiles on highways instead of rail rapid transit. Several independent research studies financed by the Automobile Manufacturers Association concluded that the automobile was indeed the dominant force in the urban transportation picture.[33] The study by Wilbur Smith & Associates asserted that maximum development of rapid-transit facilities would not diminish the needs for expanding urban freeways and in most cities future rapid transit would take the form of express bus operations on freeways.[34]

The American Automobile Association in 1961 also issued a brochure titled *Metro* whose purpose was to "answer half-truths, misstatements and distortions of fact being leveled against urban highway transportation."[35] It warned against massive expenditure of motor vehicle tax revenues to support public mass transportation.

32. U.S. Congress, Senate, *Urban Mass Transportation Act of 1963, op. cit.*, p. 76.
33. See Walter Y. Oi and Paul Shuldiner, *An Analysis of Urban Travel Demands* (Chicago: Northwestern University Press, 1962); Stanley L. Warner, *Stochastic Choice of Mode in Urban Travel: A Study in Binary Choice* (Chicago: Northwestern University Press, 1962); and Smith and Associates, *op. cit.*
34. Smith and Associates *op. cit.*, pp. x, 153.
35. Institute for Rapid Transit, *Newsletter III* (January 15, 1962), p. 7.

The publications of the Automobile Manufacturers Association and AAA were often cited in a variety of contexts. For example, a representative of the Ford Motor Company speaking on the subject "Business Responsibility to Local Government" at the 1961 Annual Conference of the Texas Municipal League included the charge that the rail rapid-transit interests sought an end to further expressway construction. He said that if urban road programs kept up with twentieth-century needs, congestion problems could be solved.[36]

In short, it appeared that the automobile interest groups preferred to educate decision makers and the general public to the benefits of the highways, automobiles, and buses; to emphasize that rail rapid transit was applicable only to a few cities; to avoid fighting the concept of "balanced transportation planning" as embodied in the federal legislation; and, to wait until specific projects were proposed and fit their strategy to the circumstances of the individual community. Their ultimate objective was to insure that, in a given urban area, highway construction was not displaced by investments in mass transportation.

PLANNERS AND ACADEMICIANS. Both the American Institute of Architects and the American Institute of Planners submitted letters to the Congressional hearings on urban mass transportation. Each supported the legislation, especially the provision that approved projects must conform to an urban plan.

Another important interest group working at the national level should be mentioned at this point, even though this organization did not appear at the hearings. In the early 1950's the Highway Research Board, a subgroup of the National Academy of Sciences, began to turn its attention more closely to urban problems.[37] In 1958 it set up a conference cosponsored by the American Municipal Association and the American Association of State Highway Officials. The conference agreed that planning must include all levels of government, be a continuing activity, and be carried through to the capital improvement stage.

In 1961 the Board issued a report titled, "A Key to Change: The Needs of Urban Transportation Research," which identified 119 subject areas where research was needed to facilitate integrated planning. By 1964, the Board's activities in the urban field had increased to the point where a Department of Urban Transportation Planning was established. The committees within this department were to encourage and coordinate research on the subjects of (1) organization and administration of urban transportation planning; (2) land-use evaluation; (3) community values; (4) transportation system analysis; (5) urban measurements; and, (6) future concepts. The department was to maintain close liaison with the National Co-operative Highway Research

36. *Ibid.*, p. 5.
37. The following discussion of the Highway Research Board was taken from Pyke Johnson, "The Human Side of Urban Transportation," *Traffic Quarterly*, **XVIII** (July 1964), pp. 321–334.

Program (NCHRP), the Department of Health, Education, and Welfare, and other government agencies, so as to channel available funds into research projects. It was anticipated that the reports would provide a "more intensive look at urban transportation and its interactions upon the social, economic, esthetic, and political sides of community life." The Urban Transportation Department was to "deal with research leading to policy formulation rather than to policy decisions or technical procedures."

U.S. CHAMBER OF COMMERCE. The only major opponent of the legislation to testify was the United States Chamber of Commerce. The Chamber reported that it had sent a questionnaire to 2,700 local chambers throughout the nation. Out of a total of 1,129 only 21 chambers favored federal grants. Of these 21, only one chamber represented a city with a population greater than one million people. In addition, the survey found that 73 percent of the respondents wanted no federal aid whatsoever. Therefore, the Chamber concluded that mass transportation was a problem in only a relatively small number of cities and did not constitute a national problem. The Chamber's testimony provoked a great deal of discussion as to the methodology and implications of its study. Senator Williams commented, "I think the survey you conducted is really inadequate as a test of opinion, because of those who did not choose to reply."[38] The spokesman for the Chamber retorted that 1,129 did reply and the 50 percent response was high by any survey standards.

The position of the national Chamber was further clouded by a statement of a spokesman for the Greater Boston Chamber of Commerce:

> I have been advised that the U.S. Chamber of Commerce is opposing the bill, but I wish to assure you they do not represent the feeling of the Greater Boston Chamber of Commerce in this matter, nor, I dare say, would they represent the voice of the chamber of commerce of the other major cities who are most likely affected by such things.[39]

AMERICAN FARM BUREAU FEDERATION. The American Farm Bureau, representing 1,607,000 farm families, supported the U.S. Chamber of Commerce's position, claiming that urban mass-transportation aid would add to the unhealthy trend for federal expenditures to increase relative to the Gross National Product. The Bureau's testimony was symptomatic of an undercurrent of resistance to the legislation. It was rumored that the primary reason for the aforementioned delay in the House vote was the reluctance to spend federal funds solely for "big city" mass transportation.[40]

38. U.S. Congress, Senate, *Urban Mass Transportation Act of 1963*, *op. cit.*, p. 142.
39. *Ibid.*, p. 107.
40. See *Congressional Quarterly Weekly Report*, XXI (week ending December 20, 1963), p. 2219. During the session the important Area Redevelopment Bill was pigeonholed in both the Senate and House, following defeat of a similar measure in the House. This action indicated major resistance to federal urban aid programs at that time.

RAILWAY PROGRESS INSTITUTE. The Railway Progress Institute was the spokesman of the railway equipment and supply industry. Its 122 member companies included firms specifically interested in mass transportation, including the St. Louis Car Co., Pullman-Standard, and others. The RPI approved the urban mass transportation aid program and asked for the improvement of rail systems, either commuter railroad or rapid transit.

The suppliers played an important part in the passage of the Act. It was rumored that a letter from Governor Scranton of Pennsylvania to the Pennsylvania delegation urging passage of the bill stemmed in part from pressure of railway suppliers located in his state. Shortly after this letter, Representative Saylor (R. Pennsylvania) offered an amendment requiring that all contracts under the bill provide for the use of products manufactured in the United States only. This amendment was adopted by the House along with its approval of the bill on June 25, 1964. When the Senate voted on the House-amended bill, there was some concern over the rigid requirements of the Saylor amendment, but in order to retain the support of the Pennsylvania Senators and other sympathetic Republicans, the Saylor amendment was adopted.

LABOR. The final strong interest groups represented railroad and mass-transportation workers. Each group favored federal aid, but wanted its own interests protected. For example, the mass-transportation company labor unions feared public acquisition of private companies, and in this respect echoed the position of the American Transit Association. The railway labor representatives spoke out against the use of federal funds to deprive a worker of his job. They noted that if the aid encouraged abandonment of commuter railroad operations and the extension of rapid-transit routes, railroad workers would be displaced. The pleas of the labor groups did not go unheeded. The Urban Mass Transportation Act of 1964 included provisions for (1) preservation of transit worker rights, collective bargaining benefits (including pensions), and privileges; (2) job protection for railroad workers equivalent to that existing in the cases of railroad mergers and acquisitions (up to four years protection of income); (3) assurance to employees of acquired companies that they would have their rights preserved and, if laid off, have priority on re-employment; and, (4) paid training or retraining programs.

URBAN PASSENGER TRANSPORTATION ASSOCIATION. Even the brief listing of the variety of interest groups gives an indication of the complexity of the process of establishing a pool of funds for urban mass transportation at the federal level. One structural device that facilitated trade-offs between the interest groups and permitted the groups to exercise their maximum pressure was the formation of the Urban Passenger Transportation Association. This association included urban-metropolitan governmental interests, labor, and the mass transportation industry. It has been credited with being instrumental in the passage of the bill.

CULMINATION: THE URBAN MASS TRANSPORTATION ACT OF 1964

The final version of the legislation included only $375 million for the capital aid program on a two-thirds federal basis; authorized the use of $30 million of the $375 million for 100 percent federal grants for research, development, and demonstration projects; provided for relocation assistance; protected private transit companies and labor; and, bowing to pressures from rural congressmen, limited federal aid to any one state to 12.7 percent of the funds.

There is little question that further research on the legislative history of the bill would yield significant information as to the process of obtaining federal capital aid for vital services in our largest cities. Relevant questions might include the process whereby differing viewpoints within the government were resolved; the formation and functioning of the Urban Passenger Transportation Association; the interplay between the executive and legislative branches; and the attitudes of interest groups striving to obtain a pool of funds as contrasted to the same groups as need perceivers.

In the author's opinion, the study of Box 3 of Figure 7-1 should not assume high priority. It would appear more relevant to understand the stages of need perceived (particularly by planners) and perhaps most important, how the pool of funds is ultimately used; that is, specific project approval (Box 5).

AID AT THE STATE LEVEL

Several states, including Massachusetts, New York, New Jersey, and Pennsylvania, have established pools of funds for mass-transit systems and commuter railroads. The legislation in Massachusetts is of interest because Boston is one of the few state capitals that is also the largest city in the state. Thus, the state legislature in Massachusetts was perhaps more responsive than those in other states to pleading for mass-transportation funds.

The key interest groups were the city government of Boston, the surrounding towns in the Boston area, the Metropolitan Transit Authority which provided surface and rapid-transit service in the Boston area, the commuter railroads serving Boston, and a few other cities and towns that were experiencing failing public transportation.

Unfortunately, it is not possible at this time to document clearly the events leading to passage of the measure. It might well form the subject of a promising case study inasmuch as the confinement to one state would make data collection more feasible.

It is significant to note that the question of individual project approval was sidestepped when the legislation was considered. There was strong pressure to specify that funds would be used for rail rapid transit in the Boston area along designated corridors, but the enacted legislation specifically left the question of routes and technology (buses, monorails, or rail rapid transit) for the administrators of the newly created Massachusetts Bay Transportation Authority to decide. Thus, as in the case of the federal legislation, the elements of specific project approval (Box 5) were bypassed during the struggle to get funds (Box 3). It is reasonable to assume that no one wanted to risk rocking the boat and losing all chance for funds by inflaming specific interest groups.

Detailed Planning

Ideally, detailed planning should precede specific project approval in the decision-making process. The objective of the detailed plans would be to provide decision makers with relevant information to be evaluated according to established criteria. For example, the detailed plan for a rapid-transit line would include data on route, power, equipment, service standards (running time and headways), costs, revenues, patronage, and suggested methods of financing the project.

Two major problems arise at this stage. What happens when a major decision maker is confronted not only by a host of projects proposed by need perceivers, but also by a variety of detailed plans? Second, what should be the sequence between the availability of funds and detailed planning? A plan could well stimulate the establishment of funds and specific project approval. But if the availability of funds becomes the critical issue and the detailed plan does not generate strong community support for its passage, the detailed planning is wasted. An excellent example of the issues which can emerge during the detailed planning process can be found in the Philadelphia-Kirkwood rapid-transit line.

THE DELAWARE RIVER PORT AUTHORITY EXPERIENCE

In 1951–52, the states of Pennsylvania and New Jersey agreed in principle that the Delaware River Port Authority should construct a rapid-transit line from Philadelphia and Camden into the New Jersey suburbs.[41] (This would be an example of a need perceived, Box 1, in the present model.) The Authority had funds for detailed planning and engaged the firm of Parsons, Brinckerhoff, Hall and McDonald to prepare a detailed rapid-transit plan. In 1956 their plan was delivered to the Authority. It recommended a $242 million system composed of a transriver tunnel and three rail routes

41. This discussion of the Philadelphia-Kirkwood line is taken in large part from Institute for Rapid Transit, *Newsletter* II (April 3, 1961), and *Newsletter* III (March 30, 1962).

in New Jersey. The Port Authority stated that it could not finance a project of that magnitude and the planning continued.

The firm of Klauder & Associates was then hired by the City of Philadelphia to evaluate the Brinckerhoff study. Their report, delivered in March 1959, proposed an $89 million system using the existing Delaware River Bridge rapid-transit line to Camden rather than the transriver tunnel, but preserving the three routes (of the Brinckerhoff study) in New Jersey. Part of the New Jersey routes would be single track. An all double-track system would cost $115.5 million.

Significantly, the Klauder study forecast that one of the three Jersey routes, Haddonfield-Kirkwood, could operate at a profit even after debt service. At this stage, the Port Authority saw financial feasibility emerging, and commissioned a third firm, Simpson & Curtin, to review both previous studies. The Simpson & Curtin report was completed in January 1960. It proposed a $44.6 million line to Kirkwood using the Delaware River Bridge. This proposal, like the others, included forecasts of passengers, revenues and expenses, and preliminary details as to power, signals, track, and so forth. The proposed capital expenditures were deemed feasible by the Authority, and its Transportation Committee prepared a final report for approval by the Governors of New Jersey and Pennsylvania, relying heavily on the recommendations of Simpson & Curtin.

During this same period, the W. C. Gilman Company was engaged by the Public Service Coordinated Transportation Company, which operated extensive commuter bus service from Philadelphia to New Jersey over the Delaware River. Of course, Public Service feared that the Port Authority rail commuter line would divert many of its riders. The Gilman report found that bus service would be adequate for the expected passenger volumes and that the cost of improvements to facilitate bus traffic would be less than investments in rail rapid transit.

In addition, the $4.5 million Penn-Jersey Transportation Study, sponsored by federal and state funds, was in the midst of its massive multimillion planning study for the greater Philadelphia urban area. This group was charged with developing a transportation plan consistent with expected changes in land use, population, and travel volumes. In January 1962, Penn-Jersey presented five possible plans for evaluation by federal, state, county, civic, and business leaders. The plans were the partial product of the study's work up to that time. They included (1) a rail-dominant system with heavy use of the Reading and Pennsylvania railroads' commuter lines, (2) allowing railroad transportation to decline and add express highways on a crisis-by-crisis approach; (3) expanding the mass-transportation system using rapid transit, railroad, and express bus; (4) phasing out rail service by 1985 and relying on buses to handle mass-transportation demands; and, (5) retaining Philadelphia's rapid transit system, but handling mass transportation elsewhere by buses. It should be noted that at that time these plans were only being presented for discussions. It was anticipated that the plans could not be evaluated before late 1962.

Also, in January 1962, the officials of the Port Authority and the Governors of Pennsylvania and New Jersey approved the construction of the Kirkwood extension. Governor Meyner of New Jersey suggested some modifications that were incorporated into the final plan.

The Philadelphia experience is important because it demonstrates the extreme differences of opinion at the detailed planning stage of a proposal, the interaction between detailed planning and financing, and the interrelationship between detailed plans and the overall regional planning effort. Detailed plans disagreed as to whether rail rapid transit or buses were best suited for transportation between Philadelphia and South Jersey. There had to be several detailed plans made before financial feasibility was achieved. But perhaps most fascinating, each of the detailed plans was prepared and evaluated before the plans of the all-inclusive Penn-Jersey Transportation Study could be costed through simulation.

Comparatively little is known about the process of developing detailed plans. The necessity of studying this function would hinge on the analysis of Box 5, Figure 7-1 (specific project approval). If, in fact, the detailed plan is the dominating factor in the ultimate decision, then those responsible for the plan would be at important "leverage points" in the mass transportation investment process.

Specific Project
Approval

At this stage of the investment process, what was perhaps once deemed the unrealistic musings of the planner become translated into reality. Some individual or group with legitimate authority says "yes," and the project moves into the dirt-and-shovel stage (complete with appropriate ribbon-cutting ceremonies).

Unfortunately, generalizations as to this stage of the process are extremely difficult. The problem is that each project is invariably accompanied by a unique set of circumstances surrounding its approval. Often the "uniqueness" hinges on personalities within the political or commercial communities who have strong interests in particular solutions to urban transportation problems, or on the existence of geographic constraints (for example, San Francisco Bay crossings) which intensify an urban area's transportation crisis.

Two observations can be made, however. Most of the interest groups active at the need-perceived or approval-of-funds stages return to exert pressure on the major decision makers. This activity will be discussed shortly.

In addition, the method of financing stands out at this stage, for it determines *who* will make the final decision. At one end of the spectrum are those transit companies, both public and private, which have the internal resources (or borrowing power) to undertake the investment. In such cases, the decision makers will be the executive board (and bankers if necessary) and the interplay of interest groups will be relatively small. A good example is the aforementioned investment by the Chicago railroads in new commuter railroad equipment.

It should be noted that even internally financed decisions in urban mass transportation may result in controversy. In Cleveland, the Transit Board in 1964 voted to use replacement reserve funds to extend the rapid-transit system despite the strong objections of the general manager, who preferred to see the funds used for replacement of maintenance facilities and purchases of new buses.[42]

Investments in mass transportation that require government or taxpayer financing encounter more complex forms of approval. In New York City, transit capital projects must be approved by the city government. In Massachusetts, prior to the establishment in 1964 of the Massachusetts Bay Transportation Authority, rapid-transit extensions had to be approved by the state legislature. If the extensions were made into a town outside the MTA district, approval also had to include a voter referendum. San Francisco's Bay Area Rapid Transit District similarly had to secure approval from the legislature (to form the District), Boards of Supervisors of the participating counties, the District's Board of Governors (including county and city representatives), and the 60 percent of the electorate. The enactment of the Urban Mass Transportation Act of 1964 will add to the complexity of the decision process. The Department of Housing and Urban Development, as noted, now has the authority to withhold the two-thirds federal contribution from specific projects that are not essential to the program for a unified, coordinated, urban transportation system.

Having spotlighted the locus of major decision making, we may now consider the pressure groups that act on the decision maker. This section of the chapter will then close with two case studies which demonstrate the complexity of the decision-making process.

INTEREST GROUPS AT THE SPECIFIC PROJECT LEVEL

The major characteristic of interest-group activity at the specific project level is its intensity. As the specific project "hits closer to home" abstract statements such as "we need an East-West rapid-transit line" are replaced by "don't send that track through my backyard." If project approval and the method of financing are lumped into one package (as contrasted with deciding

42. Schneider, *Marketing Urban Mass Transit*, pp. 158–159.

how a given pool of funds is to be allocated), the intensity of these groups is that much greater.

It should be noted that in general these groups are treated as though they had clearly defined, almost self-evident, and virtually unitary interests. As the reader will see when we deal with the pro-automobile interest groups, this is not actually so. Circumstances (largely the topography of the San Francisco Bay Area) produced a revision of this group's original perceived self-interest. Experience in the study of interest groups has indicated that they have a multiplicity of interests that are subject to redefinition. It may very well be that one of the major functions of detailed planning is to define the interests of the potentially involved groups and possibly in a direction distinctly different from the one the group might have anticipated. The main intent of these comments is to alert the reader to the fact that the very circumstances under which a group's conception of its self-interest evolves provide a promising context for investigation.

TRANSIT COMPANIES. Obviously the company that has proposed the project will fight for its approval using the detailed plans discussed in the previous section. In certain instances (particularly when the transit company is publicly owned) the transit officials will be well versed in the political process and use personal experience as well as "scientific data" to obtain approval. On the other hand, transit companies which stand to be hurt by the investment can be expected to battle the proposal. They, too, will come armed with detailed plans, and usually claim that they can perform the task at a lower cost to the public.

COMMUTER RAILROADS. It was found earlier that the commuter railroads joined with the mass-transit companies to obtain federal aid. At the specific project-approval level this harmony can cease, for improvements in either mass transit or commuter railroads draw patrons from each other as well as from the private automobile. Thus, the Chicago & Northwestern fought in 1961 against extension of the Chicago Transit Authority's Milwaukee Avenue rapid-transit line, and that same year, the Pennsylvania Railroad resisted efforts by the Philadelphia Transportation Company to extend an expressway bus service.[43]

PRO-AUTOMOBILE INTEREST GROUPS. There has been a shift in the attitudes of the pro-automobile interest groups at the specific project level. At one time, these groups were adamant in their stand against raiding the public treasury to benefit urban mass transportation.[44] Recently, in some cities with extreme

43. *Ibid.*, pp. 110–113.

44. For example, in 1957 and 1959 the Chicago Transit Authority submitted proposals for expansion of the mass-transportation system to be financed by the combination of CTA revenues, motor fuel taxes, and real estate taxes. CTA said that it was unable to finance the investment from its own resources and, being an autonomous agency, had no power to draw on public funds. In both cases the state legislature voted down the plans, in large part because of grass-roots pressure of the Illinois branch of the American Automobile Association.

traffic congestion, automobile-oriented groups have occasionally endorsed mass-transportation improvements. For example the California State Automobile Association publicly supported the Bay Area Rapid Transit District proposal and the policy of using Bay Bridge tolls to construct the transbay subway tube. More typically, the new stand has been to support mass-transportation improvements (particularly the use of buses) *and* to continue the highway program. Of course this implies strong criticism of any plans that attempt to substitute mass-transportation facilities for highways.[45]

PUBLIC OFFICIALS. As noted in the need-perceived section, some public officials have promoted mass transportation heavily, whereas others have shied away from outward support. This is understandable, for until recently the image of mass transportation has been one of crowded, uncomfortable, slow vehicles coupled with increasing fares. Now, the attitudes of central city officials are changing, particularly as federal and state financial aid shares the burden of the expensive rapid transit facilities. In addition, public concern over the questions of air pollution and highway safety has made support of mass transportation more palatable politically. At worst, central city public officials will hold out for modifications in the final plans to prevent serious dislocations to neighborhoods or to secure better central city service (for example, more stations). Suburban officials, however, generally remain hostile unless the tax burden is negligible or unless their residents in large part commute to the central city.

OTHER PUBLIC AGENCIES. As noted in the sections on planning and federal approved, many public agencies can have a vital interest in a specific project. They can approve it, oppose it on general principles, or suggest modifications. For example, the quasi-public turnpike and parking authorities might well oppose mass-transportation investments on the grounds that they were unnecessary for the community. (Of course, from their point of view, mass transportation could divert their business.) The department of public works might similarly fight the project or might cooperate so as to produce a better coordinated highway mass-transportation network. An excellent example of the latter was the development of the Chicago Congress Street Expressway with rapid transit in the median strip. A similar facility is being constructed as a part of the San Francisco Bay Area project.

GENERAL PUBLIC. Pressure from the general public takes two forms. The most active comes from groups located along the proposed route. As in the case of the Philadelphia-Camden line extension, this pressure resulted in

45. An excellent report on the resistance of pro-automobile interest groups to a specific project can be found in *Congressional Quarterly Weekly Report*, **XXI** (week ending October 4, 1963) pp. 1727–1737. In this case the project was the proposed rail-transit system in Washington D.C. The highway groups were particularly concerned over the delays in pushing ahead on portions of the expressway network.

modifications of the design so as to eliminate overhead fills ("Chinese Walls"). In other instances, neighborhoods will request shifts in station locations, either to prevent traffic congestion or to improve access.

The second form of public action comes from the pro- or anti-spending groups which accompany all municipal spending proposals. Their messages can range from, "We must build for a better city," to "More taxes mean more graft for public officials."

BUSINESSMEN AND THE FINANCIAL COMMUNITY. This group can also act in several ways: individually, through community organizations, through a firm or institution, through political or regulatory channels, or via the chamber of commerce. Those who stand to be critically injured or aided by the proposal will probably act in one or all of the above ways.

Although one would think that business, commercial, and financial pressure would be quite valuable in achieving approval of specific projects, the subject has not appeared often in the literature. George Sternlieb's survey of businessmen in the *Harvard Business Review* found that 62 percent of the respondents reported that their companies participate actively as a company in community projects, but that major specific involvement is limited.[46] Whether the activity included working for better mass transportation was not indicated.

The Committee for Economic Development in 1960 called upon business-men to participate more actively with local officials and other groups in setting goals for the community and guiding metropolitan affairs. The CED specifically cited the aforementioned Greater Boston Economic Study Committee's rapid-transit study as an example of desired business involve-ment.[47] In a more recent report, the CED warned businessmen that the nation's large cities faced decay unless rail rapid transit were subsidized. The controversial report (which included nine dissents of the fifty-man policy and research committee) said that businessmen could better view problems in "area-wide terms" than elected public officials, and that they therefore should be active members of transit-planning institutions.[48]

It has been suggested in this section that at the specific project-approval stage, self-interest becomes extremely important. Thus, in Cleveland, it has been rumored that one of the contributing factors to the defeat of the down-town distribution subway was the disagreement within the central business district retail community over the location of the subway. On the other hand, some downtown businessmen will support any proposal to improve access to

46. George Sternlieb, "Is Business Abandoning the Big City," *Harvard Business Review*, XXXIX (January-February 1961), p. 6.
47. Committee for Economic Development, *Guiding Metropolitan Growth* (New York: Published by the Committee, 1960), pp. 45–47.
48. Committee for Economic Development, *Developing Metropolitan Trans-portation Policies*, (New York: Published by the Committee, 1965).

the central business district. In the aforementioned controversy between the Pennsylvania Railroad and the Philadelphia Transportation Company concerning the extension of PTC's expressway bus operations, one representative of the downtown merchants was asked by the railroad's lawyer at the Public Utilities Commission hearing if the existing railroad commuter service between the suburbs and central Philadelphia was beneficial to the merchants (The lawyer implied that the expressway bus service would destroy the rail routes.) The reply was: "Another means of transportation, another means of conveyance, but if the PTC or horseback or anything else will serve its purpose, then let them.[49] The support of the central city business community in Philadelphia was instrumental in the decision of the PUC to approve the PTC express bus service.

When it is recalled that the U.S. Chamber of Commerce implies that businessmen in large cities do not want federal aid for mass transportation, it would be of interest to explore this question in greater depth; to find out what businessmen's attitudes toward mass transportation are and if they translate attitudes into action at the specific project approval stage in their local community.

PRESS. The press can be expected to support the general concept of mass transportation, but encounters problems when a choice must be made between alternatives. It is difficult to say at this stage whether press support is effective in generating grass roots and political support for mass-transportation projects. Certainly it can potentially aid project approval through the education process. But, if the press is rigidly "big city, pro-railroads or transit" in tone, regardless of the tax implications, intense suburban hostility can be generated and/or intensified.

PLANNERS, CONSULTANTS, ACADEMICIANS. These interest groups have been discussed previously in other sections of this chapter. It would not be an understatement to say that differences of opinion can be extreme at this stage. As stressed before, the question is, to which planners, if any, do the decision makers listen?

TWO CASE STUDIES OF SPECIFIC PROJECT APPROVAL

SAN FRANCISCO. The problems of trans-Bay traffic congestion in San Francisco came to a head following the end of World War II. By 1949, enabling legislation was passed for a rapid-transit district. Preliminary studies costing $800,000 were undertaken during the years 1951–1956. These studies resulted in completely new enabling legislation for the now-existing San Francisco Bay Area Rapid Transit District. Between 1957 and 1961 the District spent almost $5 million developing detailed engineering and financial

49. *Pennsylvania Railroad Company* v. *Pennsylvania Public Utility Commission,* Record, Superior Court of Pennsylvania, October term, 1962, No. 153, p. 79a.

plans for a $1 billion rapid-transit system. The design features of the rapid-transit network (air conditioning, high speed, seats-for-all) were given extensive publicity.

The aforementioned 60 percent voter approval in the November 1962 referendum did not come easily. Two of the five counties involved in the project withdrew from the district before the referendum. In the summer of 1962 the county board of Contra-Costa County also came perilously close to withdrawing. Only the favorable recommendation of the Governor persuaded the pivotal board member to vote in the affirmative.[50]

B. R. Stokes, general manager of the Rapid Transit District, discussed the successful elements of the District's strategy to convince the ultimate decision makers, the voters, to approve the plan. He listed ten factors as follows:

1. Create technical liaison committees of planners and public officials in each county and city involved.

2. Gain public understanding of the problem.

3. Devote special attention to leading community and civic leaders and encourage formation of a Citizen's Committee to aid in selling the system to the public.

4. Be frank. If the rapid-transit system is expected to cost $800 million, don't ask for less simply to ensure passage.

5. Recognize that the struggle may take a long time and there will be strong opponents.

6. Invest in preliminary studies to provide guidelines to the basic solution to the problem.

7. Rely on independent consultants and keep the permanent staff at a minimum.

8. Rely on dedicated citizen leadership which would include a respected board of directors of the transit facility.

9. Gain the support of automobile interests through an emphasis on co-ordinated, balanced transportation.

10. Don't debate the type of equipment to be used. That should be an engineering decision not a political decision.[51]

A statistical study of the vote patterns by county in the Bay Area referendum has shown the difficulty in generalizing about consumer attitudes toward

50. For details on the San Francisco experience see Institute for Rapid Transit, *Newsletter* IV (December 15, 1963); Alan K. Browne, "Financing Mass Rapid Transit: The California Experience," *Traffic Quarterly*, XVII (January 1963), pp. 46–56, and "A Fool's Chance," *Metropolitan Management, Transportation, and Planning*, LX (November 1964), pp. 33–35.

51. B. R. Stokes, "How San Francisco Passed the $792 Million Transit Bond Issue," *Metropolitan Management, Transportation, and Planning*, LX (November 1964), pp. 33–35.

rapid transit. Homburger correlated the percentage of affirmative votes with six variables: distance from census-tract centroid to nearest rapid-transit station, median income, percent of workers not using mass transit for work trips, percent of housing units occupied by owners, percent of housing units in structures of four or less units, and percent of housing units where one or more automobiles were available.

Perhaps the most interesting finding was the difficulty in obtaining correlations between affirmative votes and the variables. In San Francisco County support was strongest from census tracts with low proportions of owner-occupied dwellings, whereas distance from the rapid-transit line was a minor factor. In Contra-Costa county the exact opposite was true; distance played an important part in affirmative responses and the impact of home ownership was low. There were no strong correlations of any kind in Alameda County. The study did find pockets of local opposition in Albany and El Cerrito because of the controversy over the elevated route.[52]

It should be noted that the San Francisco experience corresponds to the author's model in the sense that there was a perception of needs, preliminary planning, and the creation of a financial mechanism for supplying funds. On the other hand, because the final decision took the form of a referendum, the financing and specific project approval stages were in effect merged.

NEW YORK CITY. An excellent example of the complexity of the decision-making process can be found in the problem of solving the transportation crisis in the Queens–Long Island corridor of New York City. The problem is simple, yet frustrating.[53] During peak hours, the subways are jammed, sections of the Long Island Railroad are operating at less than capacity, and the Long Island Expressway is clogged with automobiles.

In March 1963, the New York City Transit Authority proposed an East River tube at 76th Street plus three local subway lines in Queens. At the same time the Citizen's Budget Commission proposed a single-track tunnel under the East River at 61st Street with three-track operation on existing lines. The New York City Planning Commission looked at both plans and recommended a 59th Street East River tunnel linked to the Long Island Railroad and subways under Madison Avenue and Second Avenue.

In May 1963, following a conference called by the Mayor of New York City, it was decided to move ahead with a tunnel at 61st Street as soon as possible. Shortly thereafter, in June 1963, the Housing and Home Finance Agency of the federal government approved a $3,185,000 grant to study the

52. Wolfgang S. Homburger, *An Analysis of the Vote on Rapid Transit Bonds in the San Francisco Bay Area* (Berkeley: University of California Institute of Transportation and Traffic Engineering, 1963).

53. The following discussion stems in large measure from Joseph McC. Leiper, "Queens–Long Island Corridor: Urban Transportation Laboratory," *Traffic Quarterly*, XVIII (July 1964), pp. 335–348.

Queens–Long Island corridor. Among other tasks the HHFA project was to evaluate various alternative tie-ins to the 61st Street tunnel and provide guidelines for future transit projects.

The Queens–Long Island Demonstration Project's Policy Committee included the Mayor of New York City, the Chairman of the New York City Planning Commission, the Chairman of the New York City Transit Authority, the President of the Borough of Queens, the President of the Long Island Railroad, the Nassau County Executive, and the Chairman of the Tri-State Transportation Committee. This latter group, also federally financed, was charged with evaluating overall area transportation requirements in the New York metropolitan region much in the same manner as the Penn-Jersey Transportation Study in the Philadelphia area.

By October 1963, the City's Board of Estimate agreed on a 64th Street location based on engineering studies conducted by the New York City Transit Authority. There followed a wave of protest, particularly from the Rockefeller Institute, which claimed that subway train vibrations would render useless its delicate scientific instruments. Not until early 1965 was the problem resolved. In late January it was announced that the Board of Estimate had approved the Transit Authority's plan for a $30 million tunnel at 63rd Street rather than 64th Street.

Yet, the battle was not over. During 1965, the Citizen's Budget Commission challenged the 63rd Street location in the courts, and the NYCTA ordered another study of the 61st Street location. The consultants again recommended 63rd Street, and in early 1966 Mayor Lindsay called for immediate construction at that site.

It is important to note that the 63rd Street tunnel will probably be constructed before the final results of the Queens–Long Island Demonstration Project and Tri-State Transportation Committee's Studies are known. Thus, as in Philadelphia, key specific projects have been approved before the completion of an overall plan that should constitute theoretically the "normative statement of needs perceived."

Implementation and Feedback

Often a study of the decision-making process ends with the approval or disapproval of the proposal. Yet, approval is only one element of the process. There may be technical or legal difficulties of implementation. For example, a citizen's suit blocked the start of construction of the aforementioned Philadelphia-Kirkwood line for months.

Perhaps more important is the ability of the operating agency to transform approved plans into reality. Too often the public reads that the most modern transportation system in the world has been approved, but a year later finds that the new system is little different from the unpleasant existing lines. In these situations, it is not surprising that the feedback to decision makers results in unfavorable attitudes toward future mass-transportation projects.[54]

There is no need to belabor this point. Subjects for study would include the extent to which modifications are made in the "jet-age" plans during the process of construction. What interest groups are consulted before these changes are made? Are the consumer-oriented planners who may have participated in the original plans still available with the power to make recommendations? Are the leverage points at which the decision is made at Box 5 the same as those which are critical at the implementation stage?

It seems reasonable to conclude that grass-roots support hinges on transforming the image of urban mass transportation from a necessary evil (characterized by noise, dirt, high fares, and slow speed) to a modern component of today's transportation scene. Today we find approved plans, such as those of San Francisco, promising a new image. It remains for the transportation organization to implement these plans.

Summary
and Conclusions

This chapter has examined the process of investing in urban mass transportation facilities. Six elements of the process have been identified for analysis: need perceived, preliminary planning, approval of funds for projects in general, detailed planning, specific project approval, and implementation. The analysis has shown that the decision process is highly complex, because many interest groups are involved and these groups are active at the local, state, and federal levels.

At the present time the major trend in the process has been the increasing participation by the federal government in the problem. The federal funds should herald a period of increased investment in mass-transportation facilities. On the other hand, the federal funds will be accompanied by an important "leverage point," the approval of the Department of Housing and Urban Development.

The author has found that there has been little research on how decisions are made, despite reams of studies of urban mass transportation.[55] The bulk

54. For a more extended treatment of this subject by the author see Schneider, *Marketing Urban Mass Transit*, Chapters 6 and 7.

55. An exception which should be a model for future research is Michael N. Danielson, *Federal-Metropolitan Politics and the Commuter Crisis* (New York: Columbia University Press, 1965). This study concentrates on obtaining a pool of funds at the federal level.

of the available studies concentrate on traffic forecasting, technological innovations, and financial feasibility of proposed projects. He has concluded that much could be learned about the general problem of allocating our nation's resources to urban areas through study of the decision-making process surrounding investments in mass transportation.

Specifically, he would recommend concentrating initially on the need-perceived (Box 1) and specific project-approval (Box 5) stages of the model. There are a great many interest groups which perceive needs, and these groups return actively at the specific project approval stage. In the interim, a host of planning activity—some good, some poor—takes place. In addition, a tremendous number of facts, opinions, and half truths circulate among the "leverage points." The evidence to date suggests that the major "leverage point" hinges on the method of financing the specific project. The important decision makers thus include local and state political officials, the Department of Housing and Urban Development, transit company and railway executives, financial and business leaders, and at times the electorate. These are influenced by each other as well as by planners and consultants, automobile and highway interest groups, civic groups, and other special purpose interest groups (for example, labor, suppliers).

Throughout this chapter, at the end of the sections discussing each element of the decision-making process, the author has suggested a variety of research questions. In general, these questions concern the identification of the interest groups active at each stage of the process, the interaction between these groups, and the relative importance of each in transforming a need perceived into "bricks and mortar." Perhaps the most important questions include (1) Needs as perceived by legitimatized area transportation study groups (e.g. Chicago Area Transportation Study) have the potential of being "normative statements of needs perceived." In actuality, what is the impact of interest group pressure on area transportation plans? Are the outputs of these groups indeed normative statements? (2) What criteria are used by ultimate decision makers in the specific project approval stage? Which of these criteria are controlling, and how do the various interest groups, political, business, planners, and the general public, act so as to obtain favorable decisions? (3) What conclusions can be drawn as to the formal organizational structure necessary for the optimal planning, financing, and implementation of urban mass-transportation projects, given the steps of the decision-making process as outlined in this paper?

There will be many problems involved in undertaking research of this type. As is the case in all political science efforts, research will involve extensive field work with resulting costs. It will undoubtedly be found that many people at "leverage points" will not want to discuss their roles, particularly if they have something to hide. The mass-transportation decision-making process is in a state of flux. New institutions and individuals are entering the scene as new methods of financing investments become feasible. For example, the old-line engineering consulting firms are finding new competition for the planning of urban mass-transit systems. Individuals may not want to discuss their problems for fear that a study would "upset the applecart" and injure their chances to move ahead to become perhaps more influential.

Perhaps the most serious problem is that the unique elements surrounding project approval in each community make it difficult to generalize from a few depth case studies. It may be too much to expect that a general model (such as, Project approval = Heavily promoted detailed plan + Support of the governor + Citizens' committee + Pilot model and so on) can emerge. On the other hand, battles are more easily won when intelligence reveals the nature of the enemy. In the urban mass transportation decision process, the enemy is uncoordinated planning plus the failure to agree on objective criteria. It is hoped that a study of this type may enable those involved in the process to know themselves better and thus perhaps make better decisions.

Chapter 8

EDWARD E. FURASH

The Problem of Technology Transfer

Introduction

Since 1940 the federal government has used an ever-increasing share of our nation's research and development resources, primarily for the purpose of achieving various military, space, and atomic-energy goals deemed important to the safety and destiny of our nation. This growth in federal research and development expenditures has brought with it public and private concern that such expanded federal activity will in some fashion damage our economy, retard the achievement of cherished social goals, or harm other aspects of our national life. Some have been concerned that these federal expenditures will draw valuable scientific manpower away from the private research and development activities believed necessary to maintain an expanding economy. Others would prefer to see these funds spent on different national goals, such as education and mass transportation, or on different basic science research.

The standard reply to these concerns has been to point out that federal expenditures on military, space, or atomic-energy research and development have created a vast technology that has been or could be transferred to the civilian economy, thereby not only maintaining economic growth, but also supplying the funds to achieve other national goals. Of late, however, evidence has been presented to indicate that such "spinoffs" have been fewer in number and slower in occurrence than originally believed, and some federal agencies have been given mandates to enhance or speed up "technology transfer." The result has been a search for national policies or agency activities that could be adopted in order to *insure that the fruits of federally financed R & D will be transferred to all corners of the civilian economy.*

Technology transfer is not a policy issue in the usual sense of the term. That is, there are no warring factions that are violently for or against the transfer of federally financed technological innovation from its original use to application in the economy as a whole, as there are factions for or against urban renewal or fluoridation. Rather, the problem is how to achieve an agreed-upon and desirable goal of technology transfer, given the fact that the federal government will continue to use some share (whether larger or smaller than at present) of our nation's research and development resources. True, there are strong pro and con beliefs as to what kinds and amounts of research, if any, should be sponsored by the federal government, or whether specific projects such as the lunar landing program are worthwhile. But few disagree that, whatever the involvement of the government in R & D, it is important to spread any government-sponsored technology *that may result* throughout the economy. The issues are *whether this can be done, how to do it and at what pace, who should do it, who should control it, whether a national policy is needed,* and, if so, *what the federal activities should be.*

The purpose of this chapter is to examine these questions by identifying the individuals, groups, and organizations that participate in or influence the transfer of federally financed technology. The goal is to delineate the attitudes and predispositions of these actors and the context in which they operate so as to understand the kinds of research and information needed to aid them in developing policies that will facilitate technology transfer. The remainder of this section is directed at providing a background description of how the technology transfer problem originated and an assessment of the technology transfer achieved to date.

THE GROWTH OF FEDERAL R & D

The problem of "technology transfer" begins with the rapid increase in federal government use of our nation's research and development resources for military, space, or atomic-energy purposes. In 1942, federal expenditures on R & D amounted to some $74 million. Such expenditures are currently running at an estimated annual rate of $15 *billion.* And this $15 billion is by far the largest amount of government money spent on anything other than armament hardware. In the post-Sputnik period, federal spending for R & D has jumped nearly 500 percent in absolute size and about 300 percent in terms of its share of total federal spending. In 1956, R & D took a bit over 5 percent of the national budget. In 1965, it got an estimated 15 percent.

Even though most research and development activity in the United States is performed in private industry and universities, the great bulk of such activity is financed with federal money. In American science, the government puts up two dollars for every one dollar spent by private sources. And nearly 90 percent of the R & D activity funded by the federal government is directed at the objectives of three agencies: the *Department of Defense* (DOD); the *National Aeronautics and Space Administration* (NASA); and the *Atomic Energy Commission* (AEC). In turn, their objectives require that most of these federal R & D funds (estimated at 80 percent) be funneled into development rather than research activities, and that such spending occur in relatively few industries.[1]

As can be seen in Exhibit 8-1, the aircraft, electrical-electronics, and chemical industries employed 64 percent of all the scientists and engineers working on R & D in industry in 1962, and spent 68 percent of all funds used by industry for R & D in that same year. The federal government provided 72 percent of the R & D funds expended in these three industries in 1962, ranging from 90 percent of R & D funds in the aircraft industry to 22 percent

Exhibit 8-1   R & D Performed in Industry

| | FUNDS FOR PERFORMANCE OF R & D, 1962 | | FULL-TIME EQUIVALENT NUMBER OF R & D SCIENTISTS AND ENGINEERS (THOUSANDS) | | |
	Total $ (in millions)	% Funded by Federal Government	No. Employed Jan. 1963	% of Total	Increase Since Jan. 1957	% of Total Increase
Aircraft & Missiles	4,199	90%	105.2	31%	44.1	38%
Electrical Equipment & Communication	2,498	65	75.3	22	32.4	28
Professional & Scientific Instruments	455	49	16.3	4.8	6.1	5.2
Machinery	943	33	32.3	9.5	8.1	7.0
Rubber Products	126	25	5.1	1.5	.9	.8
Fabricated Metal Products	132	24	5.5	1.6	.6	.5
Chemicals and Allied Products	1,151	22	35.3	10.0	9.4	8.1
Primary Metals	166	8	5.2	1.5	1.2	1.0
Petroleum Refining & Extraction	302	7	8.8	2.5	1.9	1.6
Food & Kindred Products	108	5	5.5	1.6	1.4	1.2
Other Industries	1,480	n.a.	44.9	—	9.3	—
Total	11,560	58%	339.4		115.4	

Source: National Science Foundation, "Research and Development in American Industry, 1962,' NSF 63-37.

1. The data cited in this and the previous paragraph are drawn from numerous sources, the most important of which are *U.S. News and World Report* of November 25, 1963; *The Wall Street Journal* of August 26, 1964; and, various publications of the National Science Foundation, including: "Research and Development in American Industry, 1962" (NSF 63–37); "Profiles of Manpower in Science and Technology" (Series 1963, 1964); and "Federal Funds for Research, Development and Other Scientific Activities," Vol. XII (NSF 64–11).

in the chemical industry. In those industries whose total R & D expenditures are small, such as scientific instruments, small injections of federal funds can secure a large portion of that industry's R & D. A further indicator of the impact of increasing federal R & D spending is that the three industries mentioned above as having a heavy concentration of federal R & D support account for 74 percent of the increase in R & D manpower employment in all U.S. industry from 1956–1963.

A recent study by the National Science Foundation indicates that the specific R & D supported by the federal government is tied directly to changing requirements in our military and space programs.[2] In effect, a few federal agencies dictate specific goals for the bulk of our nation's R & D resources. And these resources, in turn, appear to be spent more on development activities than on research. For example, a breakdown of the $7 billion DOD budget for engineering, design, test and research (EDTR) in 1963 reveals that 4 percent was spent on research, 15 percent on exploratory development, 14 percent on advanced development, 21 percent on engineering development, 29 percent on operational systems development, and 17 percent on management and support.[3] Dr. Jerome Weisner, then science adviser to the White House, pointed out this emphasis on development in an interview reported in the February 3, 1964, issue of *U.S. News and World Report*:[4]

> We are spending about 7 billion dollars a year on military research and development. I stress the "development" because "research," the exploring of new ideas, is a small part of the cost. The big money goes into development, the building of a new ballistic-missile prototype, developing a new computer or a new radar.

The net effect of this burgeoning of federal science, then, has been to concentrate the effort of a large part of our scientific and engineering manpower on a few R & D problems whose technological solutions—hardware development rather than basic science research—are not easily used by other sectors of the economy. This situation has induced some founded and unfounded worries on the part of many groups—scientists, businessmen, economists, government officials, members of Congress, as well as the public—about everything from whether money is being spent efficiently and on the "right" research, the regional impact of research grants or the lack of them, to concerns about the effects of federal science on the economy, private industry, and the gross national product.

2. See "Federal Funds for Research, Development and Other Scientific Activities," Vol. XII, National Science Foundation (NSF 64–11).

3. See Testimony of Roswell L. Gilpatric, Deputy Secretary of Defense, before the Senate Subcommittee on Employment and Manpower (Committee on Labor and Public Welfare), November 6, 1963.

4. Reprinted from "$16 Billions for Science—Where the Money Goes," Copyright 1964 U.S. News & World Report, Inc. *U.S. News & World Report*.

CRITICISM AND RESPONSE

Although the debate over the policies and aims of federal R & D is a germane context for discussing technology transfer, it is the last matter— the impact of federal science on economic growth—that is of most relevance to the problem of technology transfer. Though, as we shall see, some of the criticism of technology transfer as a policy for federal science stems from those who really want the money spent in another research area, it is the widespread national concern about the rate of our economic growth and the recognition that technological innovation plays an important role in that growth that has led many individuals to express their concern that federal science is having an inhibiting effect on the economy and science in general. For example, in hearings before the Elliot Committee in 1964, Dr. George Kistiakowsky charged that the use of a major portion of our scientific and technical personnel on military and space problems was partially responsible for the slow growth of the civilian economy and inhibition of the growth of privately financed research and development because of the consequent rise in the cost of R & D.[5]

The evidence supporting this contention is inconclusive. Although an increasing share of technical manpower is devoted to federal R & D programs, there also has been an absolute increase in the number of scientists and engineers employed in industrial R & D. In effect, industry may be getting more technological manpower in absolute numbers simply because federal R & D has increased the size of the total manpower pool. And one cannot assume that industry would allocate more funds to R & D if fewer scientists were working on government projects. Nonetheless, the opinion that industry is being shortchanged because of federal R & D is widely expressed, and represents a clear challenge to backers of federal science.[6]

This challenge was put to Dr. Weisner in an interview when he was asked whether it concerned him that "the Government is playing such an over-whelming role in the scope and direction of all research and development in this country." After noting that some 75 percent of all scientists and engineers doing R & D work in industry are supported by federal money, he expressed the reply of many defenders of federal science when he remarked:[7]

I'm concerned that not more of these people in industry are contributing directly to the civilian economy. Yet, after considerable study of the matter,

5. See U.S. Congress, House, *Hearings*, Select Committee on Government Research, U.S. Government Printing Office, 1964.

6. See *Reviews of Data on Science Resources*, **1,** No. 1 (December 1964), National Science Foundation; and *Report of the Committee on Utilization of Scientific Manpower*, National Academy of Sciences, 1964, for two recent sources of data and reviews on this question.

7. *U.S. News and World Report, op. cit.*

I don't think that they would be contributing much more even if the Government programs weren't employing them.

In any case, I feel there is a net addition to the general welfare of the country from these activities, even though the people are supported by the Government, because knowledge obtained through Federal research and development does make a contribution to civilian industry, as well as serve Government purposes.

The challenge is that federal R & D programs in some way bring harmful side effects to the private sector of our economy and result in a retardation of our economic growth. The response is to claim that such programs will have a "fall-out" or "spin-off" or "by-products" or "spill-over" that will eventually benefit all corners of the economy and result in growth. Yet despite all the beliefs that such technological by-products will come about, the actual occurrence has been neither inevitable nor readily achievable. And this disparity between promise and fulfillment has become a source of argument in and of itself, and an impetus to finding methods for increasing technology transfer. The National Aeronautics and Space Administration's technology transfer efforts provide a good case in point.

A CASE STUDY IN POINT: NASA

Of all the federal research programs, perhaps the one that has been most visible and has come under the most criticism in terms of technology transfer is the space program and its agency, the National Aeronautics and Space Administration. There has been extraordinary interest in the potential benefits that space research might have for mankind. And one reason for this criticism is that we are spending a good deal of money on this program that many feel *we could choose to spend in other ways.*

Probably more than any other effort of comparable cost, the manned lunar landing program and other space research, unlike defense or atomic energy, is regarded as a discretionary activity. There is little need to remind the reader of the many articles that have enumerated what could be done with the $30 to $50 billion that will be spent by the time we land a man on the moon. The list of things that could be done with this sum—the number of universities that could be endowed, symphony orchestras supported, the amount of aid that could be given underdeveloped nations, the cancer research programs established, and the many other social benefits—is indeed formidable. And, if such criticism does not shake one's faith in the decision to go to the moon, it at least convinces one that this is a major national decision. Thus the critics, ranging from conservative Holmes Alexander to liberal J. William Fulbright, have pressed their doubts; and some ringing attacks have come from the halls of science and learning themselves, such as that of the strong voice of Philip H. Abelson, Editor of *Science*, asking for a "re-examination of priorities," or the polemical *Moon Doggle* by Amitai Etzioni, in which he calls the space program "an economic drag, not a propellant."[8]

The essence of their argument is that there is an implicit social cost in committing such a large share of our research and development resources to the space agency, and that the cost is measured by the foregone opportunities to develop new technology more directly applicable to industry and the consumer. Whether this argument is valid or not—and there is some evidence to say that it is not—their "opinion" is countered by the unbounded "faith" of the proponents of the space program who believe that it will stimulate the economy, finance the growth of universities, benefit civilian technology, and provide tangible economic benefits, even to the point of more than paying for itself in addition to gathering valuable scientific information and landing a man on the moon.

This concentration on the by-products of the space program is closely linked with a distinctive feature of our space activities; for a long time to come, the by-products of such space research as the lunar landing program are likely to be more tangible, demonstrable, and immediately useful than the results of the primary mission. If we were to stop the space program today, say its advocates, or even three years from today, there would be an appreciable accretion of knowledge of the universe that could be traced directly to information gathered by satellites and space probes. Communications and weather satellites will have important earthly value, but probably more knowledge and technology useful to us here on earth could be traced to the efforts to put the satellites and missiles into space. To this would be added the pool of trained manpower, the dislocation of manpower from other efforts, the growth of new communities, and the like—all produced well before the fruition of the primary lunar landing mission. NASA Administrator James E. Webb has advanced a similar argument:[9]

> The country needs the stimulus, the knowledge, and the products that will evolve from the program to land Americans on the moon. In marshalling and developing the scientific and technical resources required for manned lunar

8. For some good examples, see "Is the Moon Race Hurting Science?" *Business Week* (May 11, 1963); "Will Space Research Pay Off on Earth?" *The New York Times Magazine* (May 26, 1963); "Goodies for All in Space Program" by Holmes Alexander, *The Boston Herald* (July 2, 1964); "Is the U.S. Moon Project a Waste of Brain Power?" *U.S. News and World Report* (July 20, 1964); "Moon Madness," *Newsweek* (May 6, 1963) [summary of Abelson's views]; "Red Light," *Newsweek* (December 2, 1963) [Fulbright]; "What a Moon Ticket Will Buy," *Saturday Review*, (August 4, 1962); *The Moon Doggle* by Amitai Etzioni (New York: Doubleday, 1964); and, *The Rise and Fall of the Space Age* by Edwin Diamond (New York: Doubleday, 1964).

9. As cited in Vernon Van Dyke, *Pride and Power: The Rationale of the Space Program* (Urbana: University of Illinois Press, 1964), p. 100. The first quotation is taken from *The New York Times* (October 8, 1961), 1:1. The second quotation is from an address of October 1, 1962, NASA News Release, p. 2.

exploration, we shall be creating a technology that is certain to radiate great and diversified benefits to almost every material and intellectual activity.

. . . learning how to get to the moon, developing the technology which will be required to get there, and employing this technology for many purposes in space, is more important than the lunar landing itself.

The cumulation of all these criticisms and defenses makes understandable one of the more visible activities associated with the space program: the efforts of its supporters to stress the benefits of missile and space technology for the civilian economy. One would have to have a severe allergy to newsprint not to have read dozens of stories on this theme. The early enthusiasm for the spin-off of space technology into the civilian economy was such that critics contended that supporters of the program were promising a "free ride." And NASA itself has seized upon the mandate written in its charter by the Congress to establish "long-range studies of the potential benefits to be gained from, the opportunities for, and the problems involved in the utilization of space activities for peaceful and scientific purposes" to sponsor an extensive program of transferring its technology to commercial use.[10]

Although neither Webb nor others have attempted to justify the space program solely in terms of its secondary economic and technological effects, their enthusiastic promotion of space age spin-offs began early and continues today. Lyndon B. Johnson, a key author of the National Aeronautics and Space Act, has called the program a "second industrial revolution," and remarked that "the funds going into space research are investments which will yield dividends to our lives, our business, our professions, many times greater than the initial costs."[11] As we shall see, the business community is a strong supporter and hopeful recipient of such largesse. As one analyst of the space program's economic impact concluded:[12]

Technological progress resulting from space programs will stimulate economic growth basically in three ways:

1. . . . [By] increases in the productivity of both labor and capital . . .
2. By creating new products . . .
3. By making available new resources or by finding new uses for old resources.

Or as another early appraisal of the space program proposed:[13]

10. National Aeronautics and Space Act, Section 102, Ch. 4.

11. Van Dyke, *op. cit.*, p. 102.

12. See Leonard S. Silk, "The Impact on the American Economy," in Lincoln P. Bloomfield, (ed.), *Outer Space, Prospects for Man and Society*, The American Assembly (Englewood Cliffs, N.J.: Prentice-Hall, 1962).

13. *The Practical Values of Space Exploration* (Rev., August 1961), Report of the House Committee on Science and Astronautics, 87th Congress (Washington, D.C.: U.S. Government Printing Office 1961).

One of the most useful characteristics of the space program is that its needs spread across the entire industrial spectrum—electronics, metals, fuels, ceramics, machinery, plastics, instruments, textiles, thermals, cryogenics, and a thousand other areas. The benefits from space exploration thus have a way of filtering into almost every area of the American economy, either directly or indirectly.

NASA has attempted to validate this promise, not only through a technology dissemination program, but also through trying to identify actual spin-offs to date. In September 1963, the Denver Research Institute published the results of its NASA-sponsored survey into space program by-products, "The Commercial Application of Missile/Space Technology," listing more than 180 case studies.[14] Examples include the use of a conductive coating, heated by electric current, to prevent fogging on the X-15 windshield that led Sierracin Corporation of Burbank, California, to develop a heating coating cover for premature-infant bassinets, which maintains a constant temperature around the infant, even during examination and cleaning. And Lamtex Industries, Inc., developed advanced filament-winding techniques as a result of missile-space technology into such commercial offshoots as filament-wound pipe, tubing, and brassiere supports.

But the critics have responded to this promotion of the side benefits of space research with the reply that these spin-off pickings have been slim and nowhere near justify the cost of the program or the potential damage to the economy that such a massive government-financed R & D venture could incur. *The New York Times Magazine* featured a story with the subhead, "Concern is expressed that the space-defense research and development program not only is not yielding the 'spin-off' benefits expected, but may jeopardize economic growth."[15] And the February 1964 issue of *Space-Astronautics* contained an article querying NASA as to "Where are the 1,000 spin-offs?" pointedly criticizing NASA's five million-dollars-a-year Technology Utilization Program as a possible "foul-up" or "spin-in" program, rather than one resulting in "fall-out" or "spin-off." The gist of this article was that NASA and its supporters had promised far more than they could produce.[16] Similar statements of doubt have been expressed in the scientific and academic communities for some time, and they have now become increasingly frequent in the public press.

In effect, both sides in this debate share the assumption that there is a vast pool of new technology, endlessly created by space/defense programs,

14. John G. Welles, *The Commercial Application of Missile/Space Technology* (Denver: Denver Research Institute, 1963).
15. 'Will Space Research Pay Off on Earth?" *The New York Times Magazine*, (May 26, 1963).
16. "NASA Claims 1,000 Spinoffs. Where Are They?" *Space-Astronautics*, (February 1964).

waiting to be put to use; that not to do so is a critical waste of our nation's research and development resources. Yet transferring this technology is no simple task. For some, the responsibility lies with the federal government. As one witness put it when testifying before the Elliot Committee in 1964, the Federal government "has an obligation to develop a workable system of utilizing this enormous reservoir of scientific information so that its benefits can be transmitted to businesses both large and small in order to provide the ingredients necessary for an accelerated growth in our civilian economy."[17] The goal is clear. But the questions of whether it can be achieved, how, at what pace, who should act or be in charge, and whether a federal policy is needed still remain unanswered.

FOCUS OF THIS CHAPTER

The NASA case that we have discussed highlights a tendency of many partisans to oversimplify what is a very complex and difficult problem: *the transfer of technology developed in a special context and for a particular purpose to use in radically different contexts and for quite different purposes.* The very words used—"fall-out," "spin-off," or "by-product"—to describe the process betray the oversimplification of the many steps, translations, and persons that an idea must travel through in order to be transferred from one use to another. Whatever translations do occur are the result of much hard work, constant alertness to market potential, voluminous reading of available literature, and—perhaps most of all—the spark that exists in some men to be innovative, inventive, and creative; a spark that may be wholly dormant in others.

This oversimplification has been partly responsible for the "disappointment" expressed by some at what appears to be a small amount of technology transfer from military/space programs. Attempts have been made to trace both the general economic impact of federal R & D in terms of technology generated and specific items of hardware transferred.[18] If the pickings have been slim, it is at least in part because of difficulty in determining how big a transfer to measure as being significant as well as because we have a limited understanding of the transfer process as it relates to the peculiar technological products of military/space programs.

At least five technological transfers from federal R & D with sufficient market size to be considered significant commercially can be identified: digital computer technology, originally developed in World War II; electrical power from atomic energy; solid state (semiconductor) and related micro-

17. *Hearings, op. cit.,* p. 741 (testimony of E. Foley, Small Business Administration).

18. See Robert A. Solo, "Gearing Military R & D to Economic Growth," *Harvard Business Review,* **40,** No. 6 (November-December 1962); Dexter M. Keezer, "R & D—Its Impact on the Economy," *Challenge,* **12,** No. 3 (December 1963).

electronic devices; and, meteorological and communications satellites. On the other hand, of thirty-three technological areas listed in the Denver Research Institute study of technology transfer from missile/space technology, seven are described as having only potential commercial application, and another eight are said to have had only small commercial impact. The actual commercial sales of the remaining eighteen have been either relatively small or have reflected sales to companies within the aerospace industry, largely for aerospace applications.[19] In sum, disappointment over technology transfer is at least in part a function of what one expects to occur and whether one sees transfer in terms of significant events, numbers of events, or both.

Although there may be little disagreement as to the desirability of transferring technology from federal R & D to use in the private sector of the economy, the debate over what has or has not been achieved to date indicates considerable confusion as to how this goal is to be reached, how rapidly, and who should be responsible for achieving it. These issues will be examined in the sections that follow. The next section, Perspectives on Transfers, reviews traditional thinking about technology transfer in order to discern the ways in which the technological products of federal R & D present peculiarly different or difficult transfer problems. The third section, Actors: Groups and Organizations, identifies and characterizes the main collective participants in technology transfer, delineating the vested interests and points of view that must be mediated when establishing technology transfer policies or activities. The fourth section, Actors: Individuals, attempts to identify some elements in the transfer process that should be studied before activities or policies are set—the role of people in the transfer process and the transfer of people as a method of transferring technology. The final section, Conclusions, reorganizes the material in order to outline a number of other policy areas and issues whose solution and debate influence the ways in which one might undertake to facilitate technology transfer or establish transfer policy or activities.

Perspectives on Transfers

The problem of facilitating technology transfer is a current example of one of mankind's oldest habits—*borrowing*. The story of man is a history of borrowing ideas and artifacts from other cultures, and today's American

19. Welles, *op. cit.* Also see John G. Welles, and Robert H. Waterman Jr., "Space Technology: Pay-Off from Spin-Off," *Harvard Business Review*, **42**, No. 4 (July–August 1964).

stands at the pinnacle of cumulative winnowing and borrowing. This idea is put forth in lively fashion by John Greenway in his book *The Inevitable Americans*, in which he holds that we are the apex of a civilization that began when the first farmer pushed a dibble stick into Mesopotamian soil:[20]

> Whatever people have comes to them through independent invention—"polygenesis"—or through borrowing—"diffusion." Among the great intellectual accomplishments, the zero is a classic example of the polygenetic invention—at least three different isolated cultures produced it. The alphabet, on the other hand, is a classic example of diffusion—wherever true writing and the alphabet are found, they can be traced to their original inventors, a Semitic people who lived on the western fringe of the Near East around 2,000 B.C. Much of the making of America is due to unabashed borrowing of the inventions of others.

If such "borrowing" or "diffusion of culture" is the custom and art of mankind, then why should we have any difficulty in translating federal science/technology into usable civilian products? Why not just let our art take over and allow the inevitable to happen? The diffusion of culture is a slow process, and the inevitable transfer of federal science and technology has not happened readily thus far. The reason lies partially in the circumstances in which this new technology has been generated, its unique complexity, and the need for a special kind of perception on the part of potential users in order to effect such translations.

WAR AND INNOVATION

One can readily demonstrate that necessity is the mother of invention merely by pointing out that war and international competition have traditionally stimulated great bursts of innovation. And the peace that has followed usually witnesses the diffusion of these innovations. The tin can was invented to feed Napoleon's armies. The jet aircraft and atomic energy were developed for military purposes. As John Greenway has pointed out:[21]

> Ironically, in view of the conservative nature of the military mind, no social movement is more productive of rapid technological change than war. The most powerful force in man's existence is competition . . . and war is the essence of competition. Almost every great invention was suggested or developed by war—the first stone tools of a million years ago were weapons; the first bronze artifacts were weapons; and the first real use of the wheel and the horse was in warfare; so also with the first atomic implements . . .

20. John Greenway, *The Inevitable Americans* (New York: Alfred A. Knopf, 1964), p. 28. For an entertaining exposition of our reliance on the past for the comforts of today, see Ralph Linton's stimulating introduction to *Anthropology, The Study of Man* (New York: Appleton, 1936), in which he describes the "100% American."

21. *Ibid.*, pp. 27–28.

World War II and its continuance in the present cold war have been the greatest stimulus in history. They produced the jet engine and the guided missile; they led to the development of previous medical discoveries such as penicillin, DDT and sulfa; they are responsible for controlled release of atomic energy . . . Even greater things may be produced by the cold war . . .

Similarly, the bulk of our recent federally financed R & D is directed toward achieving cold-war, national-defense, or international-competition objectives of our government. Why then is transfer apparently more difficult to achieve today than in the past? The answer lies in the nature of the inventions created by today's science programs. Unlike the tin can or even the jet engine, many of the fruits of today's competition induced military/ space technology are not easily converted into civilian products. A missile system is not readily transferable into civilian use—even for the intercontinental transport of mail. Many of the individual inventions of federal research in missile, space, and atomic energy represent radical advancements in technology, unique and complex entities that require an intermediate process of study and analysis—*a process of adaptation*—before they can be used in the civilian economy. A brief excursion into the theoretical constructs of students of the transfer and diffusion process will help us to understand this unique situation.

DEFINING TRANSFER: SEED CORN AND SPACE TECHNOLOGY

The words *transfer of technology* can refer to any one of a number of stages through which a new idea passes until it becomes a widely used invention. Thus, when discussing the transfer of federally financed technological innovations we must specify just what it is that is to be transferred, and at what stage of the total translation process. Dr. Richard Bolt has suggested the following structure for determining what kind of transfer is being discussed:[22]

SCIENCE ⟶ TECHNOLOGY ⟶ PRODUCER ⟶ USER
discovery ⟶ transfer to ⟶ product ⟶ diffusion and
              workable idea   creation   adoption

A similar chain of events is depicted by Professor Richard S. Rosenbloom when he notes that:[23]

Science, invention, innovation, social acceptance—these are the significant links in the chain of technological change. An invention is a novel and useful

22. Minutes of the Committee on Space, American Academy of Arts and Sciences, October 10, 1963.

23. Richard S. Rosenbloom, "The Transfer of Space Technology," March 1965, for the Committee on Space of the American Academy of Arts and Sciences. *Author's Note:* This chapter has greatly benefitted from Prof. Rosenbloom's ideas, which he shared with me during my tenure as Secretary to the Committee on Space at the American Academy of Arts and Sciences.

combination of knowledge of the material universe. An innovation, in contrast, implies the *use* of an invention, which need not be new, in a manner which *is* novel in the relevant context at the time. Thus invention and innovation are distinct activities and may be be widely separated in time and space. . . . If an innovation is to be successful, it must gain social acceptance.

It is to this last point—social acceptance—toward which much of the theory and research to date on the transfer and diffusion of technology is directed. These studies have examined the process and rate at which potential users have adopted a given invention or idea. They have focused on transfer as a process of *imitation*, and have used such diverse topics as the adoption of hybrid seed corn by farmers, new drugs by doctors, diesel engines by railroads, boiling of drinking water by Indians, and purchase of air-conditioners in a neighborhood. The focus of this research has usually been on the "innovator"—studying the way in which a potential user becomes aware of, experiments with, and finally accepts or rejects a given idea or invention. Researchers in this field, the most notable of whom is Everett M. Rogers of Ohio State University, have developed extensive descriptive and explanatory theories, investigating such matters as the relation of cultural norms to diffusion rates, the characteristics of the innovator, the adoption process, opinion leadership, communications and the flow of ideas, the role of the change agent, and predicting innovativeness. In sum, these studies are directed at the process of acceptance of an innovation by potential users—that is, the adoption of *a device which already fits the needs of the situation into which it will be put.*[24]

But as both Bolt and Rosenbloom have pointed out, the transfer of technology can take place at stages other than the diffusion of a specific device among similar end users. And this distinction is important to recognizing the kind of technology that is being transferred most of the time from federal science and development programs to private industry: *ideas, technology, and inventions that do not have a direct application in this new context.* Thus, at the end of the chain, transfer is the diffusion of a specific product mainly by imitation of other users in similar circumstances, while diffusion or transfer at other stages in the chain occurs primarily by means of *translation* or *analogy*: the adaptation of the technology or principle embodied in a given product to a new context and a new product.

In the case of missile/space technology, most of the transfers that occur happen somewhere in this middle part of the translation chain—the "technological ideas" embodied in a given aerospace application are reconverted to a new civilian product, or the "technological know-how" of aerospace is embodied in a new civilian product. Professor Rosenbloom has stated this as follows:[25]

24. See Everett Rogers, *Diffusion of Innovations* (New York: Free Press, 1962).
25. Rosenbloom, *op. cit.*

In looking specifically at the utilization of technical by-products of military and space research and development, we find: (a) utilization of the midrange of general technology looms large in relation to useful applications of either specific inventions or basic science; (b) that analogy as well as imitation will play an important role in most successful transfers; and (c) that both *a* and *b* have important implications for what can and cannot be done to promote and facilitate transfer.

Welles and Waterman come to a similar conclusion from their study of spin-off from missile and space technology:[26]

> Our findings show that *intangible spin-off* (from missile/space technology) *is far more important than tangible spin-off* . . . By the time space-developed information is incorporated into some commercial process or material, it has usually been combined with information from many sources, and the chain of events is next to impossible to unravel . . . Thus, intangible spin-off can contribute to the invention of an entirely *new* product, process or material. . . .

And, as we shall see later, an important factor in the transfer of technology through transformation or analogy is the creative imagination of an *individual* who can perceive the application.

OTHER WRITINGS

There are, of course, a great many writings and discussions of the process of technology diffusion that we have not discussed here. Much of this writing is devoted to economic analysis of the impact of the rate of technological innovation on economic growth. Although writings in this area by such authorities as W. Rupert Maclaurin, David Novick, Simon Kuznets, John Enos, Lynn White, and Robert Solo are important, their effect on the particular problem of technology transfer that we are concerned with here is mainly in terms of providing a context for debating the importance of facilitating technology transfer.[27] In effect, the impact of their work is to heighten

26. Welles and Waterman, *op. cit.*, p. 108.

27. W. Rupert Mclaurin, "The Sequence from Invention to Innovation and Its Relation to Economic Growth," *The Quarterly Journal of Economics*, LXVII (February 1953); "The Process of Technological Innovation: The Launching of a New Scientific Industry," *American Economic Review* (March 1950); David Novick, "What Do We Mean by Research and Development?" (Santa Monica; RAND, 1959); Simon Kuznets, "Inventive Activity: Problems of Definition and Measurements," National Bureau of Economic Research, 1960; John Enos, *The Rate and Direction of Inventive Activity* (Princeton, N.J.: Princeton University Press, 1962); Lynn White, *Medieval Technology and Social Change* (New York: Oxford University Press, 1962); Robert A. Solo, "Gearing Military R & D to Economic Growth," *Harvard Business Review*, **40**, No. 6 (November 1962); Fritz Redlich, "Innovation in Business: A Systematic Presentation," *American Journal of Economics and Sociology*, X (1951), pp. 285–291.

whatever urgency is felt as to the necessity for seeing to it that every ounce of "transfer" is drained from federal science in order that we may be sure to maintain our nation's economic growth.

We have noted that traditional research and theory about the diffusion of technology are mainly concerned with the diffusion of ideas and products to potential users in circumstances similar to the original innovation and that this concern is not germane to most of the problems in translating federal research and development into civilian products. However, there are two conceptual areas in this material that seem relevant: the rate of innovation and the role of individual behavior. One of the frequent statements in this literature is that the *rate of diffusion* of an innovation can vary greatly from circumstance to circumstance. Rogers ties the rate of diffusion to the innovation itself, and notes that five characteristics affect its rate of adoption:[28]

> *Relative advantage* is the degree to which an innovation is superior to the ideas it supersedes. . . . *Compatability* is the degree to which an innovation is consistent with existing values and past experiences of the adopters. . . . *Complexity* is the degree to which an innovation is relatively difficult to understand and use. . . . *Divisibility* is the degree to which an innovation may be tried on a limited basis. . . . and *Communicability* is the degree to which the results of an innovation may be diffused to others.

Along these same lines, Edwin Mansfield explains that about 50 percent of the variations in the rates of adoption of twelve innovations in the coal, steel, brewing, and railroad industries by relating adoption to (1) a measure of profitability, and (2) measures of the extent of interaction with other firms about the innovation.[29] A brief speculation about the characteristics of the missile and space technology to be transferred, for example, indicates that its very nature may cause its diffusion to be slow and cumbersome: its relative advantage is hard to perceive; it is expensive to experiment with; it is radically new, complex, and difficult to comprehend by those outside the industry; and, there is a low interaction between aerospace companies and other parts of American industry.

Similarly, the extensive research done on the character of the "innovator" may have some worthwhile insights for understanding the kind of man who will be able to undertake transfer by *analogy*. Mclaurin notes that his most important ingredient will be "entrepreneurial skill," and Rogers characterized him by noting that:[30]

28. Rogers, *op. cit.*, p. 146.

29. Edwin Mansfield, "Technical Change and the Rate of Imitation," *Econometrica*, **29**, pp. 741–766. See also Edwin Mansfield, "The Speed of Response of Firms to New Techniques," *Quarterly Journal of Economics* (May 1963).

30. Rogers, *op. cit.*, p. 304; Mclaurin, *op. cit.*, p. 97–111.

The dominant value of innovators is venturesomeness. Innovators appear to gain interpersonal security by being more venturesome than other members of a social system. Therefore, innovators are frequently viewed as deviants from the system's norms. . . . In terms of the situational field within which innovators operate, they may not perceive their decisions as venturesome. Innovators frequently bypass change agents and use more cosmopolite sources of new ideas.

Is this the same kind of man who will perceive analogies for missile and space technology so that he can apply it in his own industry? And note one special dimension of this theoretical model of the innovator: he frequently bypasses change agents in preference to his own channels of information. This last characteristic could have special importance in a situation where disseminators of new missile or space technology appear to be relying heavily on an "official" communication channel.

CONCLUSIONS

Obviously, it would be impossible to survey and analyze in depth the great amount of research on technology diffusion that has been accumulating for the past fifty years—certainly not for an essay of this scope. But our brief journey through some selected writings indicates that there are descriptive and predictive theories in this research lode that could be useful in understanding the various actors and circumstances that will be presented in the sections to follow.

First, we can realize that the traditional definition of diffusion as the transfer of technology by imitative processes is insufficient for understanding the more difficult problem of the acquisition, development, and utilization of technology in a context different from that in which it originated; this process requires the use of analogy. In effect, the diffusion of federal research and development appears to be a very special case in the theory of diffusion, a case on which relatively little direct research has been done, but on which numerous leads can be provided.

Second, we find that the very nature of the technology that we are trying to transfer may itself slow down the transfer process. At the least, this is food for research and thought. Certainly it must cause us to place in sharp focus any attempt to speed up or "facilitate" such technology transfer and cause us to discount both claims that much transfer has already occurred and claims that little will ever occur.

Third, the existing theory of diffusion may have a good deal to contribute in terms of understanding the behavior of the innovator in this new transfer situation. Even though the traditional concepts of "innovator categories"— for example, innovators, early adopters, early majority, late majority, and laggards—may not be directly applicable to the new "analogy" transfer situation, the writings in this field do contain a wealth of observations about human behavior that should be culled in order to design further research.

Actors: Groups and Organizations

The purpose of this section is to identify and characterize the major groups and organizations that participate in or, influence the process of technology transfer, and to depict their relevant attitudes, policies, and activities. The focus of this discussion will be the three Federal agencies that account for nearly 90 percent of all federal R & D expenditures: the Department of Defense (53 percent), the National Aeronautics and Space Administration (25 percent), and the Atomic Energy Commission (10 percent). These three agencies have an "invested interest" in the transfer of technology, since they produce the technological innovations to be "transferred." Other government agencies and groups, such as the Department of Commerce, will be discussed in terms of their "vested interests" in the control, facilitation, or success of technology transfer. The attitudes and activities of the recipient of all this federal technological largesse, the business community, will be discussed, as will the many "interested parties" to policy formulation on technology transfer, such as Congress, the press, labor unions, local and state governments, and various public organizations.

THE DEPARTMENT OF DEFENSE

Although it is by far the largest federal R & D user, the Department of Defense has maintained that its job is to defend the nation and not to concern itself with the "by-products" of the vast amount of research and development activity it purchases in private industry. In a more positive sense, it has maintained that the civilian fruits of its R & D are the property of the industrial contractor as reward and incentive for taking on government work. The unspoken belief behind this policy is that if any civilian applications are going to be made, they will be made by the company that knows the most about the innovation (the contractor) and which has some extra advantage (patent protection) to encourage the development of civilian products.

In support of these beliefs, the DOD does not actively *promote* the dissemination of its technology to nondefense users, though certain technological information is available on request through its Directorate of Technical Information (Defence Documentation Center), and DOD reports are distributed through the Department of Commerce Office of Technical Services information system. Of greater importance, however, is that the DOD has traditionally practiced a "license policy" in regard to patents. Under such a policy, the U.S. government obtains an irrevocable royalty-free license, and the contractor retains patent rights and the right to collect royalties on commercial applications. (This policy is followed by a number of other agencies.)[31] This policy is in conflict with that of the National Aeronautics and Space Administration, and all federal agencies are under a special October 1963 Executive Order to establish uniform guidelines. By and large however, there has been little change in policy, since the order leaves open the path for an agency to seek the best interest for itself.

In recent years, however, with the increased cutbacks in military spending, the Department of Defense has concerned itself with a special kind of technology transfer: the employment of idle defense facilities in other kinds of work. Again, while the DOD does not see that its responsibility is to find other work for defense contractors, its Office of Assistant Secretary for International Security Affairs is charged with planning in relation to arms control and disarmament. One of the Deputy Assistant Secretaries in this office, Mr. Arthur W. Barber, speaking on the application of defense skills to domestic problems, encouraged defense contractors to go into some other line of work in the face of defense spending cutbacks:[32]

> I believe there is a chance, and opportunity, for those who are willing to change, and your choice is not whether you will change. The bids and the success in marketing will go to those who recognize the nature of the change fastest and appear in the marketplace with the appropriate products.

Mr. Barber went on to cite a number of projects into which defense contractors might transfer their skill, such as programmed public health, automated highways, mass air transportation, and the like. At the same time he noted that there were many barriers to such wholesale transfer of defense contractors to other publicly sponsored activities, not the least of which are public and contractor attitudes:[33]

> If we are to encourage creativity and private corporate interest in public non-defense areas, we must create programs in which industry can participate and make a profit, and the last is all important. I can think of nothing which would more stimulate the shifting of R & D and industrial resources to public non-defense expenditures than some administrative reforms which could make

31. Lee E. Preston, "Patent Rights Under Federal R & D Contracts," *Harvard Business Review*, **41**, No. 5 (September 1963). Others using license policy: Civil Aeronautics Administration, General Services Administration, Weather Bureau.

32. "Some Thoughts on the Application of Defense Skills to Domestic Problems," speech given at the Third Annual Management Conference on Marketing in the Defense Industries, American Marketing Association and Boston College, published in *The Next Five Years in the Defense Industries* (Boston: Boston College, 1964).

33. *Ibid.*

it possible to make a profit by putting the best minds of this country on these problems.

I am surprised at many of my liberal friends who at the same time preach conversion of industrial concerns and then are shocked to think that someone might be interested in making a profit by developing better schools, better hospitals, water purification plants . . . Profits and the public interest need not be a contradiction in terms . . . Success will depend as much upon visions, imagination, and courage—courage most of all, for every new idea must begin as a minority opinion.

Despite these ringing encouragements to its contractors, the DOD does not believe that it has any direct responsibility to undertake conversion activities or even, at present, to allow conversion costs as a part of defense contracts. It is, obviously, directly concerned with the employment of those displaced by the closing of government operated facilities, but only a small portion of these are retrained for "transfer" into other industries.

Finally, there are those within the federal establishment who would have the Department of Defense use its vast purchasing power to encourage and underwrite technological innovation in the civilian economy. For example, in 1963 the White House Panel on Civilian Technology recommended such action by the DOD to stimulate the use of new technology in the building field. Michael Michaelis, former executive secretary of the panel has noted that[34]

Something like 20,000 houses are built every year on military bases and these are houses, not barracks. They could be built outside the multiple [building] code system, and this should mean that the Defense Department could be relatively free in terms of what it can introduce in the way of new building technology. The Defense Department is beginning to act on this idea—with what it calls Project 12: setting performance specifications to reflect modern, even experimental, building materials and techniques. The resulting houses will be a fine living laboratory, under controlled maintenance —so that we can measure performance. . . . And don't forget consumer demand. Let's say that service personnel take to these houses. They see that they're better than the houses on Main Street: "Why can't I buy a house like the one we had in the Army?"

In sum, the DOD has followed two concerns insofar as "technology transfer" is concerned: vesting the patent rights to particular innovations in the contractor as a reward and encouragement to create civilian products, and transferring the "technological know-how" of defense contractors into other nondefense activities. A third concern, using its purchasing power to improve products normally purchased from the private sector of the economy has only recently emerged.

34. Michael Michaelis, "Obstacles to Innovation," *International Science and Technology* (November 1964).

THE NATIONAL AERONAUTICS AND SPACE ADMINISTRATION

Since its inception, the National Aeronautics and Space Administration has been deeply committed to transferring its technology into widespread use in the civilian economy as part of its mandate to utilize space activities for peaceful and scientific purposes. As James Webb, NASA Administrator has said,[35]

> We in the Space Agency do not seek to justify our program on the basis of the industrial applications which flow from it. . . . since we are committed to this great effort in space, however, a responsibility exists to glean from it the maximum benefits which can be obtained.

And this responsibility was put into operational terms by Dr. George L. Simpson, Jr., Assistant Administrator of Technology Utilization and Policy Planning, when he noted that "NASA is committed to a hard, driving effort to transfer the useful fruits of our research and development effort to the private sector of the economy in as quick and useful a way as possible."[36]

This effort begins with the NASA patent policy and ends with a four-million-dollar-a-year program for disseminating its technology. NASA's patent policy is a "title policy" in which patent rights become the property of the U.S. government (NASA), assigned to the head of the agency.[37] NASA's dissemination policy requires that any interested parties obtain a royalty-free nonexclusive license. Under certain conditions a firm can obtain an exclusive license at NASA's option. In practice, very few firms have obtained exclusive arrangements, though some have gone to the original inventor.

NASA's technology transfer program is vested in its Office of Technology Utilization charged with the mission of identifying and evaluating advances in technology resulting from work supported by the Space Agency, and disseminating this information in the most effective manner to potential users. The Office of Technology Utilization sponsors a number of programs aimed at (1) *identifying* useful technology by reports of innovations from contractors, searching NASA literature, and surveying advances in specific technical fields; (2) *evaluating* the potential usefulness and feasibility of transfer for selected technological advances (using outside consultants), amd selecting those that should be promoted by the OTU; (3) *developing* regional facilities for disseminating technology by cooperative ventures with universities and others in the storage, retrieval, interpretation, and adaptation to local industry of NASA technology; (4) *supporting* relevant research

---

35. Speech to the Oakland Conference on Space, Science and Urban Life, March 1963.

36. 1964 NASA Authorization Hearings, Committee on Science and Astronautics, U.S. House of Representatives, No. 3, Part 4, p. 3182.

37. Preston, *op. cit.* Other users of this policy include the Departments of Agriculture; Health, Education and Welfare; and Interior.

projects on technology transfer, R & D management, and the long-range implications of the space program.

Through its Office of Scientific and Technical Information, NASA operates a vast system for reporting new technology to the public through its Scientific and Technical Aerospace Reports (STAR). To keep important innovations from being buried in the flood of STAR material, NASA attempts to winnow out advances from its own in-house research facilities through the use of "technology utilization officers" at each facility, through evaluations of STAR and other material by outside consultants, and by requiring its contractors to report new technology to NASA. This last matter has become a problem for both NASA and for industry, with there being considerable contractor expenses involved in such reporting. This reporting requirement is written into every contract negotiated by NASA with a prime contractor and requires him to report innovations, improvements, discoveries, and inventions made in the course of the contract—a considerable extension of previous requirements for the reporting of patentable inventions.

Once a significant innovation or invention is identified by NASA's OTU or independent contractors, it can be given speedy dissemination through a "Tech Brief" sent out via the OTU mailing list, to trade publications, and other channels. On occasion, NASA will report a group of innovations in a given technical area by publishing a "state-of-the-art" booklet, such as its "Selected Welding Techniques."

Some 35 percent of the OTU budget is spent on identifying and evaluating potentially transferable technology. And, for reasons given above, NASA has had difficulty in getting its contractors to report new technology. If complete compliance should occur, in fact, NASA's evaluation system would be inundated by data. The Astro-Nuclear Laboratory of Westinghouse Electric Corporation reported to the OTU a ratio of 0.5 to 0.8 patentable inventions per man-year of engineering effort. Given the 60,000 engineers and scientists working for NASA in 1964, and using the lowest reporting ratio, the OTU would have to deal with some 30,000 reports annually.[38] In effect, this problem of identifying and reporting technological innovation would be translated into an even more difficult dilemma—how to evaluate and disseminate all this information.

One of NASA's problems has been to match its information with the needs of potential users. It has tried to do this through the STAR reports and other publications of the OTU. The assumption behind this technique is, in effect, that potential users will search through the various information sources to find technology useful to them. Recognizing that this procedure does not result in a speedy dissemination of technology, NASA has attempted to experiment with matching user needs and information dissemination through participation in several experimental efforts.

38. As reported by Rosenbloom, *op. cit.*

The first of these was the study by the Denver Research Institute discussed earlier in this chapter. This attempt to identify spin-off was undertaken before NASA had established its technology utilization program in full, and could not be considered a fair measurement of what such a program could accomplish. However, the optimism of this report appears to have encouraged NASA to believe that a straightforward documentation program would be successful. The documentation program has been described above.

The next effort was the funding of a program at the Midwest Research Institute aimed at displaying NASA technology to companies in the Midwest, away from the technically sophisticated areas of the East and West Coasts. Companies were invited to participate actively in MRI meetings at which NASA innovations were presented. This program was established in an effort to interest companies in actively searching through NASA release documents.

The more recent emphasis has been toward dissemination through regional centers, primarily universities. The most important of these has been the Aerospace Research Application Center (ARAC) at the University of Indiana. At this center, an attempt is being made to link NASA technical information to the research and development of specific companies in the Indiana region. In effect, the OTU directs its attention to identifying, evaluating, and selecting promising inventions, and then disseminating these inventions in various ways. The ARAC approach starts at the other end of the transfer circuit by concentrating on identifying user problems and then searching for the relevant technology stored in its computer memory banks. Though OTU documents are the major source of its information, ARAC does not limit itself to NASA technology, and has used information from the Defense Documentation Center and the Atomic Energy Commission.

ARAC began operations in 1963 with twenty-nine participating companies, each of which pays a subscription fee for the service. NASA is estimated to pay up to 50 percent of the cost of this program. Each company has assigned to it a representative from ARAC, usually a graduate student at the university, who is thoroughly versed in the company's needs and interests. When a problem is posed to him by the company, he programs the ARAC computer to search for relevant material, and transmits this material, appropriately annotated, to the company. Other regional centers are planned, perhaps as many as fifty. Several other organizations such as Wayne State University, the University of Pittsburgh, and North Carolina Science and Technology Research Center have been conducting experimental programs of evaluation and transfer under NASA auspices.

Finally, NASA has recognized that it must understand the process by which users of technology acquire new information. To this end, it has sponsored studies in this area by the Committee on Space of the American Academy of Arts and Sciences, under the direction of Professor Richard S.

Rosenbloom of Harvard Business School. These studies have probed such matters as the ways in which engineers within a large, decentralized corporation learn about new technology in another part of the company, and the way in which document titles aid or retard a researcher in obtaining and paying attention to new information.

To recapitulate, NASA has developed a complex system for gathering, evaluating and disseminating its technological information in order to achieve its goal of rapid transfer of the fruits of NASA R & D to the private sector of the economy. NASA has viewed dissemination as mainly a process of making information available for the potential user to acquire, such as through its STAR reports, trade publications, or even traveling "technology transfer" shows by the Midwest Research Institute. And NASA has attempted to measure the success of this dissemination system through sponsoring studies of space-program-generated spin-off, such as that cited early by the Denver Research Institute. More recently, NASA has recognized that the mere publication and so-called dissemination of information may be insufficient to achieve the rapid rate of technology transfer that it desires, and has sponsored user-oriented search devices and active transfer experiments such as ARAC and studies of how potential users acquire technological information.

THE ATOMIC ENERGY COMMISSION

Like NASA, the Atomic Energy Commission has been vitally interested since its very beginnings in the peaceful applications of its technology: atomic energy. Although it has practiced considerably information dissemination through its Division of Technical Information and the Commerce Department's Office of Technical Services, the AEC has spent most of its budget for applications on developing actual processes for using atomic energy which could then be imitated by private industry. Thus the AEC has promoted applications of radioisotopes, including developing particular application techniques and licensing them, commercial use of nuclear power for generating electricity, including the building of prototype plants, and the like. The AEC has backed its applications policy with a patent policy in which the AEC has rights to all inventions arising under its contracts. In practice, the AEC retains the patent rights only for inventions in the atomic field, and allows patents on subsidiary developments to pass on to the contractor with a royalty-free license for government use.[39]

One of the larger programs undertaken by the AEC has been its Power Reactor Demonstration Program. Through the use of direct and indirect subsidies to industry, the AEC has helped establish the United States nuclear power industry. Whether private industry and private power companies have

39. Preston, *op. cit.*

joined in this program because of fear of public power or through recognition that fossil fuel resources may soon be exhausted does not matter. This program makes available to industry such large facilities as the Materials Testing Reactor and the Engineering Test Reactor, and provides basic research and development subsidies to reactor designers. In addition, the AEC supplies basic technical design data, as well as materials, fuels, and such services as fuel reprocessing, at relatively low cost until industry can take over this work without subsidy.

The AEC also allows private industry to send technical personnel to Brookhaven, Argonne, and Oak Ridge National Laboratories in order to acquire experience in AEC techniques. Since 1962 the AEC has supplied a consulting service to industry through its Office of Industrial Cooperation. Consulting services are available to industry on a daily rate basis.

The AEC has repeatedly used "demonstration devices" in encouraging industry to apply atomic energy. In some cases these demonstrations have been necessary to prove the safety of the technique proposed. In others the demonstrations have served to substantiate the economic feasibility of the projects undertaken. The effect has been for the AEC to bring atomic energy uses to a point where such applications could be diffused throughout private industry by imitation of the AEC demonstration project. This technique has also served to provide subsidies for expensive atomic energy research.

A good case in point is the application of atomic radiation to such matters as sterilization, food perservation, and creating new products. Although many private companies manufactured equipment that could produce atomic radiation suitable for commercial experimentation, little research was being done in industry on such applications, and most of these machines were being used for teaching and theoretical research. The AEC pioneered by sponsoring studies on the impact of radiation on various materials such as wood, or on radiation as a catalyst in chemical reactions.

Such preliminary research was sufficient to start other federal agencies or private industry off on their own. For example, the Army Quartermaster Corps has pioneered in food preservation through irradiation, and its irradiated bacon and potatoes have been approved by the Food and Drug Administration for field use followed by approval for domestic use. The FDA has recently approved the use of irradiation to destroy insects in wheat and wheat products. In other food areas, industry has needed more encouragement to see that end uses were practical, and the AEC, for example, has just opened a plant for experimental irradiation of seafood in Gloucester, Massachusetts. This plant will be available to all companies in the industry. Swift & Company is considering irradiating meat.

In some areas, industry has taken the lead. Ethicon, a division of Johnson & Johnson, has been using irradiation for seven years to sterilize packages of plastic tubing for hospitals. W. R. Grace & Company is using a stream of

electrons to change characteristics of plastic packaging—creating poly-
ethylenes that are five times stronger than other plastic packaging materials.
But despite all the incentive for industry in such applications, the AEC has
had to pioneer in end uses in order to encourage industrial investment.
One of the latest of these is the development of Novawood®, a new combination of wood and plastic, which, when irradiated, becomes durable and
mar-proof. The AEC selected Vitro Corporation of America to build a pilot
plant to manufacture the new material.[40]

One reason put forth for industrial apathy to AEC technology transfer
attempts is the question of who owns the patent rights to any commercial
invention made by industrial researchers using AEC facilities or working on
AEC contract. As noted, under current practice these are vested in the AEC,
though certain subsidiary developments are given to inventors on a royalty-
free license basis. It appears that this problem, common also to DOD and
NASA transfer efforts, will have to be dealt with if industry is to be encouraged
to risk further development of government originated technology.

The AEC Technical Utilization Program is currently funded at $300,000
per year. The AEC has published for a number of years quarterly reports
which are state-of-the-art surveys describing research progress in various
fields. These are written with the particular objective of giving industry a
broad view of AEC technology.

The AEC appears to be making progress in the peaceful application of
atomic energy. But whatever progress has been made has been built over
twenty years. Because of public fears of the effects of atomic radiation and
industry difficulties in perceiving profitable atomic energy applications, the
AEC has taken on the role of demonstration in order to facilitate technology
transfer. This role has been relatively easy for the AEC to assume, in that its
charter directs such peaceful applications and involvement as a major mission.

THE DEPARTMENT OF COMMERCE AND OTHER
FEDERAL AGENCIES

The Department of Commerce and several other agencies, such as the
Small Business Administration, can be said to have vested interests in the
field of technology transfer. That is, they purport to represent various segments of the economy and have developed their own communications system
for disseminating technological information to these segments. As a result,
they have an interest in participating in any type of technology transfer or
diffusion activities undertaken by the agencies that create new technology
(and can be counted on to comment on, oppose, or cooperate in such
activities as circumstances may dictate) in order to preserve their role in
technological growth.

40. See "Atomic Radiation Role Widens in Making New and Better Products,"
Wall Street Journal (November 24, 1964).

The most important of these organizations, the Department of Commerce, participates in technology transfer in several ways. First, it participates in the diffusion of technology through its Area Redevelopment Administration programs. These programs are directed at the revitalization of local and regional industries through infusions of new technology and capital. Second, the Department of Commerce's Office of Technical Services is the focal point of a technology information dissemination system to all of American industry. This office began by making German and Japanese research data captured in World War II available to U.S. science and industry. It now acts as a clearing house for unclassified R & D reports from the Department of Defense and other agencies, and for technical translations. There is some evidence to indicate that the clearing-house activities of the Commerce Department may soon be vested in its Bureau of Standards. While each of the prime generators of federal R & D maintains independent information distribution systems to meet its own needs, all three, and especially the DOD, also participate in the OTS activities. Third, the Department of Commerce appears to believe that it should play a strong role in the transfer of federally financed technological innovations, and, for the past few years, has proposed the establishment of a Civilian Industrial Technology Program in the Commerce Department. This program, which would establish an agency devoted to active participation in industrial development of new technology, has not received Congressional backing. This failure has been attributed to a number of factors including the opposition of other agencies, Congressional reluctance to fund such an extensive program, and personal antipathies. None of these factors can be verified. The view behind this proposal, however, is that industry needs a facilitating agent to help it develop new technology or absorb missile and space technology, and that in view of the Commerce Department's understanding of American industry, it is the place to locate such an activity.

The Small Business Administration is also interested in the dissemination of new technology for at least two reasons. First, it is often called upon to invest in new businesses—businesses using new technology. Therefore, it would like to see these businesses make the most of whatever technology is available in order to insure their success. Second, it has a channel that can be used to disseminate technological information to particular kinds of businessmen, a goodly number of whom are innovators. With this in mind, the SBA has already cooperated with the major AEC or NASA programs in order to extend their impact on small business.

THE UNITED STATES PATENT OFFICE

The United States Patent Office and the Commissioner of Patents also have a vested interest in participating in and promoting the dissemination of technology. While the patent system is devised to protect exclusive use of innovations for economic reasons, it has been traditionally used by United States companies as a vehicle for searching out (and getting around) new technology. In effect, the patent office and patent system have for a long time been functioning as *de facto* vehicles for the dissemination of new technology. And there are those who believe that the Patent Office should have a strong hand in any system devised to disseminate federally generated technology simply because the American business community is already attuned to the system and knows how to get information out of it.

Of late, the huge number of patentable innovations flowing from United States companies to the patent office has created a troublesome processing backlog, a backlog serious enough for one publication to suggest that if you "take a close look at the patent system in the U.S. . . . you find it's deep in trouble, swamped by a flood of useful new ideas that people just can't get at."[41] This situation has created increasing scepticism from some sections of Congress and the academic community as to the usefulness of the patent system in disseminating technology on a broad scale. Strong—though unprovable—defense has usually come from those who believe that the protection offered by the patent system has been essential to economic growth by rewarding those who will push new technology into use. In fact, they say, this protection is so essential that it was written into the Constitution by the founders of the republic, who established that Congress shall have the power[42]

> To promote the progress of science and useful arts by securing for limited times to authors and inventors the exclusive rights to their respective writings and discoveries.

This situation has resulted in a debate over whether patents really do contribute to economic growth by sheltering the development and application of new technology, or whether they are a drag on the economy by providing a device that industry can use to hold innovations off the market in order to protect investments in the old ways of doing things. This debate has currently focused on the widely different patent policies of the three prime federal R & D agencies, and whether they should be made to adhere to a uniform policy and, if so, what policy. Some believe that federally generated technology will be most rapidly transferred by vesting it in patents granted to the company developing the innovation under government contract, or by granting development rights to selected companies. This method, they claim, will protect the heavy investments needed to put this technology to use, thereby encouraging economic exploitation. Others hold that technology financed by the government belongs to the public, should therefore be made available to all comers, and that such free access is the fastest way to achieve technology

41. "Invention—Is It Keeping Up?" *U.S. News and World Report* (July 15, 1963).
42. Article I, Section 8, paragraph 8.

transfer and stimulate economic growth.[43] These issues, as we shall see, have been given considerable attention by the business community and in Congress. As noted, the three agencies are under executive order to adopt a uniform policy, and this policy may have an important effect on facilitating or inhibiting technology transfer.

Whatever the solution, it is interesting to note that the Commissioner of Patents, David L. Ladd, has recognized that the technological needs of the times have changed, and that the future demands some kind of central clearing house for technical information—a role he believes is suited to the Patent Office:[44]

> I think that 20 to 30 years from now—maybe sooner—the role of the Patent Office as a central clearing house for technical information is going to be as important as its function in examining and granting patents. This function has got to be taken on somewhere, whether it's the Patent Office or the National Science Foundation or the Smithsonian Institute or the Department of Defense—somebody has got to take this on and make the information available.
>
> We visualize a system so far advanced that the information will be coded in a central bank in Washington, available for transmission in pictorial images transcontinentally—as a matter of fact, internationally . . . Some folks laugh, but we mean it.

UNIVERSITIES AND NONPROFIT INSTITUTIONS

Last on our list of organizations with a vested interest in technology transfer are the universities and nonprofit research institutions. In a sense, these organizations also have an invested interest in technology, for they are the creators of some of the innovations available for dissemination. Although they devote a considerable portion of their facilities to performing federally financed basic science and R & D, they have participated minimally in formal systems for disseminating such technology to the private economy.

The universities have always had a strong role in the diffusion of technology in the United States. As the seat of basic science, they have led in creating new knowledge and have been the focus of business and government support for the conduct of basic research. Traditionally, the findings of their research efforts have been diffused informally through scholarly publications,

43. An analysis of the true role of patents in innovation or of the nature and effects of the prevailing government policies is beyond the scope of this discussion. It is sufficient to note that these policies will have an important role in facilitating or inhibiting technology transfer. Useful discussions of this cloudy issue can be found in Robert S. Wright, "U.S. Patent Policy and Government Research," *Bulletin of the Atomic Scientists* (December 1963); Preston, *op. cit., Harvard Business Review;* "From the Thoughtful Businessman" (letters to the editor on the Preston article), *Harvard Business Review* (January–February 1964), p. 43.

44. *U.S. News and World Report, op. cit.*

learned societies, and the like. The establishment of an institutionalized technology dissemination system by the government does not threaten university leadership in research; but it does affect its relationship to national industry. For this reason, several universities and technology institutes are endeavoring to serve as focal points for information-distribution systems, believing that such institutions are ideal mediators between government and industry and that new information should be vested with them. At least one generator of federal technology—NASA—believes strongly that the universities should become focal points for active dissemination of federally generated and other technology, and supports a number of university programs.[45] In practical terms, this has meant considerable research on information storage and retrieval techniques, and studying the ways in which such information can be made available in a form readily usable by industry.[46] An excellent example of such university pioneering is the University of Indiana's ARAC program, described in the section on NASA.

The universities have also participated in the transfer of government financed R & D in another fashion. The best example of this participation is Massachusetts Institute of Technology, whose involvement in federal R & D programs—the World War II Radiation Laboratory, the Instrumentation Laboratory and Lincoln Laboratory, and the independent, nonprofit MITRE Corporation—has inadvertently made it a prime source of technology transfer and the creator of economic health for an entire region.

There are those who maintain that M.I.T.'s Radiation Laboratory created to develop radar and guidance systems, is the starting place of the electronics revolution in America. Among them is Dr. H. Guyford Stever, President of Carnegie Tech. Dr. Stever believes that the laboratory had two effects: (1) its immediate technical advances for military use, and, (2) "the even longer lasting effect of a tremendous spurt in research in physics and electronics as the group spread its knowledge and techniques around the country."[47] Dr. Stever is pointing out an important vehicle for technology transfer: *moving people around.* And his contention is born out, for looking over a sampling of names of former members of the Radiation Lab, we find not only himself but other prominent scientists such as Vannevar Bush; Ivan Getting, president of Aerospace Corporation; Lee Dubridge, president of California Institute of Technology; Lee Hayworth, director of the National

45. Programs have been funded by NASA, directly or indirectly, at Wayne State University, the University of Pittsburgh, University of Indiana, North Carolina Science and Technology Research Center, and University of Missouri.

46. A good deal of research on technology transfer is now underway—both sponsored and unsponsored—in the academic community. This is especially true when one includes traditional work on diffusion of innovation. What is interesting to note is that there appears to be a minimum of communication or transfer of thinking among these groups at the present time.

47. Interview with Dr. Stever reported in the *Boston Globe* (November 15, 1964).

Science Foundation; Joseph Platt, President of Harvey Mudd College; and Julius Stratton, President of M.I.T.

The nonprofit institutions—RAND, MITRE, Jet Propulsion Lab, and the like—also have an interest in facilitating technology transfer. These organizations have been created to fulfill the government's unique military and space R & D needs, in competition with private industry and as a supplement to it. In certain respects, spin-off from these organizations will help justify their existence at a time when their economic function and worth are under attack.[48] Representative Wright Patman and others have charted the growth and economic impact of the nonprofit organizations, and there is considerable resistance to further extension of this kind of organization to other federally supported activities. Whether such organizations are a benefit or detriment to the civilian economy could become an issue, one in which their role in technology transfer would be involved. Finally, these organizations themselves are a subject for transfer: can they be shifted into other activities?

THE BUSINESS COMMUNITY

The receptacle of all these efforts, the business community, is enthusiastic about technology transfer. However, we might consider business attitudes toward the space program more closely.

In 1960, Professor Raymond Bauer, of The Harvard Business School, and I surveyed the subscribers to the *Harvard Business Review* on their attitudes toward the space program. In 1963, I repeated that survey.[49] In both studies, businessmen believed strongly that the national space program is both worthwhile and important. And their enthusiasm for the space program is tied closely to their belief that it will pay off handsomely in products for our everyday lives, and an even greater expection that the space program will revolutionize our technology.

There has been extraordinary enthusiasm on the part of businessmen in the potential benefits that space research might have for mankind. For example, more than 75 percent of the executives responding to the *HBR* surveys in 1960 and 1963 agreed with the following statement that reflects enthusiasm

---

48. See "Tax-Exempt Foundations and Charitable Trusts: Their Impact on Our Economy," a Subcommittee Chairman's Report (Wright Patman) to Subcommittee No. 1, Select Committee on Small Business, House of Representatives, 88th Congress (U.S. Government Printing Office).

49. Raymond A. Bauer, and Edward E. Furash, "The Opinions Held by Business Executives About Space Activities," in D. Michael (ed.), *Proposed Studies on the Implications of Peaceful Space Activities for Human Affairs* (The Brookings Institution, Washington D.C.: 1961). Raymond A. Bauer, "Executives Probe Space," *Harvard Business Review* (September 1960). Edward E. Furash, "Businessmen Review the Space Effort," *Harvard Business Review* (September 1963).

for the space program: "Outer space is the new frontier. Research and exploration will have profound and revolutionary effects on our economic growth."
These executives also believe that the space program will produce specific
tangible payoffs. These expected payoffs can be divided into three categories:
(1) research and development payoffs that will have benefits on this planet;
(2) payoffs from the earth-circling satellites; (3) payoffs that are dependent on
man's traveling to outer space. More specifically, 88 percent of those responding in the 1963 survey believed that new medical and biological knowledge
was a "very likely" or "almost certain" payoff from space research. Some
86 percent felt this way about robot devices; 82 percent about new mathematics
and physics; 81 percent about compact nuclear power plants; 79 percent for
new fabricating materials, and 73 percent felt that "new products for our
everyday lives" were "very likely" or "almost certain" to happen. Every one
of these examples was considered more likely to happen by those responding
in 1963 than by those who had responded in 1960.

Furthermore, some 71 percent of all respondents in the 1963 survey
indicated that they expected an eventual application of space-generated
knowledge *in their own companies*. And 25 percent said that space research
knowledge was *already* being applied in their companies (up from 20 percent in
1960), with another 11 percent expecting applications within the next two
years. However, only 10 percent believed that such applications will be the
direct result of the space program research and development, while 59 percent
said they will come as a by-product, and 31 percent indicated "both." If
nothing else, these data indicate some kind of awareness that space technology
will have to be *adapted* before being used in the civilian economy.

There are, of course, those in the business community who for various
reasons oppose the space program, but few of them will rule out space research as a generator of useful civilian technology. Enthusiasm is not confined
to businessmen and scholars who believe that space research will produce
wonders on earth, but includes investors who have put their hard money on
their faith in spin-off from space research: COMSAT, resulting in a stampede
for stock in a situation where tremendous difficulties had to be overcome
before the system could operate, to say nothing of showing a profit; Barnes
Engineering, whose perceptive president, R. Bolling Barnes, has translated
space-originated concepts of infrared sensors into a hot steel micrometer and
the medical thermograph, bringing active trading in the company's stock.[50]

Despite all this promise and faith, industry as a whole has been slow to
adapt federal R & D to civilian products. The National Academy of Sciences
came to this conclusion when it stated:[51]

50. "Barnes Engineering Company Stock Activity Stirred by Thermograph
Report," *The Wall Street Journal* (September 25, 1964).
51. *A Review of Space Research*, Publ. No. 1079 (Washington, D.C.: National
Academy of Sciences—National Research Council, 1962).

Despite the popular impression, industry at large has been relatively slow to introduce new products arising from the atomic-energy, missile, or space technologies . . . The major inhibiting factor [is] the uncertainty of the profitable return required to attract risk capital and the need for return on investment within a relatively short time span.

These sentiments have been echoed by those within industry. As *Printer's Ink* observed, "One of the most pressing problems today is the need to translate the developments achieved through government-supported research into goods of direct use to consumers. Little has been accomplished in this direction."[52]

One of the reasons given for this slowness in adapting space technology to consumer products is NASA's patent policy. In reality, this policy is a very touchy issue in the business community, for it raises a very fundamental question: *Who should benefit from civilian applications of government-financed research?* There appears to be more heat than light generated on this issue, as can be seen in Exhibit 8-2, for the 1963 *Harvard Business Review* survey of executives indicated that there was no consensus on the matter.[53]

Exhibit 8-2 Who Should Benefit from the Civilian Applications of Government-Financed Research?

Possible Solution	Percent of All Respondents Giving This Solution
a. The government should hold the patent or rights and establish a government agency to develop and sell civilian products or applications.	1
b. The government should invest the patent or rights for civilian applications in some kind of a joint government-private enterprise corporation.	3
c. The government should hold the patent or rights and let all companies use them for civilian applications, the users paying the government a royalty.	20
d. The government should hold the patent or rights and let all companies use them for civilian applications free of charge.	31
e. The patent or rights for civilian application should remain wholly with the company doing the research to exploit it as it sees fit, but the company should pay the government some kind of royalty.	16
f. The patent or rights for civilian applications should remain wholly with the company doing the research to exploit as it sees fit.	12
g. The solution to this problem depends on how much money the government has invested in each individual case.	12
h. Other solutions.	5

Source: "Businessmen Review the Space Effort," *Harvard Business Review* September-October 1963.

52. Walter Joyce, "Why So Few Really New Products?", *Printer's Ink*, Part I, Feb. 1, 1963.
53. Bauer and Furash, *op. cit.*

4% proposed solutions that entail the government "going into business."
51% proposed solutions that have the government keep the rights to civilian use, putting the applications into a common pool for all to use either free of charge or for a royalty.
28% proposed solutions that vest the civilian rights in the company doing the government research either with or without some reimbursement to the government.
17% proposed that the solution to this problem depends on how much money the government has invested in each individual case or some other solution.

As one might expect, this lack of consensus reflects some strongly held, conflicting opinions. At least to one group of businessmen, the presence or absence of patent protection will be a factor in their entrepreneurial evaluation of whether it is worth their while to develop a given innovation. It is not likely that the final federal policy on this matter—the major federal R & D agencies are under an executive order to work out a common policy—will satisfy everyone. This policy, even the heat of the current debate itself, may be sufficiently unsettling to have an adverse effect on facilitating technology transfer.[54]

These same executives were also asked "what method is the fastest way to put such new ideas and inventions into consumer or industrial use?" Their replies:

Method 1: "Let the company that discovered the product or process exploit the civilian or industrial uses."   39%
Method 2: "Have NASA or the military inform all companies about the product or process and encourage them to exploit the civilian or industrial uses."   40%
Method 3: "It is difficult to say which method would be faster," [and other answers] . . .   21%

To some degree, industry's failure to adapt space technology to commercial products reflects the behavior of those companies in the best position to take advanatge of the technology: the aerospace industry. The key problem is that most aerospace companies simply are not oriented toward the detection and exploitation of opportunities in consumer or industrial markets, and lack appropriate experience and staff when so inclined. This blind spot prevents them from perceiving the consumer and industrial needs that could be filled by their innovations.

Lee E. Preston found that North American Aviation, the largest recipient of federal R & D contracts from 1949–59 and a purely aerospace company, was far less successful than General Electric, the second largest contractor during the same period and a primarily commercial company, in extracting commercial profit from patents obtained in the course of doing R & D for the government. He concluded that[55]

54. See Preston, *op. cit.* and Wright, *op. cit.*
55. Preston, *op. cit.*, p. 200.

At a minimum, one would say that effective commercial application by the inventing company would occur only when that company had a substantial commercial business to which the patented invention could be applied.

Even when such noncommercially oriented companies do come up with a good commercial innovation, their attitudes and lack of industrial market experience will often hamper marketing it. Thus even after the Fairchild Camera and Instrument Company had adapted space technology to create a prototype home video tape recorder, it put the invention up for licensing (unsuccessfully), commenting that "this machine does not fall into Fairchild's present marketing pattern and the company hopes that some other concern will adopt and produce it."[56] Similarly, though Bell Aerosystems has tested its patented "electronic stethoscope," a space program spin-off, it is not intending to produce it itself, but has offered the invention to medical electronics companies. "It's not in our line," a Bell spokesman has noted.[57] On the other hand, company orientation can *make* its new products succeed, such as in the case of the Barnes Engineering Company's infrared micrometer to measure the diameter of hot steel rods. Barnes' President R. B. Barnes sees the company in the infrared technology business, not aerospace, and pushes the company to market infrared devices in all situations possible— even medicine, as it does with its thermograph.[58]

This lack of success in technology transfer by American aerospace companies highlights an important fact: *most government-financed R & D takes place in industry itself.* The information does not have to cross some great gulf of time or space to be translated into a commercial product. Technology transfer can—and sometimes does—occur within the originating company, though not to the satisfaction of those who would want it to occur at a faster pace, with more success, and with many more companies involved.

It would be unfair to conclude our discussion at this point, for it leaves the impression that translating government-financed technology into civilian products is a unique problem for business and that the fault lies in a failure to recognize the importance of this new technology. This is not the case. If we put technology transfer into the context of business R & D as a whole, we find that it is a special case of a very old, widespread industry problem: the management of innovation. Whether it is labeled "problems of R & D management," or "new product development," or "organizing for research," or whatever you like—the problem of evaluating new products and bringing them to fruition has yet to be solved well in industry. Of course, there is an extensive literature on new product development, much of it devoted to long

56. "Do It Yourself Reruns," *Business Week* (April 18, 1964), p. 186.
57. "Bell Aerosystems Develops a New Stethoscope," *New York Times* (May 8, 1964).
58. R. B. Barnes, "An Industrial Derivative from the Space Program," 3rd National Conference on the Peaceful Uses of Space, Chicago, May 1963.

lists of do's and don't's; and a great deal of research is being carried out on this topic.

It would be fruitless to review these materials in depth at this point, for their very existence alerts us to recognizing that the technology available to industry from government-financed R & D is *just one more source* for a company. True, the company may not be well attuned to using that source, but even if it were, the technology perceived would still be subject to the vagaries and standards of traditional product-development practices.[59] In sum, industry itself has no sure-fire method for bringing even its own ideas to complete and rapid success. This situation led one observer, Donald A. Schon, to note that "it is in the nature of a large organization to oppose upsetting change and innovation," and that such change is introduced only by having a strong champion in the organization.[60]

This champion must be an individual who is sufficiently intrigued by a new idea to be willing to do the work of preparing as complete an evaluation as he can, and then, with the facts in hand, selling his new idea. The champion may or may not be the inventor of the particular technique or device. This man, perhaps more accurately described as an entrepreneur, may appear anywhere in the transfer sequence, from the inception of a new idea to the marketplace. What appears to be most important, however, is his personal interest in the idea, his enthusiasm for transferring it into actual practice, and his personal ability to persuade other individuals to use it. This entrepreneur, then, serves as a bridge between the idea and a real market need. He is the mechanism for persuading others that this idea will fit the need. Without the entrepreneur, the transfer process is a situation in which those who have developed aerospace technology are searching for persons to use it in different markets, yet these persons do not realize that they need the innovation.[61]

In closing, it is important to note that although we have been discussing the business community as if it were a homogenous entity, it is not. Within the community there will be firms that attach special importance to policy decisions concerning technology transfer. Among them would be defense

59. For example, one such traditional standard is to ask whether the new product "fits into the existing product line"; uses the materials, facilities, distribution channels, or markets of existing company products; gives some extra plus to existing products by "filling out the line"; or makes use of the firm's distinctive know-how in some way. And, of course, the most important measure of all: will we make a profit?

60. Donald A. Schon, "Champions for Radical New Inventions," *Harvard Business Review*, **41**, No. 2 (March 1963).

61. For a more complete discussion of this concept, see section of this chapter, "Actors: Individuals." See also concept of "techno-entrepreneur" in W. R. Purcell, Jr., *Commercial Profits from Defense-Space Technology* (Boston: The Schur Company, 1964–1965).

contractors and others with a vested interest in patent policies; professional commercial R & D and consulting organizations which are in competition with government technology as a source of new products and which currently retail such technology to industry; and those firms in the industries most affected by government money.

INTERESTED PARTIES

There are many organizations in our society that are "interested parties" to the process of technology transfer or to policy decisions about technology transfer. Some of these groups, such as Congress, may have great power to effect technology transfer; others, such as consumer communications media, will merely report the passing scene. Our purpose here is to identify them and depict briefly their possible interests.

CONGRESS. For all the reasons that Congress is interested in anything that happens in the United States, it has been and will be interested in this topic. Because technology transfer is a matter for executive policy setting, Congress finds it within its power to investigate, regulate, and even legislate on this issue. Naturally, Congress is interested in order to assure itself that taxpayers' dollars are being used in the most efficient fashion, with the least amount of bias, and for the good of the nation. Congress is also concerned about technology transfer because such transfer contributes to national growth which, in terms of Gross National Product, is a current concern.

Of late, Congress has been intensely concerned with the issue of who should benefit from the commercial applications of R & D innovations. Senator Russell Long of Louisiana has advocated strong legislation that would vest all patent rights for inventions made under federal R & D contracts in the government. His objective is to "not have some robber baron getting the benefit of the Government's money . . . it will be for the benefit of 190 million people."[62] Senator Long has already achieved remarkable success in introducing restrictive patent riders on R & D programs such as the Water Resources Research Act of 1964. But he has been unable to change the behavior of the Department of Defense in awarding patents to R & D contractors as a reward and incentive for doing government work, or to keep NASA from granting patent rights to contractors when it deems it in the national interest to do so.

The debate, as noted earlier, is between those who believe that patent protection is the best route to encourage companies to undertake commercialization of innovations developed under federal R & D contracts, and those who want to prevent a few companies from getting a monopoly on the fruits of federal R & D. Senator John McClellan of Arkansas has introduced

62. For a comprehensive view of this legislative situation, see "New Curbs Are Sought on Patents Stemming from U.S. Research," *Wall Street Journal* (June 1, 1965), p. 1.

legislation that would permit a flexible policy on the part of the agencies. His plan is to specify three categories of contracts: those in which the government would automatically take title to inventions, including patents stemming from work aimed at developing a specific commercial product (fertilizer, drugs, etc.) for the government itself; those in which the contractor retains title because the government is capitalizing on his extensive commercial know-how; and, those in which the answer is so uncertain that the federal agency decides on a case-by-case basis after the invention has been identified and its potential value determined. At present, the Justice Department opposes any bill that will automatically vest patent rights in advance of discovery.

Congress is also concerned about technology transfer because it relates, albeit indirectly, to the latest form of pork barrel: the allocation of federal funds for science and R & D. Legislators have come to understand that federal funds for science affect local and regional prosperity. They need only observe the electronics industry of Massachusetts, the aerospace complex of California, and the NASA centers in the South to realize the potency of this new pork barrel. Furthermore, if spin-offs occur, they will probably occur in the region where the original government funds were spent. For all these reasons, then, we can also see that local and state governments can become "interested parties" to technology transfer. There have been several battles to date over the location of NASA facilities.[63]

COMMUNICATIONS MEDIA. The communications media are interested parties to technology transfer in two ways. First, they purvey entertainment to consumers, and set tastes and expectations. Second, they transmit information to businesses. In this first sense, these media recognize that the new, the novel, and the changing have always been important forms of entertainment for American public. News about new products, great inventions, and life fifty years from now, fill our newspapers, magazines, and even the exhibit halls of the World's Fairs. These media prepare the public for the never-ending flow of new products to be turned out by American industry, and create an atmosphere which encourages technology transfer. As for business, trade publications and information services facilitate technology transfer by purveying technological information itself.

OTHER GROUPS. Obviously, interested parties also include public organizations—such as the National Science Foundation, the National Academy of Science, or the National Planning Association—that sponsor research on, discussions of, or evaluations of technology transfer. We have cited elsewhere,

63. See Ian Menzies, "Science Funds Pork Barrel?" *Boston Globe*, (February 19, 1964); "The Latest in Pork Barrel: Science Funds," *Science*; Dr. Charles Kimball, "Why the Midwest Is Lagging—and What Can be Done About It," *U.S. News and World Report* (August 10, 1964); John Lear, "Global Budgeting for Science," *Saturday Review*, (November 23, 1963).

for example, the contribution of the National Academy of Sciences in assessing business progress in technology transfer. We have also cited the impact of the work by Robert Solo for the National Planning Association on the relationship of R & D to national growth. The N.P.A. is continuing to study technology transfer with a project under the direction of Sumner Myers. This project is directed at identifying the sources of information used by companies in achieving innovations, in an attempt to discover technology transferred from missile and space programs. A case-study approach is being used.

In the academic community, a good deal of interest has been evoked in studying the transfer process and methods for facilitating the process. Research is underway at such diverse institutions as Harvard Business School (R. S. Rosenbloom, C. Orth and others); Princeton (M. Tannenbaum, for the National Academy of Sciences on behalf of the DOD); Stanford (C. Vesper); Cornell (Scala); Dartmouth (B. Quinn); University of Missouri (Thayer); and M.I.T. (E. Roberts and others). This research covers such matters as studies of the role of the individual in the transfer process, studies of the role of the organization in facilitating or inhibiting technology transfer, and methods for storing and retrieving technological information that will facilitate transfer.

If our purpose were to produce a completely exhaustive list of interested parties, we could go on to discuss the effects of technology transfer on such groups as organized labor (by affecting employment or work), farmers, or the general public. But for the scope of this discussion, their interests are too peripheral for further detailed consideration.

Actors:
Individuals

Up to now we have been discussing technology transfer as if packages of knowledge were being tossed between various organizations. Nothing could be further from the truth, for the core of technology transfer is *communication* —and this means people. As the President's Science Advisory Committee has put it, "transfer of information is an inseparable part of research and development."[64]

PARTICIPANTS IN THE TRANSFER PROCESS

The key to the transfer of missile and space technology to civilian uses is the communication of people—how they search for information, how they

64. *Science, Government and Information*, Report of the President's Science Advisory Council (Washington D.C.: U.S. Government Printing Office, 1963).

react to presentations, how they think things through, how they perceive innovations. Putting it another way, if you invent a better mousetrap people will not necessarily beat a path to your door. They may not be able to find your door or understand that what you are selling is a mousetrap.

With this in mind, we must recognize that with the exception of a few lone tinkerers and entrepreneurs, most of the people participating in the transfer of technology—scientists and engineers—will be part of large research and development organizations. But even if they are members of small organizations, their problems will be the same: how to find out what's new, what's relevant, what's useful. And given the sheer volume of technological information to be culled, this is no easy task. In the first half of 1964, NASA's STAR reports contained some 10,000 items plus some 8,000 items in the International Aerospace Abstracts. And this was just the beginning.

It has been estimated that there are some 30,000 scientific periodicals currently being published, with a worldwide total of perhaps six million printed pages. Estimates of the number of significant technical documents published annually in all engineering and scientific fields in the world range as high as 1.5 million. There are about 300 abstracting and indexing services in the United States, and these services covered 950,000 titles in 1963 (vs. 437,000 in 1957). And Dr. Adkinson of the National Science Foundation believes that they *may* cover 1 to 1.5 million items a year. About 100,000 unpublished technical documents are produced by or for the federal government in the course of a year.[65]

Whether these reports all contain useful information or not, it is impossible for any one individual to cope with even a part of them. The researcher must therefore limit his search to some tried-and-true methods: asking friends and acquaintances; reading trade publications he likes, or using an index or abstract that he knows. In sum, he uses a form of selective perception—or does he behave in some other way? *Understanding how people—and especially scientists and engineers—search for information, then, is an essential step in facilitating technology transfer.*

But even if we know how they search for information and can put it before them, how do we know they will read it? This is a very special problem in the case of transmitting technology, which is usually in the form of ideas of *highly specialized* product forms. For unlike ordinary information about pills, seed corn, or air-conditioners, we cannot know in advance who will be interested in it. We can tell doctors about new medicine, farmers about a new type of corn, and homeowners about air-conditioners. But telling engineers and scientists about missile/space technology is *trying to inform someone you don't know how to locate how to solve a problem he doesn't have as yet.* This special characteristic of most government-financed technological information demands that the disseminator label and store the information in a way that

65. Rosenbloom, *op. cit.*

will encourage wide use. For as we have noted earlier, the information to be transmitted is *technology*—not a specific product—and the way in which it will probably be put to use is by *analogy*.

Translating technology by analogy may require a very special kind of person. This notion has been summed up by Rosenbloom as follows:[66]

> To the extent that secondary innovation must come by analogy, rather than by imitation of the source innovation, we must contend with a new element of the process—creative adaption—and hence a different problem. The practical significance of this difference is, we believe, great; not only have we added an additional step in the process, but the one which is added is essentially an inventive act, one requiring creativity and imagination. Facilitation of the creative adaptation of an invention is clearly a different kind of problem from facilitation of the adoption of an invention in imitation of the original inventors.

Thus the development of a micrometer to measure the diameter of hot steel rods in the course of production, using infrared components developed originally as horizon sensors in satellites, and the invention of the "thermograph," using this same principle to measure "hot spots" in the human body as a diagnostic device, supports the hypothesis that the key to transfer is analogy.

And this analogical ability is vested in a man—someone who is perhaps so saturated with his technology that he reaches out to any and all problems to find applications. What kind of a man he is, we do not know. Neither do we know if he can be trained to think in this manner. But from industrial experience we know he is a man capable of championing a new invention, of being the entrepreneur who acts as the bridge between end use and the technological idea, a man who will have the stamina to see the project through to completion, and possess the ability to persuade others that it is worthwhile. Finding out more about him will be important to facilitating technology transfer.[67]

PEOPLE AS A RESOURCE

Although technology transfer has been thought of primarily as the movement of information, it can also be conceived of as the movement of people—the application of individuals trained in government-financed research to new activities. There are those, in fact, who maintain that the greatest spin-off from federally financed R & D will not be particular inventions, but a phalanx of trained engineers and scientists who can put their talents and methods to work on a host of unsolved problems—such as water shortages,

66. Rosenbloom, *op. cit.*; see also, Purcell, *op. cit.*
67. See Donald White, "Entrepreneurs Cited As Key to Conversion," *Boston Globe* (November 13, 1964).

transportation, and air pollution—in our society. Now this seemingly beneficial result disguises a critical problem for our nation; for what this statement really indicates is that there are thousands of engineers and scientists wholly dependent on federal R & D expenditures for their livelihoods, and that cutbacks in space and defense R & D spending will put these men out of work, at least until they can find jobs in private industry or until new projects are funded. This is why the state of California once asked its aerospace firms to bid on $500,000 worth of research to study ways in which the state can solve some of its earthly woes, such as freeway snarls, juvenile delinquency, and management of waste materials.[68]

Federal R & D expenditures have created more than a research army. They have also created a unique business-government system for carrying out the various research programs, new economic entities in American life— the corporation that does most of its business with the government or the non-profit organization doing only government work. These kinds of companies are not insignificant: depending on the category, from 70 to 90 percent of government expenditures for R & D (especially those for space and defense) are spent through these firms or organizations. In sum, we have huge numbers of engineers and scientists employed by firms or organizations whose major work is carrying out federally financed research and development.

The specific name of this new business-government system is not important. Whether we call it "the project system," "the aerospace industry," the "defense industry," or "administration by contract," the effect on the lives and work of scientists and engineers is the same. These men work for and are trained for life in a special organization—an organization whose attitudes, standards, mores, values, and atmosphere can be quite different from those of other businesses. In other words, we have created a distinctive system for carrying out government-financed research and development, and we have trained thousands of men and women to work within that system.

In this situation lies the kernel of a transfer problem. Because these men have been working in very special organization situations, because they have been trained to do very specialized scientific jobs, they are not readily transferable to other parts of our economy when federal R & D expenditures are cut. Thus, whenever there are cutbacks in defense spending, they affect thousands of engineers working on defense related R & D.

There are many reasons why these engineers and scientists are not readily absorbed by other segments of industry, and most of them relate to the work habits and attitudes developed in government work.

First, the work of scientists and engineers on government-sponsored R &

68. See *Wall Street Journal* (November 19, 1964); "Plan Sought to Shift Defense Brainpower to Big Public Projects," *Wall Street Journal*, (October 7, 1964); "Aerospace Firms Seek to Turn Their Talents to Curing Urban Ills," *Wall Street Journal* (June 9, 1965), p. 1.

D projects is usually more specialized and focused than it is in private industry. As an RCA official once pointed out, "Many of our top scientific people in defense work just can't handle jobs in our color-TV production lines in the Midwest. Besides, we don't have a big surplus of jobs going begging out there."[69]

Second, these men are frequently accustomed to working on projects where unlimited financial support is available and where they can achieve early advancement to management status with high pay. This is usually not the case in industrially financed R & D. When a management research firm compared research costs under defense contracts with costs for commercial markets, it found that the typical defense-research operation requires four to five times as many scientists per sales dollar as the normal commercial operation. Now, this finding does not necessarily reflect inefficiency. It does reflect the faster pace of government work and the fact that the scientific work for the government is quite different and more complicated and requires more personnel to get it done. This points out that men coming from government R & D will carry with them ideas and attitudes about how to get a job done or how much to spend on a job that are in conflict with industrial standards. Considerable adjustment would be needed by both parties, especially when one realizes that such men might often not meet industrial seniority standards for management position or find a pay scale that matches government R & D. The difficulties of such changeovers are well illustrated by this excerpt from an interview with an unemployed engineer:[70]

> I've been out of a job since last July. I was making $13,000 a year, but I've offered to work for half that. No luck. One personnel chief refused to take me on for a $7,000 job on the grounds that I would be bored. He said I would know more than the boss in my section, that I'd be unhappy and soon quit. I wish he'd let me be the judge of that.

Third, these men tend to be isolated, with little or no experience with civilian markets or association with the business world. Because of this, they are viewed by business as being "impractical" or not "profit oriented," an unfair accusation, but nevertheless an attitude that makes absorbing them into industry difficult.

Engineers themselves are aware of this transfer problem. In 1964 when 2,500 men were laid off, engineers at Boeing Aircraft in Seattle recognized the retraining need and asked management for four hours off per week in order to read and broaden their technical and managerial abilities.[71]

A more positive view is needed, however, in order to solve the engineering unemployment problem. Part of this positive view is to recognize that the

69. "Defense Cuts Bring a New Kind of Job Crisis," *U.S. News and World Report* (May 18, 1964).
70. *Ibid.*
71. *Wall Street Journal*, (May 7, 1964).

business-government system created by government R & D projects is *unique*, and that, as such, it has certain characteristics of potential value to other national activities or problems. This system has evolved a viable method for accomplishing government goals primarily through private means. In a world in which we wish to maintain free enterprise, this is no mean accomplishment. And further, we must recognize that this system has been able to accomplish huge undertakings, manage them successfully, and, on the whole, bring them to fruition.

To those who would like to disband the entire apparatus, there is little solace to offer. First, it is doubtful whether such a large establishment would ever allow itself to be disbanded. Organizations and industries have a vested interested in maintaining themselves, and this situation will be no exception. Second, the social dislocation caused might be too high a cost for us to pay. Of course, while we would like to see decreases in federal spending, we must recognize that such decreases are not to be measured in dollars alone, but in fewer jobs and a possible business recession. Any such reduction can come with justice only after we have prepared the way for these men to be absorbed in private industry. Third, the record for converting the government R & D defense industry to industrial or consumer activity has been a poor one. As Carl Frische, President of Sperry Gyroscope, put it, "It would be difficult to find or name any significant example of the defense/space oriented segment or company which has successfully converted from government production to industrial or consumer activity."[72] And little wonder when, for example, a firm like North American Aviation estimates that it could find $15 million in civilian business over the next three years. And North American Aviation is a mighty complex with two billion dollars in government business.[73]

The solution, of course, is to find other things for this industry to do, which is easier said than done. Ideally, one would hope that new products available from space and defense R & D would create tremendous civilian opportunities for these companies and organizations. As we have seen, the development of such products is not a simple task, and the industry does not seem oriented to making such developments.

Conclusion

The problem of transferring the fruits of Federal R & D to all corners of our economy has received a good deal of attention, particularly because of the increasing share of our nation's research and development resources being used for federal R & D. And the debate over other policy issues related to

72. *U.S. News and World Report, op. cit.,* (May 18, 1964).
73. Peter B. Greenough, "Scientists Role Shifting in U.S.," *Boston Globe* (May 19, 1964).

federal R & D—its effect on our rate of economic growth, its impact on business, and patent policies—has placed even further emphasis on facilitating technology transfer as a solution to other problems. But technology transfer is not a policy issue in the usual sense of the term. There are no interests, individuals, or groups at loggerheads over whether technology transfer is a good thing. There are some doubters who wonder if anything of great import can be accomplished, but the goal of technology transfer is commonly agreed upon as being desirable. If there are any arguments over technology transfer, they relate to who is going to play the major role in disseminating federal technology and what is the best technique for facilitating technology transfer.

Although there are many interested parties who want to help facilitate technology transfer, it is important to remember that no one of them has the power to do more than provide circumstances, encouragements, and systems that will help the *business community* to transfer federal R & D into fruitful commercial applications. Unless the federal government or other interested parties is going into business, the actual technology transfer process is beyond their direct influence and control, *for it occurs within business enterprises.*

The role of information in formulating technology transfer policy, then, is quite different from that of usual policy issues. In a normative sense, policy issues can usually be related to particular groups holding "pro" or "con" opinions. And in such situations the role of an agent providing information to participants in the policy formulation is that of providing information at leverage points—that is, determining *who will be influenced by what information at a given point in the policy process.* While this formula is valid when thinking about policy issues that impinge on technology transfer, it does not apply to the problem of technology transfer itself because there is a good deal of confusion on the part of those who want to facilitate technology transfer as to what is to be accomplished, how to facilitate it, and who should control the facilitating mechanisms. Although the issues of control and establishing formal transfer activities may become typical policy problems subject to the injection of information at leverage points, they will not become so until after the first two confusions are clarified.

At this stage in the formulation of technology transfer policy, the first step should be to clarify the objectives and to provide an understanding of the transfer process, and both should serve as preludes to the formulation of any specific technology dissemination system, policy, or organization to be placed in the hands of one group or another.

CLARIFYING THE ISSUES AND OBJECTIVES

Those who want to facilitate technology transfer give many different reasons for their interest: to aid our rate of economic growth; to relieve the impact of federal R & D on the business community; to prevent the waste of a vast pool of technology; to provide additional benefits to the nation beyond the primary R & D mission of a particular project; and many others. This diversity of objectives, when it is coupled with the even greater diversity of those who are interested in facilitating technology transfer, cumulates to create *a situation in which there is general confusion as to just what technology transfer is supposed to accomplish.*

In effect, while various organizations and individuals state that they are trying to facilitate technology transfer, they really do not share common frameworks as to what amount, kind, nature, or speed of technology transfer is to be achieved. Our first information need, then, is to order and enumerate the different points of view and their sources in an attempt to achieve some kind of mutual agreement as to what the goals of technology transfer are. As we noted earlier, disappointment over the amount of technology transfer achieved depends on what one hoped would be accomplished to begin with. The importance of transfer and the urgency attached to facilitating it are affected by the content, status, and heat of the following continuing debates:

1. *National science policy*, including the kinds of science to be supported by the Federal government, the balance between sciences in that support, and the impact of such support on manpower, private research and development, and other such matters.

2. *Economic growth*, including the degree to which our economy is matching desired goals, whether current science policy is contributing to economic growth through manpower allocations or technology creation, and discussion over the regional distribution of federal science funds with their attendant impact on regional economies.

3. *Patents*, including decisions as to who should benefit from the civilian applications of government-financed research and development, and the need for patents to encourage economic growth.

In addition, what one expects to achieve through technology transfer appears to be related to the kind of "vested" or "invested" interests that one has. Obviously, each agency funding federal R & D to some degree sees it to its interest to facilitate technology transfer if only in order to provide an additional reason for its primary mission. The more an agency relies on spin-off to justify its primary mission the more zealously it will attempt to control technology transfer in order to insure that something will occur. Those agencies with "vested" interests in the dissemination of technological information also have particular points of view as to what can be achieved and have their own interests to be protected in any dissemination system or policy they advocate. A monitoring of the opinions of key decision makers both in the Federal Government and elsewhere on the subject of technology transfer might provide key information.

UNDERSTANDING THE TRANSFER PROCESS

A second critical need is understanding the transfer process itself. Although one can debate the amounts of transfer that have actually occurred, there is little disagreement that more transfer is desirable. Yet, whatever transfer has been achieved has primarily come about in a "natural" fashion— without major programs to facilitate transfer. Thus it is important to understand both the barriers to transfer and the transfer process itself before we set any policy or activity to facilitate transfer.

In this chapter we have identified a number of barriers to the transfer of technology:

1. There is a marked and increasing divergence between much of the federal technology that has been developed (especially missile and space technology) and the needs of the civilian economy. Transfer must occur by *analogy* rather than by *imitation*.

2. There is a lack of adequate communication between the body of technology generated from federal R & D and potential users.

3. The increasing volume of technological data generated from federal R & D programs is making the process of searching for information in this technology cumbersome, uneconomic, and unappealing.

4. There are traditional ways of doing things, as exemplified by business practices, building codes, and work rules, that inhibit innovation in general.

If we are to develop a policy or system to facilitate technology transfer, there is a crucial information need in understanding the process itself and the barriers to transfer. With this in mind the key areas in which further information might help policy formulation are in understanding the following matters:

1. How scientists, engineers and others go about searching for new information and relate themselves to existing information systems.

2. The institutional features and decision rules of business organizations that affect the adoption of innovation.

3. The role of the "entrepreneur," the "champion," or the "insightful individual" in achieving technology transfer by analogy. Are there situational determinants that affect the ability to perceive technological analogy?

4. The manner in which the nature of federal R & D technology itself affects dissemination. Is it readily communicable? How can it be presented in usable fashion? Is such technology too esoteric to hope for transfer? Is analogy the only method by which it can be transferred?

5. How technological innovation affects economic growth and the impact of subsidiary issues, such as patents, on innovation and growth.

6. The institutional and cultural barriers to innovation.[74]

7. The various ways in which national information dissemination systems

74. For an interesting exposition on this topic, see Michaelis, *op. cit.*

can be developed. Should the agencies merge their activities into one center? What institutions could participate more effectively? What data storage and disbursement techniques will have to be developed? In what ways can we improve our ability to handle the flood of documents now being published?

8. The role of mass media and business publications in stimulating transfer through promoting higher consumer expectations or through disseminating technology. Consumers are constantly subjected to a flood of media information on "your life tomorrow," or "spin-off from space research." How does this affect the rate of technology transfer?

9. To what degree is technology transfer affected by business ideology and the willingness of the business community to accept government incursion in the economy in the form of sponsored R & D? How is this affected by business reaction to the growth of nonprofit research institutions and in-house government research agencies? Will business react to the possible threat of government entry into the private commercial markets in order to achieve technology applications? What is the role of patent policy in this situation?[75]

A NATIONAL POLICY

Our third need really occurs only after sufficient information has been amassed from the kinds of studies outlined above to make technology transfer evolve into a more traditional policy issue. At this point, one can expect that pro and con positions will develop on the following kinds of issues—and the role of information will be to influence key decision makers at specified leverage points:

1. To what degree is technology transfer a responsibility of the federal government? Can transfer objectives be achieved without a federal policy?

2. How should this policy embody various points of view as to who should benefit directly and indirectly from public funds spent on federal R & D?

3. Which federal agency or group should control the information dissemination system, the financial incentive systems, or other such devices that will be used to facilitate technology transfer?

Obviously, these are just a few of the policy issues that will be raised. To a degree they are issues already being discussed in terms of other policy matters—federal science policy, patent policy, impact of federal R & D, and the like. Since decisions in these areas will ultimately affect technology transfer, one further role for the information agent is important. The progress of these key issues and debates should be monitored, not only to provide an understanding of how they will affect technology transfer, but also to provide key decision makers on these issues with current information on technology transfer. After all, the state of knowledge about technology transfer is itself an input to decision making on these other issues.

75. See Raymond A. Bauer, "Keynes via the Back Door," *The Journal of Social Issues*, **XVIII**, No. 2 (1961).

Chapter 9

THEODORE GEIGER and ROGER D. HANSEN

The Role of Information in Decision Making on Foreign Aid

Introduction—Assumptions and Scope

This chapter is intended to contribute toward better understanding of the factors that enter into the process of making decisions on United States national policies and goals.[1] Our approach is empirical rather than theoretical. We focus on a particular area of national decision making—the foreign aid program—and seek to identify and evaluate the relative importance of the various factors that play a role both in the formation of national attitudes regarding this activity and in the policy and operating decisions made in the Executive Branch and in Congress concerning it. However, this chapter is only exploratory in nature. Neither time nor manpower has been available to undertake the detailed research and analysis necessary for a thorough investigation of the process of national decision making on foreign aid. We hope that the ideas and suggestions presented herein will be regarded as tentative conclusions to be tested in the course of a more extended research

1. This chapter was completed in June 1965. For a later and more developed analysis of some of the subjects treated here, see Theodore Geiger, *The Conflicted Relationship: The West and the Transformation of Asia, Africa and Latin America* (New York: McGraw-Hill, for the Council on Foreign Relations, 1967).

study and not as findings that have been definitively demonstrated in this paper.

Within the present framework particular attention is paid to the role of information—that is, empirical data and analytical concepts relevant to them—in decision making on foreign aid. It is generally assumed in the United States that there exists a positive correlation between the amounts of information disseminated to decision makers and the public on national policy problems and their willingness to undertake the prescribed actions for coping with them. In many cases, this expectation is valid; more and better information does directly increase support for programs designed to realize national goals. In others, however, the relationship does not hold; the better the understanding of the difficulties and uncertainties involved in trying to achieve a particular policy objective, the greater the reluctance may be to attempt it. Such a reaction is often a rational response to recognition that the costs and time required to realize the goal are greater, or the benefits thereof are likely to be less, than originally anticipated. Sometimes, however, a practicable objective may be abandoned through disappointment and frustration when better information reveals that expectations of easy and rapid results have been highly unrealistic. One of our tentative conclusions is that such loss of morale could eventuate from greater public and elite-group understanding that their optimistic expectations regarding the foreign aid program have in many respects been unfounded.

Our major assumption regarding the role of information is a truism of contemporary sociology that is not always recognized by decision makers themselves. It is that their willingness and ability to seek and utilize particular kinds of information are never determined solely—and in many cases not even mainly—by purely intellectual considerations. In the case of foreign aid, much of the information used in decision making is rationally determined; that is, it can be pragmatically demonstrated that there is an objective connection between the particular sets of ideas and empirical data used in the decision-making process and the economic and social phenomena which the policy makers are trying to influence. If this were not so, decisions would be divorced from reality; and because it is so, relevance, comprehensiveness, and accuracy of the information utilized are essential elements in the effectiveness of decisions in influencing the actual course of events. However, two other kinds of factors enter importantly into determination of the particular types of information believed to be relevant to decisions and of the particular ways in which this information is used in the decision-making process.

The first set of factors arises from the cultural system.[2] It is from the

---

2. As used in this paper, the terms *society, culture, cultural system, social system, economic system, political system,* and their interrelationships follow the definitions suggested in A. L. Kroeber and Talcott Parsons, "The Concepts of Culture and of Social System," *American Sociological Review,* 23, No. 5 (October 1958), pp. 582–583.

cultural system of their society that decision makers acquire the basic categories of thought by which they perceive and attach significance to external social reality, the values and norms in terms of which they formulate goals, the rules governing their efforts to achieve them, and the standards for judging their performances. Each society—and, indeed, each subgroup within a society—inculcates in its members a distinctive set of categories in terms of which certain social (as well as physical) phenomena are perceived and others are not perceived, and particular meanings and connotations are attached to those perceived. At the same time, each society encourages the acceptance by its members of a distinctive value system and set of norms which help to determine motivations and attitudes, individual and social behavior, and personal and social objectives and expectations. For methodological purposes, it is often convenient to distinguish these two sets of directives of the cultural system as (1) those declaring what is believed to exist, and (2) those prescribing the values and norms of the society, that is, what ought to exist. However, values and norms *per se* are "facts of life" influencing individual and group attitudes and behavior and, therefore, also have an existential character. These cultural factors are particularly important in the formation of popular and elite-group attitudes toward foreign aid.

The second set of factors arises from the nature of the institutional system. It embraces the effects on the information sought and utilized of the characteristics of the organizations within which the decision-making process occurs, and of the environment within which those organizations operate and interact with one another. This set of factors is particularly important with respect to foreign aid decision making by the Executive Branch and Congress. In each case, the organizational structure and methods of functioning, the characteristics of the personnel involved, and the external relationships of and pressures on the institution influence the choice and use of information. These institutional factors interact with rational, intellectual considerations and with cultural influences to determine the specific ways in which decision makers utilize the information that they believe is relevant to their purposes.

Throughout this paper, the term foreign aid refers to what is generally called economic aid—that is, intergovernmental transfers of economic resources either as loans or as grants, and the financing by the U.S. government of technical assistance activities in the recipient countries. We are not concerned with military aid provided by the U.S. government to its allies and friends abroad. As stated in the preamble to the Act for International Development of 1961, the U.S. purpose in providing economic aid is to

> . . . help strengthen the forces of freedom by aiding peoples of less developed friendly countries of the world to develop their resources and improve their living standards, to realize their aspirations for justice, education, dignity, and respect as individual human beings, and to establish responsible governments. . . .

> Accordingly, the Congress hereby affirms it to be the policy of the United
> States to make assistance available, upon request, . . . on a basis of long-
> range continuity essential to the creation of an environment in which the
> energies of the peoples of the world can be devoted to constructive purposes,
> free of pressure and erosion by the adversaries of freedom.

In short, we assume that the major objective which the United States seeks to achieve today through the provision of foreign aid is the economic and social advancement of the less developed countries in Africa, Asia, and Latin America. However, in practice, economic aid is also given or withheld by the United States in order to obtain more immediate political advantages. The particular kinds of information relevant to such shorter-term foreign policy decisions are significantly different from those relevant to the longer-term decisions regarding economic and social development and, hence, are not specifically covered in this discussion. However, we may note that short-term foreign policy considerations are important influences on decisions regarding aid to foster longer-range economic and social development, and—though less often and much less effectively—*vice versa*.

The first part of this chapter sketches in broad outline the historical and cultural factors underlying American attitudes and expectations regarding foreign aid and, within this context, describes briefly the national interest rationale for this activity and the results of public opinion polls and other studies of attitudes on foreign aid. The second and third parts analyze in broad outline the relationships between the specific types of information sought and utilized and the institutional processes and constraints of the Executive Branch and Congress, respectively. A concluding section notes problems on which further research might be desirable.

In effect, this division of the subject matter enables us to distinguish and consider separately the three major subsystems within American society that are involved in national decision making on foreign aid. The first and most pervasive is the large subsystem within which both popular and elite-group attitudes on foreign aid are formed. The two smaller subsystems, the Executive Branch and the Congress, are differentiated within the larger subsystem, and are the institutions in which policy and operating decisions on foreign aid are made. Although, for analytical purposes, each subsystem is discussed separately, their intimate interrelationships should be kept in mind.

National Attitudes and
Opinions on Foreign Aid

Since the beginning of the Lend-Lease Program in 1941, a majority of Americans polled have supported foreign aid when asked such questions as

"Are you for or against foreign aid?" and "Do you feel that we should help underdeveloped countries whether they can pay us back or not?" Over the past twenty-five years, the percentage favoring aid has fluctuated between 50 and 70. The results of three of the most recent nationwide polls were: 1958, 51 percent in favor; 1963, 58 percent in favor; and in 1964, 50 percent in favor.[3] The remaining respondents in each poll include those with no opinions as well as those opposed; in 1963, for example, those opposed to foreign aid constituted 30 percent.

Opinion surveys over the past ten years have indicated significant positive correlations between the degree of detailed and accurate knowledge about the foreign aid program (though not about its relationship to economic and social development) and the extent of approval of aid as a concept, of support of the amount requested for it by the President, and of favorable attitudes toward most of the specific aid efforts of the United States since World War II. The less a respondent has known about aid, the more inclined he has been to disapprove of it.

However, all indications point to the fact that most of the people polled have little knowledge about the size or nature of the foreign aid program. In a 1963 poll, only 9 percent of the respondents came within one billion dollars of the correct figure of four billion dollars in estimating the program's size. Over 25 percent guessed that the program was at least three times its actual size. When queried in 1958 that "foreign aid is spent for different purposes; can you name some of these?" only 11 percent mentioned both military and economic assistance; 24 percent named various purposes included in economic assistance; 5 percent noted purposes applicable only to military aid; and the rest—60 percent—either failed to reply at all or gave only incorrect or irrelevant responses.

The views of the general public about foreign aid are held with a minimum of intensity, and are often unstable. Many of the same people polled year after year swing from support to opposition and back, indicating a lack of commitment to either position. In other instances, it may mean that the individual polled has not formed an opinion until asked the question. This low intensity and instability of opinion help to account for the large swings in percentages of support by party affiliations as one or the other party becomes the national administration and, therefore, responsible for foreign aid. It also documents the low interest in the concept of foreign aid as a national activity and is closely correlated with the lack of knowledge about the program.

In recent years, support for most aspects of foreign aid has been slightly

3. The statistical data presented here on national opinions on foreign aid were obtained through the courtesy of Alfred O. Hero, Jr., of the World Peace Foundation, who is preparing a comprehensive study on this subject. The authors assume full responsibility for the presentation and interpretation in this paper of the data made available by Mr. Hero.

higher among Democrats than Republicans. However, the low intensity of support for it means also that knowledge of the views of influential political leaders has a marked effect on the responses of their party affiliates. For example, when a question names a prominent Republican as favoring foreign aid, the Republican respondents typically show a greater percentage of support for the program than do the Democrats polled. When a well-known Democratic leader is similarly identified as supporting foreign aid, a higher proportion of Democrats will usually favor the program than if no name is mentioned in the question. However, partisan differences in expressed opinions have seldom been as large as 12 percent.

Geographically, support for the program is highest in the Northeast and West. The South is generally the lowest in percentage of support and has the highest percentage of respondents with no opinions. One reason for this difference is that smaller proportions of Southern Negroes than of Southern whites have favored foreign aid, a situation which reflects particularly their lower average education and their own lack of decent living standards. However, there is usually no more than a 10 percent spread in the level of support for foreign aid between any two geographical areas in the United States.

Degree of support for foreign aid is most highly correlated with level of education. The percentage of college graduates polled who favor the aid program is almost 70; this figure drops off rather rapidly as the level of education diminishes. For example, in a 1963 poll, 70 percent of college graduates, 59 percent of those completing only high school, and 52 percent of those with an elementary school or less education favored foreign aid. The next most highly correlated factor is socioeconomic status or occupation. Again, the higher on the income ladder, the greater the percentage of support among the groups polled.

No more than 10 per cent of those polled ever mention long-term economic development as a reason for supporting foreign aid; and, of that percentage, two thirds are college educated. The reasons most often cited by the great bulk of the respondents is some secular or religious form of humanitarianism and charitable obligation. Hence, these people tend to favor much more heavily those program activities (that is, technical assistance and the shipment of food and medicine) which contribute directly to the welfare of people abroad as compared to capital investment projects and other activities designed to accelerate economic growth.

Thus, aid as a means for economic and social development is apparently neither well understood nor strongly supported by the American people. The vast majority of those polled, who favor foreign aid for charitable and humanitarian reasons, are much less firmly committed to this national effort than are the ten percent who support it for reasons of economic development. Because their principal motivation for approval of economic aid is humanitarian, the great majority of Americans have difficulty in grasping the long-term nature of the activities involved and tend to express the opinion that the aid program has gone on long enough. They are more likely to favor one-year, as opposed to long-term, appropriations and to suggest that the amounts involved be reduced.

CULTURAL FACTORS IN ATTITUDES AND OPINIONS

All Americans, whatever their attitudes concerning foreign aid, have formed their opinions under the influence of the cultural traditions and values that distinguish American society. For the educated upper-income and occupation groups—the elites—who support foreign aid, the values and norms and the prescribed beliefs about the nature of social change are both important. For the public generally, however, only the values and norms expressed in the concept and activity of foreign aid have much significance, since most people have little interest in the nature of the development process and how it could be influenced. Because the normative aspect is important for both groups, we may offer first some suggestions as to the particular values which appear to contribute most significantly to the formation of attitudes on foreign aid. Some of these values are rooted in the pervasive Judaeo-Christian ethos of Western culture as a whole; others are related more particularly to the distinctive characteristics and historical experiences of the American subculture.

Two aspects of Christianity appear to be particularly important in motivating and justifying the foreign aid activity—the missionary responsibility and the obligation of charity.

The age of discovery and expansion which began in the fifteenth century expressed, among other motivations, the desire to bring the gospel—the "good news" of salvation—to the heathen living beyond the borders of Christendom. Although other motives and interests often weakened and nullified the missionary urge, it nevertheless played an important role in the establishment of European control first over the New World and later over Africa and Asia. As early as the sixteenth century, Dominican, Franciscan, and Jesuit missionaries in the New World recognized that their work of salvation among the heathen required not only instruction in the faith but also improvement of the material conditions of the people they were seeking to convert. In Spanish America, the Church—particularly the missionary orders—made repeated efforts to prevent the enslavement of the Indians by the *conquistadores* and to abolish or alleviate the *encomienda* system under which the Indians were forced to labor as serfs of the Spanish settlers.[4] In regions beyond the areas of European settlement, such as Paraguay and the United

4. See Lewis Hanke, *The Spanish Struggle for Justice in the Conquest of America* (London: Geoffrey Cumberlege, Oxford University Press, 1949).

States Southwest, the missionary orders organized and administered model Indian communities based on Christian principles. They also fostered education and the use of more productive agricultural and handicraft techniques.

Protestant missionaries also manifested a similar concern for the material as well as the spiritual advancement of new and prospective converts, particularly when missionary activity expanded in Africa after the mid-nineteenth century. David Livingstone is perhaps the best known of these early Protestant missionaries who systematically undertook improvement of the health, education, and productive techniques of African converts. Over the past one hundred years, this concern for the material advancement of the inhabitants of Africa, Asia, and Latin America has assumed a larger and larger place in Christian missionary activity, both Catholic and Protestant.

Paralleling and reinforcing the Christian missionary responsibility has been the Christian concept of charity, particularly in its Protestant version.[5] The Catholic view of charity has always been primarily concerned with the donor rather than the recipient. While recognizing that charity relieved the sufferings of the poor and unfortunate, Catholicism has nevertheless regarded the essential religious element in it as the performance by the donor of an individual act of sacrifice—an "imitation of Christ." In contrast, the Protestant concept of charity, most fully developed among the Calvinist sects, focused on the effects of charitable actions upon the recipients. Calvin, Knox, Wesley, and their followers frowned upon individualistic and impulsive acts of charity as capricious, sentimental, and self-serving. Instead, they advanced the idea of "efficient good works," that is, organized charity specifically designed to help the recipient help himself. Charitable acts not aimed at assisting self-help were regarded as wasteful and, hence, immoral. Moreover, recipients have to demonstrate their worthiness to receive charity, a qualification embodied in the notion of the "deserving poor" who followed advice and were hard-working, respectful, and grateful.

This Protestant concept of charity has played a major role in attitude formation in the United States. Not only has it tended in recent decades to influence the rather different Catholic idea of charity but, stripped of its religious context and justification, it permeates the American approach to all social welfare activities both at home and abroad. Moreover, its influence has been reinforced by the Protestant concept of the "trusteeship of wealth," of which Andrew Carnegie was perhaps the leading American proponent and practitioner.[6] According to this notion, the possession of great wealth by an individual or a nation is not only an evidence of salvation and a reward for

5. The relevance for our purpose of the differences between the Catholic and the Protestant concepts of charity and of implicit and explicit faith discussed here, was suggested by Benjamin Nelson of the New School for Social Research.

6. Andrew Carnegie, *The Gospel of Wealth*; edited by Edward C. Kirkland (Cambridge, Mass.: The Belknap Press of Harvard University Press, 1962).

effort but is also a trust which must be used in effective ways for the benefit of people less fortunate but deserving of assistance.

In addition to the influence of the Christian missionary obligation and the Protestant concept of charity in the formation of U.S. popular and elite-group attitudes toward foreign aid, an important role has been played by the distinctive American sense of mission as it has evolved from a purely religious concept in the seventeenth-century Puritan settlements into its modern secular form. Though related basically to the Christian missionary urge, the American sense of mission has special characteristics of its own. The Puritan settlers believed that they were establishing in the New World the first truly Christian society since the days of the primitive Church—in the words of John Winthrop, "a city upon a hill" for the rest of the world to see and imitate.

Since the late eighteenth century, this concept has been increasingly secularized. In the course of the nineteenth century, it took the form of the conviction that the best features of Western civilization were brought from Europe by the original settlers and, under the unique conditions of freedom and equality prevalent in the New World, flowered into a new society that was superior politically, economically, and morally to any other evolved upon this planet. Today, there is a pervasive belief in American society that the "American way of life" provides a model for other nations to imitate if they wish to enjoy the benefits of political freedom and a high and rising standard of living. America's mission in the world is further to perfect this paradigm of the good society and to help other nations which sincerely wish to model themselves upon it. Foreign aid is regarded as a means whereby the American way of life can be spread to all parts of the planet.

Also relevant in this connection are the implications of the difference between the Catholic idea of implicit faith and the Protestant idea of explicit faith for attitudes toward the non-Christian societies of Africa and Asia. Both in its religious form and through its influence on secular concepts, this difference has played a significant role in contemporary United States expectations regarding economic and social development abroad. Strongly rooted in the natural-law concepts of classical philosophy, Catholic theology has always emphasized the view that the capacity for faith, and hence the knowledge of good and evil, are a natural endowment of all peoples by virtue of their common creation and humanity. In consequence, both faith and morality existed before the Incarnation of Christ, and there can be elements of true religious belief and morality in non-Christian religions, past and present. This view has predisposed Catholic missionaries to a marked degree of tolerance of many features of the traditional cultures of Africa, Asia, and Latin America. In contrast, Protestant theologians, particularly among the more evangelical Calvinistic sects, have rejected the concepts of natural law and of implicit faith, insisting that there can be no morality before or without Christ. Their view has been that true conversion requires explicit faith, which is demonstrated by abandonment of the traditional culture and adoption of a completely Westernized way of life.

This difference helps to explain the readier acceptance in Africa and Asia of Catholicism as compared with Protestantism, especially in societies whose cultures diverge most markedly from that of the West and which continue to possess a vitality of their own. However, the significance for our purposes of this difference lies in its implications for contemporary concepts of development. In the nineteenth and twentieth centuries, the United States has been the home of evangelical Protestantism, and today provides most of the resources for the widespread missionary activities of these sects throughout the non-Western parts of the world. Their insistence upon the need and the possibility of total Westernization as a sign of explicit faith is also reflected in secular United States expectations that the less developed countries can and should, by a deliberate act of will, rapidly and easily transform themselves into replicas of Western societies. The Protestant commitment to explicit faith also helps to account for the fact that positivistic ideas and expectations have proven to be so congenial to Americans, as will be discussed below.

These concepts and convictions—rooted in the distinctive Christian ethos of Western society, though largely secularized in the United States today—constitute the major cultural factors entering into the formation of American attitudes toward foreign aid both in the population as a whole and among the elite groups more directly interested or engaged in the national decision-making process. However, in the case of the elite groups, several other very significant cultural factors are involved which may be briefly noted here.

The great political, economic and social reform movements in American society during the last 150 years have gradually fostered awareness of the social implications of individual and group activities and acceptance of corresponding responsibilities for social improvement by political leaders, businessmen, professionals and intellectuals, and other elite groups. Aspects of this transformation of values and expectations that seem to be particularly relevant to elite-group attitudes on foreign aid include the "social gospel" movement in the liberal Protestant churches; the spread of humanitarian liberalism and cosmopolitanism among elite groups generally; the decline of isolationism and the rise of internationalist sentiments of various kinds (for example imperialistic, liberal, revolutionary); and other universalistic movements in American social and political thought.

With the emergence in the course of the twentieth century of the United States as the strongest and richest nation on the planet, these developments—infused and reinforced by certain aspects of Christian social doctrine—have also helped to foster among many members of elite groups a sense of guilt regarding the disparities between American wealth and power and those of other countries, thereby contributing to the desire to provide assistance for economic and social advancement abroad.

In addition to the influence of the cultural system on popular and elite-group values and expectations, it has also provided the conceptual framework by which social reality is perceived and interpreted. This framework has played a significant role in the formation both of opinions and expectations regarding foreign aid and of the policies and operating programs of the United States government in this field. Among the most important with respect to foreign aid are the ideas commonly identified as American positivism.

Owing to their cultural heritage and particular historical experiences, Americans have developed a strong conviction in their capacity to solve problems through the application both of common sense and of scientific knowledge. Even though these two methods are often at variance, Americans believe that virtually all problems can be solved either by ordinary people cooperating with one another on the basis of commonly accepted ideas, or by groups of experts equipped with the latest scientific know-how and ample funds. Regardless of their inconsistency, these distinctive American attitudes —which we may designate, respectively, as common-sense and technocratic positivism—have been major factors in the unprecedented economic and technological achievements of American society. But, they also continually engender unrealistic expectations and a tendency toward utopianism. American positivism in both of its forms has played an especially important part in forming the self-images of American elite groups and in stimulating their willingness to fulfill the roles expected of them both at home and abroad. The elite groups provide both the decision makers and the personnel for the United States foreign aid effort, and their positivism constitutes a key element in their motivation for, and their sense of the validity of, this activity.

Moreover, American technocratic positivism has increasingly placed central emphasis on economics and technology as the two forms of scientific knowledge most relevant to explaining and improving society. Perhaps the most articulate expression of this tendency can be found in the work of Thorstein Veblen, who combined earlier technocratic ideas of Simon Patten and other nineteenth-century American positivists with the Marxist notion that the economic system determines the cultural, social, and political systems. In practice, Americans have generally not ignored the major influences of noneconomic factors on their own economic system, particularly in the making and execution of economic policy. Nonetheless, economics has usually been regarded as the supreme policy science not only in the United States but also throughout Western society; and most of the kinds of improvements in society sought under the Western value system either consist of or require as a precondition increases in or redistribution of economic resources.

In addition, economic theory has for methodological reasons generally made the assumption of *ceteris paribus* with respect to cultural, social, and political factors that, in effect, has fostered a tendency to ignore them in the empirical application of theoretical analysis. Hence, in a society dedicated to progress and confident of its ability to achieve it by rational means, there is a natural tendency to regard the economic system as autonomous and economic changes as somehow more fundamental than, and automatically inducing, changes in the other systems. We shall see later how these convictions—embodying to an important extent the perceptual and conceptual biases of American culture—have had a major influence on the ideas, procedures and expectations of the personnel participating in our foreign aid effort.

These values and ways of perceiving society inherent in American culture help also to explain the anomalies and ambiguities in popular and elite-group opinions on foreign aid. Space permits only a few brief illustrations.

One anomaly is the use of so-called hard-headed national-interest rationales (explained below) as the main official justifications for foreign aid, particularly before the Congress, and the accompanying apologetic downgrading of humanitarian considerations despite the fact that the latter are the reasons most often cited for supporting this activity by the public generally. Even more pronounced are some of the ambiguities that have arisen in opinions on foreign aid. As we have seen, Christian ethics, humanitarian liberalism and internationalism, the sense of mission, and the sense of guilt form a major part of the motivation for providing aid to poor countries. Yet, many Americans in whom a favorable attitude toward foreign aid has been engendered by these normative factors will also express opinions critical of—and even hostile to—the foreign aid program largely in consequence of the expectations derived from the Protestant concept of charity and the American forms of positivism. The result has been such reactions as "those countries only waste our aid," "they don't take our advice or follow our example," "they aren't grateful for what we are giving them" and suggestions that, in consequence, the aid program be reduced in size and duration or even abolished.

The disillusionment regarding foreign aid that has been spreading among elite groups and national decision makers in the past few years also results in part from these ambiguities. The lack of development progress in many recipient countries and the declining United States influence over their participation in world political affairs have raised serious doubts about the validity of the national interest rationale and contradict the deeply held positivistic and rationalistic convictions of United States elite groups. Within the academic and independent research community, increasing involvement in recent years in research and technical assistance activities under the foreign aid program has further contributed to this disillusionment owing to direct experience both of the difficulties of the development process and of the frustrations entailed by the institutional characteristics of the United States foreign aid agency. Although for some, the remedy for these disappointments and frustrations is a manyfold increase in the size of the United States foreign aid effort, others advocate transferring operating responsibility for the program to the World Bank, UN agencies, and other international organizations, and a small but growing number believe that it should be drastically reduced or even terminated.[7]

THE INSTITUTIONAL SETTING OF FOREIGN AID ATTITUDES

Against this background of the concepts and values that enter into American attitudes on foreign aid, we may now sketch briefly the rational, intellectual considerations involved and the institutional factors influencing the kinds of information available to the public generally and to elite groups. Neither popular nor elite-group support for foreign aid would be sufficient to ensure that this activity would be carried on unless national-interest considerations were widely believed to dictate the same course of action as that indicated by the other values and expectations of American society outlined above. There are three main types of national-interest rationale.

The first is the anti-Communist line of reasoning, widely used by proponents of foreign aid in the decision-making process—particularly in Congress—and in efforts to influence public opinion on the subject. It argues that foreign aid enhances United States influence over the policies and orientation of the recipient countries and thereby discourages them from aligning themselves with Moscow or Peking in world affairs. Although the argument is believed to be strongly persuasive in its appeal to concern for the national safety and prestige, there is little evidence that economic—as distinct from military—aid has been a major factor preventing recipient nations from supporting the Soviet Union or China in world politics or from falling under Communist control, except possibly in the few countries where United States assistance has provided a subsidy for the national budget and thereby directly helped to maintain a non-communist regime in office.

The second type of national-interest argument claims that the provision of foreign aid helps to preserve world peace and improve cooperation among nations in the solution of international problems. Foreign aid is believed to produce this effect by enhancing the economic and political capabilities of poor countries, thereby narrowing the disparities between them and the wealthy countries and inhibiting potential sources of international conflict. Of the three types of national-interest rationale, this line of reasoning is the most consistent with American cultural concepts and values and is the one most congenial to members of elite groups. However, there is as yet little

7. See the Senate Foreign Relations Committee Report on the *Foreign Assistance Act of 1965*, (89th Cong. 1st Sess., Report No. 170, for recent Congressional criticism. See also Robert A. Goldwin (ed.), *Why Foreign Aid?* (Chicago: Rand-McNally Public Affairs Series, 1963) for a variety of academic views.

evidence that the gap between rich and poor nations is being or could be significantly narrowed, much less closed, with or without foreign aid.

The third type of national-interest justification is the economic-advantage argument. It maintains that the provision of aid to recipient countries enhances their ability to supply necessary imports to the American economy and to buy increased exports from the United States. Thus, foreign aid increases employment in the United States, stimulates domestic economic growth, and raises American living standards. The validity of the economic self-interest argument can be demonstrated objectively; the direct effects of foreign aid on domestic employment and incomes have been measured and are by no means inconsiderable. Nonetheless, this is the least persuasive of the three national-interest justifications apparently because it is felt to be inconsistent with religious and humanitarian values and heightens the sense of guilt engendered by the enormous disparity between United States affluence and the poverty of the recipient countries.

Among top-level policy makers in the State Department and among many social scientists who have studied the development process and the possibilities for influencing it through foreign aid, the national-interest rationale is formulated in much more modest and realistic terms. With respect to its possible anti-communist significance, the claim is made that, by counterbalancing Soviet or Chinese aid, or by obviating the necessity to accept it, United States aid may help recipient countries to preserve their independence of both sides. In positive terms, aid helps to ensure that these countries have an opportunity—if they are willing and able to take advantage of it—to develop their own societies and cultures. It is believed that, properly conceived and administered, United States aid could exercise some—but never a decisive—influence over the development of these countries. Hence, foreign aid is in the national interest to the extent that it increases the chance that recipient countries would develop along lines compatible with the continued security and welfare of the United States.

Although, in our judgment, the chance that United States influence would be significant is large enough to justify an intelligently planned and effectively executed foreign aid program, the outcome of the development process is highly uncertain and the time perspective very long term.[8] For this reason, the latter form of the national-interest rationale is not congenial to many members of elite groups or to the public generally, owing to their positivistic convictions and utopian expectations. Hence, its use is not very successful in

8. Ironically, the chance that U.S. aid will significantly influence the course of development in the recipient countries is often diminished when aid is reduced or withheld for shorter-term foreign policy reasons. Nonetheless, the pursuit of such short-term benefits for the United States is also a legitimate national interest use of foreign aid, if it is assumed that it is the appropriate tactic in particular situations and can be applied skilfully enough to achieve the desired objective.

influencing popular attitudes and Congressional opinion. Nor does it predominate even within the United States foreign aid agency, though it does express the views of many individual staff members. As we shall see later, the maintenance of staff morale appears to require, and the institutional characteristics of the aid agency seem to foster, a much more assured, ambitious, and shorter-term conception of what foreign aid can accomplish.

The national-interest rationale in its more conventional forms is largely the product of decision makers and opinion leaders in the executive and legislative branches of the government, and a considerable portion of the data supporting it emanates from official and political sources. These include reports, press releases, and statements issued by the foreign aid agency, the State Department, and other departments of the Executive Branch; messages, speeches, and press conferences of the President; Congressional reports, hearings, and debates; and speeches, articles, and interviews of political leaders and top administrative officials. The information contained therein consists of statistics on the kinds and amounts of aid provided or proposed for individual recipient countries; descriptive materials on specific aid programs and projects; general background materials on the development needs and progress of recipient countries; and explanations of the United States objectives and policies specifically served by foreign aid.

Except for information emanating from opposition political leaders and occasionally from Congressional investigating committees, these rationales, statistical data, and descriptive materials originating from official sources are generally favorable to the foreign aid effort. Although the data made available each year are accurate, they are selected so as to emphasize positive results, actual and prospective, and to underplay ideas and information that indicate the complexities and slowness of the development process, the very limited effect which foreign aid has had upon it, and the failures of specific aid programs and projects. For both foreign policy and domestic political reasons critical comments on the policies and programs of recipient countries, and on their use of United States aid, are usually presented in recondite circumlocutions whose meanings are readily apparent only to those already familiar with the subject and this style of presentation. An additional institutional influence on the information provided by Executive Branch agencies is the inhibition induced by Congressional suspicion of domestic information programs. On several occasions, this has resulted in legislation prohibiting the foreign aid agency from disseminating within the United States materials justifying its activities and publicizing its accomplishments.

A second major source of information takes the form of publications of United Nations agencies, other international organizations, and the recipient countries themselves. The concepts and data originating from these sources deal much more broadly with the processes and problems of economic and social development, as distinct from foreign aid activities per se. They constitute the chief flow of empirical data on the actual development performance of recipient countries and on the experience with specific development techniques and prescriptions. Institutional constraints on content and style of presentation similar to those conditioning information emanating from U.S. government sources also operate with respect to data made available by the UN and other international agencies and by recipient governments.

The third source of information both on development and on foreign aid consists of the professional research undertaken in universities, independent research institutions, and by some of the commercial research organizations. This information is produced at their own initiative or for the United States government, foreign governments, and international organizations. Particularly when motivated by their own interests and purposes, these academic and independent research institutions are the sources of the most insightful, accurate, and balanced information on the development process and the role of foreign aid in it. Their publications are more technical in content and much less euphemistic in presentation than are those emanating from the two preceding sources. However, because much of this information is written by and for specialists in the various subject disciplines and is usually published in scholarly journals, technical books, and reports of limited circulation, information from these sources tends not to be available directly to the general public or even to many members of educated elite groups unless they happen to be working on or are especially interested in the subjects covered.

The final source of information on development and foreign aid consists of the articles and reports written by columnists, reporters, editorial writers, and others working for the mass media (newspapers, magazines, television), and by individuals who have traveled in the recipient countries for reasons of business or pleasure. These materials are sometimes based on firsthand investigation by the authors, at home and abroad, but more generally involve selection and simplification of ideas and data obtained from the other three sources. Information available through the mass media tends to be dramatized and impressionistic rather than statistical and analytical, and it often rests upon opinion, hearsay, and anecdote, which are not always accurate or representative. Since it is prepared specifically for as wide dissemination as possible, information from this source is much more readily available and comprehensible to the public generally, and to most members of elite groups as well, than are the data derived directly from other sources. Hence, the concepts, data, and opinions disseminated through the mass media and spread further by word of mouth, constitute the major types of information affecting public opinion on foreign aid.

In addition to the mass media, there are two other important channels through which information and opinions are disseminated both to the public generally and to elite groups. Many mass-membership organizations, such as political parties, labor unions, churches, social service organizations, citizens' groups, and the like favor or are opposed to foreign aid, and endeavor to influence the opinions of their members and of the public generally by disseminating information to them for or against the program. Farmers' and businessmen's organizations represent interest groups engaged in producing, exporting, and shipping commodities sent abroad under foreign aid programs, and hence try to keep their members informed about the subject.

The other channel is directed specifically at opinion leaders at national and local levels and at members of elite groups generally. Three kinds of organizations are engaged in this type of activity. A number of policy-oriented research institutions—such as the Brookings Institution, the Committee for Economic Development, and the National Planning Association—publish their research studies and policy statements on development and foreign aid in nontechnical language designed to be read by members of elite groups generally. The Council on Foreign Relations, the Foreign Policy Association, local World Affairs Councils, and other similar groups are engaged in educational activities on international problems, including both development and foreign aid, and provide information on these subjects through publications, conferences, lectures, discussion groups, and other means. Finally, two organizations have been specifically formed to influence the views of opinion leaders and the decisions of the Executive Branch and Congress on foreign aid: the National Council for International Development, which favors the foreign aid program; and the Citizens' Foreign Aid Committee, which opposes it.

PROSPECTS FOR ENHANCING THE ROLE OF INFORMATION IN OPINION FORMATION

Would the influence of information on the formation of public and elite-group attitudes and opinions on foreign aid be significantly greater or more important if the volume of data on this subject were expanded and the content changed or improved in appropriate ways? Although research and actual experimentation would be required before this question could be answered definitively, our preliminary inquiry indicates that such a result is not very likely in view of the roles played by the cultural and institutional factors involved.

Insofar as the general public is concerned, it is clear that the great majority of Americans do not feel strongly for or against the national foreign aid effort. The attitudes of those favoring the program are largely conditioned by the basic concepts and values of American society and not by specific information as to the purpose, nature, and results of the foreign aid activity. Undoubtedly, more information on foreign aid could be disseminated through the mass media, the principal channel of communication to the general public. But, it is questionable whether the interest of the average newspaper and magazine reader and television viewer in this subject would be sufficiently great to warrant the conclusion that he would in fact devote significantly more of his attention to it, particularly in the light of the competing entertainment and informational opportunities offered by the mass media at any given time. Nor would the general public be willing to absorb more detailed and more technical information on foreign aid than is now provided through the mass media and other channels of communication. Dramatically interesting television programs on the accomplishments of particular aid programs and projects in individual countries would probably increase the percentage of immediately favorable responses in the audience. But, it is by no means certain that such responses would persist over a long period of time or would significantly affect attitudes toward the foreign aid effort as a whole.

Information does play a significantly greater role in opinion formation among elite groups. However, there does not seem to be a dearth of data, technical and nontechnical, available to elite groups, nor are the channels for its dissemination notably inadequate. Here, too, questions of the intensity of interest in and the willingness to devote time to the acquisition of information on foreign aid are relevant and would require considerable research and experimentation before they could be answered definitively. Moreover, in view of the technocratic positivism and the tendency toward utopian expectations of American elite groups, more detailed and profound knowledge about the complexities and the slowness of the development process, and greater awareness that foreign aid is not the decisive factor in overcoming these difficulties could increase their sense of frustration and disillusionment with, rather than intensify their support for, the national foreign aid effort.

Executive Branch
Decision Making

Executive Branch decision making regarding foreign aid centers in the Agency for International Development (AID), established within the Department of State by the Act for International Development of 1961. AID has operating autonomy and initiates most policies, programs, and procedures regarding the size, content, terms, and execution of the United States foreign aid effort. However, the Secretary of State has general policy supervision over AID activities insofar as they affect the foreign policy and international security of the United States, and his responsibility is usually exercised through the area offices of the State Department. In addition, since February 1964, AID personnel concerned with aid to Latin American countries participating in the Alliance for Progress have been integrated with the corresponding State Department country desk officers under the Assistant Secretary of State for Inter-American Affairs. Resources for foreign aid are also provided by the Export-Import Bank and through the Food-for-Peace program.

The White House participates in and approves decisions affecting the foreign aid program when major issues of domestic and foreign policy are involved, for example, the size of the aid appropriation requested each year of Congress; significant changes to be made in the authorizing and appropriations legislation; the impact of the foreign aid program on the domestic economy and on the United States balance of payments; the amount and terms of aid provided to critically important countries; and so forth. Other Executive Branch agencies that participate in foreign aid decision making include the Bureau of the Budget, the Treasury Department, and the Departments of Agriculture, Commerce, Labor, and Health, Education and Welfare on policy matters within their respective areas of responsibility. These and other federal agencies also help in the planning of, and provide personnel for, technical-assistance projects financed by AID.

In this preliminary survey, it is not possible to explore in detail the various roles played by the White House and these Executive Branch agencies in decision making affecting the foreign-aid program. Hence, we shall focus primarily upon the changes in the aid agency's institutional characteristics and their effects upon its decision making. Regardless of its bureaucratic vicissitudes over the fifteen years, the United States foreign aid agency has been by far the most important locus within the Executive Branch of decision making on the objectives, size, and content of the national foreign aid effort. Its relationships with other Executive Branch agencies, with the White House and, above all, with the Congress have influenced in various ways the kinds of information which the aid agency has been willing to seek and the uses it has made of them in decision making. These influences have operated indirectly through their effects upon the institutional characteristics of the aid agency.

As we have seen, our preliminary survey has led us to the tentative conclusion that the major determinants of both popular and elite-group attitudes on foreign aid have been the values and concepts inherent in American culture. In contrast, the most important factors influencing the aid agency's decision making appear to be its institutional characteristics. Nonetheless, cultural influences are strong, although not primary, and will be noted in the course of our sketch of the effects of the agency's changing institutional characteristics.

ORIGINAL CHARACTERISTICS OF THE FOREIGN AID AGENCY

Under a succession of names, the United States foreign aid agency has had a continuous institutional existence since the start of the Marshall Plan (European Recovery Program) in April 1948, and the broad outlines of its organizational form have remained much the same. It has had a headquarters staff in Washington which is divided into regional divisions, each containing individual country desks, with functional and staff service divisions; and field missions stationed in the countries receiving aid. The forms in which the agency has extended aid have also remained much the same. Dollars have been made available on a grant or loan basis to recipient countries, which could draw upon them to meet the foreign-exchange costs of approved imports of capital goods, raw materials, operating supplies, and foodstuffs, and to pay all or part of the salaries and living expenses of American specialists engaged in technical-assistance activities. During the 1950's, the United States government also began to provide surplus agricultural commodities under Public Law 480 as grants or for payment in the currency of the recipient country. These local currency funds as well as the local currency counterparts of dollar grants and loans have in turn been used by recipient countries for various purposes, with the approval of the foreign aid agency. However, though the organizational structure and the forms of aid have remained much the same for more than a decade and a half, there have been highly significant changes in the objectives, policies, procedures, and personnel of the agency.

The new government agency (the Economic Cooperation Administration) established in April 1948 to administer American participation in the European Recovery Program was of a rather special kind. Its purpose was to carry out a widely publicized and glamorous national effort, for which it was given financial resources of an unprecedented size, a great deal of administrative discretion in their use, and freedom to hire staff outside civil service procedures and restrictions. The latter exemption made it possible for the agency to be staffed predominantly, at both policy making and senior technical levels, with people attracted from business and public life by the reputation of the Administrator, Paul G. Hoffman, and from the universities and applied professions by the reputation of the Deputy Administrator for Program, Richard M. Bissell. In addition, carefully selected career civil servants and foreign service officers from permanent government departments (for example, State, Treasury, Agriculture, and Commerce) were given temporary assignments with the new agency.

Thus the foreign aid agency was largely staffed with people of high calibre, experienced in the exercise of responsibility in business, government, and professional activities; energetic and innovative; and oriented toward maximum program accomplishment before returning to the institutions, private or governmental, in which their regular careers were being pursued. In consequence of these personal characteristics of its top- and middle-level personnel and of the absence of preexisting policies, procedures, and bureaucratic constraints, the new agency was flexible and adaptable to changing needs and capabilities; decision making was fast, realistic, and constructive; and, within broad policies fixed by the top officials, authority to make operating decisions was delegated to individuals at lower echelons with only a minimum of lateral clearances and of review by supervisors.

The agency operated on the valid assumption that its clients—the European countries receiving United States aid—were fully capable of managing their own affairs and required only an increment of financial and material resources to enable them to overcome the physical damage and economic dislocations resulting from World War II and its aftermath. In varying degree, all of these countries possessed modern economies, fully or partly industrialized, and governments capable of formulating and executing the policies and programs necessary for economic recovery. In consequence, the United States aid agency did not generally take the initiative in calculating the amounts of aid required by each country and programming the specific uses to which aid funds should be put (the exceptions were the Greek and Turkish aid programs). Instead, the agency responded to requests from the recipient countries, which were determined by them on the basis of comprehensive national recovery plans. These recovery plans, and the amount of aid from the United States implied by them, were screened each year by an international body (the Organization for European Economic Cooperation); were reviewed in detail by the United States aid missions in the recipient countries; and were finally scrutinized by the Washington headquarters staff of the foreign aid agency, which made the actual allotments to each country.

The information utilized by the European countries, by the OEEC, and by the United States foreign aid agency in this process of programming, reviewing, and allocating aid was predominantly quantitative economic data—national accounts and balance-of-payments series and projections for each economy as a whole; production and investment targets for specific industries and key commodties; and cost-benefit analysis of large-scale public and private capital-investment projects. In addition, descriptive and prescriptive analyses were prepared relating to the fiscal and monetary policies, foreign trade policies, investment and productivity promotion programs, and other activities of the recipient governments required to achieve the goals of their recovery programs. Although the choice of these types of information reflected the perceptual and conceptual biases of American culture noted earlier, they encompassed enough of the factors really at work in these societies to serve as the basis for intellectually valid and operationally effective decisions.

Moreover, the empirical validity of the concepts and data used by the agency enabled it to make some highly significant policy innovations. During the first two years of the Marshall Plan, fundamental rethinking was done within the agency on the nature of Western Europe's postwar economic and political problems and their possible remedies; on the changing political and economic relationships between Western Europe and the United States; and on the implications of the cold war for the future evolution of the West as a whole. Out of this basic re-assessment emerged two United States policy initiatives which have had major importance—the strong impetus and support for European economic and political unification, and the productivity drive, both of which have helped to stimulate the revitalization of European private enterprise and of the European economies generally. Their success resulted from the fact that the information sought and utilized by the agency accurately reflected the determinative elements in the societies with which it was concerned.

CHANGING INSTITUTIONAL CHARACTERISTICS, 1952–1962

With the end of the Marshall Plan in 1952, a new period began in the history of the aid agency which lasted for approximately ten years. During this period, the nature of its clientele changed and certain institutional developments also occurred, which together profoundly altered its characteristics and operations. These changes, in turn, had important implications for the use of information by the agency in its decision making. The relationships between institutional factors and information during the period since the end of the Marshall Plan have been both extensive and complex. Here, we can indicate only their main outlines and illustrate briefly a few of their specific manifestations.

Beginning in 1950 with the start of President Truman's Point IV program, less developed countries in Africa, Asia, and Latin America were gradually added to the clientele of the aid agency. European countries continued for a few years to be the largest recipients of economic aid even after the end of the Marshall Plan in 1952. But, by the mid-1950's, the volume of United States economic aid going to the less developed countries was rapidly increasing, and the number of aid agency personnel concerned with less developed countries grew even more sharply. By the end of the decade, only Greece and Turkey of the original European clients were still obtaining economic aid from the United States, and Greece ceased to do so early in the 1960's.

Three major developments during this period affecting the agency's institutional characteristics may be briefly noted. First, as early as 1951, an exodus began from the agency of high-calibre and experienced personnel who, with the end of the Marshall Plan in sight, wished to return to their regular careers in business, universities, and permanent government agencies. This exodus was accelerated by the large-scale reduction in the aid agency's staff carried out in 1953 by the incoming Republican administration, and was continued by the subsequent departure of many others who survived the discriminatory aspects of this "reduction in force" but were unwilling to remain in consequence of the second development. This was the series of attacks on the aid agency that began in the early 1950's, emanating predominantly from Congress and the press and stimulated by dissatisfactions of the Korean War period, McCarthyism, growing opposition to continued economic aid to European countries after the end of the Marshall Plan, the beginning of aid to less developed countries, and alleged scandals and inefficiency in aid operations. These attacks reached their peak in the mid-years of the decade and, throughout the period, the agency was only intermittently and rather half-heartedly defended by the Administration. The third development consisted of the periodic reorganizations of the agency—which largely involved changing its name rather than its structure and functions—and the appointment of a series of aid administrators, only one of whom served longer than eighteen months, some of whom were initially opposed to the national foreign aid effort, and none of whom had much knowledge of the economic and social processes occurring in the less developed countries. These three developments beyond the agency's control gradually sapped its morale, impaired its efficiency, and produced important changes in its institutional characteristics.

The voluntary or enforced departure in the early 1950's of most of the temporary personnel recruited for the Marshall Plan resulted by the mid-1950's in the restaffing of the aid agency largely with permanent civil service personnel. Some were Marshall Plan employees who decided to make a career of foreign aid work; most, however, were transfers from other government agencies and newly recruited civil servants. Hence, along with commitment to maximum program accomplishment, such as had predominantly motivated the temporary personnel of the agency in Marshall Plan days, there now developed on the part of the new career personnel a natural concern for institutional stability. This tendency, inherent in the nature of a career civil service, was reinforced by the inhibiting effects of recurring congressional and press attacks and by the periodic reorganizations, which threatened the bureaucratic positions and tenure of the agency's personnel without changing significantly the purpose or content of their functions.

This concern for institutional stability expressed itself in several ways that affected the agency's decision making. First, it was a major contributing factor in the agency's failure to work out the implications for its policies and operations of the recognized differences between the nature, limitations, and needs of its new clientele among the less developed countries of Africa, Asia, and Latin America, and those of its previous European clientele. Second, partly in response to congressional pressures and partly from its own concern to protect itself against criticism, the agency elaborated during the course of the 1950's ever more detailed and time-consuming procedures for policy making, programming, and implementation that were designed to preclude mistakes and ward off unfavorable publicity. This, in turn, necessitated increasing staff. Policy and program proposals were more and more formulated in committees, with the widest possible lateral participation, as individual officials ceased to possess or were unwilling to exercise authority; and decisions on even routine operating matters tended more and more to require specific review and concurrence by each successively higher echelon, often up to the administrator himself. As they evolved, these procedures acted as further deterrents to a fundamental review of the agency's operations, and made increasingly difficult the use of new and more relevant kinds of information in the decision process.

Both sets of changes—that is, in the agency's clientele and in its institutional characteristics—took place gradually in the course of the 1950's. Thus, there did not occur any sudden or massive change that might have stimulated or shocked the agency into awareness of the necessity of reexamining its operating assumptions and methods. Instead, it continued to operate on the assumptions that had proven valid under the Marshall Plan, and attempted to utilize methods that were effective in dealing with the European countries.

Throughout the period from 1952 to 1962, there were individuals in the aid agency who recognized that the differences between the old and the new clienteles had major implications not only for operating policies and methods but also for expectations regarding the kinds of changes that foreign aid could make possible in the less developed countries and the time required for these changes to manifest themselves. However, the bulk of the agency's personnel tended to regard these differences as simply of degree, admittedly large but requiring no fundamental changes in concepts and expectations. In effect, no important operating implications seemed to follow from the profound disparities between the new and old clients in the historical and cultural backgrounds of the societies involved, and hence in their contemporary political systems, economic and social organizations, values and norms governing their behavior, and attitudes and expectations motivating their people. The agency as a whole was, of course, aware that most of the less developed countries were newly independent and hence inexperienced in managing their own political and economic affairs. It was also aware that most of them lacked the necessary administrative, managerial, and technical skills; indeed, the explicit purpose of the Point IV Program and of subsequent technical-assistance programs was to foster the acquisition of such skills. But, even the comparatively superficial changes in concepts and operations which should have been made in consequence of the agency's recognition of the differences in experience and skills between its new and old clients received little attention, much less any serious study.

Moreover, the failure to recognize the operational changes entailed by the difference between economic and social development, the new objective to which the agency was committed in Africa, Asia, and Latin America, and economic recovery, the objective to which it had been committed under the Marshall Plan, meant that the sense of urgency that had characterized the European Recovery Program was carried over into the aid agency's relationship with its new clientele. It was assumed—indeed, often publicly proclaimed, especially to the Congress—that economic and social development must and could be rapid. Its pace was alleged to depend directly upon the volume of aid, which was regarded as the crucial factor in achieving sufficient development before a catastrophe occurred in the less developed countries as serious as the collapse that would have happened in Western Europe in the late 1940's had Marshall Plan aid not been forthcoming quickly and in massive volume. For the less developed countries, the imminent catastrophe generally envisaged was conquest by, or deliberate choice of, Communism unless the so-called revolution of rising expectations was quickly satisfied by the achievement of higher living standards.

While such assumptions remained largely unexamined and unchanged, circumstances nevertheless forced some important alterations in methods as the role of the less developed countries in the foreign aid program gradually came to predominate by the mid-1950's. The less developed countries did not have, and were not able to prepare, the quantitative data relating to their economic conditions and prospects similar to those which the agency was accustomed to rely on in considering aid requests from the European countries. However, even though this lack was widely recognized and deplored, it did not prove to be a major obstacle to decision making. During the first half of the 1950's, most of the aid to less developed countries took the form of technical assistance projects, whose merits could be judged without the use of aggregative national accounts, sector production and investment targets, balance-of-payments data, and other quantitative series and projections. Thus, both the lack of quantitative data and the specific purpose for which aid was provided combined to focus attention on the project approach. Even during the second half of the period, when loans and grants for capital investment and balance-of-payments purposes overtook and greatly surpassed technical assistance, the project approach continued to be used. It was familiar; and, as we shall see later, it was required for the Congressional presentation. But, equally important in perpetuating the project approach was the way in which it came to be carried on.

Early in the agency's dealing with the less developed countries, it was recognized that most of them lacked not only the data necessary for development programming, but also the technically trained personnel required for devising technical-assistance and capital-investment projects; for preparing them for submission to the United States government; and for administering them once funds had been approved and technical-assistance specialists recruited by the aid agency. Imperceptibly, the personnel of the aid agency tended more and more to participate in—and in many cases to perform—the tasks of project initiation and preparation, a major change from the practice during the European Recovery Program when the agency evaluated and reviewed project and program requests initiated and prepared by the Europeans themselves. The United States aid missions in the less developed countries gradually increased their staffs to include specialists in the main fields in which projects were favored—agriculture, industry, infrastructure (transportation, energy, and power), community development, public administration, and, in the early 1960's, education and housing. Not only did the staffs of the aid missions help their counterparts in the governments of the less developed countries to prepare project proposals in these fields, but they often suggested that the countries ought to have particular projects and programs. This practice was congenial to the aid agency because it made easier the task of ensuring that projects would be formulated, reviewed, and subsequently executed in accordance with the ever more detailed and restrictive procedures that the agency felt itself compelled to elaborate in order to comply with Congressional requirements and to prevent mistakes or criticism.

This relationship has been a source of difficulty between the less developed countries and the United States. For their part, the former have increasingly resented the implication that they were not really capable of running their own development programs, which had to be prepared for them by the latter in accordance with its conception of their needs and priorities. Even when the governments of newly independent nations recognized their own limitations of technical knowledge and administrative skill, they were reluctant to participate in working arrangements that blurred the distinction between the two sovereignties involved, regardless of the goodwill and sense of fellowship that usually motivated the aid agency's personnel.

Within the aid agency itself, this practice has been responsible for the development of a self-image of the agency's role which might be called the "we complex." In their discussions with one another as well as with officials of the recipient countries, the personnel of the aid agency tended unconsciously to think of themselves as the active agents not simply in providing aid but also in managing the development process as a whole. It became—and still is—common practice for the personnel of the United States aid agency to talk about "our" program for the development of country X, or how "we" are going to build schools in country Y or construct irrigation canals in country Z. Inevitably, the "we complex" magnified the agency's sense of the importance of United States aid in economic and social development and diminished its conception of the role which the recipient country's own initiative and effort had to play in this process.

The information sought and utilized by the aid agency under the project approach was conventional and familiar, though not easy to obtain. Efforts were made to utilize the same procedures and data in preparing and evaluating capital investment projects as had been developed for these purposes in the United States—essentially, cost-benefit analysis. However, in most of the less developed countries, some or all of the crucial types of information were lacking or seriously inadequate, particularly with respect to the costs of and returns on capital, to comparative production costs and their relationship to the size of the market, to the choice of technology, and to similar considerations on which data could normally be obtained in the developed market economies.

Moreover, consistent with the agency's lack of recognition of the operational implications of the fact that it was dealing with societies and cultures essentially different from its own, it implicitly assumed that the multiplier effects of capital investment would operate as automatically and on as large a scale as they do in North America and Western Europe. For example, it was not thought necessary in preparing and executing capital-investment projects to ensure that they would be organized in ways that would specifically stimulate the establishment of local suppliers of raw materials, operating supplies, components, and ancillary distributive and other services, and that would disseminate modern managerial and technical skills in the less developed economy. Studies to provide the insights and information needed for designing projects so as to achieve this objective were not systematically undertaken by the aid agency, and were only occasionally made by individual officials aware of the problem. It was implicitly assumed that the desired effects would come about without special efforts.

The information utilized in preparing technical-assistance projects was similarly limited in the main to those types of data consistent with the implicit assumption that social, cultural, and psychological differences need not be taken into account. Only very occasionally in designing technical-assistance projects were investigations conducted to evaluate the consistency between the new techniques and methods to be introduced and the existing attitudes, values, and expectations of the people who were supposed to adopt them; to identify the particular agents in each village, local, or national society who were willing and able to be innovators and whose examples would be followed by others; or to make possible the inclusion, in estimating the time span and phasing of each project, of such considerations as the rate at which traditional resistance could be overcome and the time required for new values and norms to become institutionalized and, therefore, self-perpetuating. Lack of consideration of such factors was further facilitated by the fact that systematic efforts were not made to revisit technical assistance projects at intervals after their termination in order to determine the kind and extent of innovation that had actually taken place.

Indeed, deliberate efforts by the aid agency to accumulate, evaluate, and profit by its past experiences were limited largely to refining the tactics involved in negotiating with the recipient countries on the preparation and review of projects, and to revising and increasing the restrictions and procedures imposed by Congress, suggested by the General Accounting Office, or instituted by the agency itself to ward off criticism and prevent mistakes. In effect, the aid agency has never developed a substantive "memory," and its past experiences have been systematically collected and preserved almost solely in the form of tactical, legal, and accounting precedents. Only because of the efforts of individual officials has experience been evaluated and converted into improved understanding, available to others, of the nature of the development process and of the role which foreign aid could play in it. However, we may add that with respect to the systematic collection, analysis, and use of past experiences, the agency has been no more deficient than the World Bank, the UN development agencies, and other international organizations.

The effects of these institutional characteristics developed during the decade from 1952 to 1962 were strengthened by the pervasive influence of the positivistic faith and utopian expectations inherent in the American cultural system. Intellectually, these cultural influences were expressed within the agency in a verbal activism, which substituted for a fundamental rethinking of assumptions and methods a propensity to exaggerate valid program areas into development panaceas (for example, at one time or another, technical assistance, community development, education, agrarian reform), and to reiterate fashionable clichés ("the revolution of rising expectations," "the take-off into self-sustained growth," "closing the gap between rich and poor nations") which were either misleadingly oversimplified or were beyond the limits of the possible. Institutionally, however, the agency was increasingly limited in its ability to act on such presumed prescriptions and rhetorical slogans by the growing rigidity resulting from external pressures, the change in the nature of much of its personnel, the proliferation of detailed and time-consuming procedures, and the lack of substantive leadership.

THE AID AGENCY IN THE 1960'S

A new period in the history of the aid agency began in the early 1960's. The comparatively weak commitment of the Eisenhower Administration to aid to less developed countries, and its intermittent support of the aid agency, were replaced by the assignment under the new Administration of a key role in United States foreign policy to the aid program and by the strong personal interest taken in it by President Kennedy.

In 1961, the legislation authorizing the foreign aid program was rewritten and the agency's name changed to Agency for International Development (AID). At President Kennedy's request, a major new program initiative—the Alliance for Progress—was begun to accelerate the economic and social development of Latin America, and large-scale funds were pledged for its support over a ten-year period. Greatly increased use was made of the practice, started in the mid-1950's, of contracting with private organizations (business corporations, trade unions, farm and cooperative organizations, consulting firms, and universities and independent research institutions) to assist in the preparation and to undertake the implementation of certain programs and projects financed with United States aid funds. Also in 1961, a concerted effort began to bring new personnel into the aid agency from business, the universities, and other private organizations, which resulted in the appointment of a number of new officials at policy-making and senior technical levels.

The revitalizing intent of these changes was symbolized in 1962 by the appointment as Administrator of David E. Bell who, for the first time since the departure of Richard Bissell at the end of the Marshall Plan, brought to the top leadership of the agency both professional training and substantive knowledge of the complex economic phenomena with which the agency was expected to deal.

In response to Congressional expectations and to its own more professional approach to its responsibilities, the new leadership of the agency has been concentrating the bulk of United States aid on a comparatively small number of less developed countries believed to possess the greatest potential for rapid advancement, or to be especially important to the United States for foreign policy reasons. Even though a total of ninety countries were receiving some form of economic aid at the beginning of 1965—including all forms of dollar loans and grants, and surplus agricultural commodities—more than 60 percent of total economic assistance was going to only seven countries, which were using most of the funds, directly or indirectly, for capital investment. This concentration on a limited number of countries has both resulted from and further stimulated interest within AID in attempting to understand better the economic factors involved in the process of growth and how they could be influenced.

A second development has also arisen from, and in turn contributed to, this new interest in improved economic information. It is the growing practice in recent years of development planning by the recipient countries and the related use in AID's own decision making of macro methods and mathematical models. The preparation of a comprehensive national development plan requires the same types of quantitative data as were used during the Marshall Plan—national accounts series and projections, balances of payments, sector production and investment targets, project analysis, and the like. During the last few years, considerable progress has been made by a number of less developed countries in producing data of these kinds, as well as the more basic information on which they depend—censuses of population, industry and agriculture, natural resource surveys, productivity and manpower studies, investment studies. For the first time since United States aid to less developed countries began, a substantial volume of significant and reasonably reliable quantitative data on economic and closely related factors is beginning to become available and to be used in decision making.

These two developments have made it possible for AID to supplement the project approach by a variant of the program approach originally used under the Marshall Plan. Particularly for the countries receiving the bulk of American aid, the agency has begun to allocate a growing volume of assistance funds—currently about 50 percent of total dollar aid—on the basis of their foreign-exchange deficits, as calculated within the framework of comprehensive national development plans. This portion of aid is no longer tied to specific capital investment projects but to the recipient country's development plan, or a sector program within it, and constitutes—in effect if not in name—a means of financing some or all of a planned foreign-exchange deficit.

From the point of view of economic theory, the program approach is more sophisticated than the project approach, since it focuses upon the foreign savings needed to supplement a country's own domestic savings in order to achieve a designated rate of growth. But, in practice, it rests on the assumption that the recipient country not only has prepared a valid and realistic development plan but is also capable of ensuring that the resources available —both its own and those obtained through foreign aid—would be used broadly for the purposes specified in the plan and not to finance capital flight or imports that would make little or no contribution to development. For the program approach to be effective, the recipient country must have both the willingness and the ability to steer a middle course between the extremes of no control over the use of resources and of so tight a control by the government that decision making becomes too independent of market processes, initiative is stifled, and bribery and corruption are encouraged. Effectively organized, the program approach can significantly stimulate the private sector. But, it is not a substitute for the project approach, which continues to be appropriate and desirable for financing many kinds of public and private investments and for technical-assistance activities.

The influence of technocratic positivism and other cultural factors still continues to be noticeable. For example, it helps to account for the expectation of some AID officials that policy decisions could be made regarding the allocation and eventual termination of United States aid through the use of mathematical macro models and of measurable criteria for ascertaining the extent of "self-help" by recipient countries. In theory, models can be constructed that would enable decision makers to project the future economic growth of a less developed country and to estimate the date by which domestic savings would be large enough to obviate the need for foreign savings to be obtained under aid programs. In practice, however, no model yet devised has been complex enough to take into account all of the factors involved in country development. Most existing models are highly oversimplified, if only because they must of necessity be limited to the few economic factors that can be quantified, but which are not always the most significant for economic development. Nor is it possible to build into a macro model in a significant way the diverse political, social, cultural, and psychological influences that condition the operation of and interact with economic factors.

Among the new developments in the aid agency in recent years, one of the most significant could eventually prove to be the research program started in 1961 in consequence of the efforts of a small group of officials. Since then, the size and scope of the program have grown from year to year. Most of the research is undertaken on a contract basis by universities and independent research institutions either at their initiative or at the request of the agency staff assigned to this program. It was also envisaged that the agency would conduct "in-house" research to evaluate the results of its programs and projects, but this highly desirable activity is not yet underway on a systematic and continuing basis.

The research program has encountered considerable opposition within the agency from the operating personnel. In the last few years, the operating personnel in the regional bureaus in Washington and in the country missions have received major increases in decision-making responsibility as compared with the staff personnel of the functional bureaus and offices, who are no longer free to undertake any activities affecting recipient countries without approval of the relevant country desks and field missions. Though the latter have primary responsibility for designing and evaluating projects, they tend to be sceptical about the value of research—whether sponsored by AID or by others—for improving their own decision making and are reluctant to change their procedures in order to take into account the kinds of new insights and data that could result from it. Some scepticism about the research program is justified. The research projects so far commissioned have not been designed on the basis of a systematic survey of the agency's research needs as seen from the point of view of the operating personnel in the field missions and regional bureaus. Nor has much been done to translate the results of the research already undertaken into ideas and data directly useful to operating personnel. Nonetheless, the opposition of most field-mission and regional-bureau personnel to research also reflects the influence of the common-sense variety of American positivism, as noted earlier. Institutionally, the agency's increasingly elaborate procedures and legal and accounting safeguards have impeded the research program—and have also provided opportunities for its opponents to hamper it—through excessively rigid and detailed restrictions in research contracts; delays in processing the frequent requests—necessitated by these detailed restrictions—of contractors for prior written approval by the agency of actions required to fulfill contract obligations; refusals of field missions and regional bureaus to concur in study trips to their countries by contractors' research personnel; and many other bureaucratic devices.

A step forward has recently been made in bridging the gap between research and operations—not, however, in connection with the research program, but in the technical-assistance projects conducted for the aid agency by universities and other private organizations. They are being permitted to devote to research purposes 10 percent of the funds allotted to their projects. However, no such "research component," as it is called, is being built into the projects that the aid agency designs and conducts itself; nor, so long as the field missions and other operating personnel continue to be sceptical about research, is it likely to be.

A final comment needs to be made that is applicable to much of the research activity sponsored directly or indirectly by the aid agency. So far, the orientation has largely been economic and technological—again reflecting the perceptual and conceptual biases of American culture. Even in the case of projects in so-called human resource development (for example, education and training, health, birth control, cooperatives, and trade unions) the emphasis has been predominantly organizational and technical, and very little attention has been devoted to studying the cultural, social, and political factors involved. Yet, for those who seek to influence the development process, an understanding of the crucial role of noneconomic factors is precisely the kind of knowledge for which there is the greatest need.

Until recently, the record in this respect of the universities undertaking technical assistance and other contracts for AID was no better than that of the agency itself. However, the situation is now beginning to improve with respect to the orientation of the research components in university technical-assistance contracts. Some of these projects are initiating efforts to obtain and utilize information on cultural, social, and political factors in their design and operating stages. Nonetheless, universities are also affected by the cultural system in which they exist; and, institutionally, they are composed of mutually independent subject departments which make it difficult to coordinate the different social science disciplines that would have to be brought together in an effective project.

POSSIBILITY OF IMPROVING DECISION MAKING BY BROADENING INFORMATION

This survey of certain aspects of the aid agency's history may serve to exemplify in a preliminary way the major influence of its institutional characteristics on its willingness to obtain and ability to use various types of information. We may now briefly explore what would be involved in attempting to broaden the role of information in the agency's decision making beyond the changes initiated in the last few years.

First, what kinds of information could the aid agency use that have not been and are not now being sought and utilized? As we have seen, considerable progress has been made in the last few years in increasing the theoretical sophistication of analytical economic concepts and in expanding the comprehensiveness and detail of quantitative economic data. These kinds of information can and certainly do provide more profound insights into the economic dimension of the development process and some more effective operational suggestions for using foreign aid to influence it. But, if anything has been learned about the nature of the development process, it is that economic growth of the kind being sought by African, Asian, and Latin American countries does not occur in the absence of certain changes in the cultural, social, and political systems of these societies, nor can innovations in the economic system automatically stimulate or induce the innovations required in the others. Hence, it is with respect to these noneconomic factors that the aid agency would need greatly to expand its information if it wished to improve the depth of its understanding of, and presumably the effectiveness of its efforts to influence, the development process.

However, broadening the information the aid agency seeks and utilizes to include concepts and data on the relevant aspects of the cultural, social, and political systems of African, Asian, and Latin American societies would not be easy to accomplish either intellectually or institutionally.

Economic concepts and data are the main types of information used by modern governments in decision making regarding most national goals, and economists—both within and outside official bureaucracies—are willing and able to provide it in the forms and on the specific subjects required. In contrast, except in certain limited domestic fields (public health, Indian affairs, and social welfare programs), sociologists, social anthropologists, and social psychologists are not generally employed in significant numbers by the U.S. government, nor are the academic members of these disciplines accustomed to or interested in supplying concepts and data to government officials. Apart from a few recently published general accounts of the role of noneconomic factors in development, there has not been much available in the existing literature in these fields that would be directly useful to the foreign aid agency. Whether this lack of communication between the government and these social science disciplines could be overcome, and how, are questions requiring further investigation.

Granted that the gap in communication could be bridged, the next problem is whether the existing attitudes and concepts of the aid agency are conducive to a sufficient degree of willingness to seek the broadened range of information required. Except for a few individuals, there is no evidence of a general recognition by the agency of the relevance to its objectives and activities of information on the appropriate aspects of the cultural, social, and political systems of the recipient countries. We have noted the skepticism of AID's operating personnel about its research program despite the failures that have resulted from inadequate information and understanding. For example, having originally been promoted in the mid-1950's as a panacea, community development—though still a valid program field—now has a much reduced role. This fact is attributable in part to disappointment over the meager results achieved by these earlier projects, which in most cases were organized and operated without adequate study of the cultural and social factors involved. Overcoming the inadequacy of relevant information has been made especially difficult by the fact that the separate social science disciplines involved in community development have been reluctant to work out effective multidisciplinary research approaches.

Our point is not that the aid agency has failed to undertake projects in noneconomic fields, but rather that it has failed to do what could reasonably be expected in seeking and utilizing the kinds of information on noneconomic factors that could increase the chances that its efforts would be successful in inducing continuing innovations. Another example is the currently fashionable field of educational development. As carried on today, it consists largely of the admittedly necessary activity of planning the expansion of educational systems in the light of projected manpower needs and economic resources. But, comparatively little attention is paid to studying and finding ways of taking into account the cultural and social factors important in defining educational objectives, devising educational methods, designing curricula, organizing teacher training, influencing student motivation, and providing for vocational and career guidance. Thus, neither the economic nor the non-economic programs and projects now being supported by the United States aid agency—as well as by UN agencies and other international organizations—have been based on systematic efforts to obtain and use significant information on the cultural, social, and political aspects of development.

Assuming, however, that the aid agency were to recognize the relevance of such information to its objectives and activities, could these concepts and data be effectively utilized under its existing institutional characteristics, specifically its personnel and procedures? In terms of their professional training and previous work experience, the great majority of the agency's personnel is habituated to making decisions largely on the basis of economic data. Its elaborate internal procedures for program preparation and review, and the increasingly detailed legal and accounting restrictions governing its relationships with recipient countries and private contractors are also geared to data of this type. Hence, research would be needed to determine the changes in organization, procedures and personnel which would be required before a broader range of information could be used effectively in agency decision making, and whether such changes would be politically and administratively practicable.

Finally, if all of these difficulties could be overcome, the question must still be asked as to whether the use of information conducive to better insights into the nature of the development process might not run the risk of impairing rather than improving decision making. One possible danger would be that the positivism and utopianism inherent in American culture might lead to grandiose efforts at comprehensive social engineering in the recipient countries with consequent disastrous results for United States foreign policy. Another possibility would be that improved understanding of the magnitude, complexity, slowness, and uncertainty of the changes involved in moderniza-tion and economic growth, and of the limited capacity to influence them through foreign aid, might discourage the personnel of the aid agency and thereby impair their morale and effectiveness. It would be useful to investigate the extent to which morale in a program-oriented institution, such as the aid agency, might be adversely affected by recognition that the expectations of technocratic positivism for early and substantial achievements are not likely to be fulfilled.

Congressional Decision Making

Within the Congressional subsystem of decision making on foreign aid, each of the three influences—intellectual, cultural, and institutional—affecting attitude and opinion formation is to be found in operation. In the Congressional process, our preliminary survey leads us to the conclusions that the role of rational, intellectual considerations is much less important than is commonly supposed and that it would not be greatly enhanced by changes in the volume and nature of information per se. Most of the time Congress devotes to consideration of foreign aid is spent during the committee stage, and here most of the information presented is of a rationally determined nature. However, an examination of committee hearings leads us to question the relevance of much of the information therein presented to ultimate Congressional action, as we shall see below.

Cultural considerations are of greater importance, and appear to arise from two sources. First, congressmen's opinions and attitudes are as culturally determined as those of the other members of the society. Second, most congressmen tend to look toward their own local elites—rather than to a national leadership group—for cues when forming their opinions; indeed, they seem to have little contact with national elites.[9] As their source of power and prestige remains constituency-oriented, so in large part do their views. They are influenced more by the local than by the national press, and more by local than by national business, labor, and other organizations. The local elites usually exhibit far less interest in foreign affairs than do their national counterparts; and their attitudes and opinions, which are characterized by little interest in or knowledge of foreign aid, have been outlined in the first part of this paper. Thus, most congressmen, sharing in this local elite orientation, are subject to all of the anomalies and ambiguities that the American historical experience and cultural system bring to the concept of foreign aid and hence to attitudes and expectations regarding it.

The major consideration determining the kinds of information that are used in the Congressional decision process appears to be institutional in nature. At each Congressional level—subcommittee, committee, full House

9. For the relations of congressmen to local and national elites, see James Rosenau, *National Leadership and Foreign Policy: A Case Study in the Mobilization of Public Support* (Princeton, N.J.: Princeton University Press, 1963).

and Senate—the organizational structure, the methods of functioning, and the characteristics of the leadership and other personnel seem to be the major factors determining the kinds of information that will be considered relevant to the process of Congressional decision making and the ways in which such information is used. Furthermore, the Congressional subsystem has succeeded over the years in institutionalizing a rather well-defined set of values and norms, which imposes considerable restraints upon the use of data that might from purely intellectual considerations be deemed quite relevant. Congressional attitudes concerning the project versus the program approach and the extent of Congressional control over executive branch operations are cases in point, as explained below.

PROCESS OF CONGRESSIONAL DECISION MAKING ON FOREIGN AID

Foreign aid—like all the national goals—comes before Congress in the form of a presidential program. The concept of a presidential program is a relatively new one. Although its antecedents can be traced to the administrations of Theodore Roosevelt and Woodrow Wilson, it was not until the years of Franklin D. Roosevelt's presidency that the pattern emerged clearly. Each succeeding president has accepted the responsibility for proposing to Congress a relatively detailed annual legislative program. And each succeeding Congress has recognized—in many cases explicitly—the legitimacy of and necessity for this new Executive Branch role. Faced with the complexity of modern international and domestic developments, legislative branches of government throughout Western Europe as well as the United States have been playing a diminishing role in originating legislation. Only in the Executive Branch of a modern democratic government can power and responsibility be properly focused to produce, at the speed required, program proposals which are clearly oriented toward the national interest.

Each house of Congress considers the foreign aid program twice annually —first in the authorization stage, and then in the appropriations stage. Yet, the time the average member of Congress spends considering the program is often less than one week each year. It is not unusual, for example, for both the Senate and the House of Representatives to vote annual appropriations for foreign aid in a single day.

In contrast to the average member of Congress, the committee member involved in the foreign aid decision process may spend several months each year studying the program and recommending to his colleagues a final course of action. The committee member of long standing often exhibits a grasp of the operating details of the foreign aid program equal to that of officials of the aid agency itself. As his expertise is recognized, he is in a position to influence an increasing number of his fellow legislators. The end product of this system, with regard to foreign aid as well as other programs, is often the committee or subcommittee chairman whose views, expressed in committee reports and on the floor of the House or Senate, are in themselves enough to determine the fate of the program for any given year.

There are four committees intimately involved in the foreign aid process. The two "substantive" committees are the Senate Foreign Relations Committee and the House Committee on Foreign Affairs; the two "money" committees are the appropriations committees of both houses.

The two substantive committees bring to the process a different background and set of attitudes than do the appropriations committees. For, in theory at least, they are the repositories of all foreign policy expertise in the Congress; and the foreign aid program is but one of their responsibilities in that policy area. The particular result of this institutional characteristic is that the two substantive committees tend to view the foreign aid program within the broader context of American foreign policy goals, and their membership generally includes those representatives and senators with the greatest intrinsic interest in foreign affairs.

The appropriations committees are less concerned with the foreign policy aspects of the aid program than they are with the amount of money being requested. Their subcommittees which study the program each year consider foreign aid within the context of total government expenditure rather than that of American foreign policy. Again, their approach to foreign aid reflects the institutional function of the appropriations committees to view each specific presidential program proposal as it relates to total government expenditures each year.

These differences in institutional attitudes exhibited by the two sets of committees—substantive and appropriation—are often reflected in their recommendations to their respective houses of Congress. The appropriations committees have hitherto usually recommended substantially larger cuts in the presidential program than the substantive committees. The final decisions reached in both the House and the Senate then depend on a number of variables, including the relative prestige of the committees involved, the capabilities of the committee chairmen, the strength and inclination of House and Senate leadership, and the particular "moods" of these two bodies.

The Senate Foreign Relations Committee brings to the process of Congressional decision making on foreign aid a position of prestige far superior to that of its House counterpart. The origin of this difference lies in the Constitution itself, which gives the Senate the power to advise on and consent to treaties with foreign governments. Although the Constitution says little else about foreign affairs, this single grant of power assured that from its inception the Senate would play a significant role in this area.

Despite the fact that the House Foreign Affairs Committee is now deeply involved in foreign policy making—chiefly in the area of foreign aid—it has yet to achieve the recognition and prestige that come with age. It is the Chairman of the Senate Foreign Relations Committee who is often referred to as the Congressional dean of foreign policy, and the White House and the State Department continue to display a much greater deference to the Senate and to individual senators in the realm of foreign policy than to the House of Representatives and its Foreign Affairs Committee. More important in terms of foreign aid decision making, members of the House have yet to recognize the Foreign Affairs Committee as a power within the House itself.

The ranking committee in the House involved in the foreign aid decision process is the Appropriations Committee. That Committee—which through its Subcommittee on Foreign Operations handles the foreign aid requests—is by any calculation one of the most powerful in the House. The greatest source of power of the Appropriations Committee lies in its control over all federal spending in every representative's home district. To enhance the power of the Appropriations Committee, the Public Works Appropriations Bill— the traditional "pork barrel" bill—is usually scheduled at the end of each Congressional session. Very few representatives are willing to oppose an Appropriations Committee recommendation on an issue such as foreign aid —which is relatively unimportant to many of them—while that Committee is still considering their home-district project requests.

The power of the House Appropriations Committee is further enhanced by the fact that its mode of operation is based on unity. Each of its subcommittees attempts to reach bipartisan agreement; a further effort is then made to reach unanimity in the full Appropriations Committee before a bill is reported to the floor for action. When such unanimity is reached, the Appropriations Committee generally has its way in the House.

Turning specifically to foreign aid, the key figures on the Appropriations Committee and on its crucial Subcommittee on Foreign Operations have until recently been consistently hostile to the program. In the face of this opposition, the House Committee on Foreign Affairs—on the whole sympathetic to the foreign aid program—has been obliged, in order to defend the program and to preserve what little prestige it has built, to take a position considerably nearer the predictable views of Subcommittee Chairman Otto E. Passman and his Appropriations Committee colleagues than the majority views on the Foreign Affairs Committee would have indicated.

In the Senate, a different pattern has emerged. The Foreign Relations Committee, secure in its status, has operated with more freedom to authorize whatever amount it wished without giving particular attention to the views of the Senate Appropriations Committee. In turn, the latter Committee has not been dominated by conservative sentiment as has its House counterpart. Consequently, the two Senate committees are in much closer agreement on the foreign aid program than are those in the House.

Within each of the committees—subcommittee in the case of House

Appropriations—a clear pattern of leadership is visible. In each case, a powerful chairman—varying only slightly in degree of command—guides the committee agenda, deliberations, and decisions with the assistance of a small bipartisan group of allies. In each committee, it is the chairman who presides at literally all of the foreign aid hearings and who manages the bill on the floor of the House or Senate when it is reported out by his committee.

In the Senate Foreign Relations Committee, it is not unusual for the Chairman and as few as two other members of the Committee to make the crucial decisions as to amounts to be authorized for foreign aid. Through the influence of this nucleus in some instances, and the lack of interest of the rest of the members in others, these decisions are usually confirmed by the full Committee. A similar pattern has emerged in the workings of the Senate Appropriations Committee. The only difference is that the latter committee's chairman has recently been appointing a committee member to preside at the foreign aid hearings and to manage the bill on the Senate floor.

The two House committees operate in similar fashion, although the number of committee members involved in the decision-making process is somewhat larger than in the Senate. One reason for the greater involvement on the part of House committee members is that they have far fewer committee assignments than do senators. They are, therefore, more able to concentrate on the few assignments that they do have.

The power of the four chairmen intimately involved in Congressional decision making on foreign aid is extensive. Both Senator J. William Fulbright, Chairman of the Senate Foreign Relations Committee and Representative Passman, Chairman of the House Appropriations Subcommittee on Foreign Operations and a vigorous opponent of the program, have often been referred to as "Mr. Foreign Aid" in their respective houses. But, there are constraints even on these men, as recent events have illustrated.

In the case of Mr. Fulbright, the Senator declared in December, 1964, that unless the present Administration drastically modified its foreign aid program, he would no longer manage the bill in his committee or on the Senate floor. Even though he undoubtedly supported certain changes in the foreign aid program on their merits, opposition to it—which he as Chairman of the Committee and floor manager of the bill was unable to contain—apparently forced his hand. When his suggested modifications were not accepted by the Administration, the Senator introduced his own bill incorporating them during the 1965 session of Congress. The bill, which he finally did manage, called for an end to the foreign aid program in its present form within two years.

Institutional constraints have also operated upon Mr. Passman. On numerous occasions in the past, he was able to carry the House of Representatives against even so popular a president as Dwight Eisenhower. However, in 1964, he was overruled within his own subcommittee through the efforts of the newly appointed Chairman of the Appropriations Committee, Representative George H. Mahan; and the full House confirmed that defeat. In contrast to the previous Chairman of the Appropriations Committee who had allowed his sub-committee chairmen to operate independently, Mr. Mahan played an active role in the deliberations of the Subcommittee on Foreign Operations and carried enough members with him to defeat appropriations cuts proposed by Mr. Passman. White House pressure was also in evidence during this incident, emphasizing the fact that a chairman, no matter how influential, is still vulnerable at any given time to a confluence of pressures.

The content of the information on foreign aid considered by Congress in the process of decision making is discussed below. Here, we may note that most of the information available to Congress on the foreign aid program enters the process at the committee hearing stage. In most years, government witnesses before the four committees are identical, as are their methods of presentation. Often, the same officials from the State Department and the foreign aid agency appear before each committee, and their statements reveal a minimum of variation.

A similarity from year to year in testimony by nongovernmental witnesses is also evident. Each year the same organizations, often represented by the same individuals, testify before the committees orally or by submitting a statement for the record in support of or opposition to the aid program. These witnesses represent a wide spectrum of mass organizations and interest groups as noted previously, and their opinions range from the enthusiastic support given by the AFL-CIO and church groups at one extreme to equally enthusiastic condemnation by the Liberty Lobby and the Citizens' Foreign Aid Committee at the other. The statements also exhibit great variety in terms of content. Some are well reasoned and documented; others are merely exhortations or denunciations.

Other important sources of information available at the hearings and during the mark-up sessions—those closed sessions at which the committees decide upon changes in the legislation and the amounts of aid that they will recommend for approval by their respective branches of Congress—are the General Accounting Office and the committees' own staffs. The former audits the expenditure of money appropriated for foreign aid and conducts its own investigations of the aid program, as do the committees' own staff members.

The staff of the House Foreign Affairs Committee includes certified public accountants, and specializes in work of an essentially investigatory nature. The staff of the Senate Foreign Relations Committee has a decidedly different orientation. It is the largest of the four committee staffs involved in the foreign aid decision process, with from twenty-two to twenty-five employees. Many concentrate on ordinary committee administrative procedures, preparing for hearings, answering mail, and working directly for members of the Foreign Relations Committee in whatever capacity required. However, there are generally seven or eight professional members of the staff whose work is best described as substantive. They often have considerable time to investigate the workings and results of the program abroad, to consult with leaders in the field of economic and social development, and to recommend for the Committee's consideration changes in various aspects of the foreign aid program. Their contacts with officials in the executive branch of government are extensive; the result is that they may be in a position to influence the formulation of Executive Branch presentations to Congress as well as their reception in the Foreign Relations Committee.

The appropriations committees each have a single staff member assigned to the foreign aid program. The general tendency in these committees, as previously indicated, is to view foreign aid not in terms of theory or policy but rather in terms of facts. The facts that most interest the appropriations committees are dollars—the purposes and projects for which they are spent, the tangible results of such expenditures, and any irregularities that may have occurred in the process. Hence, these committees rely more on the General Accounting Office than on their own staffs.

About these sources of information, several generalizations can be made. First, the greatest volume of information is supplied by the aid agency's oral and written presentations to the committees. Since these presentations are the crucial factor in the flow of information, they will be considered in some detail below. Second, the public witnesses seldom make much of an impression on committee members, and most of their statements are filed and never read. Only those presentations of public witnesses, usually from interest groups, that are specifically aimed at particular sections of the legislation— and are in forms that can easily be converted into amendments—stand much chance of being noticed by the committees. Third, a committee's staff contributes information to the extent to which it is called upon to do so. The staff of the Foreign Relations Committee is the only one oriented toward substantive information, and it has made significant contributions to the development of the program. The other committees' staffs concentrate primarily on routine administrative management and on auditing functions supplementary to the work of the General Accounting Office.

Though the committee hearings represent that stage of the Congressional decision-making process at which most of the information on the aid program is presented, absenteeism—particularly on the part of senators—is then at its highest. Excepting the presentations by the Secretary of State and the Administrator of the aid agency, it is not unusual to find the chairman and two colleagues representing the entire Senatorial presence at a Foreign Relations Committee hearing. Many sessions find the chairman alone in attendance. Even during make-up sessions, it is often difficult to obtain a quorum. It is at this point that the chairman and two or three of his colleagues often arrive at decisions subsequently approved by a majority of their colleagues and embodied in the committee report. Similar attendance problems are experienced in the other committees, though not to such a degree.

However, there is no necessary correlation between attendance and the absorption of information. Some members, attending at the urging of the chairman, will be working on other matters. Others will file in and out, often causing the same line of questioning to be repeated several times during a session. Still others will attend just long enough to put their criticisms and suggestions on the record, leaving before an Executive Branch response is completed. More often than not close questioning is designed to embarrass and to build into the record a case for opposition rather than to elicit information.

The end result is that there is very little constructive exchange of views during the committee hearings. Administration testimony is monotonously repetitious, and—perhaps justifiably—defensive in presentation. Congressional attendance is very poor, and the line of questioning, particularly in the appropriations committees, largely restricted to requests for explanations of why particular projects have been undertaken, of the publicity benefits which the United States did or did not derive from them, and of alleged misuse of aid funds by recipient governments, private contractors, and agency personnel.

Hearings will last a few weeks for the Senate Appropriations Committee; in the other three committees they generally extend over a period of two or more months. Only when the committees make their reports and recommendations to their respective houses are the other members of Congress likely to focus on the problem of foreign aid. At this point, several factors are liable to influence their reactions.

The first is the prestige of and unanimity within the committee reporting the bill. When the Chairman of the House Appropriations Subcommittee on Foreign Operations presents a report that has the unanimous support of his subcommittee, as well as the approval of the full Appropriations Committee, there is a strong likelihood that the bill will pass the House with no alterations. Only if the recommendations are challenged in the form of a minority report brought to the attention of the House during debate will the average member feel inclined to question the Committee's decisions.

The secrecy surrounding Appropriations Committee deliberations reinforces this pattern. Literally all the subcommittee hearings are held behind closed doors; only a very few high-ranking committeemen know what is taking place until a day or so before the subcommittee is due to report to the full House. The full committee usually approves the recommendations of its subcommittees in a matter of hours; the entire House often acts with similar swiftness. In this way, the decision of one appropriations subcommittee often becomes the decision of the House with less than a day's consideration.

However, the recommendations of the substantive committees are scrutinized much more closely.

The second factor is the attitude of the leadership within the two houses. Leadership support for—or hostility toward—any bill can have considerable influence on the outcome of full House and Senate action. In general, the shorter the length of time committee recommendations are debated on the floor of either house, the greater are the chances of their acceptance without change. Thus, leadership ability to retain control of debate and channel it toward swift action becomes a crucial factor in the foreign aid decision process. Generally, Congressional leadership is strengthened to the extent that it is operating in concert with presidential wishes and is receiving active White House support.

In the House, the Rules Committee determines the amount of time allotted to any bill for floor action. As the Rules Committee has been hostile to the foreign aid program for many years, it consistently grants more time for floor debate on the program than is requested by the Chairman of the Foreign Affairs Committee, thereby subjecting the views of that committee to vigorous attack. In the Senate, where there are no time limits on debate unless cloture is invoked, the actions of a single senator can stall plans for quick action; the end result is frequently the passage of a host of amendments to the bill to which little time for consideration has been given.

A third factor is the "mood" of the Congress. The problem of leadership is intimately connected with that of the mood of the House and the Senate. Although mood may be difficult to define as applied to those two institutions, it is an element that must be considered in determining the results of their deliberations. It is this mood which competent leadership can interpret and around which it can fashion its strategy.

The longer a debate continues, the more likely both houses are to succumb to a mood, be it favorable or unfavorable to any piece of legislation. In the case of foreign aid, the result is quite likely to be negative. Extended debate on this particular program tends to provide the one opportunity each year for many members of the House or Senate to offer their personal critiques of American foreign policy. During these debates, criticism is expressed not only by opponents of the aid program but also by those supporters who may have objections to certain aspects of it. For example, aid to the Communist countries in Eastern Europe, or to nations such as Indonesia and the United Arab Republic which are demonstrably hostile to the United States, provokes much resentment within the ranks of congressmen generally favoring foreign aid. The mood created by this debate produces constricting amendments as well as dollar cuts in the amounts recommended by the committees.

During the committee stage of the foreign aid decision process, there is information—the adequacy of which will be considered next—available upon which to act. During the stage at which the full House and Senate consider the recommendations of their committees, the role of rational information rationally presented is minimized. At this point, such institutional factors as committee prestige, leadership, and mood—factors in evidence in any institutional structure—are in control.

This is particularly the case in the general debate over foreign aid, because there are few constituency pressures brought to bear on this issue. Given the general state of public apathy on the issue of foreign aid and the lack of any strong lobbying tactics either pro or con, the average member of Congress is under less pressure than usual to reflect opinion prevalent in his constituency. His vote is, therefore, more likely to be determined by his own views and by the institutional setting in which they are formed.

INFORMATION PROBLEMS AND THE PROSPECTS FOR IMPROVEMENT

The annual Executive Branch presentations provide Congress with the great bulk of the information upon which its decisions are based. Two types of information are particularly relevant to Congressional decisions on economic aid: the general country situation reports, and the descriptions of proposed projects and loans. In the general country reports, the aid agency attempts to bring the committees up-to-date on recent changes within each of the countries receiving United States assistance. Significant political, economic and—where necessary—military developments are briefly discussed, as is the rationale for American aid in each instance. Accompanying each country report is a set of statistics measuring such factors as rates of growth of GNP; savings and investment; balance-of-payments position; population growth and other demographic characteristics; levels of education; and other series, where available.

The second type of pertinent information focuses on development grants and loans. All financial assistance falls into two categories: project financing and program financing. As explained in the preceding section, the former category covers aid that is tied directly to specified projects; the latter, funds provided to assist developing countries to pay for imports which have been designated as necessary on the basis of a comprehensive development plan or of a sector program within it.

The quantity of information submitted on development financing is voluminous. Although measurements for accuracy and usefulness are more difficult to take, certain problems are immediately evident. In the first place, the information is collected on an average of ten months before it is presented to Congress. It is often the case that information for any United States domestic expenditures program presented to Congress during a given year has been collected the previous fall, but with the foreign aid program this process has one novel aspect: the scope for significant change, which in the interim may distort that information, is far broader than with the average domestic program. Developments abroad over which the United States has little or no control, from mild inflation to violent revolution, may seriously diminish the relevance of the information previously gathered and invalidate the assumptions upon which the aid program for any given country has been based. Plans made even days prior to the Congressional presentation may suddenly be outdated.

This wide range of unpredictable and uncontrollable circumstances leads to a second major problem: all project and program proposals presented to Congress for its consideration are "illustrative." That is to say, the aid agency is under no obligation to spend money appropriated for foreign aid on the specific projects presented to Congress. The presentation includes a description of those which the agency is seriously considering, but after the money is appropriated any of these projects may be dropped in favor of new ones about which Congress is uninformed.

The rationale behind the illustrative nature of the presentation is sound. If the very unpredictability of events abroad did not alone make it so, the system of appropriation would. The aid agency submits its project and program financing requests with a total figure in mind. By the time Congress finishes with it, that figure may have been reduced by as much as 30 percent. This calls for a necessary readjustment on the part of the agency, involving the elimination of certain projects, and in some cases the substitution of others. The result is a program characterized by a great deal of flexibility in both presentation and implementation.

Thus, there are certain specific weaknesses connected with the information submitted in support of both project and program financing. Superficially at least, the informational distortions in the project approach to foreign aid are the most evident. Many of the projects submitted to Congress are never implemented. They may have appeared in the presentation with little study, and sometimes without systematic consultation with the government of the recipient country. It may later develop that the latter is not interested enough in them to pay its share of their costs. Or, it may be that feasibility studies undertaken after appropriation will discourage further efforts. It is also the case on occasion that a project may be well under way only to have the recipient government change its mind, or to have unforeseen events beyond its control prevent completion. Finally, other projects are dropped simply because Congressional cuts in the appropriation require some paring in the program.

The informational problem with regard to program financing is somewhat more complex. Here, the major flaw is not so much the illustrative nature of the proposals as it is the use of a concept whose operational implications are insufficiently understood by the Congress and for which much of the relevant supporting data is not supplied by the aid agency. The program approach, enabling a developing country to import those commodities necessary for economic growth, is sound in terms of economic theory. For a country possessing both a realistic development plan and the capabilities necessary for its successful implementation, the program approach may provide a better means for maximizing resource use than the project approach. But, only if information bearing directly upon the realism of the plan and the country's capacity to implement it is presented by the aid agency can Congress properly distinguish between a mere balance-of-payments subsidy and purposeful program financing, and judge the latter on its merits in each case.

However, it is the present practice of the aid agency to submit with each program-financing proposal merely some descriptive material dealing with the range of commodities to be supplied under the arrangement, and the importance of those items to the continued development of the recipient country. It does not discuss the soundness of the national development plan in any detail. Nor does it focus on the ability of the recipient country both to implement the program and to control imports so that the country's scarce foreign-exchange resources, whether derived from exports or from foreign aid, make their maximum contribution to development. Yet, this is precisely the type of information that is relevant if rational decisions are to be reached with regard to program financing.

Of the three major types of information supplied to Congress by the aid agency—country situation reports, and the illustrative material concerning project and program financing—the latter category exhibits the greatest room for improvement. The concept itself needs clarification as does the focus upon the recipient country's willingness and ability to devise and implement a realistic development plan. Further, the aid agency's claim that program financing allows the United States more leverage in influencing the policies of recipient countries, if valid, is highly relevant to the Congressional decision-making process. However, aid agency presentations have not yet convinced Congress on this point and until some evidence is submitted, the repetition of the claim will have little effect in the Congressional process.

Unfortunately, information regarding project financing offers no sounder ground upon which to base Congressional presentations. Because of the factors external to the initial American commitment involved in the implementation of any project, the illustrative nature of project presentations must be maintained. If there is improvement to be made in this area, it involves the methods by which the aid agency's decisions to include projects in the presentation are made. The more thoroughly the feasibility of a project is studied by the agency and the more fully it has been agreed upon with the recipient government before it is included in the Congressional presentation, the better are the chances that the illustrative nature of the presentation will be minimized, i.e., that projects appearing in presentations will be carried through to completion. However, while minimizing the inclusion of superficially prepared projects in Congressional presentations would increase the value of the information concerning project financing, it is questionable whether it would be worthwhile to put a great deal more time and resources into detailed prior studies of each project submitted to Congress. Since Congress is prone to make substantial cuts in most annual foreign aid requests, the process might result in wasted effort on the part of the aid agency and frustration on the part of the prospective recipient countries. Even granted the implementation of these refinements, information regarding foreign aid financing will continue to be tenuous, for the political, social, and economic volatility of most recipient countries often mocks the highest quality project research and analysis.

Given the nature of Congressional decision making, the question remains as to the importance of information in the process. Our preliminary survey leads us to conclude that changes in the information provided to Congress are not likely to alter very significantly the decisions made by Congress. We base this conclusion on the incompatibility that appears to exist between, on the one hand, the institutional characteristics of Congress and the attitudes and expectations of congressmen and, on the other hand, the nature and accomplishments of the foreign aid program. This incompatibility can be seen most clearly in the clash between the program's necessary flexibility and illustrativeness and the Congressional desire for control and economy.

Earlier, reference was made to the relatively recent development of the concept of a presidential program. Although Congress has conceded to the President the right to initiate legislation, it has not made that concession without parallel attempts to increase its own role elsewhere in the national decision-making process. Consequently, Congress has in recent years multiplied its efforts in the general areas of investigation of, and control over, the presidential program. Of all the existing national goals, however, none is more removed from Congressional control than foreign aid.

As we have seen, after the aid program is approved by Congress, its implementation is left entirely in the hands of the foreign aid agency and the recipient governments. Generally speaking, the flexibility of the program is so extensive that the following Congressional characterization of the process—while harsh—contains much truth: "Any budget prepared for the foreign aid program must, of necessity, be an estimate of the wildest sort. From start to finish, it is based on conjecture as to (1) the number and extent of projects which will be approved by our government and the host governments, (2) development of worldwide situations, and (3) the physical ability to spend money appropriated."[10] Although the unsettled nature of events abroad and

10. This characterization is found in the Minority Views section of the House Appropriations Committee Report on the *Foreign Assistance and Related Agencies Appropriations Bill*, 1965, 88th Cong., 2nd Sess., Report No. 1518, p. 16. Although it represents the views of the program's harshest Congressional critics, it is nevertheless in large part an accurate description of the uncertainties involved in the annual process.

the annual appropriations cuts in the program itself make this flexibility a necessity, they do little to placate Congressional concern and disapproval.

At a more specific level, the illustrative nature of the projects presented is irritating to Congress, particularly so to the appropriations committees. Most of their decision making is geared to an intensive review of specific domestic projects which will, if approved by Congress, be implemented. Their control over the process is so rigorous that major changes in projects already under way must be approved by the appropriations committees. The projects they fund are specific in detail and are implemented with a minimum of revision and delay. To this legislative pattern, the foreign aid program offers the sole important exception. The size of this exception, measured in dollars, is substantial when it is recognized that at present the program involves from 10 to 15 percent of the total funds over which Congress can exercise any real discretion each year.

Despite its inherent weaknesses, Congress prefers the project approach in foreign aid to that of the program approach. The feeling that program financing amounts to little more than balance-of-payments subsidies to recipient countries is prevalent in all of the committees. Congress has been dealing with projects for generations; it faced the program concept for the first time during the Marshall Plan era with little understanding or enthusiasm, but nevertheless went along with it. However, it is reluctant to continue to do so.

Inability to control the program does not diminish the desire of Congress to investigate the accomplishments of foreign aid; the inevitable result is that the discovery of wastefulness, about which it can do little, aggravates Congressional ire. No amount of information will alter the values and norms inherent in Congressional appropriations procedures. Project control and elimination of waste represent elemental modes of Congressional thought, and it is impossible to hold them in abeyance once each year while the foreign aid bill is being considered.

Another problem arises from the different sets of norms influencing the legislative course of the program during its consideration at the committee level. In effect, the aid agency must address its presentation to Congressional committees with widely differing standards and interests. There is, at the one extreme, the Senate Foreign Relations Committee. As we have seen, its primary interest with regard to foreign aid centers around recent political and economic developments in recipient countries, and the various ways in which these developments can be made more compatible with the foreign policy objectives of the United States. Although it shows some interest in the general types of projects and programs included in the aid presentation, it has no interest in the details of each project, or even of the majority of them. For this Committee, much of the information presented by the aid agency is irrelevant, and no secret is made of the fact that most members never "crack the books," that is, study the presentation books describing the proposed projects and programs for the coming fiscal year. It is this Committee that complains about the repetitiveness of the annual presentations, with their humanitarian overtones and warnings of "the revolution of rising expectations," rather than with emphasis, desired by the senators, on the political and economic facts crucial to a better understanding of the American national interest in various parts of the world. At the opposite extreme is the House Subcommittee on Foreign Operations. The annual books detailing illustrative projects around the world are in fact produced at the insistence of this Subcommittee. It thinks in terms of individual projects and price tags; its discussions in hearings rarely reach the level at which foreign aid as a tool of diplomacy is considered.

Thus, a presentation aimed exclusively at either of these extremes would necessarily injure the program with the other. Avoiding this pitfall, the presentation includes information for both groups and in doing so produces a mass of statistics and testimony which is, for the most part, ignored by both.

Perhaps some improvement in information is possible. There is a great deal of repetition in the presentation that is bound to discourage attendance at hearings. It is also true that there is a minimum of information focusing on the essential details of *realpolitik*. If this kind of information were put in more succinct and digestible form, it might inspire interested legislators to pay more attention to the Administration's point of view. The criticism that too much information is presented, however, seems unwarranted. As we have seen, what is of little interest to one committee may be required by another. Furthermore, much of the information that never gets to a senator or a congressman may be of value to his staff members in their work. Finally, it is not too difficult for legislators and their staffs to exercise some discrimination in their use of the material presented.

In retrospect, it would seem that with regard to annual congressional decisions on foreign aid, the role of information *per se* is of limited significance. By comparison, institutional factors appear much more important. No changes in the types or volume of information could greatly diminish the incompatibility between the necessities of the foreign aid program and the institutional procedures and cultural norms that congressmen bring to the legislative process. A growing awareness in Congress that there appears to be no terminal date in sight for the foreign aid program is gradually reinforcing the perturbation bred by these institutional and cultural factors. As a result, the prospects for continued congressional funding of foreign aid at a level substantially above recent appropriations are exceedingly dim.

Two possible developments—one internal to Congress, and the other external—might conceivably alter these prospects. Internally, any congressional reform that strengthened the role of the President in Congressional leadership would increase the prospects for favorable Congressional actions on his foreign aid proposals.

Externally, growing support for the program at the constituency level could alter the present Congressional mood regarding foreign aid. Presumably, such a development would be predicated upon an increased consumption of relevant information concerning foreign aid on the part of local—as opposed to national—opinion leaders. As has been noted, it is from this level of leadership that the average member of Congress takes his cues, rather than from national elites which generally support the program. But, bearing in mind the general level of public apathy toward foreign affairs and the marked correlation between level of education and support for foreign aid, more effective constituency support would—at best—have to wait upon a lengthy educational process to alter significantly present local leadership indifference toward foreign aid as a national goal. Given the ambiguities and incongruities in public opinion concerning foreign aid that are evoked by the deep-seated cultural values and historical experience discussed earlier in this paper, we must tentatively conclude that the prospects for such an alteration are small.

Some Suggestions for Research

Our preliminary survey again confirms the sociological principle that rational consideration is not the major process determining the role played by information in United States decision making on foreign aid. With respect to the formation of both popular and elite-group attitudes toward foreign aid, the influences of the cultural system are significantly more important. In Executive Branch decision making, social factors—specifically the institutional characteristics of the American foreign aid agency—exercise a major influence on the kinds of information that are believed to be relevant and on the ways in which the information is used. Similarly, with respect to the Congress, the institutional characteristics of the decision-making process and the attitudes and values of the people engaged in it are the major considerations affecting the use of information.

In these circumstances and with the exceptions noted below, we doubt that it would be worthwhile to devote substantial resources to comprehensive research on the role of information in decision making on foreign aid. It is unlikely that any practicable changes in the content, form, or dissemination of information on foreign aid and overseas development would significantly affect popular attitudes and opinions on this subject. Nor, in the case of the Congress, do the institutional characteristics and cultural factors governing the use of information seem likely to be modified in the next few years to an extent that would warrant an exploration at greater length of the possibilities for improving Congressional decision making by changes in the content and presentation of information.

It might, however, be useful to undertake further study of the Executive Branch use of information on foreign aid and overseas development. Our suggestion would be a study in greater depth and detail of the relationships between the choice and use of information, on the one hand, and the institutional characteristics of the aid agency and the concepts and expectations of its personnel, on the other hand. Such a study should focus, particularly though not exclusively, on those aspects of the problem that might have important operational implications. These would include:

1. Possibilities for bridging the information gap between academic social scientists and the personnel of the aid agency;

2. Experimentation with various specific kinds of information on the cultural, social, and political aspects of development to determine the particular concepts and data that would have the greatest usefulness for policy making and operations;

3. Changes in the organization, procedures, and personnel of the aid agency that might be required to increase its willingness and improve its ability to use a broadened range of information; and

4. Effects on the agency's morale of better understanding of the difficulty of its task and of the limited results it is likely to achieve.

Also, it might be useful to explore more thoroughly the extent and implications of the inverse relationship which our preliminary study has suggested between understanding of the role and limitations of foreign aid in the development process and support for the kind of program now being conducted. There has long been a widespread contention among proponents of the program that the way to increase public and Congressional support for it is to disseminate more and better information about the need for and the accomplishments of foreign aid. Often, the prescription takes the form of a demand that the administration—or somebody—formulate a new rationale for foreign aid that would be so convincing as to overcome doubt and opposition. These expectations reflect the overly positivistic and rationalistic tendencies of American culture.

Better information and more relevant rationales would, however, inevitably lead to more general recognition of the complexity, slowness, and uncertainty of the development process; of the limited role that outside aid and influence can play in it; of the not-yet available knowledge and unusual skill required to play this role effectively; and of the problematical nature of the benefits that the United States is likely to derive from such efforts. In turn, such improved understanding could result in a lessening of support for foreign aid, particularly among elite groups. Indeed, incipient recognition of some of these limitations has already produced growing doubts about the foreign aid program, as it is currently conceived and conducted, among knowledgeable congressmen, development specialists in the research community, and others.

A more thorough investigation than has been possible here of the nature and implications of the relationship between information on and support for foreign aid would have to be concerned broadly with the influence of the cultural system on attitudes and expectations and on the motivations of policy makers and operating personnel engaged in foreign aid activities. It would have to be a part historical, tracing the secularization of the concepts and values outlined in Part I and analyzing their present significance. The relationships between these cultural influences and the institutional factors in the processes of attitude formation and decision making would have to be explored in much greater detail than we have been able to do here. Such a study would be useful not only in clarifying the role and limitations of information in the decision-making process but also in yielding some insights into the criteria for devising a more realistic and effective U.S. foreign aid effort.

Index